RETAIL SUPPLY CHAIN MANAGEMENT

Series on Resource Management

RETAIL
SUPPLY CHAIN
MANAGEMENT

James B. Ayers
CGR Management Consultants
Playa del Rey, California

Mary Ann Odegaard
Michael G. Foster School of Business
University of Washington, Seattle

 Auerbach Publications
Taylor & Francis Group
New York   London

CRC Press is an imprint of the
Taylor & Francis Group, an **informa** business

Auerbach Publications
Taylor & Francis Group
6000 Broken Sound Parkway NW, Suite 300
Boca Raton, FL 33487-2742

Library of Congress Cataloging-in-Publication Data

Ayers, James B.
  Retail supply chain management / James B. Ayers, Mary Ann Odegaard.
     p. cm.
  Includes bibliographical references and index.
  ISBN 978-0-8493-9052-4 (hardback : alk. paper)
  1. Business logistics. 2. Retail trade--Management. 3. Industrial procurement--Management. I. Odegaard, Mary Ann. II. Title.

HD38.5.H86 2006
658.8'700687--dc22   2007019863

Visit the Taylor & Francis Web site at
http://www.taylorandfrancis.com

and the Auerbach Web site at
http://www.auerbach-publications.com

To the men and women in the retail supply chain—designing, manufacturing, and delivering products that enrich our lives.

Contents

SECTION 2   FORCES SHAPING THE RETAIL
SUPPLY CHAIN ENVIRONMENT

SECTION 5 ACHIEVING FINANCIAL SUCCESS IN THE RETAIL SUPPLY CHAIN

Preface

Most businesses operate as if specialization is a good thing. For example, retailer organization charts are populated by functions like sales, merchandising, distribution, human resources, and finance. Retailer suppliers—mostly distributors and original equipment manufacturers (OEMs)—also specialize but use different functions. Customarily, distributors will have warehousing and transportation functions, and manufacturers will have plant operations as well as product engineering.

A consequence of specialization has been weak processes that cross department and company boundaries. This is the central problem addressed by the supply chain management (SCM) discipline. Managers and employees practice their specialties with too little appreciation for the supply chains in which they participate. The SCM discipline requires a process view across the boundaries. New process designs go beyond tinkering with the status quo and are paradigm shifting, upsetting whole industries.

Retailing in particular is one where leadership demonstrated by companies like Dell and Wal-Mart has overcome traditional competitors. But no new model is eternal. And even Dell, Gap, and Wal-Mart must test new ways to build on past successes. At the time of writing, Dell and Gap have switched CEOs, as Wal-Mart experiments with new store formats and ways of delivering goods to stores.

This book is a resource for managers, strategists, and any others responsible for retail supply chains. These supply chains embrace brick-and-mortar stores as well as distributors, manufacturers, and providers of a wide range of supply chain–related services. For trading partners in retail to operate as a supply chain, rather than individual companies, they will need new approaches for performing the tasks necessary for supply chain success. These tasks include the following:

1. Designing supply chains for strategic advantage. This task creates "business models" that erect barriers to competition.
2. Implementing collaborative relationships inside the organization. Specialization produces local optimums but substandard service and profits at the company level.

3. Forging supply chain partnerships with trading partners up and down the supply chain. This is an "unnatural act" but increasingly a competitive "must" as companies rely on outside partners.
4. Managing supply chain information. The claims for new software confound potential users. Confusion is due to the presence of many providers and the difficulties of evaluating their claims.
5. Making money from the supply chain. Process improvement aimed at cost reduction retains its importance, but processes have to be defined along the supply chain, not at the individual company, level.

Successful retailers spread prosperity back through their supply base. To that end, the authors have formed their own partnership. Our collaboration brings together two skill sets: one in operations and another in managing retail businesses. Our mission is to match the challenges and opportunities in the retail industry with the solutions available from the SCM discipline. Managers have claimed they are besieged with so-called solutions from a multitude of advocates. Their challenges are sorting out which solutions to pursue and communicating to others up and down the chain. This book should ease the task of responding to both challenges.

Acknowledgments

Supply chain management in the retail industry is a broad topic. No two people, at least not the two authors, could produce this work without support. Suggestions, written contributions, reviews, and analytical frameworks came from many sources. We cite these throughout the book in our references. In particular we thank Douglas Hicks of D. T. Hicks & Co. for his review of Chapter 19 covering activity-based costing. We also thank Michael Gerry of ClickCommerce for his review of Chapter 18 that describes product tracking in retail supply chains. Dave Malmberg and Peter Crosby of CGR Management Consultants contributed to Chapter 21 on the topic of multicompany collaboration. Dave originated the innovations for sorting suppliers and products for the purpose of developing partnering strategies. Pete provided the case study describing the complex cold chain supply chain.

About the Authors

James B. Ayers is a principal with CGR Management Consultants, Los Angeles. He has instructed and consulted in strategy and operations improvement for clients in a variety of manufacturing, distribution, and service companies. The latter include clients delivering services in transportation, healthcare, engineering, utility, and financial industries. He has authored articles and has presented courses on product and process development as well as supply chain management. A prior book, *Improving Competitive Position: A Project Management Approach* was published by the Society of Manufacturing Engineers (SME). Books in the supply chain management series include the first and second editions of the *Handbook of Supply Chain Management* (2001, 2006), *Making Supply Chain Management Work: Design, Implementation, Partnerships, Technology, Profits* (2003), and *Supply Chain Project Management: A Structured Collaborative and Measurable Approach* (2004).

Jim holds a B.S. with distinction from the U.S. Naval Academy and M.B.A. and M.S. industrial engineering degrees from Stanford University. As a naval officer, he served on submarines. Jim is a member of the SME, the Project Management Institute (PMI), and the Council of Supply Chain Management Professionals (CSCMP). He is a Certified Management Consultant (CMC) through the Institute of Management Consultants (IMC).

Mary Ann Odegaard is a lecturer in marketing and international business and an adjunct lecturer in pharmacy. She also serves as director of External Management Programs at the Michael G. Foster Business School, University of Washington, Seattle. In this capacity she is founder and director of the Retail Management Program and of the Business Fundamentals Program for nonbusiness majors. She co-directs the Pharmacy Management Program. Her specialties include marketing strategies in retail and consumer products environments, retail management, and supply chain implications for retailers. Her current research interests span the gamut of retail strategy and include market identification and strategic response, supply chain planning for private label products, and the impact of sustainability considerations on retail management.

Previous academic experience includes faculty positions at the University of California–Berkeley and Santa Clara University where she was a founder and co-director of the Retail Management Institute. She also served as executive assistant to the vice president for business and finance at Stanford University. She holds Ph.D., M.B.A., and B.A. degrees from Stanford University.

Dr. Odegaard's retail experience includes progressive management experience at Frederick and Nelson, Seattle; buying experience at Frederick Atkins, Inc., New York City; various retail industry–related positions with IBM in San Francisco and Los Angeles; and strategic consulting in the retail and consumer products industries, as well as expert witness testimony for a variety of retail firms. She also founded and ran The Photo Place, Inc. She has published in a variety of marketing and business journals including the *Journal of Marketing Research* and currently serves on the board of directors of the University Book Store in Seattle.

THE RETAIL SUPPLY CHAIN

The five chapters in Part 1 frame what we include in the retail "industry" defined in the broadest sense. Part 1 describes the retail supply chain components and describes the industry's impact on people around the globe—in developed and developing countries.

#	Name
1.	Defining the Retail Business
2.	Success in a Retail Business
3.	Types of Retail Supply Chain Businesses
4.	Globalization: Moving toward Comparative Advantage
5.	Corporate Social Responsibility and the Retail Industry

Chapter 1 points out that this enterprise has many players, and most certainly is "more than stores." In fact, stores are the proverbial tip of the iceberg. A network of distributors, service providers, and manufacturers supports each point of sale. In many cases, the ties between these contributors are quite loose—with trading partners living in different worlds. One mission of this book is to bring these worlds closer together. If successful, the manufacturer and logistics service provider will better understand the world of the retailer, and the retailer will better understand the world of the manufacturer and service provider.

A profit model for retailers is the subject of Chapter 2. Many, in particular those upstream from retailers, may be unaware how the retailer manages its business for profitability. Chapter 3 uses the profitability framework described in Chapter 2 to illustrate the wide range of business models pursued by various retailers. Chapter 3 also reports U.S. Census data that profiles the size of the U.S. retail industry and the supply chain components that support it. Although the data describes the U.S. retail industry only, other regions and markets are likely to grow networks of a similar scale as formal retail in the form of chains takes root in new places.

The globalization topic, the subject of Chapter 4, deserves a prominent role in any discussion of retail supply chains. The chapter addresses the underlying economics of globalization, the concept of "distance" associated with doing business across country boundaries, and a methodology for "doing the math" when it comes to making global sourcing and marketing decisions.

Chapter 5 takes on the issue of corporate social responsibility (CSR) and the role of retailers. An industry with the visibility of retail is a target of efforts to "improve society." This chapter covers a variety of causes from environmental impacts to social conditions in the factories that produce merchandise. So, any large retailer must respond, and its suppliers must also fall in line. The chapter describes how to "pick and choose" in setting a direction for CSR that is consistent with a retailer's strategy.

Chapter 1

Defining the Retail Supply Chain

This chapter describes a reference model for the retail supply chain and the terminology that goes with it. This model, as shown in Figure 1.1, plays a role when there is a need for a common definition of a subject like retail supply chains. The simplified model in Figure 1.1 includes, starting from right to left:

1. Customers or end-users
2. Retailers
3. Distributors
4. Original equipment manufacturers (OEMs)
5. First-tier suppliers
6. Second-tier suppliers
7. Service providers

Not shown for the sake of simplicity is a wide range of supply chain service providers (#7). Examples include warehouse operators, transportation companies, trading companies, and customs brokers. These act to connect the other players listed. Some service providers, such as contract manufacturers, may play roles of second-tier suppliers.

In this book, the term *retail* describes final sales to mostly nonbusiness customers or end-users, often called *consumers*. However, it is important to remember that most businesses also make purchases at retail stores. Transactions in the retail domain also can be termed business-to-consumer (B2C) or business-to-business (B2B). Because supply chains for consumers can be quite long, they consist of both B2B links, such as those between first- and second-tier suppliers, and B2C links, for example, those between retailers and customers or end-users.

Because of their many variations, the terms *supply chain* and *supply chain management* (*SCM* for short) also need defining. According to Levy and Weitz, authors of a popular text on retailing, retailers carry on four major activities because they can do them more easily than the OEMs producing the products.[1] First, and most important, retailers provide an assortment of goods from which one can choose. Imagine getting a headache and having to order Tylenol directly from the manufacturer. Instead, we take our headache to the local convenience store and select from various headache remedies. Second, retailers buy in larger quantities and break these down into more consumable sizes. For example, gift shops often buy merchandise in case quantities of a dozen or more. They then break the case lots into smaller quantities and sell items individually. Third, retailers hold inventory close by and provide convenience to the customer. Finally, retailers provide services to enhance the value of the product to the customer. Gift wrapping, credit, warranties, alterations, and repair services are a few of the services that may be provided.

Successful retailers do three things well. First, a retailer must identify a niche for their offerings among all available market segments and determine a target market with an opportunity for growth. Second, retailers must design and develop an appropriate and effective retail format. Who would have thought retailer Tommy Bahama would sell Hawaiian shirts to men, women, and children at high prices in stores decorated in a tropical theme? Finally, the retailer must figure out how to establish a sustainable competitive advantage. Rarely is price a successful determinant—something else must also be offered. Costco and Wal-Mart emphasize low prices, but they have to augment this with the other aspects of the retail mix. In the case of these retailers, Wal-Mart uses its size to bargain hard for low prices and Costco buys in bulk, opportunistically.

1.1 More Than Stores

Retail supply chains include more than stores in their makeup. The nature of the supply chain will vary from product type to product type according to the characteristics of the product itself, as well as the preferences of customers and end-users. Figure 1.1 shows that customers or end-users can buy from retail stores, directly from OEMs, and from dealers or resellers who also deal directly with the OEM. Retailers and distributors refer to OEMs as the *manufacturer*, the *vendor*, or the *resource*.

Some retail supply chains include more than one intermediary distributor. This is especially true of the food industry, where freshness is a concern. For example, milk may be produced on a farm, then sold to a cooperative, which sells it to a processor, who in turn sells it to a distribution brand; it is then sold to a retailer, who sells it to the consumer. Such a distribution network or supply chain has been likened to the fire brigade, where it is faster to pass the bucket along a chain of people than to have one person carry it the entire distance.

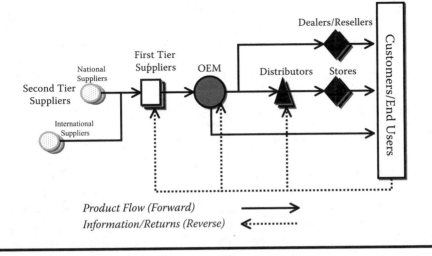

Figure 1.1   Retail supply chain.

An analogy to the supply chain is the iceberg. As consumers, we see only the part of the iceberg that sticks out of the water; most of it is hidden. Supply chains are similar. As customers or end-users, we participate in the last transaction in the chain. For complex products in particular, there would have been multiple unseen transactions among the *trading partners* who delivered the product, as detailed in the previous milk example and pictured in Figure 1.1.

Regarding Figure 1.1, there may also be a difference between *customers* and *end-users* shown at the end of the supply chain on the right. In this book, the "customer" makes buying decisions while the "end-user" actually consumes or uses the product. A wife and mother would be the customer for her household because she does the shopping; family members are end-users. Both customers and end-users influence purchase decisions. For example, the father may have health concerns for his children and insist that the mother purchase low-fat milk for them even though he is neither a consumer of the product nor the shopper making the purchase.[2]

Most of us buy much of what we use or consume at stores. But alternatives are many and increasing. We may also order out of catalogs, go online to order, or purchase from dealers, who guide us in our selections. These alternative distribution options are called retail *channels*. The store, direct, and dealer/reseller paths in Figure 1.1 are each *channels* of distribution.

Each level in a supply chain (e.g., distributor, OEM, or supplier) is called an *echelon*. Bypassing an echelon is a process called *disintermediation*. Disintermediation, in some cases, can lower cost, inventory, and lead times. Many supply chain participants, particularly distributors, are wary of disintermediation efforts that cut them out of the flow of goods. Firms trying to use a disintermediation strategy must be judicious in setting up a direct path to customers so as not to alienate existing channels.

Recently, a number of well-known apparel brands have opened up their own brand-centered specialty stores just up the street from other retailers who carry their lines. Notable examples include the previously cited Tommy Bahama and Eileen Fisher, a seller of women's apparel. These firms are said to be *vertically integrated,* controlling most of the supply chain from beginning to end. A manufacturer that engages in retail activities would be *forwardly integrated,* whereas a retailer engaged in production would be considered *backwardly integrated.*

The OEM often provides the *brand* identity for the products sold by the retailer. However, brand identity might be associated with the retail enterprise through *private label* brands designed and sold exclusively by that particular retailer. The Gap is an example of a company that carries almost all private label merchandise and uses it to develop its retail image and long-term sustainable competitive advantage. In some cases, major components of a product are branded for inclusion in other products sold at retail, such as Intel chips or Microsoft operating systems in computers sold by Lenovo, Toshiba, Dell, or Hewlett-Packard.

Another foundation for brand identity may be *extended product* features. These, not the *base* or physical products, are increasingly important in achieving retailing success. Supply chain design needs to support extended product strategies. Examples include value-added resellers of computer systems and after-market maintenance provided by automobile dealers. Starbucks, with Internet access and comfortable places to drink coffee, offers an extended product to support sales of base products such as coffee, other beverages, merchandise, and food. Their growth is partly based on consumers' perceptions of the coffee shops as a third place to go, the others being the workplace and home. A retailer who has a reputation for after-sales services provides an extended product in the form of risk reduction for its customers. The customer is certain that he or she can use the product with confidence, return unsatisfactory merchandise, or have problems fixed promptly. Chapter 6, Section 6.3 describes the importance of extended product features further.

Globalization is a hot supply chain topic. Figure 1.1 shows second-tier sources of product components as either "national" or "international." These categories symbolize the impact of global sourcing on the cost of the goods we buy and the economies of all countries engaged in trade. Globalization also opens international markets for base and extended products that fuel sales growth. Wal-Mart not only imports many of its products, but it also has opened stores in foreign countries, including China. This book deals with the subject of globalization again in Chapter 4 and Chapter 6, Section 6.4.

A possible source of confusion is the use of the terms *upstream* and *downstream* with regard to supply chains. In this book, *upstream* relates to operations that precede a point of reference. For example, in Figure 1.1, distributors are upstream of retailers. For the customer or end-user, all operations are upstream. *Downstream* operations, on the other hand, follow points of reference. So distributors are downstream of OEMs in Figure 1.1. Some companies refer to upstream trading partners as their *supply chain* and downstream trading partners as their *demand chain.*

1.2 Defining the Terms: Supply Chain and Supply Chain Management

This section defines *supply chain* and *supply chain management*. There are many working definitions of supply chain, depending on the viewpoint of the definer. Common viewpoints define the supply chain as procurement only, distribution, or as a collection of information system applications. These viewpoints mostly reflect the need for operating efficiency, not strategic advantage, from supply chain design. To understand the variation and commonality in definitions, the staff of DC Velocity (DC stands for Distribution Center) questioned a panel of 11 supply chain practitioners, whom they referred to as logistics profession "rainmakers." Table 1.1 summarizes the responses to the question, "How do you define *supply chain management* as it relates to logistics operations?"[3]

One can surmise from Table 1.1 that perspectives on SCM vary. They range from broad, planning-oriented definitions (such as #1, 3, 4, 5, and 7) to more operational ones (e.g., #2, 8, and 9). The rainmakers' responses reflect their varying roles, with those of academics and executives being broader in nature and operating executives' responses more focused on physical flows of concern to logistics professionals.

This book also takes a broad view that includes the potential for strategic contribution from SCM, so a broader definition, first of the term *supply chain,* is presented here.[4]

Supply chain: Product life-cycle processes comprising physical, information, financial, and knowledge flows whose purpose is to satisfy end-user requirements with physical products and services from multiple, and linked, suppliers.

The definition says that the supply chain is made up of *processes,* as emphasized in Table 1.1, definition #5. Figure 1.1 is a high-level picture of these processes. They include sourcing material, designing products, manufacturing, transporting, fixing, and selling physical products or services at supply chain enterprises. *Product life cycle* has at least two meanings, the selling life cycle and the usage life cycle. For long-life, or "durable," products as well as many services, these aren't the same. The selling time window may be far shorter than the product's useful life. Examples are automobiles, computers, a life insurance policy, or a 30-year mortgage. All must be supported long after newer products take the place of older ones. For this reason, product support after the sale can be an important—if not the most important and profitable—supply chain component. In these cases, the prospects for seller longevity, an extended product feature, is a factor in the purchasing decision.

Physical, information, and *financial* flows are frequently cited supply chain dimensions. However, the viewpoint, a very common one, of the supply chain as a purchasing or physical distribution network is limiting. *Information* and *financial*

Table 1.1 Practitioner Definitions of the Term *Supply Chain Management*

	Thought Leader	*Definition Summary*
1.	Theodore Stank, professor of logistics, University of Tennessee (Knoxville)	An orientation for conducting business across multiple firms with improvement in end-customer value as the unifying goal
2.	Tim Krishner, president, SeayCo Integrators, Inc., custom computer systems	How best to use the tools and reports to enhance productivity
3.	James Stock, senior professor in marketing and logistics, University of South Florida	The management of a network of relationships between independent organizations and business units
4.	John Sidell, founder of ESYNC, supply chain execution systems and consulting	As the end-to-end management of inventory and information from sourcing through manufacturing/ assembly to distribution to customer delivery and, depending on the business model, through to the end consumer
5.	Jeffrey Karrenbauer, founding director of Insight, Inc., optimization and simulation applications	The integration of key business processes from end-user through original suppliers, which provides products, services, and information that add value for customers and other stakeholders
6.	Philippe Lambotte, vice president, international customer service and logistics, Kraft Foods	Optimal management of goods and information flows from the retail shelf to our suppliers
7.	Chad Autry, assistant professor of supply chain management, TCU	Reflects business process integration across and through the boundaries of multiple firms acting together to create value
8.	Michael Fostyk, senior vice president, American Eagle Outfitters	Getting the right goods to the customer, at the right time, consistently, accurately, at the right value to the organization

Table 1.1 (continued) Practitioner Definitions of the Term *Supply Chain Management*

9.	John Gentle, retired Owens Corning leader for transportation affairs	It begins with material planning and is translated back into transportation requirements of inbound materials, warehousing of both raw and finished materials, and the transportation of the finished goods to the customer
10.	Jeffrey Camm, professor of quantitative analysis, University of Cincinnati	The old standard definition … getting the right quantities to the right locations at the right time in a cost-effective manner
11.	Dick Ward, senior staff officer, Material Handling Industry of America	Deals with the sourcing and synchronous flow, and flow is the keyword here, of all goods and materials from the very beginning of that chain to the very end, being the final consumer, and even beyond, when you consider returns

components are as important as *physical* flow in many supply chains and are examples of *reverse* flows that go in the opposite direction shown in Figure 1.1.

Also omitted from many supply chain definitions is the role of *knowledge* inputs into supply chain processes. Knowledge is the driver behind new products and new processes, the source of growth through innovation. Supply chain processes for new products require coordination of intellectual input (the design) with physical inputs (components, prototypes, factories, distribution channels, and the like). In the retail industry, such knowledge can produce better designed, more user friendly, and more stylish products. Increasingly, products sold to consumers rely on software to distinguish them. The knowledge component of our definition also includes software.

The supply chain should support the satisfaction of *end-user requirements*. These requirements give rise to the fundamental mission of supply chains—matching supply and demand. As noted later in this chapter and in Chapter 7, there may be a range of customer or end-user groups who constitute market *segments*. An integral part of SCM is designing and implementing supply chain operations to satisfy these segments.

A supply chain also has *multiple, linked suppliers*. From the customer or end-user viewpoint, a supply chain exists when there are multiple enterprises backing the last link enterprise that delivers the product or service. So, under this definition, the neighborhood barber would not constitute a supply chain while a chain of barbershops would.

As mentioned previously, the supply chain has a two-way flow. Many consider supply chains only in terms of *forward* flow from suppliers to end-users, so SCM definitions take on a limited sourcing-logistics flavor. For the physical processes, this is largely true. Only one definition in Table 1.1 (#11) mentions *reverse* flows in the form of returns. But supply chain design must include backward flows for product returns, payments and rebates, replenishment orders, repair, and other reasons. The European Union has passed regulations that require companies to be responsible for the ultimate disposal of the products they sell after their useful life is exhausted. For example, computer manufacturers have to take back and recycle parts and materials from the products that they have sold. Chapter 22 deals with reverse flows in more detail.

Services also have supply chains. Production planning for the research and development department, which produces designs not products, can benefit from the same techniques used by product manufacturers. Federal Express and UPS operate service businesses, but they employ complex supply chains to move customer shipments. A software company like Microsoft is challenged to constantly improve its product through upgrades, so it too has a supply chain for its knowledge-based product.

With the term supply chain defined, *supply chain management*, or SCM, is simply the following.

Supply chain management: Design, maintenance, and operation of supply chain processes, including those for base and extended products, for satisfaction of end-user needs.

Although easy to define, SCM is a challenge to practice. Applying this definition, effective SCM requires skills to perform the following five tasks:

Designing supply chains for strategic advantage. This task creates new "business models" that shift the basis of competition. Definition #1 in Table 1.1 comes closest to recognizing this need. The presence of needed skills to perform this task is rare.

Implementing collaborative relationships inside the organization. Specialization in focused departments of a retailer or one of its manufacturers produces local optimums with substandard service and profits for the retail supply chain overall.

Forging supply chain partnerships with trading partners up and down the supply chain. This is an "unnatural act" but often a necessary one to gain competitive advantage. Many of the definitions in Table 1.1 recognize this need.

Managing supply chain information. The claims for new software applications may confound potential users. The confusion is the consequence of having many providers and the difficulties of evaluating their claims or adapting their "solutions" to one's business.

Making money from the supply chain. Well-managed process improvement retains its importance, but processes that cross department and company boundaries have to be defined and addressed. Collaboration is the key to generating more cash from operations. Note that the tasks range from strategy-making to collaborating effectively and then to running efficient operations.

The tools and techniques in this book will help readers improve their skills in performing these tasks.

1.3 The Importance of Customer Segments

Figure 1.1 shows customers and end-users as a single block. However, customers or end-users are seldom as homogeneous as the figure implies. The block often is made up of individual groups, called *segments*. Each segment consists of customers who share buying habits and product preference, and have common needs for supply chain performance. This performance includes features like cost, quality, and responsiveness that are built into the supply chain's design.

Some marketers define the four variables that control how products are presented to different segments. These "four Ps" are product, price, place, and promotion. Decisions in these four will drive retail supply chain design. Needless to say, the number of variations for any product line is huge. The SCM "art" is in designing supply chains to support targeted-segment retail strategies. Subsequent chapters, particularly those in Part 3, will describe examples of the variations in strategy and the types of supply chain to support them.

1.4 Adding Value Along the Chain

A term that is often interchanged with *supply chain* is *value chain*, a term from strategist Michael Porter that reflects profitability at different echelons along the chain.[5] Porter uses the expression in many of the same contexts in which the term *supply chain* is used. "Value" in this case takes the form of the relative profit of each trading partner. Increasing value added is important for strategists because greater value brings higher profits and return on investment.

Profitability, or value, will vary among echelons similar to those in Figure 1.1, depending on the product. Many criticize retailer Wal-Mart for its dominance over suppliers—hence its ability to capture profit through aggressive cost negotiations with manufacturers. Many distributors fear disintermediation because their operations are not seen as "adding value" to the supply chain. The same is said of retail stores whose business suffers because of direct sales by OEMs.

For some technology products, second-tier suppliers may enjoy outsized profits, adding the greatest value to supply chain products. These tech companies possess proprietary *core competencies* that drive innovation in the end products. Microsoft and Intel have been examples for personal computers.

For other supply chains, the OEM may be the most profitable trading partner. This advantage could derive from the OEM's distribution system, its investment in manufacturing plants, or its product development capabilities. Resellers in other supply chains could enjoy high profits. This would be the case where complex systems have to be assembled from relatively inexpensive components. Another source of a highly profitable business comes from after-sales replacement parts and support. Examples are consumables like printer cartridges and razor blades.

We assume that readers of the book represent all the echelons shown in Figure 1.1, not just retail stores. The purpose of this book is to present tools that enable players at any echelon to increase their strategic advantage and, hence, value and profits. So designing operations to increase the enterprise's value in the supply chain is the goal.

Endnotes

1. Levy, Michael, and Weitz, Barton A., *Retailing Management,* 6th ed., New York, Retailing Management, McGraw Hill Irwin, 2006, p. 7.
2. Zikmund, William G., and d'Amico, Michael, *Creating and Keeping Customers: Effective Marketing,* Cincinnati: South-Western College Publishing Company, 1998.
3. DC Velocity Staff, "The Rainmakers," *DC Velocity,* July 2006, pp. 33–49.
4. Ayers, James B., *Handbook of Supply Chain Management,* 2nd ed., Boca Raton: Auerbach Publications, 2006.
5. Porter, Michael E., *Competitive Advantage: Creating and Sustaining Superior Performance,* New York: The Free Press, 1985.

Chapter 2

Success in a Retail Business

This chapter identifies factors that measure financial success for a retail enterprise and the mechanics retailers use to manage their businesses for success and some of the calculations covered are complex, even for supply chain professionals and so the reader has the option of gathering in the general concepts and referring to detail material as needed. As the chapter progresses, warnings will appear ahead of more mathematically challenging sections.

Note that this chapter discusses the retail "enterprise," not the retail "supply chain." Certainly, the supply chain that serves the retailer will benefit to the extent the retailer is successful and vice versa. Being able to collaborate with a retailer on supply chain improvements will be aided by an understanding of how the retailer makes decisions that affect its supply chain. Also, many large retailers pursue integrated strategies in which they manage not only retail assets but also the supply base. IKEA, in fashionable but good-value proprietary home furnishings, and Zara, known for its rapid turnover of fashion clothing designs, are examples. Each either operates factories or designs proprietary products for manufacturing by trading partners. Their internal production departments will benefit to the extent these companies use the tools in this chapter.

Achieving success as a retailer—as well as a supplier to retailers—requires a variety of skills, with the five supply chain management (SCM) tasks listed in Chapter 1, Section 1.2, among them. Chapter 1 also identified successful strategizing using the retailing industry's "Four Ps": product, price, place, and promotion.

2.1 Financial Statements and Analysis

Knowing how well the company is performing financially requires an understanding of basic financial analysis. Awareness of these techniques is important to any

Table 2.1   Retailer Income Statements (millions of U.S. dollars)

		Discounter	High-End
1	Gross sales	1000	35
2	Less: returns	50	5
3	Net sales	950	30
4	Less: cost of goods sold (COGS)	750	10
5	Gross margin	200	20
6	Less: operating expense	90	15
7	Less: interest expense	50	12
8	Total expense	140	27
9	Net pretax profit	60	3
Popular ratios (percent)			
10	Gross margin (#5/#3)	21%	67%
11	Expense ratio (#8/#3)	15	83
12	Pretax profit margin (#9/#1)	6	9
13	Returns ratio (#2/#1)	5	14

manager working along the supply chain. Two reports employed by all industries give details of financial performance. These are:

1. An income statement (Table 2.1), which reports operating results over a period, usually a quarter or a year.
2. A balance sheet (Table 2.2), which reports assets and liabilities at a point in time.

These two reports provide the numbers to assess profitability and to determine how effective the company is in meeting owners' investment return objectives. They also help identify opportunities for the company to improve its performance. The use of income statements and balance sheets for these purposes is definitely not limited to retail companies. Distributors and manufacturers along the supply chain can also employ the techniques described in this chapter.

2.1.1 Retail Income Statements

Table 2.1 shows two fictitious income statements—one, for a company called Discounter, representing a larger discount chain, with revenues of $1 billion

Table 2.2   Retailer Balance Sheets (millions of U.S. dollars)

		Discounter	High-End
	Assets		
Current assets:			
1	Accounts receivable	15	10
2	Merchandise inventory	150	5
3	Cash	10	1
4	Total current assets	175	16
Fixed assets:			
5	Buildings, equipment (at cost)	1000	5
6	Less: accumulated depreciation	400	1
7	Net fixed assets	600	4
8	Total assets	775	20
	Liabilities		
9	Accounts payable	80	7
10	Long-term liabilities	300	1
11	Other liabilities	5	0
12	Total liabilities	385	8
13	Owners' equity	390	12
14	Total liabilities and owners' equity	775	20
	Popular Ratio		
15	"Quick" ratio[a] (#1+#3)/#9	0.3	1.6

[a] Also called acid test, or current ratio.

annually, and the other, a smaller retail chain called High-End, with revenues of $35 million annually. The figures in the income statement in Table 2.1 don't include profit after tax because tax rates vary widely from company to company and are not relevant to this discussion.

The two companies are on opposite ends of the retail value/service spectrum. Discounter caters to value-seeking consumers in search of low prices and High-End to the service-seeking customer attracted to style and luxury. Discounter has a significantly higher cost of goods sold relative to sales (row 4 of Table 2.1) and far lower gross margins, 21 percent versus 67 percent for High-End (row 10). High-End delivers more service for the sales dollar—83 percent versus 15 for Discounter, reflected in the expense ratio (row 11). These services would include help with selection, customer education about product choices, consumer credit to finance sales, a nicer and more highly appointed shopping environment, and having ample inventory from which to choose. Pretax profit margin (row 12) is 50 percent higher for High-End, but one must consider the required investment from the balance sheet shown in Table 2.2. The returns ratio (row 13 of Table 2.1) highlights potential customer service or product quality problems, or could reflect a more generous returns policy appropriate to this retail format.

To improve income statement performance, retailers have the following fundamental options:

1. Decrease expenses
2. Increase margins by:
   - Obtaining merchandise at a lower cost
   - Raising prices
3. Sell more merchandise

The profit-improving task may not be simple. For example, consultants from McKinsey & Company report "holes in the pocket" for retailers, which show up as leaks in income.[1] They note that small leaks in income statement categories can produce large drags on earnings. This is reflected in row 11, which shows that a 1-percent decrease in Discounter's merchandise, operating, and interest costs increase pretax profit from 6 percent to 7 percent, an increase of 17 percent. Thus, attention to detail on the cost side can produce significant improvements in overall profitability. Leaks identified in the McKinsey article include the following:

- Online order discounts
- Delivery to the customer without appropriate charges
- Discounts that do not encourage rapid payment or are given without fast payment
- Cooperative advertising with the manufacturer that is ineffective
- Market development incentives to promote brands or sales to customer groups that do not work

Certainly, some components of the income statement are supply chain-related. These include the cost of goods sold (COGS), the largest expense, which comes by way of original equipment manufacturers (OEMs) or distributors. In-bound freight is added to the COGS as part of merchandise cost. Many operating expenses also cover what are commonly thought of as supply chain costs. Examples are the cost of warehousing facilities and inventory handling and carrying costs. Improving supplier quality might also reduce returns. Designing customer support processes to better match offered products with customer needs might also reduce revenue leaks that show up as returns, particularly for a company such as High-End.

2.1.2 Retail Balance Sheets

The balance sheet shows investments that support the business and the sources of financing at a particular moment in time. Assets in Table 2.2 include the credits extended to customers in the form of accounts receivable (row 1), inventory to support sales (row 2), and cash (row 3). These are referred to as "current" or short-term assets because they are items that have lives of less than one year. Fixed assets like building and equipment (rows 5–7) have longer lives. They are often shown at cost with accumulated depreciation deducted as it is on row 6. Often, this figure on the balance sheet does not reflect current market values, but rather the costs incurred at time of purchase, which may be higher or lower than current ones.

In the example, Discounter owns many of its stores and related equipment. High-End does not but relies on short-term leases for its stores and equipment and therefore, it has relatively few assets on its balance sheet. In many cases, companies also report long-term leases as liabilities. In fact, this will likely be a requirement for financial reporting. As a practical matter, most retail leases for larger companies are for at least ten years and contain renewal options. Once a retailer has built a business at a particular site, the company wants to maintain that location.

The liabilities side of the balance sheet includes both short-term, current (accounts payable, row 9), and long-term (rows 10 and 11) liabilities. For Discounter, these liabilities include the loans taken to purchase the stores it owns. High-End has few long-term liabilities because management has chosen to rent using shorter-term leases. This practice might be risky in terms of losing a lease or having a rent increase.

Owners equity is the difference between assets and liabilities. Because long-term assets are recorded on the balance sheet at historical costs, owners equity doesn't necessarily reflect existing market values. In fact, the value of the real estate assets on Discounter's balance sheet may be deeply understated compared to actual market value.

To make funding decisions when developing and evaluating various strategies, companies also calculate the "cost of capital." This is an interest rate that is determined by weighting rates paid for various sources of debt and equity capital. Any investments must return a cash flow that meets this "hurdle rate" to be approved. Chapter 19, Section 19.2, describes the application of the cost of capital to investment decisions. It also addresses the use of current market costs versus historical costs.

A popular ratio derived from the balance sheet is the acid test or quick ratio (row 15). Some lenders require borrower "liquidity" as determined by the balance sheet. Usually, the ratio assumes that inventory values are zero—hence the "acid" test. Ratios greater than one might be a lender test to assure that the borrower will have the money to repay the loan. In Table 2.2, Discounter has a low ratio (0.3) whereas High-End has a higher one (1.6).

Anand Khokha, president of turnaround company Durkee Sharlit & Associates, has had to take over and lead several retailers in financial trouble with their lenders. He points to opportunities to improve retailer cash flow and profitability:

1. Merchandising is a key factor. Making good decisions about what to buy remains the best way to increase sales and reduce inventory. Although this is no surprise, poor financial performance is often the product of poor merchandising decisions.
2. Getting the product on time is also vital, particularly for retailers who rely on high-volume seasonal sales, such as those at Christmas, or who sell seasonal products like skis, fashion apparel, and bathing suits. Processes may not assure timely deliveries.
3. Real estate is often neglected. There is a lot of capital tied up that can be turned into cash, which could be the case for Discounter. With escalating real estate values in many markets, these investments may have a higher yield than operating the retail business itself.
4. Retailers carry too many stockkeeping units (SKUs), raising inventory and tying up money. Merchandisers may seek to offer a full product range, but many of a product category's SKUs are unprofitable. Strategic analysis is required to determine the appropriate assortment width (number of product lines carried) and depth (number of SKUs within the product category).
5. Measuring category profitability is not done well. The retailer does not know what is profitable and what is not. This is particularly true for smaller companies unable to afford today's technology solutions for managing inventory.

2.1.3 Financial Analysis

A financial analysis is a starting point for turnaround experts like Mr. Khokha. The analysis seeks out opportunities for improvement and requires calculation of performance measures that combine income statement and balance sheet items. Table 2.3 provides common measures with implications for a broadly defined SCM function. The numbers aid understanding how the company operates and discovering opportunities for improved cash flow and profitability. The following paragraphs interpret some of these measures in terms of the influence of SCM on each.

Inventory turns and days of supply (rows 1 and 2). Retailers are particularly interested in inventory turnover because this tells them how many times during the year the company has used and reused its inventory investment dollars, garnering margins with each turn. Unless objectives for inventory turns are met, the company can find itself short of cash to pay its expenses and, in extreme cases, bleeding to death by depleting inventory to pay other bills. Inventory is also a common target for

Table 2.3 Financial Analysis

	Name	Factors	Equation	Discounter	High-End
1	Inventory turns	COGS/*inventory*[a]	#4/#2	5.0	2.0
2	Inventory days of supply	*Inventory*/daily COGS	#2/(#4/365)	73	183
3	A. Receivable days B. Payable days	*Receivables*/daily net sales *Payables*/daily COGS	#1/(#3/365) #9/(#4/365)	6 39	121 255
4	Cash-to-cash cycle (days)	Receivable + inventory days – payable days	#2+#3A-3B	40	49
5	Return on equity (percent)	Pretax profit/*owners equity*	#9/#13	15%	25%
6	Return on total capital (percent)	Pretax profit/*total assets*	#9/#8	8%	15%
7	Return on working capital	Pretax profit/(*receivables* + *inventory* + *cash – accounts payable*)	#9/(#1+#2+#3-#9)	63%	33%

Note: Balance sheet items are in italics, and income statement items in regular type.

[a] Some companies calculate inventory turns as net sales/*inventory.*

cost reduction efforts for supply chain reengineering. Solutions include purging slow-moving items through inventory analysis, sharing forecasts with suppliers, negotiating delivery schedules, inventory holding by suppliers, more frequent replenishment, and better forecasting. In general, many efforts by retailers attempt to forecast the optimum amounts of inventory (days of supply) that will maximize turns, minimize order costs, and avoid stockouts.

Receivable and payable days (rows 3A and 3B). Excess receivables may be symptomatic of loose credit practices or providing too much credit to customers. This is one of the "leaks" identified by the McKinsey consultants. "Firing" slow-paying customers may improve cash flow. Payables, on the other hand, provide a source of working capital. High-End makes ample use of supplier credit to finance its business. Should their suppliers' willingness to perform this service change, High-End's business model would be threatened because it would have to raise capital to finance its inventory.

Cash-to-cash cycle (row 4). This cycle captures the effect of coordinating the three working capital accounts for receivables, inventory, and payables. Early in their lives Dell and Toyota were both motivated to minimize this measure. This was simply because, at this early stage of their company's life, cash was in short supply. Dell's direct model takes an order payment from the customer and only then acquires parts necessary to build the ordered computer. Toyota has a "sell one, make one" mentality exemplified by its "pull" replenishment systems. Dell's and Toyota's approach, now labeled "lean" by practitioners, has been rewarded with high profits and market share. Many supply chain reengineering efforts use the cash-to-cash cycle to set their goals and assess changes that reduce the cycle. One such company, described in Chapter 10, Section 10.1, is furniture maker Herman Miller.

Return on capital (rows 5 to 7). Most companies use metrics that relate profits to investment. The three shown here are common. The first includes only owners' equity in the base, the second total assets, and the third working capital only. The total assets approach is the most comprehensive. Many investors would consider the 8 percent return on total capital for Discounter marginal. On the other hand, High-End's 25-percent return on equity (ROE) would be attractive to most. High-End does depend, as mentioned previously, on continued financing by suppliers.

In a period where private capital investors are acquiring retailers and other firms, candidates are surfaced by examining the income statement and balance sheet. The search identifies opportunities to convert assets into cash to pay for the acquisition. Discounter might be such a candidate. Their substantial real estate holdings may be such a source of funds. So might shortening the 40-day cash-to-cash cycle through inventory reductions, dropping slow-moving merchandise, faster collections, and having suppliers finance inventories.

2.2 Merchandise Replenishment and Budgeting

The merchandise budgeting function at the retailer level establishes a plan for buying merchandise, allocating it to stores, and planning replenishment. Retailers often utilize a "Strategic Profit Model" in assessing performance. Financial executives at E.I. DuPont de Nemours and Company (DuPont) developed the model during World War I. At the time the company, founded in July 1802, was already over 100 years old. The model is useful for retailers because it combines the effects of inventory turnover and margins on overall financial performance.

The DuPont Company, in an effort to evaluate the performance of its divisions, broke down ROE into three ratios: return on sales, sales turnover, and the ratio of assets to equity.[2] They then demonstrated the relationship between them as follows:

Return on equity = (Return on sales) × (sales turnover) × (financial leverage)

or, algebraically, with income statement parameters in regular type and balance sheet items in italics:

(Profit/*equity*) = (Profit/sales) × (sales/*assets*) × (*assets/equity*)

A subset financial parameter under the control of the merchandise buyer is the gross margin return on investment (GMROI). GMROI is the *gross margin percentage* of the merchandise multiplied by *sales-to-stock* ratio. The equation is as follows:

GMROI (%) = (Gross margin/net sales) × (net sales/*average inventory*)
          = Gross margin/*average inventory*

This measure is usually employed for a category of merchandise to produce a plan for ordering stock to support sales. It is also employed to evaluate the performance of merchandise buyers because it incorporates factors under buyer control: selling price/cost of merchandise and inventory turnover. The following discussion will include the role of GMROI in the decision making required of replenishment and inventory management processes.

2.2.1 The Importance of Replenishment Models in Retail Supply Chains

The job of juggling financial variables to optimize merchandise plans is formidable. Because the tools used for this planning are prevalent in retail store decision making, those upstream in the supply chain should understand the decision processes behind them. The retail suppliers' products and services are likely to be ordered using similar planning tools. Knowledge of these practices can produce benefits for both retailers and suppliers if they develop processes to lower the cost of doing business together. Examining the math in the performance measures should lead suppliers to ideas for improving performance and quantification of the benefits.

Merchandise budgeting does not specify exact quantities of each SKU, only the amount of money to be spent on a product line or category. In other words, the deliverable is a monetary amount to be spent in a defined budget period (usually, a few months), not the number of size 6 blue sweaters to order. The merchandise budget is constrained by the retailers' need to meet its financial objectives. Our discussion will proceed in two steps. Step 1 describes the concept behind merchandise replenishment and budgeting using an example and explains the decisions that are made using the budget. Step 2 describes how numbers required to complete the budget are calculated. This is fairly complicated; some readers may want to pass on this section (Section 2.2.2.4).

2.2.2 Merchandise Types—Staple versus Fashion

The procedures for merchandise budgeting methods may vary depending on whether the merchandise is a "staple" with predictable sales or a "fashion" category with far less sales history. Without the product history, the merchandiser will have to track actual sales more closely and adjust replenishment plans in response to actual sales. For staples, computers might do the heavy lifting.

These classifications (staple and fashion) correspond to the "functional" and "innovative" labels applied to products in Chapter 11, Section 11.2—the *staple*, to the *functional* and the *fashion*, to the *innovative*. Staples, or functional products, are those we buy every day. Examples include grocery products, basic clothing, and hardware items. Examples of fashion or innovative products include stylish apparel with a short selling window, just released movies, new electronics products, and high-end, limited production automobiles.

2.2.2.1 Staple or Functional Products

For staple products, many retailers will use automated planning systems, of which there are many choices, to manage replenishment of stock. A merchandise budget will provide planning parameters, or rules, incorporated into the software that ensure the category meets profitability goals derived from GMROI targets. What distinguishes staples from fashion items is that they are more "forecastable." Also, short-term excess inventory of durable staples, not perishable items, will generally be sold eventually, avoiding markdowns.

Supply chains for staples are engineered to deliver products as efficiently as possible. Systems for staples compute recommended *order points* and *order quantities* based on sales history and forecasts. The order point is the minimum inventory level where the item is likely to be out of stock before a replenishment order can be received. Upstream suppliers who reduce the order lead time can lower safety stock requirements for this category. Systems for staples often factor in *forecast error* or the difference between actual demand and the forecast. They then employ formulas to make adjustments. Sometimes, the forecast error is targeted for minimization. In computer calculations, seasonality factors also adjust the base "deseasonalized" forecasts when appropriate.

Most large retailers use electronic data interchange (EDI) or eXtensible Markup Language (XML) to order a wide variety of staple products. With the advent of large-scale integrated computer systems has come the ability to continuously track sales by store and region and to maintain accurate inventory counts at the retail level. Visibility in the supply chain enables automatic generation of orders without human intervention.

Michael Hugos in his work *Essentials of Supply Chain Management* classifies staple inventories into three categories[3]:

1. Cycle inventory: inventory needed between orders to meet demand, like regular quantities of men's underwear at J.C. Penney. These items are often reordered in fixed quantities when the reorder point is reached.
2. Seasonal inventory: inventory purchased and stored for anticipated future demand.
3. Safety inventory: extra inventory carried to adjust for uncertain demand during the reorder period and variations in anticipated lead times.

Hugos also suggests four ways to reduce safety stock, thereby also reducing total inventory:

1. Improve forecasting; lower forecast error.
2. Have more frequent deliveries so that lead times are reduced.
3. Reduce lead-time variability adding predictability to decision making.
4. Work with suppliers to ensure product availability including shared forecasts or providing access to in-stock status data.

2.2.2.2 Fashion or Innovative Products

When forecasting gets complicated and forecast errors increase, the merchandise may better be treated as a fashion or innovative product. It is important for manufacturers and distributors seeking out opportunities for these types of products because they bring higher margins and open new markets. Fashion/innovative products have one or more of the following characteristics:

■ Are sold in limited time windows—seasonal, new product introductions, or tied to promotional events instead of the usual one-year planning horizon
■ Are hard to forecast, requiring flexible supply chains to take full advantage of what may be unclear opportunities

- Have higher profit margins and are in market introduction or growth phases of the product life cycle
- Command higher markup percentages than staple products, typically a percentage calculated by retailers as Markup ($) divided by the retail selling price ($)
- May be recurring new models or upgrade products with a common distribution channel, such as music, movies, software, electronic gadgets, or new food items on the menu
- May have multiple retail paths to end-users and customers

2.2.2.3 Merchandise Budget: An Example

The merchandise budget, such as that shown in Table 2.4, is a tool used to plan material purchases. The table presents an example of a seasonal fashion category to be sold in a four-month period, or "window." Such products represent real opportunities for supply chain innovation, customizing business rules, and creating alternative physical paths. This can often be facilitated by collaboration between the retail store and its upstream suppliers—reinforcing the case for manufacturers and distributors to understand the retailer's planning processes.

In Table 2.4, inputs from the planner are shown in bold with shaded cells on the spreadsheet format. Initial data includes the following:

1. Beginning inventory shown on line 8 in the initial stock column ($70,000). This is a planned initial purchase from the OEM manufacturer.
2. Planning assumptions. These assumptions in the right-hand column include forecast sales (line 2) of $250,000; monthly reductions for samples, promotions, shrinkage, and employee discounts (line 4) of $25,000, or 10 percent of sales; and desired average beginning of the month (BOM) *stock-to-sales* ratio (line 6). How the stock-to-sales target ratio using the GMROI objective is calculated is described later.
3. Monthly distributions for sales and distributions in percentages (lines 1 and 3). The planner will estimate forecast sales distribution in line 1 based on the timing of promotions for the product, seasonality factors if any, and the rate of market acceptance. The approach to reductions estimates on line 3 is similar.
4. Desired end-of-month (EOM) inventory at the end of the promotion in month 4. This is $0 in the example, a seasonal category with few sales expected after the end of the four-month selling period.

From these inputs, the spreadsheet calculates expected inventory, needed replenishments and the actual average BOM stock-to-sales ratio. Although the average stock-to-sales ratio needs to be 2.0 to meet the GMROI objective, this plan shows extra stock for the first two months of the sales period. The planner makes this decision to have the stock-to-sales ratio of 2.5. The example shows that the actual ratio for the four months matches that allowed by the budget (2.0). The calculation for additions

Table 2.4   Merchandise Budget Plan for Fashion Category (Excel spreadsheet)

		Initial Stock	1	2	3	4	*Planning Assumptions*
					Months		
1	Sales distribution (percent)		15	25	40	20	100
2	Forecast sales (dollars)		37,500	62,500	100,000	50,000	250,000
3	Reductions (percent)		30	30	25	15	100
4	Monthly reductions (dollars)		7,500	7,500	6,250	3,750	25,000
5	Total consumption (dollars)		45,000	70,000	106,250	53,750	275,000
6	BOM stock-to-sales ratio		2.5	2.5	2.0	1.0	2.0
7	BOM inventory (dollars)		70,000	175,000	212,500	53,750	
8	EOM inventory (dollars)	70,000	175,000	212,500	53,750	—	
9	Additions to stock (dollars)		150,000	107,500	(52,500)	—	
					Actual average BOM stock-to-sales ratio:	2.0	

Note: Figures are in U.S. dollars except where indicated otherwise.

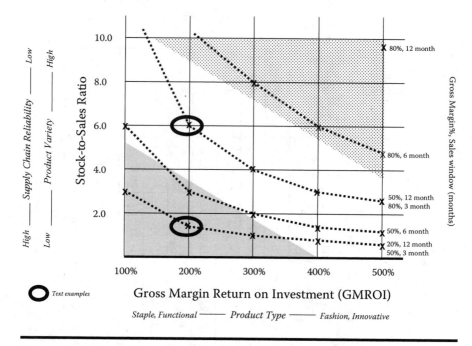

Figure 2.1   Merchandise replenishment model.

to stock (line 9) establishes an EOM inventory (line 8) sufficient as a beginning-of-month inventory (line 7) for the next month. An understanding of this procedure should enable suppliers to collaborate with the retailer on initial inventory and the replenishment schedule.

2.2.2.4 Merchandise Replenishment Model

This section, which contains some complex math, explains the relationship between GMROI and the stock-to-sales ratio that drove the replenishment plan in Table 2.4. The profitability model can help shape the type of supply chain needed for particular product variety, gross margin, and supply chain combinations. Figure 2.1 displays the relationship between decision factors that affect the merchandise replenishment and, ultimately, profitability. The horizontal axis shows the input to the model, GMROI, with values ranging from 100 to 500 percent. The vertical axis, the output, is the average stock-to-sales ratio like the figures on line 6 in Table 2.4.

The curves represent different gross margin/sales window combinations. Gross margin values of 20, 50, and 80 percent are shown. With the GMROI objective, gross margin (percentage), and the length of the sales window (months), a planner can look up the stock-to-sales ratio on the vertical axis. Staple products have lower margins—between 10 and 30 percent. Margins for fashions are higher, perhaps as much as 80 percent. Sales windows of 3, 6, and 12 months are shown. A three-month window is close to that of a seasonal or "one-shot" fashion item. A six-month window is used for planning by many retailers. A 12-month window is appropriate for an annual review of a staple or a longer-life fashion item.

The first curve applies to two scenarios: a 20 percent 12-month window and a 50 percent 3-month window. This curve applies mostly to staples, meaning stock-to-sales ratios must be kept low to achieve the GMROI goal. Moving up and to the right is a curve for 50 percent 12-month window and the 80 percent 3-month scenario window. At the far upper right-hand corner is a point for the 80 percent 12-month window product. Notice that increasing profitability and longer sales windows allow for higher stock-to-sales ratios.

Different retailers carve out strategies based on different areas of the map in Figure 2.1. Wal-Mart and the store in our example, Discounter, operate in the lower left-hand corner, and a specialty retailer such as High-End, in the upper right. The shaded area in the lower left is the domain of staples that require frequent, reliable replenishment—characteristics of well-developed reliable supply chains. The region is also more suited to product categories with less variety in terms of the number of SKUs. One can appreciate the problem of shoes versus video game consoles. A line of shoes may have five styles, four colors, and six sizes, leading to 120 SKUs. A video game console might have just two or three package options.

Having higher stock relative to sales in the upper right quadrant of Figure 2.1 protects against stockouts of more popular sizes, colors, or other product features. The upper right high stock-to-sales ratios will also insulate retailers from long or unreliable suppliers by allowing more time to react to problems. Having more stock for risk pooling provides protection against outages that go with a large number of SKUs or unreliable supply chains. In applying this technique, stock is held centrally and then dispersed to outlets as through demand-driven replenishment. Chapter 17 further describes demand-driven replenishment, including risk pooling.

2.2.2.5 Merchandise Budget Follow-Up

Several ongoing activities unfold as the merchandise budget plan goes into effect and the marketplace responds to the products.[4] These include the open-to-buy system, allocation of stock to stores, analyzing merchandise performance, sell-through analysis, and supplier evaluation. Open-to-buy systems continuously assess needs to reach the EOM stock levels planned in the budget and serve as a monthly "checkbook" for the buyer. This activity tracks goods on order and decides what needs to be spent to achieve stock levels required to meet sales goals and can be adjusted for increases and decreases in actual sales.

Store analysis tracks how specific items are doing at various locations. It also reallocates stock to stores in the case of supply chain problems. The sell-through analysis looks at specific merchandise SKUs to tune the plan to add or reduce specific SKU items and to make price changes as needed. The analysis can lead to markdowns of slow-moving SKUs before the end of the selling period. Later, Chapter 21, Section

21.4, describes an analysis methodology using the ABC approach for evaluating not only specific items but also the suppliers.

2.3 Preparing a Merchandise Budget

This section describes the processes for developing the components of the merchandise budget with the stock-to-sales ratio as the primary output. This discussion is for the more detail-inclined reader. The methods vary from typical material planning approaches used by upstream merchandise suppliers. This is input into the merchandise budget described in Table 2.4 (line 6). In that example, the target ratio is 2.0. Figure 2.2 is a guide to the process.

A merchandise budget planner should have a GMROI goal before beginning the planning process. This is step 1 on Figure 2.1. As previously described, GMROI is the product of the *gross margin percentage* (total gross margin/net sales) and the ratio of net sales over average inventory at cost, referred to as the sales-to-stock ratio. This is calculated in step 2 in Figure 2.2. Step 3 converts the sales-to-stock ratio to *inventory turnover*. The calculation multiplies the ratio by one minus the gross margin percentage to create a ratio in which both sales and stock are on the same basis. Inventory turnover is for the period (3, 4, 6, or 12 months) chosen for the marketing window for which the budget is being prepared.

For manufacturers and distributors, the term "inventory turnover" usually applies to a yearly period. Table 2.3 (line 1) calculates inventory turns in the traditional way—for a 12-month period. For the retailer's fashion merchandise, the selling period is more likely to be six months or shorter. To illustrate, Table 2.5, in the top section (lines 1–3), shows sales by month for three selling windows—twelve, six, and three months. The sales are expressed in units and assumed to be evenly distributed over the selling periods for simplicity. The table shows that the intensity of sales of the 12 units increases as the selling window shortens. This seems quite obvious, of course, but an understanding of this relationship is important to supply chain design and inventory management.

Step 4 calculates the average beginning-of-month stock-to-sales ratio used for planning merchandise purchases by month. This produces different ratios (3.0, 1.5, and 0.8) for each window, as seen in the middle of Table 2.4 (lines 5 to 7). The example assumes that the inventory turnover is 4. The equation for *average stock-to-sales* ratio is *selling window* divided by the inventory turnover as shown in the notes on Figure 2.2. Applying this ratio produces 3 units of inventory for every month as shown in the bottom section of Table 2.5 (lines 8 to 10).

Manufacturers and distributors might be confused by this terminology. As mentioned previously, their way of calculating turns, shown in the right-hand column, is on an annual basis. So their turns would be significantly higher than 4 for the 6- and 12-month selling windows. Comparisons can be made by annualizing the fashion retailer's expected turns. For example, two turns in four months is the equivalent of six inventory turns in a year.

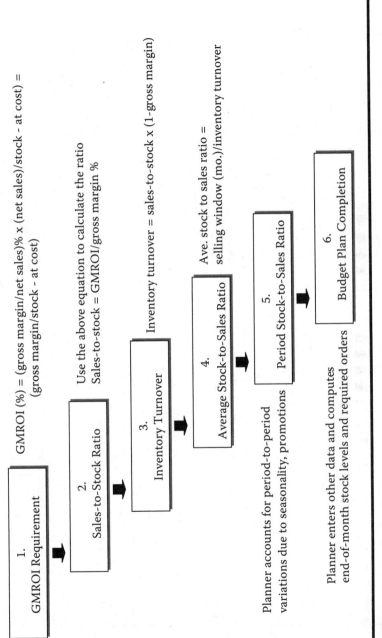

GMROI (%) = (gross margin/net sales)% x (net sales)/stock - at cost) = (gross margin/stock - at cost)

1.
GMROI Requirement

Use the above equation to calculate the ratio
Sales-to-stock = GMROI/gross margin %

2.
Sales-to-Stock Ratio

Inventory turnover = sales-to-stock x (1-gross margin)

3.
Inventory Turnover

Ave. stock to sales ratio = selling window (mo.)/inventory turnover

4.
Average Stock-to-Sales Ratio

Planner accounts for period-to-period variations due to seasonality, promotions

5.
Period Stock-to-Sales Ratio

Planner enters other data and computes end-of-month stock levels and required orders

6.
Budget Plan Completion

Figure 2.2   Merchandise budgeting process.

Table 2.5   Inventory Turnover for Various Planning Windows (Excel spreadsheet)

#		Average Sales by Month												Total
		1	2	3	4	5	6	7	8	9	10	11	12	
1.	12-month window	1	1	1	1	1	1	1	1	1	1	1	1	12
2.	6-month window	2	2	2	2	2	2							12
3.	3-month window	4	4	4										12

Average Beginning-of-Month Stock-to-Sales Ratio (window/inventory turns)

#		
4.	Inventory turnover	4
5.	12-month window	3.0
6.	6-month window	1.5
7.	3-month window	0.8

Average Beginning-of-Month Inventory Level

#		1	2	3	4	5	6	7	8	9	10	11	12	Conventional Turns
8.	12-month window	3	3	3	3	3	3	3	3	3	3	3	3	4
9.	6-month window	3	3	3	3	3	3							8
10.	3-month window	3	3	3										16

In step 5 of Figure 2.2, the planner adjusts this average month by month. These adjustments reflect promotions as well as seasonal factors. Lower stock-to-sales ratios would probably be assigned to high-sales months, and higher to low-sales months if sales were expected to vary month by month during the sales window.

These relationships are developed in the example sequence that follows, beginning with the goal setting from GMROI and using that objective to produce the other parameters, with the budget plan completion step described in step 6.

1. Use the GMROI objective to calculate a required sales-to-stock ratio. The GMROI goal may be the same for both staples and fashion merchandise. In this case, we assume the required GMROI is 200 percent. For example, low-margin underwear has a 20 percent gross margin of $500,000 on annual net retail sales of $2,500,000. To achieve the required GMROI, it must have a sales-to-stock ratio of 10. This is calculated using the following equation:

$$\text{GMROI} = (\$500,000/\$2,500,000) \times (\$2,500,000/\$250,000)$$
$$\times\ 100\% = 200\%.\ \text{So the stock level that completes}$$
$$\text{the equation is }\$250,000\text{ at cost.}$$

   For a high-margin lady's fashion, an anticipated 50-percent gross margin on annual net sales of $5,000,000 translates to $2,500,000. With the same GMROI requirement of 200 percent, the sales-to-stock ratio is 4. ($2,500,000/$5,000,000) × ($5,000,000/$1,250,000) × 100 = 200 percent. As described earlier, in the sales-to-stock ratio, the sales figure is at retail prices and the stock, at cost.

2. Convert the sales-to-stock ratio based on sales price to an inventory turnover requirement. This adjusts the sales-to-stock ratio by the gross margin for the product line. This adjustment is performed because we have used the merchandise sales price, not its cost, in the calculations. For our examples, the calculation is as follows (sales-to-stock ratio × (1 − GM)), adjusting the sales price to the cost of goods sold:

   a. Low-margin product: Inventory turnover = 10.0 × (1 − 0.2) = 8.0
   b. High-margin product: Inventory turnover = 4.0 × (1 − 0.5) = 2.0

   As shown in Table 2.5, these are the annual inventory turns based on company goals for GMROI. Inventory turnover varies by product category. For example, for one well-known specialty store, turnover in shoes is only about one time a year, whereas in junior girls' dresses, turnover approaches 13 times annually.

3. Set the average stock-to-sales ratio for the selling period. For the low-margin underwear, the assumption is that the selling period is 12 months. So the stock level at retail is one eighth the retail revenues. This is $312,500 (1/8 × $2,500,000). If the planning period is monthly, then the average stock-to-sales ratio = $312,500/($2,500,000/12) = 1.5.

For the high-margin product, the company prepares both a 12-month budget and one for a promotional three-month selling period. For the 12-month selling period, the average permissible stock would be $5,000,000/2 = $2,500,000. This doesn't mean the company shouldn't look for ways to cut this through supply chain improvement initiatives such as those described elsewhere in this book. With monthly planning and a 12-month window, the average stock-to-sales ratio = $2,500,000/($5,000,000/12) = 6.0. If the same sales were to be squeezed into a three-month period, the ratio would be 1.5. However, the planner could choose to replenish each month, buy the whole requirement at once, or split the program into two orders. Delivery for an order can also be scheduled across several months. (These results are also circled on Figure 2.1.)

4. Set beginning-of-period stock-to-sales ratios. These quarterly, monthly, or weekly figures take into account seasonality, order quantity limitations, and fluctuations in demand. They should be designed to ensure that the average stock-to-sales levels calculated previously result. These are 1.5 and 6.0 in our two examples.

5. Calculate BOM levels. This calculation is the projected sales multiplied by the monthly stock-to-sales ratio. This level is calculated by multiplying the desired stock-to-sales ratio by the forecast for consumption during the month.

6. Calculate additions to stock. These constitute the orders needed to establish EOM levels that become BOM levels for the next month.

Planned additions to stock = [(stock/sales) (planned sales)]
+ reductions + EOM Stock – BOM Stock

Reductions include planned markdowns, expected shrinkage (losses from shoplifting, damage, and administrative loss), and discounts to be given to employees. In retailing, allowances are made for these types of expected losses. However, without such planning, the store will be short of merchandise to meet their planned sales goals.

2.4 Summary

Understanding what makes a retailer financially successful is important to all retail supply chain participants. Making the retailer successful will make upstream trading partners successful as well. Retailers will be motivated by cooperative efforts to improve GMROI; suppliers who can help that effort will be appreciated. Suppliers can do much to improve supply chain links to ensure reliable, rapid replenishment of the retailer. Examining each product initiative using the analysis techniques in this chapter and the tools for supply chain design described throughout this book will enable these collaborative partnerships.

Endnotes

1. Marn, Michael V., Roegner, Eric V., and Zawada, Craig C., "The Power of Pricing," *The McKinsey Quarterly,* No. 1, 2003, pp. 27–36.
2. Bruner, Robert F., Eaker, Mark R., Freeman, R. Edward, Sjpekman, Robert E., Teisberg, Olmsted, Elizabeth, and Venkataraman, S., *The Portable MBA,* 4th ed., Hoboken, NJ: John Wiley & Sons, 2003, p. 477.
3. Hugos, Michael, *Essentials of Supply Chain Management,* 2nd ed., Hoboken, NJ: John Wiley & Sons, 2006, pp. 60–63.
4. Levy, Michael and Weitz, Barton A., *Retailing Management,* 5th ed., New Delhi: Tata McGraw-Hill Publishing Company Limited, pp. 415–425, chap. 13.

Chapter 3

Types of Retail Supply Chain Businesses

This chapter profiles financial data related to the U.S. retail industry. This data includes government sector classifications at higher levels and financial reports of selected companies at the lower levels. Every five years, the U.S. Census Bureau documents all industries in considerable detail, including the sector called *retail trades*. Summarizing this data in what the bureau calls the Economic Census leads to a better understanding of the retail industry's size in the world's largest market, how retailing fits with its sister supply chain sectors, and some of the differences between individual retail industry sectors.

The information in this chapter should be valuable to those in other countries also. First, many of them export to the United States. Second, other markets, even though smaller, could mirror the U.S. market structure as they develop. As a sign that this is the case, an article in the *Wall Street Journal* profiled the potential for growth of "organized retailing."[1] Organized retailing is defined as chain store penetration. The article quotes a study by the firm Technopak Advisors, an Indian consumer products consultancy. The study describes the different levels of organized retailing penetration in different countries—3 percent in India compared to 85 percent in the United States and 20 percent in China, a country that has become a hotbed of competition among large retail chains worldwide. Lower levels of chain penetration, as in India and China, hold promise for future growth unavailable in mature economies. The article describes Wal-Mart's alliance with Bharti Enterprises, Ltd., an Indian cell phone company, as a way to skirt Indian regulations and get a jump on competitors like Carrefour SA of France and Tesco PLC of Britain.

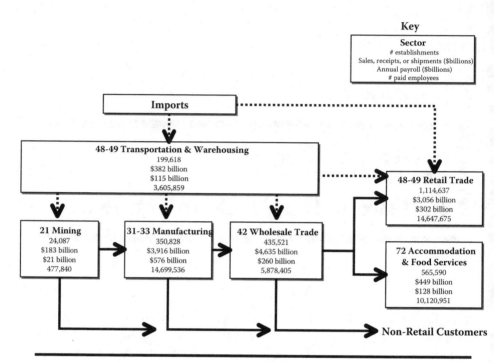

Figure 3.1   Principal U.S. supply chain sectors.

3.1 Supply Chain Component Data

The North American Industry Classification System (NAICS), run by the U.S. Census Bureau, is the successor to the U.S. Standard Industrial Classification (SIC) system. The statistics derived from the survey reveal the relative size of the retail and associated sectors that comprise the retail supply chain. Figure 3.1 displays a top-down view showing participating sectors in the retail supply chain. In NAICS, the first two digits define broad sectors similar to those shown in Figure 3.1. Subsequent three-, four-, five-, and six-digit classifications proceed to lower subsector levels. The top view includes the following sectors with their two-digit NAICS codes:

Mining (21)
Manufacturing (31–33)
Wholesale trade (42)
Retail trade (44–45)
Transportation and warehousing (48–49)
Accommodation and food services (72)

Both retail trade (44–45) and accommodation and food services (72) can be considered totally "retail" as most would define the term. Within accommodation and food services, the activity split is 90 percent for food services like restaurants, with the remainder, 10 percent, for accommodations. For simplicity the figure omits other retail outlets associated with financial institutions (banks, credit unions, savings and loan companies) and healthcare providers (doctors' offices, clinics, hospitals).

Although the supply chain serving the retail sector devotes a considerable share of its capacity to the retail sector, the chain also serves many nonretail industries such as utilities, construction, and government. The revenue figures for each sector are not value-added along the chain. In other words, the revenues for retail trades include the cost of value-adding products and services from the upstream sectors—mining, manufacturing, wholesale trade, and transportation and warehousing.

The conclusion to be drawn from the data in Figure 3.1 is that retail as an industry involves large numbers of participants in many varied industries. There are, conservatively, over 2,500,000 enterprises with over 30,000,000 employees. The profile also illustrates the "many to many" situation. That is, a lot of manufacturers and distributors, about 500,000, provide goods for sale in a lot of retail establishments—over 1,500,000. This gives rise to independent or captive intermediary distribution warehouses and other service providers, about 200,000 in the transportation and warehousing sector, which glue the pieces together by receiving from many sources and dispersing to many retail outlets. The sector provides services all along the chain for movement and storage of goods.

Much of what is ultimately sold at retail consists of imports of final products and raw materials. So this is also shown, without numbers, as inputs along the chain.

Within the box for each sector are basic statistics about that sector, which include the following:

The number of establishments or locations where business is done. For example, a single company, such as a retail chain, will have as many establishments as it has stores.
The sales, receipts, or shipments in billions of dollars for the sector.
The annual payroll for each sector in billions of dollars.
The number of paid employees, including both part time and full time.

A little math shows that the average pay (in 2002) in the retail trade sector was about $21,000. In other sectors, pay-per-employee figures are as follows: $32,000 for transportation and warehousing, $44,000 for wholesale trade and mining, $39,000 in manufacturing, and $13,000 in accommodations and food services. Note that the number of employees includes both full and part time. The comparison of retail with other industries doesn't take into account the heavy reliance of retail on part-timers. If the adjustments were available, the per-employee pay gap between retailing and other industries would likely close.

3.2 Retail Supply Chains in the United States

The retail trade category shown in Figure 3.1 includes 12 retailer three-digit subsectors from 441 through 454. Table 3.1 lists these subsectors along with brief descriptions. These classifications are broken down further with four- and five-digit categories. For example, the first category (441) breaks down as follows:

> 441. Motor vehicles and parts includes
>> 4411. Automobile dealers
>>> 44111. New car dealers
>>> 44112. Used-car dealers
>> 4412. Other motor vehicle dealers
>>> 44121. Recreational vehicle dealers
>>> 44122. Motorcycle, boat, and other vehicle dealers
>> 4413. Automotive parts, accessories, and tire stores
>>> 44131. Automotive parts and accessories stores
>>> 44132. Tire dealers

Table 3.1 profiles 12 subsectors with data as in Figure 3.1. All subsectors but the last are "fixed point-of-sales" locations, what most people call "stores." The last (454) is the nonstore category. Note that most of the descriptions in Table 3.1 list needs for equipment, advice, displays, repair facilities, and other expertise to facilitate customer purchases. These are examples of extended products as defined in Chapter 1. The retailers' markets are not limited to consumer sales but also serve business and institutional customers.

Table 3.2 profiles retail "establishments" in the United States. These are the larger retail locations, those with employees. Another category of non–employee establishments, representing 2.5 percent of receipts, also exists but is not shown here. Columns A through F are from the census data. As mentioned previously, the number of paid employees (column F) includes both full- and part-time categories. An "establishment" is a single location and is not necessarily the only location for a company or enterprise. Columns G through J are ratios calculated from columns C through F.

Retail industry size was about $3 trillion in an economy of about $10 trillion in 2002. As an employer, the industry ranked third with 14.6 million employees, behind healthcare and social assistance with 15.1 million and manufacturing with 14.7 million. Most retail locations have less than 15 employees (column I). The exception is the general merchandise store category with 62. Not surprisingly, the category includes the largest retailers. The motor vehicles and parts subsector has the highest payroll per employee. Reasons could include having more full-time staff, maintaining a sales force for high-ticket merchandise, and requiring skilled technicians to deliver repair services.

3.3 Selected Supply Chain Company Returns

Table 3.3 displays data from eight companies, a few of which are mentioned elsewhere in this book. The information in Table 3.3 comes from recent annual reports of each company available at the time of writing. The purpose of this sample is to illustrate the diversity that exists across the retail supply chain, because the companies represent different sectors. Understanding the range of differences is important for upstream and downstream collaboration to improve the supply chain. The table uses data to calculate gross margin return on investment (GMROI) in column G. The cash-to-cash cycle (column H) is also provided from financial reports. Chapter 2 describes how to calculate these parameters.

Distributors and retailers assess products, categories, markets, and companies using these measures, described in Chapter 2. Achieving excellence in the two metrics requires savvy merchandise selection, targeting attractive customers, logistics skills, and willing suppliers. The calculations use end-of-period inventory (column E), rather than average inventory prescribed in some definitions of GMROI. Because companies use different definitions of accounts and report data in different formats, the figures in Table 3.2 required some adjustments by the authors. Despite this, the sample is effective at illustrating the differences between companies.

Wal-Mart Stores, Inc., is the world's largest retail company measured by sales and operates over 6000 locations. Its strategy has centered on offering value-for-price to its customers. The 2006 report to shareholders touted growth in same-store sales of 3 percent for the year. Costco also pursues a low-cost strategy but achieves a higher GMROI than Wal-Mart. The company points to supplier financing, buying direct from manufacturers, and limiting the number of product SKUs carried to about 4000, far less than the number carried at other stores, as reasons for its superior performance. The −19-day cash-to-cash cycle indicates that Costco sells and collects its money from customers before suppliers are paid.

Gap is a clothing retailer with over 3000 stores. Its branded chains include Gap, Banana Republic, Old Navy, Forth & Towne, and Gap, Inc. Direct. The last operates the Web sites for the brands. Gap executives report that the 2005 reporting year was "a year of progress as well as challenges." Despite this, the company enjoys the highest gross margins in our selection.

West Marine, with just over 400 stores, focuses on the recreational boating industry. Chapters 15 and 16 explore the company in some detail. Its strategy calls for a high service level in terms of having available stock; hence, it has the lowest sales-to-stock ratio in the group. The service requirement also led to a low GMROI for the year, a year also acknowledged by the CEO to have been challenging. In fact, the company had operating losses.

McKesson illustrates the role of the distributor. This company uses GMROI to measure product performance, has the lowest gross margin (column D). It also carries 30 days of inventory resulting in the lowest GMROI in the group. However,

Table 3.1 Definition of NAIC Categories

Code	Descriptions of Product Category	Description
441	Motor vehicles and parts	Retail motor vehicles and parts from fixed point-of-sale locations. Typically operate from showrooms or open lots. Personnel include both sales and sales support staff to sell vehicles as well as a staff of parts experts and trained mechanics.
442	Furniture and home furnishing stores	Sellers of new furniture and home furnishings from fixed point-of-sale locations. Usually operate from showrooms and have substantial areas for presentation of products. Many offer interior decorating services in addition to products.
443	Electronics and appliance stores	Electronics and appliances from point-of-sale locations. Operate from locations with provision for floor displays requiring electrical capacity to demonstrate products. Staff is knowledgeable in the characteristics and warranties of the products and may include trained repair persons for maintenance and repair.
444	Building material and garden equipment and supplies dealers	Retail new building material and garden equipment and supplies from fixed point-of-sale locations. Display equipment designed to handle lumber and related products and garden equipment and supplies. Staff knowledgeable in the use of the products for construction, repair, and maintenance of the home and associated grounds.
445	Food and beverage stores	Sell retail food and beverages from fixed point-of-sale locations. Have special equipment (e.g., freezers, refrigerated display cases, refrigerators) for displaying food and beverage goods. Have staff trained in the processing of food products to guarantee the proper storage and sanitary conditions required by regulatory authority.
446	Health and personal care stores	Retail health and personal care merchandise from fixed point-of-sale locations. May have specialized staff trained in dealing with the products. Staff may include pharmacists, opticians, and other professionals engaged in retailing, advising customers, or fitting the product sold to the customer's needs.

447	Gasoline stations	Retail automotive fuels (e.g., gasoline, diesel fuel, gasohol) and automotive oils with or without convenience store items. These establishments have specialized equipment for the storage and dispensing of automotive fuels.
448	Clothing and clothing accessories stores	Retail new clothing and clothing accessories merchandise from fixed point-of-sale locations. Establishments have similar display equipment and staff who are knowledgeable regarding fashion trends and the proper match of styles, colors, and combinations of clothing and accessories to the characteristics and tastes of the customer.
451	Sporting goods, hobby, book, and music stores	Engage in retailing and providing expertise on use of sporting equipment or other leisure activities, such as needlework and musical instruments. Bookstores also included.
452	General merchandise stores	Establishments in this subsector are unique in that they have the equipment and staff capable of retailing a large variety of goods from a single location. This includes a variety of display equipment and staff trained to provide information on many lines of products.
453	Miscellaneous store retailers	Retail merchandise from fixed point-of-sale locations that are different from those of other sectors. Establishments include stores with unique characteristics, such as florists, used merchandise stores, and pet and pet supply stores as well as other store retailers.
454	Nonstore retailers	Nonstore examples include broadcasting of infomercials, the broadcasting and publishing of direct-response advertising, the publishing of paper and electronic catalogs, door-to-door solicitation, in-home demonstration, selling from portable stalls, and distribution through vending machines. Establishments include mail-order houses, vending machine operators, home delivery sales, door-to-door sales, party plan sales, electronic shopping, and sales through portable stalls (e.g., street vendors, except food). Includes direct sale (i.e., nonstore) of products, such as home heating oil dealers and newspaper delivery.

Source: North American Industry Classification System (NAICS).

Table 3.2   Retailing in the United States by Numbers

A	B	C	D	E	F	G	H	I	J
NAICS Code	Products	Establishments with Employees	Receipts (millions of dollars)	Annual Payroll (millions of dollars)	Paid Employees	Employees per Establishment	Receipts per Establishment ($)	Receipts per Employee ($)	Annual Payroll per Employee ($)
441	Motor vehicles and parts	125,139	801,740	64,549	1,845,496	15	6,406,796	434,431	34,977
442	Furniture and home furnishings stores	65,204	91,814	12,843	535,029	8	1,408,104	171,606	24,004
443	Electronics and appliance stores	46,779	82,228	9,330	391,015	8	1,757,797	210,294	23,861
444	Building material and garden equipment and supplies dealers	88,314	246,561	30,067	1,160,016	13	2,791,868	212,550	25,919
445	Food and beverage stores	148,804	456,942	48,686	2,838,653	19	3,070,764	160,971	17,151

446	Health and personal care stores	81,797	177,947	20,226	1,024,429	13	2,175,471	173,704	19,744
447	Gasoline stations	121,446	249,141	13,701	926,792	8	2,051,455	268,821	14,783
448	Clothing and clothing accessories stores	149,810	167,934	21,391	1,426,573	10	1,120,980	117,718	14,995
451	Sporting goods, hobby, book, and music stores	62,236	73,212	8,703	611,144	10	1,176,361	119,795	14,241
452	General merchandise stores	40,723	445,225	42,647	2,524,729	62	10,933,011	176,346	16,892
453	Miscellaneous store retailers	129,464	90,812	12,835	792,361	6	701,446	114,609	16,198
454	Nonstore retailers	54,921	172,865	17,094	571,438	10	3,147,521	302,509	29,914
	Total/Average:	1,114,637	3,056,421	302,072	14,647,675	13	2,742,077	208,663	20,623

Source: North American Industry Classification System (NAICS).

Table 3.3 Selected Public Company Data along the Retail Supply Chain

		A	B	C	D	E	F	G	H
		Reporting Year	Annual Revenue (millions of dollars)	Cost of Sales (millions of dollars)	Gross Margin (percent)	End-of-Period Inventory (millions of dollars)	Sales-to-Stock Ratio	GMROI	Cash-to-Cash Cycle (days)
1	Wal-Mart Stores, Inc.	2006	312,300	240,000	23	32,200	9.7	225	13
2	Costco Wholesale Corporation	2005	51,900	46,300	11	1,470	35.3	381	–19
3	Gap Inc.	2005	16,023	10,154	37	1,696	9.4	346	20
4	West Marine, Inc.	2005	700	495	29	312	2.2	66	206
5	McKesson Corporation	2006	88,050	84,188	4	6,920	12.7	56	12
6	Syntax-Brillian Corporation	2006	193	169	12	13	14.7	182	116
7	Li & Fung Limited	2005	6,783	6,092	10	77	88.6	901	11
8	Dick's Sporting Goods	2006	2,625	1887	28	537	4.9	137	29

distributors succeed on volume, and McKesson is one of the largest. Its use of supplier credit produces a low cash-to-cash cycle of 12 days.

Filling a different role, Syntax-Brillian describes itself as a "designer, developer, and distributor of high-definition televisions" under the Olevia brand. Syntax-Brillian is included in Table 3.3 because of its supply chain approach. The company, located in Tempe, Arizona, near Phoenix, pursues a "virtual manufacturing model." A plant in Tucson produces a key technology called "liquid crystal on silicon" or LCoS, an alternative to LCD (liquid-crystal display) and DLP (digital light processing) technologies. It relies on suppliers in Asian countries for sourced components and third-party manufacturers near to customers in many countries to assemble products. This minimizes investments in finished goods inventory by relying on "pull" signals from the market. Chapter 17 describes related concepts further. Examining reasons for the long cash-to-cash cycle might uncover opportunities for improvement.

The trading company can also play roles at multiple echelons in the supply chain. Li & Fung, a 100-year-old Hong Kong company, does this. It makes apparel and other products to support retailer brands. It also has its own branded lines. Li & Fung has the highest GMROI on a thin gross margin (about 10 percent). This is due to Li & Fung's small inventory, only $77 million. This return can be understood in light of the balance Li & Fung strikes with the other working capital accounts, receivables and payables. These were $967 million and $757 million, respectively. This produces a cash-to-cash cycle (5 days of inventory + 51 days of receivables – 44 days of payables) of 11 days.

Dick's Sporting Goods is a Pittsburgh-based retailer in the United States. *Forbes* magazine featured Dick's in its annual feature "America's 400 Best Big Companies," published in January 2007.[2] The article identifies the "best" performers in 26 industries; Dick's received the honor for the retail industry. The article cited rapid growth and prospects for further expansion. From two stores it has grown to 214 single-level and 80 two-level outlets. Sites for 500 more stores are already selected, many in currently unserved areas. Revenue growth averaged 24 percent over the last five years, and earnings grew at a rate of 38 percent. The CEO, Edward Stack, predicts more consolidation in sporting goods retailing where the top five companies control only 16 percent of the market.

3.4 Summary

This chapter attempts to capture the breadth and depth of participants in retail supply chains. An important lesson is that there are virtually infinite options for participating in retail supply chains. Part 3 is devoted to describing processes for developing or enhancing strategies for competing in this landscape.

Endnotes

1. Bellman, Eric and Hudson, Kris, "Wal-Mart to Enter India in Venture," *The Wall Street Journal,* November 28, 2006, p. A3.
2. *Forbes,* January 8, 2007, pp. 84–110.

Chapter 4

A Changing World: Moving Toward Comparative Advantage

Few topics resonate more than the effects of globalization on supply chains. Chapter 3 reported the lack of organized retailing penetration in large countries such as India and China. These countries are fertile grounds for retail chains seeking growth. At the other end of the supply chain, original equipment manufacturers (OEMs), and their suppliers in emerging economies manufacture many products. Supply chains that stretch across national borders bring political debates over whether such changes are good or bad. In rich countries, globalization means lower-cost imported goods. Consumers in these countries love a good deal; the developing country has ample capacity. On the darker side, changes in sources displace domestic producers and their jobs.

For the low-cost countries, exports bring the promise of jobs and middle class prosperity for its citizens. C.K. Prahalad, a business professor at the University of Michigan, suggests a "different set of lenses," referring to globalization as "importing competitiveness."[1] In this view, working across national boundaries spurs needed changes all along the supply chain to remain competitive.

A "global" supply chain as defined in this book simply means a supply chain that crosses international boundaries. Figure 1.1 in Chapter 1 shows physical and information flows in a typical supply chain. The OEM in Figure 1.1 imports components from international second-tier suppliers and sells its product into national markets. There are many variations of this model. A retail supply chain in a developed country likely receives many foreign-made goods directly into the retailer's distribution centers.

Although the picture of low-cost countries as producers is a common one, retailers are also eyeing these emerging markets, with their growing working class, as opportunities for new growth. Products in the supply chain might even take a U-turn from factory to retailer to consumer, all in the same country. However, this process is not automatic and depends upon political and economic conditions in these countries. In instances in which the retailer is based in the developed world, developing countries provide the "brawn" to make the product, and the retailer the "brains" to design, brand, source, and merchandise it. As each side of this balance between brain and brawn adding value seeks to broaden its contribution, the equilibrium point is sure to shift industry by industry, challenging supply chains to adjust.

Thomas Friedman in his widely read best seller, *The World is Flat*, asserts that the availability of jobs in emerging countries is not enough to bring third-world countries strongly into the world economy. He goes on to say:

> Countries grow out of poverty … when they also create an environment that makes it easy for their people to start businesses, raise capital, and become entrepreneurs and when they subject their people to at least some competition from beyond—because companies and countries with competitors innovate more and faster.[2]

The remainder of this chapter summarizes the concept of comparative advantage—a driver behind globalization—and describes a framework for decision making, for sourcing, and marketing in other countries.

4.1 Primer on Comparative Advantage

Adam Smith's *Wealth of Nations,* published in 1776, described the economics for trading across national boundaries. Smith urged any country to trade for, rather than make, goods that other countries can make more cheaply than that country could. These lower-cost countries would have an *absolute* advantage because they are more efficient at making those goods. Trading between countries with absolute advantages in certain products rewards both trading partners because each country sells to its trading partner the products it makes more efficiently.

Smith likened this concept to a "private family" situation. For example, in a doctor's household, the practice of medicine would be the "product" it produces most efficiently. Under absolute advantage, the doctor's family should trade for the other things it needs—such as groceries, house repairs, and furniture. It would not make sense for the doctor to spend time growing crops for food, doing house repairs, or building furniture. Because the doctor earns more practicing medicine, time spent on creating these other necessities doesn't make sense; also, the doctor needs to maintain his medical skills. Besides, without the doctor buying other goods and services, how could patients pay him?

Economist David Ricardo coined the term *comparative advantage* in 1817. It is counterintuitive because comparative advantage says that, even if a country has an absolute advantage in producing a good or service, it is to its benefit to buy even if it has an absolute advantage. So the doctor should stick with healthcare even if that doctor were the very best as a farmer, repairman, or furniture maker. This is because the doctor's highest contribution comes from the practice of medicine, not from other pursuits.

Ricardo's example, also a classic in economics, describes the relationship between two trading partners, Portugal and England, who exchange just two products: wine and wool. Portugal had an absolute advantage in both products in Ricardo's day. Despite this absolute advantage, the theory of comparative advantage calls for Portugal to specialize in wine while purchasing its wool from England. This is because dedicating itself to wine produces more overall value than diverting a portion of its winemaking capacity to wool production. With this arrangement, English wool makers were able to keep themselves busy and have some money to buy Portuguese wine. The Portuguese, in turn, were clothed while earning more than they would if they diverted winemaking resources to wool production.

The absolute form of advantage is easier to understand than the comparative form. If a country does everything well, why not do everything? This may seem especially true if you are a wool maker in Portugal or a wine maker in England. According to comparative advantage, both of these "misfits" must pursue another trade. The *Wall Street Journal*, in an editorial, explains further.[3] The editorial writers point out the reality that labor and capital are far more mobile than they were back in Ricardo's day. Citing economist Matthew J. Slaughter at Dartmouth University in the United States, this speed means that trade is no longer a "zero-sum game." That is, the loss of a job in the United States through outsourcing and offshoring to places like India or China is not an overall loss to the United States. This is despite the consequence of losing some industries, like winemaking in England.

A concept called "complementarity" holds that outsourcing and offshoring brawny jobs to developing countries create complementary requirements for brainy jobs in developed countries. These expand the scale and the scope of the multinational enterprise. Scale refers to growth in the functions performed in global companies due to their larger size. Scope refers to the mix of activities done in the home country, with a focus on higher-skilled activities—such as product design, branding, merchandising, and supply chain management. These displace the low-skill work transferred elsewhere. Conflict comes because those doing the low-skill work are not prepared to do the high-skill work.

Through research, Slaughter has verified the benefits of globalization with data. The findings show that, from 1991 to 2001, U.S. companies that added 2.8 million workers in overseas affiliates also added 5.5 million jobs in the United States. This growth was faster than that of less global competitors. The editorial's conclusion is that, at the company level, jobs created overseas generate jobs at home. Simultaneously, the trade brings consumers "greater quantity and variety of goods and services for lower prices."

Although the Slaughter study examined U.S. companies, the lessons aren't lost on companies in the developing world. *Forbes* magazine reports the case of Indian company Gujarat Heavy Chemicals Limited (GHCL) and its acquisition of Dan River, Inc. in Danville, Virginia.[4] Dan River, founded in 1882, designs, manufacturers, and distributes textile products for home fashions and apparel fabrics markets. At the time of purchase, the company had $250 million in sales, three plants, and 3000 workers in Danville. It was also in bankruptcy, a situation attributed to globalization forces. Indian companies, recently freed to pursue overseas investments, have cast about for companies like Dan River. However, GHCL was not after more factories (Dan River's brawn); it sought in Dan River its customers, distribution network, brands, and designers (its brains).

With customers such as Bed, Bath & Beyond and Linens 'n Things, GHCL expects a rapid payback. It intends to extend its reach by acquiring retailers around the world—having purchased $200 million chain Roseby's, a 300-store home furnishing retailer in the United Kingdom, in mid-2006. The vision is a vertically integrated chain for towels, sheets, and related products from "concept to consumer" in one supply chain.

Comparative advantage makes globalization inevitable for retailers and manufacturers in retail supply chains. This will be one of the drivers of supply chain change, as described in Chapter 6, Section 6.4. The following sections describe a methodology for assessing the viability of building a retail supply chain in a candidate country. Companies seeking to shrink their global footprints by dropping countries from their market portfolios can use the same method to evaluate their alternatives.

4.2 Concept of Distance

Globalization usually means doing business at some "distance" across international boundaries. Distance, in this context, means physical distance—between a retailer in the United Kingdom like Roseby's, for example, and a factory in China. Because the physical distance crosses international boundaries, there are other important dimensions to consider, e.g., culture, language, political systems, logistics, tariffs, currency exchanges, legal systems, and even the climate. This section describes research into the effect of these other "attributes" of "distance."

In assessing the attractiveness of country markets, some companies use a conventional tool called *country portfolio analysis* (CPA). This analysis weighs alternative market opportunities using market size measures such as per capita consumption, income, population, and market size for a particular product or product category. This produces a ranking of each country's attractiveness in terms of the market size.

Because application of CPA may ignore the costs and risks in a new market that are harder to identify, Pankaj Ghemawat recommends taking the concept of distance into other dimensions in addition to those just listed.[5] His framework utilizes research from economists Jeffrey Frankel at Harvard and Andrew Rose at

Table 4.1 CAGE Distance Dimensions

Type of Distance	Description of Factors Involved
Cultural	Language, ethnicities, religions, social norms
Administrative	Colonial ties, common currencies, political harmony, trading agreements, government policies, institutional strength (legal, financial systems)
Geographic	Proximity, common border, size of country, transportation/communication links, climate
Economic	Income similarities, cost and quality of natural resources, worker availability, infrastructure, raw materials and components, and knowledge/information resources

the University of California, Berkeley. Their research identifies other patterns in global trade. These include not only geographic but also cultural, administrative, and economic distance—producing the acronym CAGE. Table 4.1 lists the four CAGE distance types and aspects of each. In their research, Frankel and Rose found that factors other than geographic distance and income were determinants of the level of trade between pairs of countries. For example, a country link unrelated to geography, a "colony–colonizer" relationship, resulted in a 900 percent increase in trade over that observed without such a relationship.

Table 4.2 lists attributes and their impacts on trade documented by the research. For example, for item #1 in Table 4.2 a 1 percent increase in the GDP of a country such as Mexico will produce a 0.7 percent increase in trade with that country. A common border has a much larger impact, increasing trade by 80 percent as shown by item #6.

What this means is that the market potential for a U.S. retailer in Mexico based solely on GDP per capita—the country portfolio analysis approach—will underestimate potential of the market due to the effect that a common border has. Ghemawat cites the case of Tricon Restaurants International (TRI) formerly based in Dallas, Texas, and now doing business out of Louisville, Kentucky, as YUM! Brands, Inc. The company's popular food chains include Kentucky Fried Chicken (KFC), Pizza Hut, and Taco Bell. Measuring only per capita fast food consumption, TRI found Mexico to rank 16th out of 20 countries it served in market potential. Because of outsized debt, TRI was faced with the need of pruning the number of countries in which it operated. Applying the factors in Table 4.2, TRI found that Mexico advanced in market potential from sixteenth to a tie for second by adjusting for geographic closeness to its base in Dallas, a common border between the countries, and membership in a trade agreement (North American Free Trade Agreement, or NAFTA) and deducting for lack of a common language. Overall, Mexico tied for second with the United Kingdom; Canada ranked first.

Table 4.2 Attributes and International Trade Level Impacts

	Attributes Related to Distance	Effect on International Trade	CAGE Factor
1.	1 percent increase in gross domestic product (GDP) per capita	+0.7 percent per 1 percent gain	Economic
2.	1 percent increase in GDP	+0.8 percent per 1 percent increase	Economic
3.	1 percent increase in physical distance	–1.1 percent per 1 percent increase	Geographic
4.	1 percent increase in physical size	–0.2 percent per 1 percent increase	Geographic
5.	Access to ocean	+50 percent	Geographic
6.	Common border	+80	Geographic
7.	Common regional trading block	+330	Administrative
8.	Colony–colonizer relationship	+900	Cultural
9.	Common colonizer	+190	Cultural
10.	Common polity (form or system of government)	+300	Administrative
11.	Common currency	+340	Administrative

These insights enabled TRI to focus its scarce resources on the most profitable countries—in this case those closest to home.

Because trade is a two-way flow, this concept can be extended to decisions regarding sourcing, not just selling. Ghemawat explains that different distance factors will have different impacts on individual industries. Electricity, for example, is highly sensitive to administrative and geographic factors, but not at all to cultural factors. Preferential trading agreements in the administrative distance category affects textile fibers, where such agreements are common, more than they affect footwear where such agreements are less common.

4.3 Applying the Framework

Experts caution against blindly chasing "low cost" as the primary goal of going global. James Womack, who coined the term "lean" (now employed to manufacturing operations as well as supply chains) recommends application of "lean math" in making such decisions.[6] In an article, Womack listed several costs that the purchasing department often omit, including the following:

- Correction for allocated overhead costs that will not be reduced by international sourcing
- Added inventory costs to cover the distances involved
- Cost of added safety stocks to protect against disruptions
- Cost of expedited shipments that may be necessary
- Added warranty costs due to supplier learning curve delays
- Cost of engineering and social audit visits to ensure product quality and workplace standards
- The time of managers to establish and maintain the supply chain link
- Costs of lost sales and out-of-stocks due to longer lead times for material
- Costs of written off product due to the need for longer term forecasts that are more likely to result in excess stock
- Risk due to suppliers becoming competitors

Levy and Weitz in *Retailing Management* cite other hidden costs more directly of concern to retailers.[7] These include the following:

- The "panache" or style associated with higher-priced goods from a country with a better reputation for quality.
- The technical reputation of the source country.
- Foreign currency fluctuations.
- Tariffs and other taxes. The authors note that free trade zones in some countries also offer tax relief.
- Logistics costs, including the holding cost of inventories and transportation.
- Extra costs for quality assurance, including qualification of suppliers and inspections.
- The flexibility gained through quick response to changes in demand and frequent deliveries.
- Preference of customers for products made in their own country.
- Cost of policing human rights and child labor laws.

To take these factors into account, CAGE can be blended with other techniques to assess risks and opportunities in doing business in other countries. Table 4.3 uses a financial statement approach to list operating "factors of production" for application with the CAGE approach. In any analysis of sourcing, the hidden cost factors listed previously should be captured in the applicable categories in the table. Each category applies in varying degrees to different kinds of supply chain companies—to retailers, distributors, and manufacturers. The same cost categories recommended are employed in Chapter 19, Section 19.2 for the purpose of analyzing activity-based process costs for reduction efforts.

Table 4.3 Impact of Globalization on Factors of Production in the Retail Supply Chain

Improvement Categories	Description	Globalization Opportunity
Revenues	Sales of products through retail outlets, distribution services, or product sales from manufacturing.	Expanded sales or production in new countries, including those countries that manufacture for the retailer or original equipment manufacturer (OEM).
Workforce costs		
Direct labor	Labor that "touches" the product. Examples: retail sales people, purchasing, assembly workers, and material handling.	Lower-cost labor is often the motivator for outsourcing or offshoring.
Indirect labor	Labor that doesn't have a work measurement standard but supports the direct labor component. Includes store support functions.	These functions coordinate production and may increase with globalization.
Administrative/ clerical	Detached from direct activity. Managers, assistants, accounting staff, receptionists, and sales administration. Often allocated.	These tasks, especially if they are routine or don't require face-to-face interaction, are finding homes in lower-cost locales.
Technical- professional	Engineers, merchandising staff, information technology support, logistics planners, and other white-collar functions.	Often considered the custodians of "core competencies," this group is also experiencing outsourcing and offshoring to lower-cost locales. Additions needed to support operations in new countries.

Endnotes

1. Prahalad, C.K., "The Art of Outsourcing," *The Wall Street Journal,* June 8, 2005, p. A14.
2. Friedman, Thomas L., *The World Is Flat: A Brief History of the Twenty-first Century,* New York, Farrar, Straus and Giroux, 2005, p. 318.
3. Outsourcing 101 (editorial), *The Wall Street Journal,* May 27, 2004, p. A20.
4. Bahree, Megha, "The Multinational, Updated," *Forbes,* October 2, 2006, pp. 103–104.
5. Ghemawat, Pankaj, "Distance Still Matters: The Hard Reality of Global Expansion," *Harvard Business Review,* September 2001, pp. 137–147.
6. "Move Your Operations to China? Do Some Lean Math First," Interview in *Lean Directions,* the e-Newsletter of Lean Manufacturing, Society of Manufacturing Engineers, April 9, 2003.
7. Levy, Michael and Weitz, Barton A., *Retailing Management,* 5th ed., New Delhi: Tata McGraw-Hill Publishing Company Limited, 2004, pp. 441–447.

Chapter 5

Corporate Social Responsibility, Sustainability, and the Retail Industry

In 2004, the authors participated in a Sloan Foundation workshop at the University of Washington.[1] The workshop topic was the role of intermediaries in global supply chains. The sixteen academic attendees, mostly professors or lecturers at U.S. universities, represented the economics (three attendees), sociology (seven attendees), and business (six attendees) disciplines. One active discussion centered on the distribution of power among the intermediaries. Several attendees argued that retailers hold the strongest hand in the supply chain, creating a "monopsony" where they control product access to the markets.

Not unexpectedly, Wal-Mart, the biggest retailer, became the center of discussion. The question pondered by the group amounted to, "Is Wal-Mart good or bad?" The sociologists appeared to argue for "bad" because of Wal-Mart's reputed low wages and benefits and lack of employee union representation. Others, like the business representatives, argued in favor of "good" for bringing low prices to consumers and, measured by sales, doing the best job of delivering on customer requirements.

Later that year, some attendees provided their viewpoints in a Public Broadcasting System (PBS) *Frontline* documentary, "Is Wal-Mart Good for America?"[2] The documentary echoed the workshop themes and described Wal-Mart's success and methods of doing business. Topics included its rapid growth, its leverage in gaining low prices from suppliers, its sophisticated logistics, an implied "bait and switch" using low-price loss leaders on displays in its stores, and the zeal of associates in promoting high-margin merchandise. To some in society these features of the Wal-Mart model may seem like "sharp elbow," nefarious business practices; to others, they are just common sense, well executed.

The workshop and documentary remind us that the role of business is defined by its society and it changes fairly often. Brian Nattrass and Mary Altomare describe a new set of challenges in their book, *Dancing with the Tiger.* They present sustainability as one of today's foremost challenges requiring changes in today's business operating paradigm:

> Obsessed by the tyranny of the financial markets, driven to relentlessly increase sales and profits quarter by quarter, forced to match every competitor's advance ..., determined to seize market share from adversaries ..., today's corporations leave the actions needed to ensure long-term survival to someone else.[3]

Retailers are particularly close to the heat generated by public opinion on such issues. Some in society may see a company such as Wal-Mart as bad for society, whereas others have the opposite view. Of course, few companies draw the same amount of attention as Wal-Mart, because of its vast size. However, leaders in retail supply chains increasingly need to define their own company's role in the emerging world. This chapter describes the scope of what is now labeled *corporate social responsibility* (CSR) and the responses of companies in retail supply chains. According to Wikipedia, CSR is "an obligation to consider the interests of customers, employees, shareholders, communities, and ecological considerations in all aspects of their operations."

Subsequently, the chapter describes methods of aligning CSR initiatives with strategy to the benefit of both society and the enterprise. Like globalization, described in Chapter 4, the push for CSR will bring change to retail companies and their supply chains. CSR and globalization are moving forward hand-in-hand, because far flung supply chains are putting retailers "on the spot," not only for their own behavior but also for that of their trading partners.

The push has taken the form of international standards for transparent reporting of CSR goals and accomplishments. The vision for achieving this transparency is to place CSR on the same level as financial reporting. The Global Reporting Initiative (GRI) (www.globalreporting.org), an interindustry international group, has promulgated a reporting standard. The standard, described in the *Sustainability Reporting Guidelines,* encompasses what GRI calls the "triple bottom line" for economic, environmental, and social reporting. Updates to the guidelines will appear periodically; the version at the time of writing was "G3."

This chapter describes current CSR reporting and provides an overview of the initiative and its reporting requirements. It then describes a framework for focusing CSR on issues of strategic importance to the retailer and its supply chain trading partners. Finally, a case, that of Boots, Ltd. in the United Kingdom, will describe one approach to setting priorities and reporting progress using the GRI G3 guidelines.

5.1 CSR at Retailers

The trend toward increased CSR reporting is perhaps most apparent in the space dedicated to the topic in the annual reports of publicly traded retailers. Table 5.1 provides examples from the Wal-Mart Stores, Inc., and Gap, Inc. annual reports. These exemplify the scope of CSR initiative reporting retailers might embrace. The range of "good works" by both companies is wide, covering charity contributions by employees, work with suppliers, enforcement of labor standards, and environmental hazard mitigation. They point out hours spent by employees, work with international bodies, standards for and inspections of suppliers, as well as the jobs provided the company.

Another example further up the supply chain illustrates pressures on manufacturers for product improvements. It also demonstrates how one company seeks competitive advantage from their CSR initiative. *The Wall Street Journal* reports that the computer industry "slowly grows greener" under pressure from consumers.[4] The author, Lee Gomes, cites a large digital advertising reader board erected by chipmaker, Advanced Micro Devices (AMD), targeting its competitor, Intel. It states that AMD's new Opteron microprocessor uses 20 to 30 percent less energy than Intel's microprocessor. The display counts the cost of wasted energy because its chips aren't deployed in all personal computers. The article notes that other energy saving are being built into computer hardware such as LCD screens, power supplies, and operating systems that power down disk drives when they are not needed.

GRI guidelines cover sustainability topics in the categories listed in Table 5.2. Within each category are *core* and *additional* indicators. *Core* indicators are likely to be of concern to most stakeholders; *additional* indicators may be of concern to some stakeholders in certain industries. There are 79 indicators in all—49 core and 30 additional. It is important to view the guidelines as a checklist, not a mandate for full reporting. In application, a reporting company can tailor its reporting. Boots, for example, lists each GRI requirement in an index at the end of its report. The index provides its location in the report, a reference to another source like its annual report, a statement that the company is not reporting on that standard, or that the company has nothing to report.

GRI recommends that reports consider *scope*, *boundaries*, and *time* factors to assure their completeness. Scope includes the range of topics to be covered. Boundaries refer to the entities reported including company operations, joint ventures, and subcontractors. The boundary should vary with different topics. For example, for a retailer the boundary may be narrow for biodiversity—limited to company operations. But for labor practices, the boundary might be broadened—including supplier compliances. GRI provides a decision tree for standard setting, which is summarized in Table 5.3. The table shows tests for reporting different topics. If the reporting company controls the impact, metrics should be provided. If it has considerable influence, or has some influence, it should describe the management's

Table 5.1   Retailer CSR Examples

Retailer	Example CSR Citations
Wal-Mart 2006 Annual Report	"In October 2005, Wal-Mart CEO, Lee Scott, committed to associates and the public that the company will take a leadership position in sustainability."
	"Our hurricane (Rita) response efforts provide a return on investment to our business …"
	"… leadership role in improving operations, our operations, and products for our customer that will benefit the environment."
	"Our efforts … will are designed to conserve and sustain the natural resources of our planet …"
	"Did you know that in the U.S. retail channel, we are the first to make available RoHS (Retail on Hazardous Substance) compliant products?"
	"Today's consumer wants healthier and more responsible food sources. That's why we are doubling the organic and socially responsible offerings in select U.S. Wal-Mart stores."
	"Not only did Wal-Mart bring much needed jobs (to Evergreen Park Illinois)—25,000 applications for 325 store positions—but, in addition, the village benefited from the $35,000 we donated to local charities."
Gap, Inc. 2005 Annual Report	"Gap, Inc. employees volunteered nearly 155,000 hours last year to benefit charitable causes."
	"The elimination of trade quotas in 2005 created a dramatic shift in our industry, as retailers now have the opportunity to consolidate their sourcing base. We are collaborating with other stakeholders to help manage the impact of this shift on economically challenged regions."
	"We will continue to support global efforts that promote economic development, improve factory conditions, and help ensure healthy communities where we do business."
	"As a major apparel retailer, improving working conditions in garment factories approved to do business with us continues to be one of our top priorities."
	"Through organizations such as the MFA Forum, the Ethical Trading Initiative (ETI), and Social Accountability

Table 5.1 (continued)   Retailer CSR Examples

Retailer	Example CSR Citations
	International (SAI), we continued working with partners from the private, government and nongovernmental sectors to address some of the garment industry's most intractable standards, such as the need for a universal set of labor standards."
	"And perhaps most important, we took another step toward building labor standards directly into our business practices by piloting our new integrated Vendor Scorecard that will enable our sourcing team to consider labor standards along with factors such as speed and quality when determining where to place orders."
	"In total, Gap, Inc. made more than $23 million in cash and in-kind contributions last year, while employees donated approximately 155,000 hours of their time to causes they care about."
	"In 2005, we announced our goal as a voluntary member of the U.S. EPA's (Environmental Protection Agency) Climate Leaders program to reduce greenhouse gas emission by 11 percent per square foot between 2003 and 2008."
	"We also continued working with suppliers to monitor wastewater for laundry facilities against the apparel industry's voluntary water quality guidelines."

approach to the issue. It also recommends reporting in narrative form when influence is limited, but the condition provides a "challenge" in some form for the organization. "Time" refers to the activity during the reporting period, reporting both positive and negative long-term effects. Section 5.4 provides examples of reporting against the GRI standard.

5.2 CSR Link to Strategy

Academics and consultants recommend making societal concerns integral to company plans for its processes and its products. The growing CSR movement requires substantive, formal processes for managing what will likely be multiple, simultaneous efforts at different levels of the organization. This section describes two frameworks for linking CSR with strategy provided by prominent management thought leaders.

Table 5.2 Sustainability Indicator Categories

#	Indicator Category	Description	Representative Indicators
1.	Economic (EC)	Includes capital flows among stakeholders and economic impacts of the organization throughout society; supplements conventional financial reports. 9 performance indicators—7 core and 2 additional.	Direct economic value generated and distributed (revenues, operating costs, wages, taxes, etc.) Defined benefit obligations Payments to local suppliers Local hiring of workers and senior management Infrastructure investments
2.	Environmental (EN)	Impact of the organization on ecosystems, land, air, and water. 30 performance indicators—17 core and 13 additional	Materials used/percent recycled Energy/water consumption Impact on biodiversity (the ability to sustain a variety of species) Emissions of greenhouse gases and ozone-depleting substances Waste generation and water discharges Mitigation of product-related impacts; Reclamation of product packaging
Social Categories			
3.	Labor practices and decent work (LA)	Protocols in this category are those promulgated by the United Nations and other standard setting bodies	Total employment and employee turnover Collective bargaining agreement coverage

		14 performance indicators—9 core and 5 additional	Rates of injury, lost time, fatalities, and absenteeism Hours of training provided per employee by category Percentage of employees receiving performance and career development reviews
4.	Human rights (HR)	Measures gauge the degree to which human rights are weighted in investment and source selection decisions 9 performance indicators—6 core and 3 additional	Percentage and total number of contracts with human rights clauses or that include human rights screening Total number of incidents and action taken Identification of locations where freedom of association and rights to collective bargaining may be in jeopardy Operations at risk for violation of child labor or forced labor standards
5.	Society (SO)	The impact on the community in which the enterprise operates. Examples: bribery, monopolies, and undue political influence 8 performance indicators—6 core and 2 additional	Management of issues of related to the impact on the community of company operations Management of risks and incidents of corruption Role in public policy development and related positions Number and amount of fines and nonmonetary sanctions
6.	Product responsibility (PR)	The effect of company products and services on customers, including health and safety, needs for information and safety, the effects of marketing, and labeling, and personal privacy 9 performance indicators—4 core and 5 additional	Life cycle stages in which health and safety impacts are assessed and percentage of products and services covered Requirements for labeling and other information and percentage of products and services subject to the requirements Number and amount of fines for noncompliance

Note: Abbreviations of the category are shown in parentheses.

Table 5.3   Boundary Setting Decision Tree

Degree of Control Over the Entity	Significant Impact? (Yes or No)	Performance Data	Disclosures of Management Approach	Narrative Reporting of Issues and Dilemmas	No Report
1. Control	Yes	•			
	No				•
2. Significant influence	Yes		•		
	No				•
3. Influence	Yes			•	
	No				•

5.2.1 Link between CSR and Competitive Advantage

Michael Porter, the widely read strategy thinker at Harvard University, and Mark Kramer, a cofounder with Porter of the FSG Social Impact Advisors and the Center for Effective Philanthropy, recommend making CSR strategic.[5] "FSG" is derived from the organization's former name, foundation strategy group. Michael Porter was also the originator of the term *value chain* and developer of the activity system tool described in Chapter 13.

In their award-winning article, Porter and Kramer note that most CSR efforts are disconnected from business needs. Essentially, they are reactive to external stakeholders or critics. There is little in the way of a *shared value*, a form of win-win, for society and the enterprise. A core reason is often that activists target visible, usually successful, corporations to attract attention, even if those corporations can make little impact on the causes they support. Company responses, according to the authors, have been cosmetic public relations and media campaigns. Even worse, such criticism may develop a reaction in the company that puts it at odds with CSR goals, initiating a zero-sum game with no net gain for society. In this environment, the company does what it has to do to look good, and the private businesses fall short in fulfilling their potential to benefit society while adding value for shareholders and employees.

The authors examine the current ways companies justify CSR initiatives and find them wanting. They identify four common methods: moral obligation, sustainability, the license-to-operate, and reputation. The moral obligation assumes that "doing good" is good for business. Sustainability is associated with minimizing environmental damage. The license-to-operate applies to industries such as mining where approvals are needed to set up operations. In the absence of this necessary approval, the "license" justification devolves into responding to pressure groups, forfeiting control over the CSR agenda. Improving one's reputation seeks to gain external approval.

Unfortunately, these four justifications are "outside in" and provide no framework for setting CSR priorities that support company strategy. Porter and Kramer point to a common weakness of all the four approaches: each justification approach focuses on the "tension between business and society rather than their interdependence." Successful businesses need a healthy society that provides the climate for successful operations. Likewise, a healthy society needs successful businesses to satisfy peoples' needs and efficiently use resources. A shared-value CSR effort that also includes "inside out" priorities should benefit both society and the enterprise. This leads to a healthier company that provides jobs, pays taxes, and produces products society needs.

Porter and Kramer recommend thinking of social issues as being of three types:

1. Generic issue. Response to social issues in this category is "good citizenship." They do not affect company operations or its competitiveness at least in the short term. Global warming and AIDS might be examples.
2. "Value chain" impact (including what this book defines as the "supply chain"). Affects company day-to-day activities. There are two types—mitigation of harm and strategic transformation of the value chain. The boundary is either inside the company or along its chain in the upstream or downstream direction. An example is recycling material that reduces costs at a plant. Another is developing a new product that uses recyclable components and that can be efficiently manufactured minimizing consumption of raw materials and energy.
3. "Strategic philanthropy." Issues that affect an underlying driver of company competitiveness in locations where the company works. This category changes the "competitive context." The authors cite Microsoft's partnership with the American Association of Community Colleges to relieve the shortage of information technology workers.

Porter and Kramer note that a car manufacturer might consider CSR investments to reduce the spread of AIDS as a type 1 generic impact, whereas a pharmaceutical company might consider it a type 3 competitive context impact. One test of the type 3 situation is that the company investment will be seen as a means to differentiate it from competitors.

The authors then divide CSR initiatives into *responsive* and *strategic* categories. Table 5.4 summarizes the split between the two types. Addressing generic issues is responsive. It is likely this is the case with many current efforts due to the absence of

Table 5.4   Responsive and Strategic CSR

Type	Social Issue	Responsive CSR	Strategic CSR
1	Generic	•	
2	Value chain mitigations	•	
2	Value chain strategy reinforcement		•
3	Competitive context		•

links between CSR and strategy. A type 2 mitigation effort may make the company less of a polluter or violator of human rights, but it is mostly meant to stay out of trouble and is not strategic. Some type 2 efforts can reinforce a strategy, like AMD's new microprocessor mentioned earlier or a strategy developed with the activity system tool described in Chapter 13. A type 3 effort will use company capabilities to improve in some way the environment in which the company competes. It is also likely to "move the envelop" by providing distinctive ways of serving society that distinguish the company.

5.2.2 Private Companies and Social Issues

In another article, consultants from McKinsey & Company also urge companies to anticipate the changing CSR landscape.[6] The authors call attention to the constantly moving nature of the "social contract" between society and the business enterprise. Figure 5.1 shows three types of CSR responsibilities in this environment: formal, semiformal, and frontier expectations. The formal contract includes regulation, taxes, contract structures, and product liability. Laws, treaties, and the like put these in place. The informal contract lies in expectations, not laws or regulations. An example is the responsibility to maintain labor standards in global supply chains.

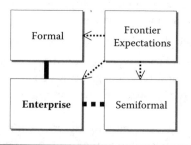

Figure 5.1   Social issues environment.

Frontier expectations have less direct threads to the enterprise. An example is the responsibility of food manufacturers for obesity. If people eat too much or the food is "over-caloric," where does the responsibility lie—with the restaurant or the consumer? Today's frontier expectations can turn into tomorrow's formal and informal social contract, as shown by arrows in Figure 5.1. The authors argue for more business intervention in the shaping of these expectations.

5.3 Framework for Classifying CSR Activities

The previous sections suggest a way toward better management of CSR activities. Table 5.5 consolidates the ideas presented in this chapter for the purpose of gaining control over the company's CSR agenda. The authors of both the cited articles in Section 5.2 describe this need. For a company in the retail supply chain that has undertaken or plans to undertake CSR initiatives, the classification approach will assist in the following ways:

- Provides an inventory of existing efforts to facilitate coordinated responses
- Produces a list of candidate issues to address in the future through research or brainstorming
- Leads to setting new priorities, such as dropping some efforts and initiating or renewing others
- Assists in communicating with internal and external stakeholders

The columns provide for listing existing and proposed CSR efforts. Then the type, driver, and reporting requirement under GRI guidelines can be discussed and determined. Some examples from Boots, Ltd. are shown in the columns and discussed in the next section.

5.4 Boots Ltd.—CSR/Financial Report Convergence

In early 2006, Boots, a company in the United Kingdom that dates back to the 19th century, reported in some detail about its CSR efforts. This was not Boots' first report, but it was a one that clearly explained its efforts in terms of GRI G3 guidelines. By way of background, a merger in 2006 resulted in a company with 3,000 retail outlets in 17 countries. Boots also supports 125,000 retail customers with its wholesale and distribution business. Many of these are independent pharmacists. Products include bath and body, skincare, cosmetics, and haircare categories. Its 2006 annual report disclosed sales of over £5,000 million ($8,900 million) and profits, before financing costs and taxes, of about £369 million ($660 million). Its gross margin ROI (GMROI), an important retail supply chain metric described in Chapter 2, was 228 percent.

Table 5.5 CSR Activity Classification

#	Name of Boots CSR Activity	C GRI Category	D Type of CSR	E. Origination	F. Driver	G. Reporting
1.	Pension plan obligations	EC	2	O	F	3
2.	Total materials used	EN	2 and 3	I	S	3
3.	Energy efficient products and services	EN	3	I	S	3
4.	Skills management/lifelong learning	LA	3	I	S	2
5.	Supplier human rights screening	HR	1 and 2	O	S	2
6.	SunSmart campaign	PR	4	I	E	1
7.	Change One Thing anti-smoking campaign	-	1 and 4	I	E	1

Figure 5.2 Boots' Strategic Pillars.

The company supports the idea that CSR is strategic and that initiatives need to be integrated with business goals. They point to five "strategic pillars" that drive company efficiency. Figure 5.2 shows each pillar along with a brief description. The company motto, "Trust Boots," also signals commitment to CSR. The company identifies 21 CSR issues in four categories: *our marketplace, our communities, our people,* and *our environment.* Table 5.6 lists the issues by category. The company uses this structure to report its CSR initiatives. In its 2006 report, it disclosed its intention to add "healthy living" to the list. This initiative covers efforts to increase the nutritional content and labeling of the foods Boots sells and its commitment to help customers quit smoking.

The purpose of the list in Table 5.6 is to provide readers with content examples of a company's robust program progress report and to demonstrate the recommended CSR portfolio profiling tool. To that end, the authors populated Table 5.5, based on information provided in the Boots' CSR report. We realize that another participant or observer might make a different interpretation. The following paragraphs describe each CSR item briefly:

1. Pension plan obligations. The sale of a business allowed Boots to more fully fund by £85 million its pension plan for employees. This signaled a "commitment to ensuring the long-term financial health of our people." Although noble, this is a basic obligation.
2. Total materials used. The initiative seeks to cut landfill waste from product packaging, in-transit packaging, and store waste by 20 percent in five years. Use of recyclable material for displays is also promoted. Boots also challenges store requests for more disposal bins. The progress reported was a 7.5 percent reduction in the first 3 years.

Table 5.6 Boots' CSR Issues

Our Marketplace
Ethical investment Corporate governance Supplier verification Customer safety/access Cause related marketing

Our Communities
Community healthcare Charitable giving Education Employee fund-raising Employee volunteering

Our People
Women in the workplace Diversity Training and development Health and safety Employee forums

Our Environment
Chemicals Sustainable products Energy Biodiversity Waste and recycling Transportation

3. Energy efficient products and services. Boots used a variety of innovations to reduce fuel consumption required for transportation. These include double-deck trailers for longer distances, drop trailers, and having the fleet delivering to stores backhaul incoming Boots material by stopping at suppliers. Another component is to employ vehicles that burn more efficient fuel mixes.

4. CO_2 emission reductions. Boots achieved a reduction of emissions by 22.9 percent to a level of 37 tonnes (1000 kg or about 2200 pounds per tonne) per £million of sales. This was done by attacking energy consumption across the company.

5. Supplier human rights screening. According to Boots, the rise of the "ethical shopper" demands that the 550-plus suppliers follow ethical human rights and environmental practices. With only a few exceptions, reviews were completed.

6. SunSmart campaign. Boots makes and sells products for sun protection. It delivered advice for safe sun exposure to virtually all the schools in the United Kingdom. This included a contest to draw lots for playground shade shelters worth about £2000.

7. Change One Thing anti-smoking campaign. This program was launched in early 2006 to increase store traffic after the holidays. It was based on the premise that many had New Year's resolutions to quit smoking. 2,000,000 participated leading to 500,000 committing to giving up smoking. The campaign also boosted the "Healthcare first" pillar in the Boots strategy.

The sample demonstrates one company's effort to put its sustainability reporting on the same level as its financial reporting. Of particular note are the last two that are most likely to change the competitive context or the way customers view the company. Such efforts are increasingly essential for customer-facing retailers. This reality should be a signal upstream in the supply chain to trading partners.

5.5 Summary

Many of the CSR examples in this chapter are not limited to a single company. But the retailer is often the target of organizations agitating for a better society through sustainability and other CSR dimensions. That force will be felt up the chain; being capable of controlling the negotiation between society and private industry requires more attention to the situation. This means having an inside-out plan rather than reacting to outside-in mandates.

Endnotes

1. Sloan Foundation Workshop Series, Marketing, "Merchandising, and Retailing: The Role of Intermediaries in Global Value Chains," June 7–9, 2004. Sponsored by the University of Washington Business School.
2. Smith, Hedrick and Young, Rick, "Is Wal-Mart good for America?" Frontline program available at http://www.pbs.org/wgbh/pages/frontline/shows/walmart/, Hedrick Smith Productions, 2004.
3. Nattrass, Brian and Altomare, Mary; *Dancing with the Tiger, Learning Sustainability Step by Natural Step*, Gabriola, British Columbia, New Society Publishers, 2002.
4. Gomes, Lee, "Prodded by Consumers, the Computer Industry Slowly Grows Greener," *The Wall Street Journal*, June 14, 2006, p. B1.
5. Porter, Michael E. and Kramer, Mark R., "Strategy and Society; The Link Between Competitive Advantage and Corporate Social Responsibility," *Harvard Business Review*, December 2006, pp. 78–92. The article was the 2006 first place winner of the annual McKinsey Award for the best article in the *Harvard Business Review*.
6. Bonini, Sheila M.J., Mendonca, Lenny T., and Oppenheim, Jeremy M., "When Social Issues Become Strategic: Executives Ignore Sociopolitical Debates at Their Own Peril," *The McKinsey Quarterly* (online journal of McKinsey & Co.,) 2006, Number 2.

FORCES SHAPING THE RETAIL SUPPLY CHAIN ENVIRONMENT

2

The five chapters in Part 2 cover topics that play a role in the design of retail supply chains.

#	Name
6.	Drivers of Supply Chain Change
7.	Paths to the Customer: What is the Retail Supply Chain?
8.	Supply Chain Risk
9.	Retail Supply Chain Metrics
10.	The Decision-Making Needs of Supply Chain Participants

Chapter 6 describes a model that joins together seven drivers of supply chain change. These drivers act on supply chains of all types and include the following:

1. New product/process technology—an external driver
2. The innovation cycle from internal or external sources
3. Extended product design—base products and associated services
4. Globalization of sourcing and markets
5. Flexibility—the ultimate supply chain capability
6. Process-centered management
7. Collaboration among trading partners along the supply chain

Chapter 7 moves from the simple model of the retail supply chain described in Part 1. This model reflects retail's complexity where many manufacturers supply many points of sale. Emerging markets and wide-flung sources of merchandise increase the level of risk in supply chain operations, the subject of Chapter 8.

Responses to the changes include the growth of new metrics (Chapter 9) and information systems solutions (Chapter 10). The chapters inventory available choices and describe ways for readers to pick the metrics and the information technology solutions that fit their business requirements.

Chapter 6

Drivers of Retail Supply Chain Change

This chapter describes six drivers fueling change in retail supply chains. Most of the transformation witnessed today can be traced to one or more of these drivers. In marketing, these are often called *uncontrollable variables*. The drivers arise from multiple causes: competition, regulation, economy, society or social evolution, and technology (CREST). Table 6.1 presents a working definition of each of the drivers discussed in the next section, and Figure 6.1 models the connections among them.

The chapter also illustrates a framework for defining requirements for flexibility, the cornerstone of supply chain design, whose requirements are a driver of supply chain change. Supply chain features needed to achieve flexibility are pervasive, encompassing product offerings and design, the logistics network, and employee capabilities.

6.1 Drivers Are Important

Drivers are generally beyond the power of individuals to influence. People embedded in supply chain operations seldom connect change drivers to the tasks they perform daily. However, the need to adjust to these forces is always present, even if the need is unseen. Here we describe these drivers and explain how they compel changes in the retail supply chain. Those formulating projects to improve retail supply chains should understand and acknowledge their projects' "roots" in the form of drivers. This acknowledgment will lead them to identify and address important issues that increase chances for success.

Table 6.1 Supply Chain Change Drivers Defined

	SCM Drivers	Definitions
1.	Innovation	Technical advances in both product and process. Examples include material technology, production equipment, software, and artistic input
2.	Extended product design	The necessity for features and services beyond the base, or physical, product. Often driven by commoditization of the base product
3.	Globalization	Having to source or sell across international borders. Includes trade for raw materials, manufacturing, distribution, and marketing/sales
4.	Flexibility imperative	The advantage gained from effective responses to market and technology changes. Examples include product mix, volume, base product design, and extended product features
5.	Process-centered management	A focus on multicompany business processes for designing or improving organizations and systems
6.	Collaboration	Using intra- and intercompany cooperative efforts to meet mutual goals. Exchanging transaction information between partners. Joint development and improvement of supply chains

Innovation, in Figure 6.1, pushes the change process forward, so we place it first in our sequence. Innovation is affected by changes in product and process technology. These are external to the supply chain. The fruits of collaboration among supply chain trading partners also promote innovation, an internal source. The three drivers, *extended product design, globalization,* and *flexibility imperative,* shape the direction, scope, and form of products and services and the supply chains that deliver them. Two-headed arrows connecting these three drivers signify simultaneous, coordinated responses. In effect, the output of innovation is "digested" and transformed into requirements for retail supply chain process designs and the collaboration required to implement and maintain them.

The next driver is what we call *process-centered management,* encompassing the requirements for new supply chain processes—processes that cross both internal department and intercompany boundaries. Crossing these boundaries challenges the traditional organization-centric or budget-centric paradigm in most companies. The process design encompasses enabling organization designs and technologies. These, in turn, define needs for *collaboration,* the last driver. Collaboration among supply chain partners sets in motion more innovations in the form of continuous improvements and more far-reaching changes.

Figure 6.1 Drivers of supply chain management (SCM) change.

"Where are the company boundaries?" is a question asked about Figure 6.1. In other words, "Are the drivers internal or external to a single company?" The answer is, "Both." The drivers act on industry supply chains. However, the need for any one company to react will depend on the driver and its effect on the industry and the company. For example, *new product/process technology* innovation likely originates outside the company and its immediate trading partners. *Collaboration*, on the other hand, is between one's own company and its trading partners, so it's contained within the supply chain. The following sections discuss the drivers and how each plays a role in motivating supply chain change.

6.2 Innovation Driver

The model in Figure 6.1 shows innovation as the "engine" of change, affecting both products and the processes needed to produce them. An innovation in product technology, such as nanotechnology or improvements in diesel engines for automobiles, will act on current supply chains for related products and services. A totally new product could require new suppliers as well as new ways to distribute a product.

A process innovation, such as RFID, shipping containers, or supermarket shopping carts, alters the way the product is produced or distributed, making it better or lowering the cost of shipping, handling, and storing it. Other examples include changing relationships in the supplier base itself, such as vendor-managed inventory that results in bypassing distribution centers or, conversely, adding distribution points; and cross-docking at warehouses.

Product, process, and supply chain innovations interact. The interactions can overlap or be sequential in their timing. Unfortunately, development of new products, changes in process technology, and the pursuit of new markets are often the responsibility of different departments in a company. This division of responsibility is a barrier to coordinated implementation. Those responsible for the innovations may come together only by happenstance or when things are obviously not working well. At the National Retail Federation Annual Conference in January 2007, 90 percent of trade-show booths were devoted to showcasing non-Web, or E-commerce, technology solutions. This suggests that there are many areas of the retail supply chain that need improvement.

Without innovation, the push for supply chain change would be much more limited than it is. Product innovation increases the value of products to customers. The reward is more than a minimal profit over cost—the kind of profit enjoyed by product innovators such as those in the pharmaceutical (new drugs) and technology industries (Microsoft, Google). Clothing retailer Zara has also honed its process for adopting new styles quickly; Au Bon Pain does the same with sandwiches. As described in Section 4.1, the Indian company GHCL is integrating the supply chain for bed and bath products. Profits from the stream of new products fund new investment, enrich producers, and fuel more innovation.

Another driver arises from process innovation. Even without new products or markets, few can stand still in the face of competition. This is particularly true for low-margin products where distribution costs are a high share of the sales price. This is a powerful driver because low-cost operators in markets set the standard. Also, as process innovations decrease costs and improve service, products become more affordable, increasing the ability of customers to buy them and expanding the available target market.

The consulting firm McKinsey captured the effects of process innovation by examining U.S. retail sales leader Wal-Mart.[1] The author of the study, Bradford Johnson, notes that in 1987 Wal-Mart had only a 9 percent market share, but was 40 percent more productive than competitors as measured by sales per employee. By 1995, through "big box" stores, electronic communication with suppliers, low prices, and central distribution centers, Wal-Mart had a 27 percent share and a productivity advantage of 48 percent.

From 1995 to 1999, competitors played catch-up, but Wal-Mart maintained its edge. McKinsey's study summarized how Wal-Mart achieved the gains through changes in both product and process.

- *Managerial innovations* that did not involve information technology. An example is cross-training employees to increase flexibility in their assignment and the hours they work.

- *Focused IT investments* that enhanced Wal-Mart's low-price objective and did not include more recent investments in real-time sales data collection and dissemination.
- *Higher-value goods* matched to the market's desire for upscale products. For example, the $30 shirt costs as much to handle and sell as the $20 shirt, but is far more profitable.

Wal-Mart illustrates the innovation driver for supply chain projects. The company uses its supply chain capability to identify products that yield the highest profit. For a retailer bringing thousands of products to market, pegging profitability at the product level is a vital, and often daunting, task. Relying on data, not the intuition of buyers and merchandisers, is the key. Chapter 19 recommends a process using activity-based costing to achieve this objective.

What about a company with only a few products where there's no confusion where profitability lies? This is often the case when the product is based on intellectual property (IP) that provides a monopoly of sorts. A *Wall Street Journal* article described the implications of this product category.[2] The article notes that the products based on IP are fundamentally different. Almost all the cost is in development, and almost 100 percent of every sales dollar is pure profit after the initial investment in development is paid off.

Is SCM important in cases where the cost of the base product is close to zero? There are at least three ways supply chain considerations support such proprietary monopoly products.

1. *The introduction of "killer" products.* Effective supply chain processes speed moneymaking products to market. Glitches that delay product introduction are tantamount to leaving money on the table. Also, such software products require, according to Bill Gates of Microsoft as quoted in the *Wall Street Journal* article, "monopoly power." This results only if you become an industry standard by being first to market. Without that dominating position, up-front investments will be total losses, not total profits. The supply chain may make the difference in establishing this position ahead of a competitor.
2. *Reduction of unseen lost sales.* Reducing lost sales requires adequate supplies to meet demand. Products produce no profit if the sale is lost due to a stock-out. This is so important to Wal-Mart that it has a program called *remix* for handling fast-moving staple products. Chapter 12, Section 12.3, describes this program further.
3. *Extensions of product life.* The innovative product is not innovative forever. If costs are not reduced as it matures, it may die a sudden death. Squeezing cost out of the supply chain is a duty of supply chain managers.

Steven Wheelwright and Kim Clark have defined different types of product and process change.[3] Table 6.2 shows types *A* through *D* from Clark and Wheelwright;

Table 6.2 Types of Product/Process Development Projects

Type	Examples	Extent of Product Change	Extent of Supply Chain Change
A	Existing product enhancements Derivative products Variations on similar products	Minor changes Different content/same form Few, if any, supplier changes	Incremental or no change Single department involved Requires material management changes
B	Next-generation product New platform	Major changes likely Supplier changes more likely	Next-generation process Multiple departments involved Likely supply chain impact
C	Radical breakthrough	New core product Probable new suppliers and chain	New core processes New supply chain more likely
D	Research/advanced development	Leads to new core product New suppliers/chain likely	Design requires new core processes New supply chain more likely
E	Partnership projects	Likely to require a new supply chain if product is new	Supply chain change involving partners likely

E is this book's authors' addition to recognize the "partnership" project, which contains its own issues. The table recognizes that each project will vary in terms of the product and process change involved. For example, an *A*-type project involves minor changes in both dimensions. *A*-changes are like Rhino Entertainment's compact disc (CD) releases of its wide variety of previously released tracks or new menu items at sandwich maker Au Bon Pain. The companies' flows of new products are routine events, and the product introduction process is repeated over and over.

B projects are more ambitious. They often involve the "next generation" of a base product. The continual upgrading in personal computers is an example. A product change in the *B* category could result in the same effect on the process dimension, or needed processes could remain the same. The *C* project is the "breakthrough" in either product or process. In retailing, the growth of Internet sales is an example of a *C* project on the process side. *D* projects represent the "fuzzy front end" of product and process development. Managers may choose how much supply chain planning is required. *E* projects are efforts with multicompany participation. These bring other issues discussed elsewhere in this book, primarily Part 4.

Table 6.2 describes the impact on the retail supply chain from either new products or new processes. A next-generation process resulting from a *B* effort can happen even if there is not a great deal of change in the product itself. Likewise, a next-generation product may require only incremental process or supply chain changes.

Manufacturing companies use the term "concurrent engineering," or CE for short, to describe simultaneous development of manufacturing processes and products. Note that most efforts are confined to manufacturing at a company and do not address broader supply chain issues. CE speeds up product introduction. It is the opposite of the "over-the-wall" approach of engineering departments handing product designs to the production department—or increasingly to suppliers. For many products, delays are just as great when handing a design to the procurement department charged with finding suppliers. The need to consider the capabilities of supply chain partners adds another dimension to the CE concept. Now it is not only tooling and material that have to be considered, but also other issues such as distribution channels and inventory policy. CE for the entire supply chain particularly fits in the case of *B*, *C*, and *E* products. In these cases a new product is more likely to be accompanied by a new supply chain.

6.3 Extended Product Design

Figure 6.1 illustrates how product or process innovations feed the next SCM driver, *extended product design*. Our definition in Chapter 1, Section 1.2, describes the supply chain as "product life cycle processes comprising physical, information, financial, and knowledge flows whose purpose is to satisfy end-user requirements with physical products *and services* from multiple, linked suppliers." For many products, there can certainly be a lot of services, and such services are a source of differentiation.

Figure 6.2 depicts the base and extended products, and lists the supply chain links—retailer, distributor, original equipment manufacturer (OEM), or supplier—that might provide each service. In Figure 6.2, the physical product is the "base product," and with it the services help to form the "extended product." For several services, such as *product availability* and *warranties,* more than one link along the chain may play a role. For product availability, the retailer or the distributor or both could be responsible.

A *Wall Street Journal* article confirmed the trend by stating that "manufacturers find themselves increasingly in the service sector."[4] The article attributes the trend to manufacturers having to provide services because that is "where the money is." Few products and services are commodities in the strictest sense. However, for many, extended product features may outweigh the importance of the base

Base Product Features

Retailer
•Size/shape/form factor
•Options/features

Distributor
•Size/shape/form factor

OEM Manufacturer
•Obsolescence risk
•Styling
•Ease of use
•Options/features
•Size/shape/form factor
•Product quality
•Connectivity/standards

Component Suppliers
•Technology
•Product quality

Extended Product Features

Retailer
•Dealer quality
•Technical assistance
•Availability/delivery/selection
•Warranty
•Brand image/reputation
•Ease of doing business
•Financing
•After-sale service
•Returns handling

Distributor
•Availability/delivery/selection
•Product line availability
•Returns handling

OEM Manufacturer
•Brand image/reputation
•Technical assistance
•Warranty
•Updates
•After-sale service
•Ease of doing business
•Returns handling
•Repair/replacement parts availability

Component Suppliers
•Repair/replacement parts availability

Figure 6.2 Base and extended product.

product, which customers may view as indistinguishable from competing brands. General Electric's former CEO, Jack Welch, portrayed service development associated with hardware production as fundamental to his success as the CEO.[5]

In an ideal world, supply chain managers methodically monitor the product and process innovations coming their way. They then design supply chains to incorporate each innovation. Or, in a slightly less ideal world, the managers slot each innovation into the "best-fit" supply chain already in place. However, in many instances, managers fall short of achieving either of these situations. In fact, base product and extended product management, like other related functions, are also often in separate departments. For example, base products may be the responsibility of R&D, engineering, and manufacturing departments, whereas marketing and sales shape extended products.

Many managers also assume that every product innovation must fit existing supply chains. Inertia, hard-to-change information systems, required behaviors, and functional barriers make it hard to adjust current practices. Everyone is used to the way things work now; additionally, expensive investments in systems, staff, and facilities may be needed for the new product. However, ignoring this driver will put the company at risk. Chapter 13 explains the activity system approach to developing extended product processes.

6.4 Globalization

Chapter 4 described the economics of comparative advantage behind globalization. By adding jobs and payrolls, social good also arises from globalization through growth in multi-country supply chains. For supply chain managers, globalization influences range from upstream suppliers to downstream customers. For smaller manufacturers who export to other countries, their executives must not only ensure that the production lines are running but also that currency risks are hedged.[6] The shift to "offshore" sourcing, often to cut material cost, provides opportunities for jobs and investment in developing countries. When this occurs, globalization puts money in people's pockets, widening markets for company products. For example, the market in China for cars is growing, even for luxury models. Many sales in China today are to first-time buyers—and often for cash.

Rich Karlgaard, publisher of *Forbes* magazine, describes the state of the world's growing prosperity.[7] He notes that the U.S. economy grew 30 percent in the five years after the 9/11 attacks on the World Trade Center and Pentagon. This is in spite of the fact that these attacks were designed to "destabilize" economic life in the western world. He notes that the global economy did even better than the United States, growing 47 percent in the same period.

Long-term growth can also be documented on a per capita (per person) basis. On a per capita basis, in 1500, as the Renaissance began, per capita gross world product was $800 in current dollars. Three centuries later, in 1820, it had increased only to $950. However, by 2006, it had grown substantially to $9500. However, this growth has been unbalanced with higher per capita incomes in the developed world—about $30,000. So, there are many stuck in poverty, particularly in Africa and India, where incomes remain at the levels they were at in 1820.

Karlgaard refers to the imbalance as "immoral and obscene," given the deprivations at the bottom of the income ladder. He points to the spread of technology, communications, and "ideas" such as those of Adam Smith as being responsible for growth in the rich regions. The implication is that globalizing markets enabled by supply chains may be the mechanism to spread this wealth.

Narayana Murthy echoes these thoughts.[8] Murthy is the retired chairman of Indian technology services firm, Infosys Technologies Limited. Murthy reports that the company started on the premise that globalization would make the world "as wired and open as a trading floor." The founders' premise was that this globalization would bring a competitive advantage to low-cost skilled workers.

Murthy's company has grown, in 25 years, from virtually nothing to a $20-billion firm with 58,000 employees. He describes how India, at the beginning, was bogged down in a culture of bureaucracy. His startup faced obstacles like a two-year delay to buy a computer and two to three years to get a telephone line. These are examples of "distance" as defined in Chapter 4. His advice, upon retiring, is to pursue fresh ideas with vigor, maintain a meritocracy, and to benchmark operations and products against the best competitors continuously.

6.5 Flexibility Imperative—the Ultimate Capability

The last driver arising from innovations is the retail supply chain flexibility imperative. Absence of flexibility infers a static supply chain that is unable to "flex" as changes in the environment require. Product designs, competitive responses, sales levels, and customer requirements rarely stay the same for long. Although the environment has many moving parts, many companies attempt to fulfill customer requirements with a "one size fits all" approach. They fail to take into account the needs of different customer segments, the necessity of providing extended product features, and the ever-changing base products.

Flexibility is a term with different meanings to different people. However, its importance raises the need to define the word and what it requires in supply chain design. For this to happen, management must be prepared to respond in three ways:

1. *Mindset.* The company must recognize the need for defining flexibility formally, and what kind of flexibility is needed for the business.
2. *Long term.* Management must be skilled enough to match supply chain design, including supply chain capacity, with customer expectations. If it is not willing to do so, management must be prepared to drop customers. In growth markets, management must monitor the marketplace to quickly adapt to changing customer needs.
3. *Short term.* Management must understand the markets they choose to serve well enough to define requirements for response time and production flexibility.

The needed responses are interdependent. That is, a company must have #1 to get #2; and it must have #2 to get #3. The next sections explain each further and their implication for retail SCM.

6.5.1 Management Mindset

If one accepts that change in variables such as product demand and product mix will occur in the marketplace, then one must accept that building flexibility into the supply chain is "imperative." The flexibility imperative becomes the foundation for achieving objectives in any of the other traditional supply chain metrics such as cost and lead time. Being flexible gives the ability to move to where the supply chain needs to be with regard to reliability, responsiveness, cost, and asset utilization.

Without flexibility, to cope with change, there can be no ongoing reliable delivery, responsiveness to customer demand, efficiency, and effective use of assets.

Describing the absence of the correct mindset is easier than defining its presence. Symptoms of such an absence include the following:

- Company strategies are silent on the topic of flexibility.
- Departments in the supply chain are frozen and unlinked. Separate budgets exist for functions—marketing, sales, purchasing, manufacturing, and distribution—without regard to the processes they share.
- Supply chain is defined as warehousing, transportation, and other physical handling of products. Manufacturing, product design, marketing, and inventory management are not included.
- The primary measure for supply chain managers is cost. A common example is "supply chain cost per dollar of sales."
- Management pursues an inventory reduction program. Inventory is an effect, not a cause. It is the by-product of supply chain processes and can't be reduced unless supply chain processes are changed.
- The company measures buyers on unit costs of purchased material, omitting other cost factors such as returns and quality.
- Lost sales due to out-of-stock situations are not estimated and tracked. No one is accountable for them.
- Inventory and other assets are considered "free" because their costs are not weighed in performance measures.

The presence of any of these conditions should raise alarms. However, absence of any of the symptoms is not sufficient for achieving a management mindset. Management should also articulate the types of flexibility needed for the business such as that described in the following section.

6.5.2 Defining Needed Flexibility

David Upton has recommended a methodology for incorporating flexibility into manufacturing systems.[9] His definition of flexibility as follows:

> Flexibility is the ability to change or react with little penalty in time, effort, cost, or performance.

The framework for flexibility can be translated from the manufacturing level, where he proposed it, to trading partners such as distributors and retailers. Upton recognizes the problems that go with defining flexibility. Just saying, "We need to be flexible," is inadequate due to the many possible interpretations. To fill this gap, Upton defines flexibility as having three "dimensions" defined by answers to questions. Table 6.3 summarizes the framework and provides examples.

Table 6.3   Characterization of Flexibility

	Component	Description	Examples
1.	Dimension	What is it that requires flexibility?	Different input materials Mixes of product Different volumes
2.	Time horizon	What is the period over which flexibility is required? • Operational—seconds to days • Tactical—days to months • Strategic—months to years	Operational—schedule changes, daily shipments, order response time Tactical—quarterly changes in mix, use of materials, number of SKUs to carry to support a product line Strategic—long-range changes requiring capital or new systems
3.	Element	In what way should we be flexible? • Range—by how much the dimension (#1 above) must be able to change • Mobility—low transition costs for moving in a range • Uniformity—the ability to be consistent over a range	Range—volumes of output or deliveries, sizes of product, SKUs breadth, merchandise models Mobility—having low setup costs to change product mix or to add or discontinue merchandise SKUs Uniformity—the ability to maintain a certain standard such as delivery time, cost, or merchandise availability

■ Question 1 asks what parameter requires flexibility, that is, in what dimension is flexibility needed. APICS identifies product mix, design changeover, product modification, volume, rerouting, and material usage in the product as flexibility dimensions for a manufacturer. Some of the same dimensions exist for retailers and distributors. Other dimensions include delivery lead time, support from extended product services, and product-line breadth and depth.

■ The answer to Question 2 identifies the "time horizon." Upton uses operational, tactical, and strategic for short (seconds, minutes, and hours), medium (hours, days, and weeks), and long time horizons (weeks, months, and years). Whether short means seconds or hours depends on the product, industry, and position along the supply chain.

Figure 6.3   Taxonomy for flexibility—an example.

- Question 3 addresses "elements" of flexibility. Upton describes three elements under which most flexibility requirements fall. They are *range, mobility,* and *uniformity.*

A range element specifies the limits of performance. For example, if volume flexibility (dimension) over a short period is sought (time horizon), the range will specify the high and low operating volumes. Mobility refers to the lack of a penalty in moving from one state in the range to another. For example, if there is little cost in moving from 100 units per hour to 150, then mobility is high. On the other hand, if it is very difficult to make this change, mobility is low. Uniformity refers to the performance over a range. For example, if the move from 100 to 150 units causes little change in the quality of the product, then flexibility is high with respect to quality.

Figure 6.3 illustrates a flexibility specification. The example is a sandwich shop that requires supply chain flexibility in multiple dimensions, including product mix, volume, and customer response time. The sandwich shop operates in one of the most demanding retail situations, build-to-order, in terms of the need to provide quick, consistent responses to customers.

- Product mix changes are required over an operational timeframe that, in this case, is daily. The element of flexibility is mobility. So, any product mix can be made each day with the supply chain moving quickly to produce one unique product after another. A sandwich shop exemplifies this type of flexibility in a short timeframe measured in minutes, because the staff must assemble any sandwich on the menu as soon as the customer places the order.
- "Product volume" in our example is the ability to change overall volume up or down in a tactical, or intermediate, timeframe. For the sandwich shop, this period could be monthly. So, the sandwich shop, like other retailers, adjusts its schedule up or down across a range of expected business levels. If the shop were across the street from a college, then the number of workers would be

higher during the school year and lower during summer vacation. The range component specifies the product volumes used to set staffing levels.

■ "Response time" provides a strategic standard that is competitive in the market served by the organization. This dimension is likely to be as important to manufacturers and distributors as it is to retailers. It is a uniformity element, meaning that customer response time must be uniform over the range of volumes in which the supply chain must operate. So, the sandwich shop must provide uniform service, building each sandwich within minutes at both high- and low-volume levels. In fact, McDonalds and other fast-food retailers track the time it takes to serve each customer and hold employees responsible for achieving targeted rapid customer service.

A sandwich vendor who doesn't make to order but stocks retailer shelves with prepackaged sandwich varieties has a different problem. It must try as best it can to get the mix right. Also important is ensuring that the right quantity is on hand to serve the customer willing to take a second or third choice. Forecasting in the case is for delivered sandwich, not their components—like the build-to-order sandwich shop. Starbucks must determine how many pastries and what kind they will have on hand in each of its cafes each day. However, the goal is to order the right quantities of each type of pastry such that nothing is left at the end of the day.

Contrasts in product mix flexibility requirements can be seen in the strategies of major retailers. Nordstrom, the clothing retailer, presents a broad product mix to its customers with individual departments targeting slightly different customers. A range of offerings is a merchandising goal. Retailer Costco, a discounter, buys in bulk whenever product is available. Consistency in offering low-cost merchandise, not a broad range, is the flexibility goal. Chapter 3, Section 3.3, described differences in performance, many of which are driven by choices about flexibility.

Flexibility specifications are imperative because they drive design of supply chain processes and shape collaboration with supply chain partners. These include capacity, inventory, and merchandising decisions along the retail supply chain. Static specifications are not acceptable. The Upton method described earlier makes possible the definition of ranges of operations and expectations for customer service. Also, many CEOs seek some kind of visual cockpit to monitor their operations. One based on defined flexibility parameters such as those in the example should be part of such a cockpit.

6.6 Process-Centered Management

Examining end-to-end processes without taking on too much at once has gained currency. Awareness of the importance of processes is not new. Reengineering, Total Quality Management (TQM), lean, and Six Sigma are all mature initiatives aimed at process improvement. Yet there is often tension between those wanting to focus on end-to-end processes and functional managers who implement local improvements in their departments. They do this because their measurements encourage local improvements, and changes are easier because they control the departments and their direction.

Jack Welch, in the previously cited interview, talks about "world peace" projects requiring complex information technology.[10] In his first decade as General Electric's CEO, he approved many of these projects. His term, *world peace*, refers to the over-hyped promises made to sell the projects. When promised results never materialized, Welch became far more skeptical. In his second decade as CEO, only projects that produced tangible, fast results moved forward.

What is the implication for SCM? Is top-down end-to-end, or bottom-up local the right model for retail SCM projects? Table 6.4 describes three scenarios framing how projects for supply chain improvement are formulated, justified, and managed. Scenario #1 in Table 6.4 is bottom-up, originating in the department. A project might be the purchase of a machine tool in the manufacturing department. "We will cut our labor by 20 percent," is a claim that might describe expected results from such a project. It is likely a local savings, just involving that portion of the process where the machine is used. It is not necessarily true that overall process cost will be reduced at all, especially when the cost of capital for the machine is taken into account.

Scenario #2 is top-down at the business unit level, with projects that cross department boundaries. A customer relationship management (CRM) system is an example. This technology could be deployed at the retailer, distributor, or manufacturer level. "We shall increase our sales 5 percent," might be a claim of success for the system. However, an auditor might have difficulty tracing any "hard" return revenue increases to the system. Scenario #3 is "beyond" top-down because it extends past company boundaries. Projects in this category seek to reduce multi-company process cost across trading partners.

To be effective at the supply chain level, a process focus, i.e., top-down end-to-end, is a necessity. Reasons include avoiding local optimums at the expense of the overall system, the interdependence of departments and businesses in the supply chain, and the advantages of shared knowledge to solve problems. But there are also many obstacles that include physical separation, suspicion, inadequate cost accounting, counterproductive performance measures, and lack of skills or numbers. So, collaboration to improve processes is not easy. But the beginning is a process-centered focus that includes supply chain partners. Parts 4 and 5 recommend methods to bring about a supply chain process-centered focus.

6.7 Collaboration

The end-to-end process approach leads to the need for collaboration across internal departments and company boundaries. Few dispute the need for collaboration in

Table 6.4 Scenarios for Developing Supply Chain Projects

	Level	Sponsorship	Examples	Goal	Justifications
1.	Function	Department head	Machine tools, new production equipment	Department improvement	Return on investment, savings
2.	Business unit	CEO	Enterprise systems, expansions/contractions	Business unit improvement	Revenue increase or cost reduction
3.	Supply chain	CEO, customer, supplier, alliance	Information sharing, investment sharing	Multicompany competitiveness	Revenue increase or cost reduction

improving supply chains. Like flexibility, the term *collaboration* can mean different things to different people. Certainly, both companies on either side of a supply chain link must agree to the form of collaboration.

6.7.1 Definitions of Collaboration

A big push for collaboration is technology based. To many practitioners, the term *collaboration* is a code word for *information sharing*, which is in turn a code for *new systems*. To meet the demand, many supply chain information software applications have emerged to support collaboration. These products enable sharing of production and inventory data, online auctions, market places for buying and selling, and production planning along the supply chain.

It should be no surprise, then, that definitions of collaboration have an information technology tone. Table 6.5 shows the definitions of collaboration by industry analysts who, at the time of the presentation, represented three prominent research organizations.[11] All three analysts described collaboration as a three-stage process. The levels begin with simpler forms of information sharing that are relatively easy to automate. They proceed to higher levels that involve joint decision making. These may be aided by technology, but are essentially powered by management decision-making processes that are difficult to automate.

Of the three, the version from Navi Radjou captures the widest range of decision-making activity going beyond transactions to supply chain structuring. It also most clearly covers collaboration processes such as strategy setting and cost sharing of investments needed to compete on a supply chain basis. This view has been reinforced since the time of the presentations as reflected by efforts by the Supply Chain Council and the Collaborative Planning, Forecasting, and Replenishment (CPFR*) initiative reported in Chapter 15, Section 15.2.3.

6.7.2 Stage 3 (Multicompany) SCM

What general structure might collaboration take between two or more trading partners? An earlier article outlined a vision for "Stage 3" supply chain collaboration efforts.[12] The term "Stage 3" comes from the third, or supply chain, level as shown in Table 6.4. Multicompany collaboration features include the following:

1. Shared goals that include strategic and tactical improvements. An example of the former is increased market share; an example of the latter is lower product cost or reduced inventory.
2. A team effort that includes representatives from participating companies on a full-time or part-time basis.
3. As needed, an honest broker to facilitate the effort. This can be a trusted team member or third party such as a consultant.

Table 6.5 Definitions of Collaboration

Company	Company Represented		
	Yankee Group	AMR Research	Forester Research
Analyst	Jon Derome	Larry Lapide	Navi Radjou
Level 1	Exchange of structured data	Execution (routine documents such as purchase orders)	Monitor. Watch the process together
Level 2	Free-form interactive sharing (Web tools, chats, online)	Information sharing, mostly one-way	Manage. Coordinate activities.
Level 3	Process collaboration (structured, mix of human and automated exchange)	Collaborative relationship (joint planning and scheduling, coordinated execution)	Optimize. Joint decision making. Win-win partnerships across network

4. A multicompany CEO or senior management steering committee. This group would be responsible for the results of the collaboration.
5. Contracting that distributes costs and rewards based on contributions. Negotiations over costs and profits shouldn't fall back on standard buyer–seller price negotiations but be guided by a model of supply chain costs using techniques such as those described in Chapter 19.
6. Process integration using appropriate technology and continuous improvement. An important component could be synchronizing the supply chain replenishment cycle.

Item 6 on the list also closes the loop as shown in Figure 6.1, taking collaboration back to further supply chain innovation—with ideas coming from inside the supply chain. A Stage 3 effort shouldn't be a one-shot affair. After the initial effort, improvements should continue. Once established, the supply chain partnership becomes a source of innovations.

6.8 Know Your Drivers

This chapter addresses the factors that make supply chain change a way of life. Some companies will be slow in comprehending which of these drivers affect them most. However, the drivers will be there, exerting a force for change whether it's recognized in the organization or not. Supply chain partners delivering functional, low-technology products seek innovations in processes. These could result in globalization of sourcing and innovations in tracking and transportation. A technology product supply chain, on the other hand, must react to innovations coming from manufacturers in the supply chain. In any change, retailers in contact with customers and end-users should transmit market preferences back through the chain.

Endnotes

1. Johnson, Bradford C., "Retail: The Wal-Mart Effect," *The McKinsey Quarterly*, 2002, Number 1.
2. Murray, Alan, "Intellectual Property: Old Rules Don't Apply," *The Wall Street Journal*, August 23, 2001, p. A1.
3. Wheelwright, Steven C. and Clark, Kim B., *Revolutionizing Product Development*, New York: Free Press, 1992, p. 49.
4. Ansberry, Clare, "Manufacturers Find Themselves Increasingly in the Service Sector," *The Wall Street Journal*, February 10, 2003, p. A2.
5. Welch, Jack, A conversation with Jack Welch, *MSI Executive Series* (Internet broadcast), April 16, 2002.
6. Phillips, Michael M., "Ship Those Boxes; Check the Euro!" *The Wall Street Journal*, February 7, 2003, p. C1.
7. Karlgaard, Rich, "The World's Accelerating Prosperity," *Forbes*, October 2, 2006, p. 29.
8. Murthy, Narayana N.R., "Clear Conscious-Clear Profit," *The Wall Street Journal*, September 29, 2006, p. A16.
9. Upton, David M., "The Management of Manufacturing Flexibility," *California Business Review*, Winter 1994, pp. 72–89.
10. Welch, Jack, op.cit.
11. Lapide, Larry, Derome, Jon, and Radjou, Navi, Analysts' panel discussion, *Supply Chain World North America: Extending Collaboration to End-to-End Synchronization*, April 2002.
12. Ayers, James B., Gustin, Craig, and Stephens, Scott, "Reengineering the Supply Chain," *Information Strategy: the Executive's Journal*, Fall, 1997 (14/1), pp. 13–18.

Chapter 7

Paths to the Customer

New markets, new products, and shifts in end-user needs require new or updated supply chain responses. Chapter 6 described the drivers of supply chain change. Responding to these drivers appropriately entails multiple dimensions of supply chain planning and design. Table 7.1 lists seven—several of which many companies may not associate with supply chain management (SCM). The reader should also note that the list applies for all roles in supply chains—retailers, distributors, suppliers, original equipment manufacturers (OEMs), and service providers. The importance of any one dimension will vary for any particular combination of supply chain role, product, and market. For example, *product design* and *capabilities and capacity* are more important for manufacturers than distributors, yet they have a very direct impact on retailers in the form of appropriateness for the market. However, too often some dimensions are overlooked altogether in companies with a narrow view of SCM. This chapter explores these dimensions and describes important decision categories for each.

7.1 Meeting Market Needs—Dimensions

As implied in the previous paragraph, an SCM function with "deep roots" will contain processes that address the applicable dimensions listed in Table 7.1. The timeframes, in the second column of Table 7.1, will depend on the role-product-market combination. A *long* timeframe will likely exceed one year and could be as long as five years. For example, longer terms are characteristic of new technology product development, whereas an *intermediate* timeframe applies to product upgrades. A long-term timeframe would also apply to a middleman distributor whose strategy is to offer extended product services to manufacturers and retailers. Intermediate

Table 7.1   Meeting Market Needs—SCM Dimensions

#	Market-Need Dimensions	Timeframe	SCM Relevance
1.	Product portfolio	Long	Mix, technology, breadth and depth of line
2.	Product design	Long	Configuration, reliability, complexity, options
3.	Capabilities and capacity	Long	How to produce/source, logistics; need for partners
4.	Competitive responses	Intermediate	Competitors, strengths, and weaknesses
5.	Product channels	Intermediate	Customer preferences for acquiring the product
6.	Customer risk concerns	Intermediate	Returns, service and repair, technical support
7.	Matching supply and demand	Short	Flexibility requirements, information sharing

timeframes are generally measured in months. For a retailer, planning for the holiday season could have an intermediate planning horizon. *Short* term is hourly, daily, or weekly and the usual domain of conventional, narrowly defined SCM.

The *product portfolio* (#1), a long timeframe dimension, includes decisions by the manufacturer for both the base product and extended product services. For a logistics service provider such as UPS and FEDEX, it includes pursuit of those services that retailers and manufacturers may want to outsource. For retailers it involves merchandising decisions regarding products and brands their stores and other outlets will carry, including new products heading to market from manufacturers. *Product design* (#2) will obviously concern the OEM of the base product and its suppliers. New designs bring the need for adjustments in manufacturing processes and the supplier base, important supply chain features. Product design may also affect distributors and retailers if the product can be assembled, labeled, or otherwise processed en route to the end-user. Collaboration between retailer and manufacturer is necessary for private label brands where the retailer, instead of the manufacturer, designs the product, and the manufacturer produces to these specifications. Certainly, the rollout of new products brings the need for information exchange, if not outright collaboration, to estimate demand all along the chain.

Responses in the *capabilities and capacity* (#3) dimension range from no change to radical change in the case of new products. This dimension also applies in planning regional expansions to new markets or countries as part of a manufacturer or retailer growth plan. Because technology is evolving so quickly, radical supply-chain changes are expected over the next few years. At the 2007 National Retail Federation Annual Conference, Steve Ballmer, CEO of Microsoft, stated:

> The young generation has grown up in a connected world which will continue to revolutionize how people shop. Any time they walk in your store, they will expect you to be able to deal with all their gadgets. They will expect to be the center of attention of any business that tries to serve them.[1]

A new process technology such as radio frequency identification (RFID) also fits in this dimension. These technologies entail collaboration because they require installation of technical capabilities all along the retail supply chain. Chapter 18 addresses the subject of supply chain visibility in greater depth.

Any planning, including that for the supply chain, should consider *competitive responses* (#4). This is particularly true if management seeks, or needs to seek, competitive advantage from its supply chain design. This book, in Part 3 and Chapter 13 in particular, recommends activity systems to establish unique, hard-to-copy processes. Deciding what *product channels* (#5) are needed to reach end-users arises from customer preferences and market standards established by competitive responses. This dimension may or may not be associated with the supply chain function. For many manufacturers, for example, decisions on channels are the responsibility of the marketing function. However, supply chain professionals must implement these decisions and do so in an economical manner.

Customer risk concerns (#6) have ramifications for supply chain design. Risks exist all along the chain. The ease of returning a purchase—to a store in the case of an Internet purchase, for example—may be a factor in the purchase decision. The customer perceives less risk in making the purchase. For complex, large-price-tag purchases, such as an automobile or a computer, customer service and repair support are a concern and can play a big role in brand selection by the customer. This brings into consideration the supply chain for repair and replacement parts and the service facilities to install them. For example, one of the authors purchased a vehicle that was involved in a very major accident six days after purchase. The insurance company decided that it should be repaired rather than replaced. Because it was a brand new version of its model, it took more than six months for the repair parts to reach the United States and another month for the repairs.

Poor SCM of repair parts can result in greatly dissatisfied customers. Chapter 22 describes the repair and replacement parts and services environment. If use of the product requires new ways of working or new skills, then the quality and accessibility of product support will be an SCM issue. The risk dimension also includes supply chain vulnerability to security threats and the potential for substandard working conditions in offshore factories far upstream in the chain.

The final dimension, *matching supply and demand* (#7), encompasses operational activities along the chain. Few would doubt this is an SCM domain. The discussion of supply and demand is deferred to Section 7.4 and other chapters, particularly those in Section IV.

7.2 Procter & Gamble Case Study

P&G demonstrates how one leader addresses the dimensions listed in Table 7.1 The company, headquartered in the United States, has $68 billion in global consumer products sales and is a significant supplier for major household retailers such as Wal-Mart, Target, and major grocery chains.[2] In fiscal year 2006, about half those sales were in the United States with the other half in Europe, Asia, and "developing geographies." There are few companies of P&G's size. However, its success offers lessons to those operating at a smaller scale. In fact, reaching such a size in terms of the number of customers, countries served, and products is, in large part, due to executing effective supply chain processes and systems and superior brand strategy.

P&G's 2006 annual report and an earlier article from consultants McKinsey & Company describe its financial performance from 2002 through 2006.[3] P&G growth ensued from both internal, organic growth and through acquisitions. The largest acquisition, in October 2005, was Gillette, another U.S. consumer products company. As described later, fast integration of acquisitions into P&G processes contributed to the company's success. Much of this integration included information systems capabilities. During the five-year period, sales, including acquisitions, grew from $40 to $68 billion, net earnings from $3.9 to $8.7 billion, and earnings per share from $1.46 to $2.79. Sales for existing businesses, without considering the Gillette acquisition, often referred to as "organic" sales, grew 6 percent in fiscal 2006.

In 2006, P&G had 22 brands selling over $1 billion annually. These include those acquired with the Gillette acquisition—Braun (shaving and hair removal), Gillette (razors and related products), Duracell (batteries), and Oral B (dental hygiene products)—with the remaining in a number of product categories, including well-known brands such as Charmin (tissues), Folgers (coffee), Pringles (food), and Tide (detergent). P&G identifies what they consider their strengths. These are listed as follows and mapped to the applicable SCM dimensions from Table 7.1:

■ Shopper and consumer understanding (dimensions 1, 2, 5, and 6 in Table 7.1)
■ Branding (dimensions 4, 5, and 6)
■ Innovation (dimensions 1 and 2)
■ Go-to-market capability (dimensions 3, 5, 6, and 7)
■ Global scale (dimensions 3, 5, and 7)

CEO Alan G. Lafley cites "executing with excellence" as the key element in P&G's success. To be effective, this execution must be supported by "disciplined strategic choices, a structure that supports the strategy, systems that enable organizations to work and execute together, a winning culture, and leadership that's inspirational."[4]

Addressing the seven supply chain dimensions will go a long way toward achieving this environment for any company. Lafley warns against incremental improvements that lead to complacency. "You can get used to being a player without being a winner. There's a big difference between the two." Lafley manages P&G growth by focusing on what he refers to as "the core." The core consists of business components that provide the best opportunities to achieve financial objectives. To qualify, a core business must be a global leader capable of meeting growth and cash flow objectives. For P&G, the core businesses in mid-2006 were fabric care, baby care, feminine care, and hair care. P&G growth strategies according to its annual report include:

- Growth in the core businesses—more sales to big markets employing P&G's core strengths and technologies
- Pursuit of fast-growth, high-margin business with global leadership the goal
- Emphasis on growth in developing markets to serve more low-income customers

Lafley particularly emphasizes that the need to be in touch with customers is the same for any product in the portfolio. Such contact reveals product portfolio expectations, desirable product features, channel preferences, and customer risk concerns. To ensure P&G fulfills its commitments, the company spends over $200 million a year for 10,000 market research studies. The company also identifies what it calls "moments of truth" in customer contacts with P&G products. The first moment of truth occurs when the customer purchases the product; the second, when the customer decides whether use of the product has delivered on its promise.

P&G also seeks to have its customers "pull" new products out of the company's product pipeline. The alternative is to have P&G product developers "pull" new products to its customers by directing much of its sales promotion and advertising to the consumer rather than the retailer. He notes that, at one point, the company spent, in its efforts to push new products at consumers, over $200 million in "skunk works" product development. This wasn't working. Lafley put the customer first and restored the customer-pull approach to setting product development priorities. Later, this chapter (Section 7.5) describes the quality function deployment (QFD) tool, a method for translating the "voice of the customer" into product and supply chain features.

Lafley describes the need to integrate acquisitions and products into P&G systems and procedures. With regard to the Gillette acquisition, he notes that P&G "integrated systems in 26 countries, spanning five geographic regions, and representing 20 percent of sales" in about eight months. This integration provided common back-office methods for order taking, product shipping, and payment processing, and resulted in significant efficiencies.

7.3 Role of Specifications

A start toward the environment described by CEO Lafley is to specify what kind of supply chain you want. To meet market needs, the specification process for supply chain design should be ongoing, incorporating the seven dimensions. Vague higher-level goals such as "excellent customer service" may exist in any supply chain company, but these are seldom translated into consistent specifications for operations. The principal, if not the only, control in many cases is the budget—a monetary figure, not a clear blueprint for process development. These situations are common when supply chains grow with the business without formal definitions of what they should do.

Specifications for supply chain design play the same role they do in designing a product. Designers or users begin the design of an automobile or a computer with such a specification. For totally new products, there may be little customer experience to guide the effort, so the designer creates a specification based on common sense, customer inputs, and a formal statement of requirements. The QFD process described later in this chapter is another way to generate needed inputs.

A company such as P&G brings to market a continuous stream of new products to improve the profitability of its "core." Many can be introduced into existing supply chains serving the end-user. Others, however, will need new or modified supply chains. The dimensions in Table 7.1 serve as a template listing the specifications that reflects market needs.

Table 7.2 lists examples applying the template to three principal supply chain roles—manufacturers, distributors, and retailers. Items on the list, labeled "Supply Chain–Related Decision Categories," are candidates for consideration as a shared SCM function, not just a marketing, manufacturing, or technology function. A forum for deciding how to meet market needs is a brainstorming session by a team representing these stakeholding functions.

Each of the principal links—the manufacturer, the distributor, and the retailer—has different concerns, examples of which are shown in the column headings of Table 7.2. Some decision categories will be common to different roles, and others will not. Certainly, a manufacturer must pay close attention to the base products they design. The distributor, being a midchain service provider, has similar concerns with the service needs of upstream and downstream trading partners. Without these, the "plain vanilla" distributor that limits itself to physical handling of merchandise could disappear.

A common retailer concern is often the profit each product will generate for the corresponding investment in shelf space or store area. Gross margin return on investment (GMROI) as described in Chapter 2, Section 2.2, is often used to measure this return. The annual reports of many retailers also report "revenues per square foot," a metric frequently used by merchant teams to choose between competitive products. Merchandise cost used in the calculation of gross margin includes the freight portion of supply chain costs. Table 7.2 is guided by these concerns in identifying decision categories that determine whether success will be achieved or not. The best use of the table for readers is to select the decision categories important to their own businesses. From these selections, they can specify requirements for their supply chains.

7.4 Nature of Demand

Meeting market needs, at the most fundamental level, requires an understanding of "demand." This is dimension 7 in Table 7.1. Figure 1.1 in Chapter 1 presents a "simplified" picture for physical and information flows in a supply chain. The illustration is a fairly common way to identify supply chain "players." These links in the chain are called *echelons*. In the example, there is a major supplier often referred to as an original equipment manufacturer, or OEM. Most real supply chains are more like Figure 7.1, labeled the "supply chain reality" and showing only physical flows.

In the real supply chain, pathways are complex on both upstream (incoming) and downstream (outgoing) sides of the several OEMs competing in the market. Note that segments displace the single market view of customers shown in Figure 1.1. Each segment makes its own demands for product configuration, channels, technical support, delivery options, and other supply chain features. One message of Figure 7.1 is that many supply chain players may be far removed from end-user demand. Some can barely see past their own upstream and downstream trading partners.

Research reported in *Supply Chain Management Review* points to the problems of defining demand in real supply chains.[5] The authors, John Mentzer and Mark Moon of the University of Tennessee in Knoxville, researched over 400 companies.

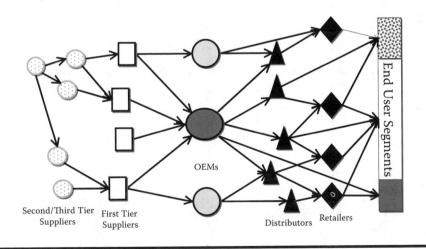

Figure 7.1 Supply chain reality.

Table 7.2 Specification Template Decision Categories

#	Market Need Dimensions	Supply Chain–Related Decision Categories		
		Manufacturer (concern: base product success)	Distributor (concern: service offering success, GMROI)	Retailer (concern: profit per square foot, GMROI)
1.	Product portfolio	Technology expertise to maintain New products/purging existing products Replacement parts strategy	Attractive markets/customers Base and extended products to offer Regions/customers to serve	Fit with marketing strategy Expected demand/shelf space allocation Profitability/pricing In-house brands to carry
2.	Product design	Product base features Models/options needed Extended product features	Organization capabilities/skills/facilities Customer expectations for service and cost Opportunities for premium pricing	Potential for customer dissatisfaction Need for technical support Return policies and support
3.	Capabilities and capacity	Make or buy Processes/technologies required Capacity planning Collaboration strategy/trading partner links	Systems required Hardware investments Transportation requirements Supplier/customer links Vendor-managed inventory	Direct or through distributor Information sharing Schedule coordination Internal or external distribution centers

4.	Competitive responses	Basis for competing Technology leadership SWOT[a] analysis Activity system design	Competition from suppliers, retailers, other distributors Activity systems design	Market strategy/activity system design Product line exclusivity Product turnover Degree of supply chain integration
5.	Product channels	How to reach attractive markets Need for product customization Information technology requirements	Customers/regions to serve Channel-specific services to provide Plan for incoming/outgoing merchandise	Store and nonstore alternatives Direct to store delivery Needs for upstream customization
6.	Customer risk concerns	Ability to return product Guarantees and warranties Part availability/obsolescence Retailer/dealer roles	Liability Handling of returns Requirements for lead time Requirements for delivery reliability	Availability planning/inventory policy Guarantees and warranties Recycling Factory working conditions
7.	Matching supply and demand	Demand patterns Lead-time expectations/supplier capabilities Downstream information sharing Seasonal inefficiencies	Lead-time expectations Systems requirements Trading partner information sharing Seasonal inefficiencies	Product availability Manufacturer/distributor reliability Upstream information sharing Seasonal inefficiencies

[a] Strengths, weaknesses, opportunities, threats. Applying the tool should identify issues related to the product introduction.

They conclude, "Supply chain managers have only a hazy idea of what really drives demand." This reality is the consequence of the multi-echelon property of supply chains where raw materials and products follow convoluted paths similar to the ones shown in Figure 7.1.

Mentzer and Moon remind us that there are different types of demand. *Independent demand* is "the amount of product demanded (by time and location) by end-use customers of the supply chain." APICS, the Educational Society for Resource Management, defines independent demand as "that which is unrelated to the demand for other items." Examples include finished goods, parts for testing, and service parts. In Figure 7.1, independent demand from end-users at the far right of the figure suck product from the supply chain. The major suppliers, or OEMs, supply the channels that flow through distributors, go direct to retailers, or make direct sales to customers.

Dependent demand is directly related to the product and includes the components listed in the product bill of material (BOM). The OEM and its suppliers provide the production capability to support dependent demand. Sometimes a part will have both dependent demand as part of the final product and independent demand as a spare part. To meet market needs, one theoretically need not forecast dependent demand if one has access to data on independent demand. A practical difficulty is the complexity involved in gathering information from all the points of consumption—both from trading partners and end-users. This is particularly true in a retail supply chain with many points of sale to customers.

To demonstrate the level of waste this "fogginess" causes, Mentzer and Moon describe a hypothetical four-echelon supply chain—retailer, wholesaler, manufacturer, and supplier. To support these sales for a month, the retailer projects a sales forecast of 1000 units. However, the outlet then hedges its forecast by adding a 10 percent safety factor for its immediate supplier, the wholesaler. The authors assume that other echelons also hedge their forecasts by adding a 10 percent safety stock cushion to what they expect to sell. In this case, the extra inventory that accumulates over the chain will exceed 100 percent of the needed supply. So, to support final sales of 1000, 1105 units of safety stock in excess of the 1000 actually needed will accumulate along the chain.

The authors recommend forsaking the traditional forecasting that assumes that each partner's demand is independent. In place of this, partners should utilize end-user sales for their production decisions by communicating this demand throughout the chain, an application of the demand-driven supply chain concept developed in detail in Chapter 17. One of the benefits of P&G's effort to standardize its transaction processes is that it removes clutter that obscures demand and supply in the chain.

A barrier to sharing is that the source of the information, the retailer, has the least amount of safety stock—only 10 percent. So it has that much less motivation to participate. The upstream inventory, including its cost, is invisible to it. Another barrier is the inability by those upstream echelons to access and manipulate the data even if it is available. Large computers may be part of the answer. An article reports the discussion of panelists at a conference on high-performance computing (HPC) sponsored by the Council on Competitiveness in September 2006. The Council pursues measures to increase the level of U.S. innovation. Panelists included representatives from both P&G and Wal-Mart.

Nancy Stewart, Wal-Mart's chief technology officer stated, "It's an advantage if suppliers can link into Wal-Mart systems and perform their own analyses using Wal-Mart's complex tables." According to Tom Lange, P&G's director of corporate modeling and simulation, barriers to supplier use exist regarding software licenses, technical capabilities, and middleware that enable supply chain members to extract data that is useful for decisions.[6]

The tidy model of computer links from all points of sale to the dozens of manufacturers involved in producing a product faces all kinds of hurdles. These range from formidable capital investments in computer gear to the necessity for sophisticated technical support infrastructure. This has been described as the "many-to-many" problem. Figure 7.1 supports these observations. By tracing the arrows, first- and second-tier suppliers find their components employed in the products of multiple OEMs. These in turn sell to different market segments with some going directly to end-users whereas others sell their products to distributors. Also, retailers must be depended upon to provide the information required. Some, like Wal-Mart, may do so willingly. Others are unable to by virtue of their own existing systems. Others may consider such information competitively sensitive, not to be shared because competitors could gain access to it.

A phenomenon related to excesses in inventory along a supply chain is the "bullwhip effect." This occurs when a supply chain experiences wide swings in production and inventory despite a relatively steady level of final demand. The reasons include the just described tendency to hedge, time lags, lack of information sharing as discussed by the panel, poor information quality, and the planning systems and decision rules along the chain.

A third type of demand, *derived demand,* results from final product sales that are not linked directly through the BOM. For example, a second-tier steel supplier company may monitor auto sales to make its own production forecasts. Increases or decreases in auto sales say a lot about future demand for steel.

Mentzer and Moon recommend a "demand management" function based on an understanding of these types of demand. Recommended responsibilities for the position include the following:

- Internal and external information sharing including marketing function initiatives such as promotions.
- Assessment of customer and product profitability. The function would eliminate both products and customers who are not profitable.
- Supply chain relationship management in which performance improvement benefits are shared.

■ A sales and operations planning (S&OP) process that includes sales forecasting, planning, and replanning. A multifunction group charged with providing forecasts, rationalizing products and customers, capacity management, and production scheduling should execute the process. There is more on this in Chapter 15, Section 15.3.

These recommendations open the topic of possible roles for the supply chain manager, which could be broader than that of the "demand manager" recommended above. The broader role would entail inbound and outbound sides of the organization—as well as internal operations.

7.5 Quality Function Deployment (QFD) Tool

Quality function deployment (QFD) is a technique to translate requirements—defined by customers or end-users—into specifications for a product or service. Opportunities to use QFD include product design by manufacturers as well as, for process and extended product service design, by manufacturers, distributors, and retailers. A Design Team can use Table 7.2 decision categories to set the boundaries for the QFD effort.

According to the *QFD Handbook,* the name—which often leaves English speakers scratching their heads—is a Japanese phrase with three characters.[7] The characters have the following meanings:

1. Qualities, features, attributes
2. Functions or mechanisms
3. Deployment, evolutions, diffusion, or development

The handbook summarizes, "QFD means deploying the attributes of a product or service desired by the customer throughout all the appropriate functional components of an organization." The QFD tool accomplishes this through a series of structured matrices that begin with the "voice of the customer" and translate that into product or service features. The supply chain is a service that delivers products and other services, so QFD can also be employed to specify supply chain processes to flesh out a strategy for serving customers.

7.5.1 QFD Overview

QFD "forces" designers to consider customer needs important to the product or service design. Customer requirements can be developed by survey or by assumptions made in the absence of formal research. This lowers the risk of leaving something out and is particularly appropriate for very new products or services. According to *The QFD Handbook,* properly executed QFD offers the following benefits:

Figure 7.2   QFD house of quality.

1. It transitions customers' jargon into technical specifics.
2. It links the customer with the design of the product, service, or process.
3. The QFD process enhances the productivity of a diverse Design Team by assuring no customer requirement is either overemphasized or omitted.

At the center of the QFD approach is the "house-of-quality" matrix shown in Figure 7.2. The analogy of the house arises from the shape—several square matrices topped by a triangular roof. The house encapsulates what is known about customer requirements, their importance, and the product or supply chain features needed to meet those requirements. Customer requirements (labeled #1 in Figure 7.2) from surveys, questionnaires, market research, or internal knowledge become the "what" of the house (#2). That is, the characteristics that the supply chain must consider to satisfy the customer. Examples are speed, variety, and product support. These requirements are weighted in terms of customer priorities.

An example used in QFD training sessions is a cup of coffee. Base product features include the shape and size of the cup, the temperature of the coffee, the insulating wrap around the cup, and the type of beans used to brew the coffee. The supply chain and extended features include options for service time, serving size, variations in ingredients, promptness of service, and ambiance of the location. Starbucks is an often-cited example of a company using supply chain and extended features to turn a functional product (cup of coffee) into an innovative one (multiple options, ambiance, lounge chairs, Internet connections, music, and so forth). An example related to the base product is Starbucks' extra effort in buying coffee beans. Their coffee suppliers must be geographically located within certain latitudes (between the Tropic of Capricorn and Tropic of Cancer) and altitudes (1300–1800 m) to meet their standards for taste.

The team should weight the requirements in the order of importance (also performed in #2). A common approach is to assign percentages to each factor, with all factors adding to 100. For example, the most important feature might have a weight of 30, the second, 20 and so on. An important contribution of this exercise is that it forces the Design Team to define who its customers are and their priorities. The team might also prepare multiple matrices—one for each customer segment. Conjoint measurement is a technique commonly used to estimate individual customer importance weights. These can then be aggregated by segment and an overall ideal point estimated for each segment.

In the case of coffee, market research might find the customer values both product and supply chain features. For example, *taste* might be the first-ranked quality, earning a 40 percent, and *comfortable ambiance*, the second-ranked with 20 percent.

The "why" (#5) is a competitive assessment on the right of the matrix in Figure 7.2. The evaluation displays the company position against competitors on each customer requirement. The information should show company product and supply chain positions in terms of the features most wanted by customers.

The "how" is a list of supply chain or product features listed along the top of the matrix (#3). If the purpose of QFD is to evaluate the current supply chain, then these hows could represent the existing (as-is) supply chain. In designing a new process or supply chain, the hows can be features in the "to-be" supply chain. A how in the coffee business could be product variety and aspects of the interior design of the stores. Another how might define flexibility requirements to assure service levels as described in Chapter 6, Section 6.5.2.

The relationship matrix (#4) links the customer requirements (the "what's," #2) with the design features (#3), (the hows). Coffeehouse lounge chairs (a how), for example, will contribute strongly to *comfortable ambiance* (a what). In the case of responsiveness in product delivery (also a what), a customer requirement for 5-min service would provide an important specification for the staffing process (the how). The supply chain design must provide enough servers to limit line length.

In the relationship matrix (#4), design features are evaluated in terms of their contribution to each customer requirement. So a supply chain design feature that contributes significantly gets a higher weight than one that contributes to a lesser degree. There are many scales used to quantify the relationships. One calls for a 9-3-1-0, ranging from strong to weak to no support at all, for a customer requirement. The correlation matrix (#6, the roof of the house of quality) indicates reinforcing or conflicting supply chain features. An example might be the conflict between costly inventories to provide short turnarounds required to be responsive and the need for cost reductions required to be efficient.

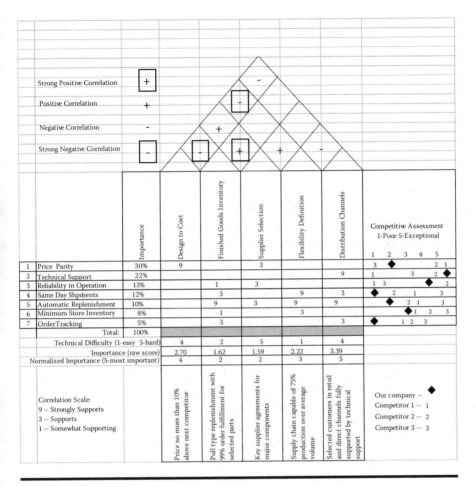

Figure 7.3 An example of quality function deployment (QFD).

The output of the house is the "how much" (#7). This quantifies what needs to be done and provides the team an incentive to rethink design features. For example, the coffeehouse may need to add varieties to its product lines and more lounge chairs. The preference here is for specificity. So the requirement for lounge chairs might be expressed in relation to customer traffic; thus, a rate of sales of forty customers per hour requires at least eight lounge chairs.

7.5.2 Supply Chain QFD Example

Figure 7.3 displays a filled-in house of quality completed by a Design Team of a fictitious manufacturer, Delta Technology. Delta's product, a multifunction printer for small offices, is sold through a variety of channels—retail office stores, equipment resellers, and direct through the Internet. Delta has decided to upgrade its existing supply chain. In preparation for the redesign, it has queried the retailers and resellers it serves and gathered their inputs about what customers seek in the product. For the purpose of this example, there are no important differences between the weights for features provided by retailers and resellers.

The first output of the survey is a list of seven customer requirements, or whats. In this case, these included both product—such as reliability in operation—and supply chain features. These are listed along the left side of the matrix in Figure 7.3. Based on interviews with users, the Design Team ranked the requirements in terms of importance to customers.

A second product of the survey enabled the team to assess where it stood with respect to its three largest competitors. This is displayed on the right. Delta, from the competitive assessment, ranks high in technical support (requirement 2) and reliability (#3). It is, however, seen as "expensive" (#1). Although customers believe Delta's product is worth more, it is considered "pricey" as indicated by a low rank for price parity on the competitive assessment. Delta also ranks low in all the categories that would be considered as key supply chain elements. These include keeping customers supplied in a timely way (#4 and #5). This causes customers to keep more merchandise stock on hand than they think is necessary (#6); they would like to see these stocks reduced. Order tracking (#7), a low priority with a 5 percent weight, would be a nice but not entirely necessary feature. It might be a "catch up" needed to stay in the game, but it wouldn't add materially to overall competitiveness.

The Delta Design Team next devised five supply chain features as part of a strategy (whats) for dealing with the challenges presented by the survey. These are shown in columns along the top of the matrix.

- Design to cost. A product redesign that was constrained by the need to be more cost competitive. Success means product costs are closer to, not necessarily less than, competitors.
- Finished goods inventory. A decision to employ inventory buffers in the form of Delta finished goods to enable faster responses to orders.
- Supplier selection. Reassessment of existing suppliers and selection of fewer, more capable partners willing to cooperate in meeting new response goals.
- Flexibility definition. An effort to formally make needed trade-offs in production capacity, product price, inventory, and order taking to meet customer expectations.
- Focused distribution. Use of profitability data and activity-based costing (ABC) to determine the most profitable customers and channels. There is a concern that being all things to all people diluted the company's efforts. (Chapter 19 describes activity-based costing further.)

The Design Team noted that some whats conflicted with each other while others were mutually supporting. For example, the decision to increase finished goods inventory would add to cost, so in the correlation matrix there is a "strong negative" relationship between finished goods inventory and design to cost. On the other hand, supplier selection and finished goods inventory have strong positive correlation. This would be the result if suppliers would carry parts in their own finished goods inventory to cover upswings in demand at Delta. The same possibility also creates a positive correlation between supplier selection and flexibility definition. A negative correlation exists between distribution channels and flexibility definition. This is because Delta would presumably tailor its supply chains to profitable customers and customer groups. This would result in different flexibility requirements for different customers and customer groups, a potentially difficult situation to manage.

The Design Team next assessed the correlation between the whats and the hows. They decided to use the 9-3-1-0 scale, with 0 credit, shown by a blank, given when correlations were absent. The calculation multiplied the correlation by the importance percentage on the left to yield a raw score for importance at the bottom of the matrix. So the design-to-cost feature supports the price parity (#1) customer requirement. A "9" appears in the matrix at the intersection of the requirement and the feature. At the bottom, the *importance* (raw score) sums the products of the combinations. This produces a rating of 2.7 (30 percent × 9) for the design-to-cost feature.

The team also assessed the degree of difficulty in implementing each element of the strategy on a scale of 1–5 with 5 being the most difficult. An importance rating on a scale of 1–5 with 5 the most important provided a normalized importance score. This importance level was awarded to the focused distribution feature. This insight should help the team to concentrate its attention on the most important elements of the strategy.

The final step produces the "how much" specification at the bottom of the matrix. This part of the matrix compiles conclusions about what has to be done to create an effective supply chain or product. It should be as specific as possible. For example, Delta's products were awarded a premium price in the marketplace, but there was a limit to how far this would carry them. So the team created a design-to-cost goal of no more than a 10 percent price premium compared to the next competitor. Prior to this decision, product development had no "price constraint" around which to design the product.

For finished goods inventory, the team set a "fill rate" specification of 99 percent for selected parts. These would be high-turnover, critical parts. Supplier selection would be guided by the willingness of suppliers to enter agreements to support the strategy. Working together to lower unessential inventory through collaboration on ordering and response times would be key.

A cornerstone of flexibility definition would be setting a band for production. Delta, as a premium-priced offeror, decided to build in enough flexibility to handle peaks in volume. By examining historical data, the Design Team defined the upside capacity capability as 75 percent over average volume. The team could use any or all the following to achieve this flexibility specification: extra shifts, overtime, added capacity, and inventories. The last specification was to develop custom extended product features tailored to large customers or large segments. These fulfillment centers would include order taking, order tracking, technical support, and customer billing.

7.6 Summary

Discovering paths to the customer is not simple. It involves all seven of the SCM dimensions listed in Table 7.1. Unfortunately, the responsibility for addressing these dimensions, if there is any at all, is vague in most companies. The chapter presents arguments for a strategy by companies of considering its SCM function as a logical participant, or even "owner," of these dimensions. Understanding the basic nature of demand in various channels and how to turn customer requirements into product features and supply chain processes will be an essential SCM role.

Endnotes

1. Albright, Mark, "Future Shop," tampabay.com, February 5, 2005.
2. Information in this section is from the P&G Annual Report for the fiscal year ending June 2006.
3. Gupta, Rajat and Wendler, Jim, "Leading change: An Interview With the CEO of P&G," *The McKinsey Quarterly*, Web exclusive July 2005.
4. Ibid.
5. Mentzer, John J. and Moon, Mark A., "Understanding Demand," *Supply Chain Management Review*, May/June 2004, pp. 38–43.
6. Conway, Steve, "HPC (High Performance Computing) and Supply Chain Management," *HPCwire*, September 15, 2006.
7. ReVelle, Jack B., Moran, John W., and Cox, Charles A., *The QFD Handbook*. New York: John Wiley & Sons, 1998.

Chapter 8

Supply Chain Risk

This chapter addresses operating risk along the supply chain. The risks addressed here are inherent in either supply chain design or execution, and include such events as dock strikes, hurricanes, and accidents. For example, products on the way to New Orleans' retailers at the time of Hurricane Katrina could not be delivered, and were either destroyed in the floods or diverted to other locations. Millions of dollars were lost as a result.

A second category of risk, project management risk, is encountered in managing efforts to develop or change the supply chain. Examples in this second risk category include missing requirements when setting up a distribution system, introducing a new product and forgetting about the supply chain, the perils of installing or upgrading an information system, or embarking on a relationship with an unknown trading partner. Such "project" risks are not covered here but are the subject of a related book in this series.[1]

Market needs for products and delivery vary over a wide range. For example, a "need" for the lowest-cost product will encourage high-cost producers to outsource to low-cost producers—often in faraway places. Currently, this is the situation in much of the U.S. apparel industry where local wage rates make it feasible for clothing manufacturers in the United States to compete only in the highest-margin products. A decision to go to distant sources, in turn, adds risks such as those related to lengthy transportation links, delivery uncertainties, theft of intellectual property, currency exchanges, and so forth. Assuming these risks requires a conscious or unconscious trade-off that evaluates the benefits of the move against the risk of losing market share because of costs.

So, supply chain risk often becomes one of the hard-to-quantify factors faced in the seven of supply chain management (SCM) market need dimensions listed in Table 7.1 (Chapter 7). These are product portfolio, product design, capabilities and capacity, competitive responses, product channels, customer risk concerns, and matching supply and demand. However, supply chain risk is present in all the dimensions.

The quality function deployment (QFD) tool, described in Chapter 7, Section 7.5, provides for identifying and weighing those trade-offs using the roof, or correlation matrix, in Figures 7.2 and 7.3. Often, avoiding a risk of one type, such as the loss of market share from a too high product cost, brings on others, for example, having a lengthy (in terms of both distance and time) supply chain from a far-off low-cost contract manufacturer.

Risk is a term with multiple meanings; one can take his or her choice of definitions from a number of sources such as those on the following list:

- Thorndike–Barnhart dictionary. A chance of harm or loss; the amount of possible loss
- Wikipedia. A concept that denotes a potential negative impact to an asset or some characteristic of value that may arise from some present process or future event
- APICS, the educational society for resource management. Uncertainty associated with the research, development, and production of a product, service, or project
- Project Management Institute PMBOK[2]: An uncertain event or condition that could have a positive or negative effect on a project's objectives

The definitions use *chance, potential, and uncertainty* to describe risk. *Uncertainty,* the authors believe, best captures the concept of risk in a single word. As the definitions indicate, uncertainty is not confined to negative outcomes; it also includes the possibility of things going better than expected—for example, a risk that sales will exceed forecasts.

APICS, the Association for Operations Management, has also defined the term *risk pooling.* Pooling in this context is important in supply chain planning. Risk pooling refers to the collection of stock in a central location to protect against stockouts. This inventory supports multiple points of sale, not just one, as customers make purchases. This results in lower inventory than required if the inventory were dispersed to points of sale, a practice common in the retail industry. For example, Target brings all of its imports from Pacific countries to a warehouse facility in Lacey, Washington, where it is held for distribution around the United States.

Forecasting becomes extremely important in such a system. A technique called *postponement* involves not committing merchandise in terms of its final configuration or its final destination until the latest possible time. This saves money and reduces the risks of stockouts. Chapter 17 describes this technique as a fundamental tool of creating the demand-driven supply chain.

Editor Francis Quinn of the *Supply Chain Management Review* (SCMR) has summarized research on supply chain risk performed at Dartmouth College.[3] His article reports an interview with Eric Johnson of Dartmouth's Center for Digital Strategies. The article calls attention to the variety of risks faced by managers in retail supply chains, particularly those from disruptions in information flow. Table 8.1 lists risks cited in the article plus others associated with managing supply chains. In keeping with the idea that meeting market needs has several dimensions, we associate risk with one or more market need dimensions of SCM described in Chapter 7, Table 7.1.

The list in Table 8.1 is a good start for establishing formal processes for considering risk. Readers can add risks they need to address as part of their own supply chains. Table 8.1 shows three risk categories:

1. *Location/trading partner selection risks.* Uncertainties that go with decisions about where and with whom to partner. It includes the risks that go with adding partners in other countries to a supply chain.
2. *External supply chain production/logistics risks.* Risks that lie outside the control of the supply chain. Examples are disruption due to weather-related emergencies, labor market instability, quality of infrastructure, foreign exchange fluctuations, adequacy of legal institutions, and material availability.
3. *Internal supply chain production/logistics risks.* Risks inherent in the company's and its trading partners' product portfolio, markets, processes, and infrastructure. These may be susceptible to fixing or mitigating if recognized.

The following sections explain each risk category further.

8.1 Location/Trading-Partner Selection Risks

The cited SCMR article argues that the best way of mitigating risk lies in trading-partner selection. No doubt that is true, but what risks and trade-offs should one assess in selecting trading partners? The category lists several. Intellectual property violations (#1), counterfeiting (#2), and information leaks (#8) are associated with partner honesty and attention to security issues. One may also find a potential trading partner in a region where contracting/legal institutions (#3) are weak. Insufficient oversight (#4) addresses management weaknesses that lead to poor business practices, such as missing promised delivery dates. A partner may also have financial difficulty (#5) that could affect the delivery of vital parts or result in lost sales in attractive markets.

Internal management issues also include lack of technical capabilities (#6) and unaligned incentives (#7). The former may be critical to a new product in the case of a scarce production capability, or in terms of having the capacity to produce sufficient volumes for the designated market. With regard to incentives, every company will have its distinct culture. That culture may, and very likely will, place different values on the same goals you put first. Mitigation of these risks lies in the process of selecting partners and on the specifics of the partnership

Table 8.1 Supply Chain Risks

Location/Trading-Partner Selection Risks	Product Portfolio	Product Design	Capabilities and Capacity	Competitive Responses	Product Channels	Customer Risk Concerns	Matching Supply and Demand
			Market Need Dimensions[a]				
1. Intellectual property violations[b]	•	•		•			
2. Product counterfeiting	•	•		•			
3. Contracting/legal issues			•				
4. Insufficient oversight			•				
5. Financial difficulty			•				
6. Technical capabilities weaknesses	•	•	•		•	•	•
7. Unknown unaligned incentives[b]			•		•	•	•
8. Proprietary information leaks[b]	•			•	•	•	•

External Supply Chain Production/Logistics Risks							
1.	Foreign exchange reverses					●		
2.	Labor disruptions					●		●
3.	Weather consequences					●		●
4.	Information infrastructure weakness[b]	●	●			●		●
5.	Material availability	●	●					●
6.	Liability—labor-related		●	●	●	●	●	
7.	Liability—environmental		●	●	●	●	●	

Internal Supply Chain Production/Logistics Risks							
1.	Market misses	●	●		●			●
2.	Insufficient production capabilities		●	●				●
3.	Quality performance weaknesses		●	●			●	●
4.	Synchronization failures					●		
5.	Forecast error consequences				●	●	●	
6.	Physical bottlenecks		●	●			●	
7.	Delivery variation (lead time)[b]			●	●	●	●	●
8.	Returns handling capabilities missing	●	●	●		●	●	

[a] See Chapter 7.
[b] Risks mentioned in *Supply Chain Management Review* article.[3]

agreement. Part 4, Supply Chain Process Improvements, recommends methods. Chapter 16, Collaboration with Supply Chain Partners, is particularly relevant.

8.2 External Supply Chain Production/Logistics Risks

This category encompasses factors outside the company and its trading partners. Factors are geographic, social, legal, and financial. The presence of any risk is usually embedded in the country or region. Labor and environmental liabilities may pose a customer relations risk. This occurs when news of a retailer's partners' poor labor practices and harmful chemical emissions are widely publicized. Situations such as this have triggered retailer audits of trading partners to ensure compliance with the norms of the retailer's customer base. Chapter 5 described the challenges retailers face in fulfilling societal expectations. One path for companies is to experiment by starting to produce or sell in a region, then expanding there if successful.

The risk of material availability (#5) is placed in this category. Often shortages exist globally, so the risk will be a general one and will equally, though adversely, impact all industry participants. However, sometimes materials will be less available in a particular region or country than they are in a traditional supply chain. This risk applies to differences in availability, not general shortages, and can result in either competitive advantage or disadvantage. For retailers producing large amounts of private label merchandise, such as GAP or Old Navy, such risks can be substantial.

8.3 Internal Supply Chain Production/Logistics Risks

This category is the most "controllable" in terms of the decisions made in building a supply chain. The risks on this list should also be a part of the supplier selection process. Parts 4 and 5 on supply chain process improvements and collaboration recommend mitigations for these types of risk.

Market misses (#1) relate to deviations from expectations for the success of new products or old product sold into new markets. The risk arises when too much or not enough is produced to meet market demand, and the supply chain can't make the necessary adjustments. This is different from forecast error consequences (#5), which refers to shorter-term errors in estimating end-user demand.

Insufficient production capabilities (#2) can be shortfalls in capacity or the ability to perform an operation. Inadequate capacity is a physical constraint; however, a shortfall in the ability to perform is a management inability to use capacity that's available. Causes can be quality related, a lack of appropriately trained workers, or insufficient material. Physical bottlenecks (#6) has a broader meaning because bottlenecks can include production, logistics, and supplier limitations. Quality performance weaknesses (#3) add cost to cover process waste, limit capacity, and pose a threat of selling defective products to customers.

Synchronization failures (#4) and delivery variation (#7) will affect the smooth running of the supply chain, especially if the chain is tightly linked. The authors believe that these factors are rarely considered in building supply chains. The vision for addressing this situation is the subject of Chapter 17 on demand-driven supply chains. The working of the demand-driven supply chain is abetted by having multiple partners "synchronized" in terms of the replenishment cycle. This creates a rhythm in the chain, whether the period used is daily, weekly, monthly, or quarterly. West Marine, described in some detail in Chapter 15, sought to synchronize its supply chain. Toyota parts operations, through fixed-interval milk runs, synchronize operations as described in Chapter 17.

Toyota also points to delivery time variability as a major obstacle to achieving efficiencies in the supply chain. The Toyota example cites variation in arrival times at its manufacturing plants and warehouses as detrimental to its goals for its "sell one—move one" approach to replenishment. Variation in lead times, not the length of the lead times, is the greater enemy.

The lack of returns handling capabilities (#8) should be considered where such resources might be needed. Likely cases include critical, complex components and situations where the return loop needs to be fast. For example, a laptop computer made in Taiwan shouldn't have to go back to Taiwan for a warranty repair.

8.4 Supply Chain Risk—Summary

Risk management issues pervade SCM functions. Supply chain designs that address risks require an understanding of the risks involved and the feasible alternatives to minimizing their effect. For retailers, risk can result in late and unseasonable deliveries such as not receiving holiday inventory (Christmas, Chanukah, Kwanza) until February, long after the holidays are over, making the merchandise basically unsalable. Subsequent chapters will describe ways to manage risk through avoidance in partner selection or insurance policies that take the form of extra capacity or inventory.

Endnotes

1. Ayers, James B., *Supply Chain Project Management: A Structured Collaborative and Measurable Approach*, Boca Raton: St. Lucie Press, 2004.
2. PMBOK: *Project Management Body of Knowledge*, 2000 Ed.
3. Quinn, Francis J., "Ready For the Digital Future?" An interview with M. Eric Johnson, *Supply Chain Management Review*, July–August 2006, pp. 26–32.

Chapter 9

Retail Supply Chain Metrics

This chapter explores retail supply chain performance definition and measurement. In particular, it points out likely differences in performance measures among companies along the chain. It also describes how supply chain managers in a company might connect their performance measures to their organization's retail format and its strategies for competing. This need is acknowledged in the Supply Chain Council's Supply Chain Operations Reference (SCOR) model. SCOR describes, as a best practice in SCM, an enabling process to align the supply chain plan with the financial plan. The approach in this chapter is one way to accomplish this objective.

Retail *format* is the term commonly used to describe what business a retailer is in and who its competition is. Levy and Weitz define the term retail format as follows:

> The retailers' type of retail mix (nature of merchandise and services offered, pricing policy, advertising and promotion program, approach to store design and visual merchandising, and typical location.)[1]

Stores with similar formats are seen as belonging to the same format category. Within a category, stores are usually seen as having similar inventory turnover strategies. Example formats include convenience stores, department stores, big box retailers by merchandise category, supermarkets, and discount stores. Stores with similar retail formats are often considered to be competitors, but in this era of "scrambled" merchandising, customers may actually choose stores with different formats when making a purchase. For example, someone needing to purchase a headache remedy could choose to go to a supermarket, chain drugstore, small pharmacy, convenience store, or a discount store.

Factors such as other concurrent product needs, distance to the store, severity of the pain, time spent in the store, and pricing may be more important store selection criteria. But for most retailers, retail format serves as the cornerstone of corporate strategy. As a result, format is a strong driver of appropriate metric selection not only at the retailer but also by upstream supply chain partners.

Figure 1.1 in Chapter 1 shows the "echelons" in the typical retail supply chain. One immediately sees that there are often large numbers of participants, as well as many types of participants. With regard to types, the figure, starting on the left, shows second-and first-tier suppliers, original equipment manufacturers (OEMs), distributors, and retailers. In addition, there are numerous providers of transportation, customs brokerage, information technology, freight forwarding, and delivery services. Li & Fung of Hong Kong, Federal Express, Expediters International of Washington, and UPS are prominent examples of service companies. Software vendors such as Microsoft offer specialized applications for retailers, distributors, and manufacturers. With so many different roles, strategies and measures of performance vary from echelon to echelon, retail format to retail format, and company to company. Thus, measurements of success for a retailer most likely differ from those of a supplier, OEM, distributor, or service company.

9.1 Metrics Problems

Metrics are important because they define performance expectations and supply chain performance in terms of strategy fulfillment, as long as supply chain operations metrics are aligned with the strategy. Debra Hofman, a benchmarking expert at AMR Research, Inc., has described challenges for measuring supply chain performance.[2] She lists the following problems observed in companies surveyed by her firm:

■ *Too many metrics.* This creates confusion, costs a lot to maintain and, in many cases, actually inhibits taking appropriate action.

■ *Metric debates.* Those being measured debate the value of a proposed metric, what organizations should be measured, and even how to calculate the metric.

■ *Changing metrics.* New metrics are introduced over existing metrics in the name of improvement, but they cause confusion.

■ *Old data.* Lags exist in gathering and acting on metrics, reducing the effectiveness of metrics in guiding interventions. Just because it's measured doesn't mean it's controlled.

■ *Gaming.* "You get what you measure," is an often repeated observation about metrics. This shortfall applies when those being measured manipulate the system to improve their measures.

The SCOR model reinforces the theme of metric proliferation. SCOR consists of high-level process descriptions that users employ to evaluate the completeness of processes in their own companies. These include planning, executing, and enable processes. SCOR's generic "executing" processes include SOURCE, MAKE, DELIVER, and RETURN. Another category, ENABLE processes, includes performance measurement and alignment of metrics with company financials. Together, all the SCOR process descriptions contain over one hundred metrics that practitioners might employ to measure the health of individual processes. SCOR does not advocate using them all, but their existence is emblematic of the multitude of choices. Many users err on the side of inclusion when selecting metrics for their own processes, a fault noted by Ms. Hofman.

Ms. Hofman also observes that companies have different levels of performance measurement maturity. Mature companies that are effective at measurement know what to measure, have in place processes to measure, and can access and act on the data in a timely way. Understanding what to measure, in the view of the authors, requires that supply chain metrics align with strategy, a goal discussed later in this chapter. Having processes to measure means actually reporting performance; and having access and acting on the data means managers are guided toward appropriate actions in time to make a difference.

Hofman also defines supply chain metrics at three levels:

- *Ground level for correction* for assessing processes and addressing problems as they occur. The hundred plus process metrics in SCOR are options for this level.
- *Diagnostic mid-tier level* exemplified by the cash-to-cash cycle that applies to most businesses. Components are accounts payable, inventory, and accounts receivable.
- *Assessment top tier level* for enterprise evaluation. Examples from Ms. Hofman's article are forecast accuracy, perfect order performance, and the cost of managing the supply chain.

The authors believe that the process of developing metrics should be "top down," beginning outside the supply chain realm with company strategy and then progressing to these three levels. The strategy should link with the highest level (assessment) in the hierarchy just described, and then deploy downward to the diagnostic and ground levels and should always reinforce the designated retail format. For example, Wal-Mart's main strategy targets the lower 25% of the population in income and touts low prices and a lean supply chain. Their metrics must reflect this, and participants in Wal-Mart's supply chain are expected to support the giant retailer's goals. Some Wal-Mart suppliers will function well in this environment whereas others will not. The conclusion to be drawn from this is that large participants, in this case the retailer, can exert a lot of power on the supply chain at each echelon. The following section describes a framework for matching top tier supply chain assessment level measures with company strategies for competing.

9.2 Alignment with Strategy

A framework, utilizing a concept called the "driving force," will help explain alignment of metrics and strategy. Michel (Mike) Robert, the founding partner of Decision Processes International (DPI), consults on strategic planning using his distinctive framework. Mr. Robert's observation is that strategic planning is often not done at all or, where it is done, is done poorly. As a solution, he proposes a "strategic thinking" process described in his book, *Strategy Pure & Simple II*.[3]

According to Robert, companies tend to fall into one of four categories based on having operations that support or don't support strategies. From worst to best the categories are:

1. Operationally incompetent. Uncertain strategic vision
2. Operationally incompetent. Explicit strategic vision
3. Operationally competent. Uncertain strategic vision
4. Operationally competent. Explicit strategic vision

Robert goes on to state that having a strategic vision does not include paper-producing exercises that do little more than produce strategic planning paperwork. The operations dimension refers to the execution of daily tasks, the operating processes that execute the strategy. The best-run companies, Type #4 in the preceding list, are good at both visualizing a strategy and executing it. Others are good at neither task (Type #1); in the absence of a coherent strategic vision, it's obvious that operations can't be shaped to fulfill that vision.

Operations in some companies can actually be quite efficient (Type #3). However, they may not be effective in strategic terms. Robert believes this is the case for most. The first reason for this situation is that many executives come through company ranks and lack the strategic perspective. A second reason may be that measures focus excessively on ground-level or mid-tier processes without links to strategy. A coherent strategy suitable for linking with ground-level processes is absent.

A third reason applies to U.S. markets. Robert notes that domestic markets may be too familiar and homogeneous. A manager in a smaller country, who must operate in multiple, varied markets, will probably have superior strategic skills. Going after new, unfamiliar markets forces deep strategic thinking. As a fourth reason, the company may blindly pursue growth and market share as ends. Necessary strategic choices don't get made. Chapter 13 describes the activity system approach to making such choices.

Robert observes that additions to global capacity have transformed economies from relative scarcity to surplus capacity. He terms these the old push (scarcity) and the new pull (excess capacity) economies. Interpreting Robert, the pull economy with its increased competition requires supply chain innovation. The customer is king, not the producer. Product life cycles are short. Market segmentation has progressed to market fragmentation. The need for efficient manufacturing has given way to the need for flexible manufacturing.

Robert's insight is that there is one single *driving force* that is the "strategic heartbeat" of the business. It is the determinant of company products, market segments, customers, and geographic focus. Robert identifies 10 possible strategic drivers, which are listed in Table 9.1. One of these 10, and only one, is central to the way a company operates, according to Robert. People in the company may or may not be aware of their own driving force. In fact, they may believe they actually pursue, and have to be good at, all 10!

According to Robert, underlying factors such as quality, customer service, and profitability are "givens." This is #11 in Table 9.1. All companies serving the market must perform well at the givens; most improvement activity in a company pursues improvements in the "given" category. These companies are likely operationally competent but lacking in strategic vision. SCOR metrics are measures for these essential processes. Achieving competitive levels as measured by SCOR metrics is necessary, but not sufficient for measuring success in retail supply chains.

Competitive advantage centers on managing activities associated with the driving force—what Robert refers to as "areas of excellence." Within this framework, potency in the marketplace is measured by the contribution to "areas of excellence" where the company excels over competitors beyond the "givens." For example, a project to automate product configuration processes between the customer and company's salesperson could be strategic in one company and not strategic in another. In a company with a technology-driven (Type #5) or a natural-resource-driven (Type #8) strategy, it would not be strategic even though it might lower costs or improve customer service in the "givens" group. But the project in a product concept (#1) or sales/marketing-driven (#6) company would likely be strategic.

Managers in a company with ongoing projects and with options for new ones can apply the driving-force framework to rank the potency of their projects in terms of supporting strategy. A simplified categorization is shown below.

Potency Rating	Contribution
High	Supports an area of excellence
Medium	Supports a "given" area of improvement
Low	Maintains a basic capability

We can estimate the potency of reengineered supply chain processes on organizations with different driving forces. Table 9.1 does this with example project objectives listed in the right-hand column. These serve as a test for candidate projects. If an existing project fulfills the listed objective, it is likely to support the company's

Table 9.1　Driving Forces for Strategy

#	Driving Force	Examples	Areas of Excellence	Supply Chain Improvement Objective
1.	Product/service concept	General Motors/cars, IBM/ computers, Boeing/aircraft	Product development Sales/service	Assure material support for improvements and service
2.	User/customer class	*Playboy* for men, Johnson & Johnson for doctors, families	User research Customer loyalty	Design supply chains for tailored product offerings to the targeted users
3.	Market type/category	American Hospital Supply for hospitals, Disney for families	Market research Customer loyalty	Design chains to deliver product categories to the target markets
4.	Production capacity and capability	Capacity: hotels, airlines, paper mills Capability: job shops, specialty printers	Operating efficiency Substitute marketing[a]	Find integration and cost reduction opportunities throughout the chain
5.	Technology know-how	Dupont in chemicals, 3M, Sony	Technology research Application marketing	Design supply chain concurrently with technology development. Bring new products to market fast
6.	Sales/marketing method	Avon for door-to-door selling, QVC Home Shopping Network	Sales recruitment Selling effectiveness	Assure the sales department has reliable material supply

7.	Distribution method	Telephone companies, department stores, food wholesalers, Fedex	System effectiveness System organization	Support sales force and product delivery. Reduce cost. Assure product constraints, like cold chain, are met
8.	Natural resources	Oil and mining companies	Exploration Conversion	Improve logistics between source and conversion points
9.	Size/growth	Companies driven by growth for growth's sake	Volume maximization Asset Management	Consolidate and improve resource utilization. Seek economies of scale
10.	Return/profit	Conglomerates, leveraged buyout companies, hedge fund-owned companies	Portfolio management Information systems	Increase asset/working capital utilization. Support new services
11.	"Givens"	Product quality Low-cost manufacturing Basic levels of customer service Growth and profit	Pursuit of operating efficiencies to maintain parity with competitors	Maintain state-of-the-art processes

[a] Refers to increasing the share of one's own product over substitutes. An example is printed corrugated containers over adhesive labels.

driving force. If a company has no supply chain project that supports its driving force, management should reconsider the strategy or look for new projects.

Most supply chain literature, including Ms. Hofman's article, describes production-driven companies (#4). This reinforces the view that supply chain design is really not strategic but is in the realm of the "givens." Certainly, ground-level metrics in models such as SCOR do this, calling to mind the manufacturer with its networks of suppliers, distribution, and retail customers. As Table 9.1 indicates, however, there are many ways in which supply chain improvements can help companies with other driving forces. The next section describes how the driving forces in a cross section of companies playing different supply chain roles might vary.

9.3 Definitions of Supply Chain Success

The most intensely sought-after performance goals for supply chain companies are likely to be visible in reports to shareholders and the press. Table 9.2 summarizes reported performance from companies, many of them market leaders, across the retail supply chain spectrum. This list of eight provides examples for those searching for better ways to measure supply chain operating performance. Also, several are used later in this book as case studies for various aspects of supply chain operations. Also included is a reference by number to the driving force in Table 9.1 that's reflected in the measure. Identifying the driving force is a good foundation for designing supply chain performance metrics suitable to the company's role in the supply chain.

The first two examples are from manufacturers. Procter & Gamble (P&G, Example #1) seeks growth in a variety of ways, one of which is "organic" or internal growth. This is growth in the current business and excludes that added by takeovers, divestitures, and foreign exchange gains. A reading of P&G's reports indicates that growth is an important, if not the foremost, measure of business health. This level of organic growth, along with help from acquisitions, is expected to increase earnings-per-share at a double digit (10 percent or more) rate. (See Chapter 7, Section 7.2.) Herman Miller (#2), on the other hand, redesigned its supply chain to speed product to customers while minimizing its capital requirements. It did this by fundamentally altering its financial measures to account for capital, particularly inventory and receivables. This redirection forced a new focus on shortening process cycle times for order taking through installation of its office furniture systems on customer sites. (See Chapter 10, Section 10.1.)

Examples #3 and #4 are both supply chain service providers—to shippers in the case of Expeditors (#3), and to retailers in the case of Li & Fung (#4). The two companies have succeeded in attracting customers who seek "one-stop shops" for services. Expeditors (#3) provides air and ocean shipping along with customs brokerage and other services. A determinant of profitability is filling the cargo space they purchase. Li & Fung offers an array of supply chain services for soft goods such as apparel, and selected hard goods. These include all the activities needed to deliver finished products to retail outlets. Li & Fung positions itself to its largest market, retailers in the U.S., as an alternative to having a captive sourcing department. *Forbes* magazine calls Li & Fung a "vital bridge between East and West."[4] Expediters and Li & Fung seek higher profit margins reflecting increasing value added to their customers.

McKesson (#5) follows a similar path. It operates in the supply chain for pharmaceuticals and health and beauty aids sold at retail. This supply chain is a many-to-many relationship with numerous manufacturers—2,000 medical surgical suppliers and 450 pharmaceutical manufacturers—on the supply side, and numerous points of sale—200,000 physicians and 25,000 pharmacies—on the demand side. McKesson offers physical distribution and many supporting "value-added offerings" for managing supply chain inventories for retail chains and individual stores. General pharmacy business consulting is one of their services: keeping their retail customers in business keeps McKesson in business!

Three retailers focus both on return on assets and on customer service. Foot Locker (#6) has a long-term goal against which it reports to shareholders. This is the revenue generated for each gross square foot of store space. This measure, very common in retailing, meets the simple and actionable criteria discussed in Section 9.1.

Wal-Mart (#7), in late 2006, had to cut back on its growth to increase its profitability. A strategy change that curtailed capital expenditures grew from investor fear that top-line sales growth would occur without corresponding profits. This could be interpreted as a shift in strategy from a #9 Size/growth focus to #4 Production capacity focus. West Marine (#8), on the other hand, stresses service for the 50,000 items it carries in a retail chain of over 400 stores. Product lines include equipment for sail and powerboats, apparel, and staples like paint and rope. Its business also includes wholesale service to other retailers that accounts for 7% of sales. It has many ways of reaching customers—through large superstores (25,000 sq. ft.), traditional stores (6,000–8,000 sq ft) focused retail outlets called Express stores (2,500–3,000 sq. ft.), the Internet, and, when all else fails, fulfillment via overnight shipments from regional warehouses. Chapters 15 and 16 use West Marine as a case study for multicompany collaboration.

9.4 Mid-Tier and Ground-Level Metrics

With awareness of the driving force, a company can select metrics that match their strategies. This selection has two dimensions.

1. Selecting metrics that are needed in the business matched to the driving force
2. Deciding what level in Ms. Hofman's hierarchy they belong to: top level assessment, mid-tier diagnostic, or ground-level process problem correction

Table 9.2 Assessment Metrics Used by Supply Chain Companies

#	Company	Supply Chain Echelon Driving Force	Source	Metric	Reported Performance
1.	The Procter & Gamble Company (P&G)	OEM Manufacturer #9. Size/growth	Investor Relations Frequently Asked Questions, October 2006	Organic Revenue Growth (percentage) (excludes acquisitions, divestitures, and foreign exchange)	Range of 3 to 5 percent growth
2.	Herman Miller	OEM Manufacturer #10. Return/profits	Case Study at HYPERLINK "http://www.sternstewart.com/action/miller.php"	EVA® (Economic Value Added). Debt to Capital Ratio	Ratio managed between 30 and 35 percent
3.	Expeditors International of Washington, Inc.	Logistics Service Provider #4. Production capability	2005 Annual Report, Management's Discussion and Analysis	Same store growth in revenue and profit with profits depending on revenues from air and ship capacity	16 percent revenue 25 percent operating income
4.	Li & Fung Limited	Consumer Products Export Trading Company #3. Market type/category	2005 Annual Report, Management Discussion	Total margin as a percent of sales reflecting "higher-value-added-supply chain model," particularly in fashion markets with differentiated designs	9.64 to 10.65 percent

	Company				
5.	McKesson Corporation	Healthcare and Related Products Distributor #2. *User/customer class*	2006 10-K Report	"To maximize distribution efficiency and effectiveness" for several customer segments	Six Sigma tools
6.	Foot Locker, Inc.	Athletic Footwear & Apparel Retailer #4. *Production Capability/Capacity*	2005 Annual Report	Sales per average gross square foot	$350
7.	Wal-Mart Stores, Inc.	Global Retailer #4. *Production capacity & capability*	"Wal-Mart Announces Fiscal 2008 Growth Plans—Company Balances Returns with Growth" October 23, 2006 press release	"This store selection process will .... drive higher returns by focusing on locations that make the most efficient use of capital"	Zero percent growth in capital expenditures for fiscal 2007
8.	West Marine, Inc.	Boating Supplier Retailer & Wholesaler #7. *Distribution method*	2005 Annual Report	Reliable in-stock availability of merchandise	Overnight shipment to back up other channels

Note: EVA is the registered trademark of Stern Stewart & Company.

Column A in Table 9.3 displays common business level and supply chain metrics or metric families. Supply chain practitioners will recognize many of these metrics that are divided into service, operation, and financial categories. Also included are metrics associated with the overall business—such as *Market share* and *Total cost of ownership*. The rationale for their inclusion is that supply chains must support their retailers' objectives reflected in these metrics as well as their own. Shown in Column B are the echelons—Supplier (S), OEM (O), Distributor (D), Retailer (R), and Service Provider (SP)—most likely to deploy the metric as an assessment level gauge of business success, the top level of the metric hierarchy.

Selecting the "vital few" metrics for the assessment level will trim the number of metrics tracked, addressing the problem of proliferating measures. Column C associates driving forces with appropriate assessment level metrics. This doesn't mean that other metrics shouldn't be put to work at the diagnostic level (column D) or process level (column E). If metrics are broader and have multiple determinants, they should be diagnostic-level metrics. When a diagnostic metric falls below goals, the root cause may not be associated with a single process failing. On the other hand, some metrics can and should be associated with individual processes at the process level (column E).

9.4.1 Service Metrics

Most advisors encourage their clients to start their reengineering projects by understanding customer requirements. So the service category is first in Table 9.3 with 11 metrics. *Market share* (#1) is the broadest metric. Its inclusion is justified by the fact that high market shares go to companies that provide the best value to the market, broadly defined as products, service, and price. All the echelons, regardless of the driving force, might deploy this as an assessment level metric for the supply chain. Of course, other factors beyond the scope of supply chain operations will affect market share—particularly if the company has a lead position in offering innovative products as described in Chapter 11. As a general statement, however, either a slippage in market share or a goal of increased market share calls for an examination of how supply chain design should support that goal.

The *Perfect order* (#2) has its origins in the logistics field. "Perfect" means all items ordered are delivered on time and order-related paperwork is also perfectly executed. This metric is usually associated with OEMs and Distributors, although the metric can travel to other echelons. An enterprise focused on distribution channels should pay close attention to execution. Enterprises focusing on customer classes or market categories would also strive for perfect orders as a high-level goal.

Order fill rate (#3) and *On-time delivery* (#4) are components of the perfect order. But their importance will be elevated in the case of some companies with certain driving forces. Having predictable lead-times is mandatory for many suppliers to retail stores and distribution centers. Reliable delivery within defined windows reduces customer disruptions at the store or warehouse. Others should use these metrics at the diagnostic level because there are usually multiple causes of shortfalls. *Delivery lead-time* (#5) measures responsiveness in addressing customer requirements. The shortest lead-time often wins the competitive battle for many products.

Return rate (#6), *Backorders* (#7), and *Backorder frequency* (#8) indicate mismatches in demand and supply. They also might reflect problems in collaboration along the chain for sharing information about end-user demand. *Return rate* exceptions might be due to defects, overordering, salesperson error, or the lack of penalties for returning merchandise. The number or percentage of *Backorders* in certain products should lead to reviews of forecasting and production plans. *Backorder frequency* in total or by merchandise category indicates systemic problems, supplier bottlenecks, or forecasting shortfalls.

Volume flexibility (#9), *Mix flexibility* (#10), and *Product-line breadth* (#11) are key in determining supply chain performance. Chapter 6, Section 6.5, described the "flexibility imperative," and these metrics measure how well flexibility needs are met. In constructing such metrics, managers should consider the tool described in Section 6.5. Certainly, shortfalls in other service category metrics may be due to insufficient supply chain flexibility.

9.4.2 Operating Metrics

There are many metrics in this family, particularly in tools such as SCOR. The list in Table 9.3 contains metric families related to quality and productivity. Service and flexibility are addressed in the previous section. *Product quality* (#12) is interpreted narrowly in terms of form and function and broadly in terms of features that "please" or "delight" end-users. It is certainly vital to the manufacturing companies that design and produce the products, as well as to service providers along the chain. *First-pass quality* (#13) and *Process capability* (#14) are both indicators of the reliability of processes—whether they are deployed in producing the base physical product or providing extended product services. Chapters 19 and 20 describe these metrics in greater detail. *First-pass capability* finds application in manufacturing. It measures the percentage of products completed without any rework. *Process capability* is closely related, and the target of Six Sigma efforts. A process rated high in capability produces few defects.

Floor-space productivity (#16) is usually expressed in monetary terms, such as sales dollars per unit of area (square feet or square meter) or gross margin per unit of area. Foot Locker, in Table 9.2, reports this measure in its annual report. The metric captures the productivity of investments in real estate—the stores where products are carried. It does not address productivity through other channels such as Internet sales. However, different metrics can be used to measure Internet sales productivity, probably based upon return on assets required. Other driving force examples in this chapter describe how supply chain participants, namely Expeditors International and Li & Fung in Table 9.2, seek higher-value product mixes. In these cases, a similar measure to retail floor space productivity could be adapted to substitute contribution or gross margin on sales that involve higher value product mixes.

9.4.3 Financial Metrics

As most readers know, financial measures rule decision making along the supply chain. They are particularly important in enterprises pursuing sales growth and profit. There are many variations in this family of metrics, but for retailers these are often reported as total revenue figures for the company or for "same store" operations. The latter removes the impact of new store sales on the metrics and measures "organic" growth. The Financial Metrics section of Table 9.3 lists several. *Total cost of ownership (TCO)* (#17) is a popular metric for durable products that require supply chain support after the sale. This support includes technical advice, maintenance and repair, upgrades, and disposal. Many products are even sold on the expectation that the service provided after the sale will compensate for a low initial price. Supply chain managers should be involved in goal setting and measurement of the TCO. Electronics retailers such as Best Buy have developed a product replacement/repair program that operates much like "product insurance" in order to participate in this piece of the pie.

Revenue growth (#18), *$ New product revenue* (#19), *Profit growth* (#20), and *Total operating cost* (#21) are basic measures of profitability. Chapter 19 advocates a methodology for measuring growth and profits by product or product category using activity-based costing. Many metrics address the investment required to support sales. These include the remaining metrics #22 to #26. The following paragraphs describe each briefly. Chapters 2 and 3 introduced several as they apply to retailers.

The *Cash-to-cash Cycle* (#22) metric is the time, usually in days, between cash outflows to create a product to the time when customers' money is collected. It is calculated as work-in-process (WIP) inventory plus accounts receivable less accounts payable. Many supply chain efforts seek to reduce this period. Dell is known for being able to collect from the customer before acquiring the parts necessary to build the computer, resulting in an impressive cash-to-cash cycle. *Inventory turns* (#23) also captures the speed of processing through the supply chain. It is measured as cost-of-goods-sold (COGS) divided by average inventory. Some use sales prices instead of COGS to make the calculation.

Return on investment (ROI) (#24) measures gross margin or profit as a percent of the investment required. This investment can be total assets or equity investment. *Gross-margin ROI* (#25) is a tool for retailers that is calculated as gross margin divided by average inventory. This metric measure is under the control of the merchandise buyer at the retailer and was described in detail in Chapter 2. *Residual*

Table 9.3 Metrics Use by Driving Force

| | | | Driving Forces (Table 9.1) | | |
	A Metric/Metric Family	B Echelons Used for Assessment[a]	C Assessment Level	D Diagnostic Level	E Process Level
Service Metrics					
1.	Market share (%)	S, O, D, R, SP	All		
2.	Perfect order (%)	O, D	#7	#2, #3	All others
3.	Order fill rate (%)	O, D	#2	All others	
4.	On-time delivery	S, O, D, SP	#2, #3, #6	All others	
5.	Delivery lead-time	S, O, D, R, SP	#2, #3, #5	All others	
6.	Return rate (%)	O, R	#2, #3	All others	
7.	Backorders (#)	O, D, R		All	
8.	Backorder frequency	O, D	#1, #2, #3	All others	
9.	Volume flexibility	S, O, D	#4	All others	
10.	Mix flexibility	S, O, D, R, SP	#1, #3	All others	
11.	Product-line breadth	O, D, R	#1, #2, #3	All others	
Operating Metrics					
12.	Product quality	S, O, SP	#1	All others	
13.	First-pass quality	S, O	#1, #4		All others
14.	Process capability	S, O	#4		All others
15.	Labor productivity	S, O, D, R	#4		All others
16.	Retail floor space productivity	R	#6, #7, #10	All others	

Table 9.3 (continued)   Metrics Use by Driving Force

A Metric/Metric Family	B Echelons Used for Assessment[a]	Driving Forces (Table 9.1)			
		C Assessment Level	D Diagnostic Level	E Process Level	
Financial Metrics					
17. Total cost of ownership (TCO)	O, R	#1, #2	All others		
18. Revenue growth (%)	O, R, SP	#3, #5, #6, #9	All others		
19. $ New product revenue (%)	O, R	#1, #5	All others		
20. Profit growth (%)	O, R, SP	#2, #6, #10	All others		
21. Total operating cost	S, O, D, R, SP	#4, #8		All others	
22. Cash-to-cash cycle	O	#3, #6, #7	All others		
23. Inventory turns	O, D, R	#6, #7		All others	
24. Return on investment (ROI)	O, D, R	#10	All others		
25. Gross-margin ROI (GMROI)	D, R	#2, #3	All others		
26. Residual income, EVA®	S, O, D, R, SP	#4, #7, #8	All others		

Note: EVA® is the registered trademark of Stern Stewart.

[a] Echelons: S—Second-Tier Plus Supplier, O—OEM Manufacturer, D—Distributor, R—Retailer, SP—Service Provider.

income, EVA* (#26) captures asset cost by converting the value of an investment into an equivalent cash flow expense. *EVA* stands for Economic Value Added and is discussed further in Chapter 10 in the Herman Miller case. The application uses the enterprise cost of capital expressed as an interest rate and the lifetime of the assets involved. The effect is to convert working capital and fixed asset capital costs into equivalent period expenses. Chapter 19, Section 19.2.2, shows the impact of different assumptions when converting capital costs to equivalent uniform annual costs.

9.5 Supply Chain Metrics—Summary

Successful supply chain companies involved with retailers must monitor factors important to their success. Recognizing the driving force is a major step in identifying the needed measures to monitor the business, including the expectation for supply chain performance. It's also an important step in reducing the number of metrics. There are as many variations as there are businesses. Few, however, use the concept of the driving force to establish the foundation for measures. Doing so will clarify missions and simplify the management process. Clear definition of appropriate supplier metrics that reinforce the needs of the retail format will drive the success of all supply chain members. .

Endnotes

1. Levy, Michael and Weitz, Barton A., *Retailing Management*, 6th ed., New York: McGraw-Hill Irwin, 2007, p. 612.
2. Hofman, Debra, "Getting to World-Class Supply Chain Measurement," *Supply Chain Management Review*, October 2006, pp. 18–24.
3. Robert, Michel, *Strategy Pure & Simple II*, New York: McGraw-Hill, 1998, pp. 58–72.
4. Meredith, Robyn, "Global Trading at the Crossroads," *Forbes*, April 17, 2006, pp. 45–47.

---

* EVA is a registered trademark of Stern Stewart & Company.

Chapter 10

Meeting the Needs of Supply Chain Decision Makers

This chapter closes Section II on Retail Supply Chains with a description of the needs for supply chain decision makers. The decisions discussed here determine the short- and long-term direction of the decision makers' enterprises. Examples range from placing orders and scheduling manufacturing operations in the short run to designing transportation networks, setting store inventories and pricing merchandise—all longer-term decisions. These and many other decisions are embedded in processes that require structure in the form of organization, information systems, and policies. Chapter 9 described supply chain metrics, which also guide decision making. But there is a need for translating broad objectives into mechanisms for making decisions.

10.1 New Decisions at Herman Miller

A case illustrates how a new financial goal brought on supply chain changes that resulted in new processes and decision-making roles. The company was called Miller SQA headquartered in Holland, Michigan, and at the time of the transition described here was a division of Herman Miller, Inc. Herman Miller is a major manufacturer of office furniture that includes desks, filing cabinets, chairs, and panel systems found in offices, healthcare facilities, and homes throughout the world. Herman Miller, with fiscal 2005 sales of over $1.5 billion, produces made-to-order systems for an office or healthcare facility installation and made-to-stock products for retail stores. Since the case implementation in the late 1990s, Herman Miller has dissolved the SQA division and adapted the streamlined approach described here broadly for all its make-to-order business.

Miller SQA, with sales about $300 million, filled the "value" end of the Miller product line. SQA incorporated its goal to be "simple, quick, and affordable" into the name of its business. This seemingly "best of all worlds" objective required an extensive overhaul of the SQA supply chain. The Miller effort was motivated by its twofold needs for internal financial improvement—particularly, earning more on its investment in inventory and facilities, and capturing increased market share in a competitive industry.

At the beginning of the supply chain overhaul, the industry commonly delivered orders in four to six weeks. In addition, the delay for installation at the customer's site, often by the local dealer who sold the system, could be one or two weeks. All this time was required for a product that could theoretically be manufactured and installed in hours, not days or weeks. The long waits cut revenues because some customers canceled their orders during the waiting period and added to Herman Miller's receivables. The old Miller shipped from finished goods inventory, or, when it had to build to order, from a large raw material inventory kept on hand. This make-to-stock approach, one that relies on finished goods inventory to fill orders, is common among manufacturers in retail supply chains.

The SQA receivable and inventory "investments" lowered the company's business performance. Of particular note, Miller was adopting a financial measurement tool called EVA* (Economic Value Added, which was briefly discussed in Chapter 9). EVA takes into account the cost of assets such as inventory and receivables. So, the cost of capital required to support inventory, warehouses, and factory capacity would be charged against SQA's profits. As a result of its supply chain reengineering, Herman Miller raised its return on investment considerably—tripling its EVA to $40 million, resulting in an increase in stock value from $11 to $36.

The project drastically cut the time Miller took to fill an order, making corresponding cuts in the inventory and receivables committed to support sales. The result was inventory reductions of 24%.[1] This also satisfies customers by responding quickly when the customer places an order. Fast response means that customer money is collected sooner, leading to a 22% receivables reduction. With the new method, the company can make to order rather than make to stock, eliminating finished goods inventory and reducing the large raw material inventory.

In the new process, SQA also ordered materials from suppliers to build exactly what the customer wanted because they had the order in hand. This meant that their whole supply chain became "demand driven" rather "forecast driven." In a forecast-driven supply chain, managers must have a crystal ball to "guess" future demand. This was an especially good opportunity in a company such as Miller that

---

* EVA is a registered trademark of Stern Stewart & Company.

offered customers many product options. No two orders for office furnishings were alike in terms of size, color, and mix of products.

This was not a quick changeover; the project took about two years to complete. To do this, Miller SQA required shifts in supply chain decision making and the systems to support them. The project manager, William Bundy, in discussing the impact of the supply chain project on Miller, compares his company with Dell Computer, the seller of personal computers and other computer hardware. [2] "Dell succeeds not because it has the latest product technology but because it has built a 'service model' that builds to customer order and delivers with great speed and reliability."

Miller SQA looked at the lead time it wanted to reduce and identified three major components, each with its own challenges:

1. Customer contact to order entry
2. Order entry to shipment (manufacture)
3. Shipment to installation

At Miller, manufacturing (Component #2) consumed only 20% of the lead time. So, to make dramatic improvement, the company had to reduce all three lead-time components, including sales and material supply as well.

An important part of the initial plan was to partner with a third-party logistics provider, Menlo Logistics. Menlo staffed a separate material-staging facility—called the Production Metering Center—where logistics into Miller's production facility could be handled. The logistics specialist, Menlo, brought expertise in transportation and warehousing to the supply chain. By cutting raw materials to the bone, bringing them into the Metering Center only in response to actual customer demand, Miller could produce an order in eight to ten hours and plan to do it only two hours before production started. Because orders consisted of a variety of color-matched products that used different production lines, this was not a simple coordination task.

To become what it wanted to be, Miller had to make choices about its financial and customer service-related goals. It had to stop being a follower and become a leader by being different from its competitors. The result was a hard-to-copy set of distinctive supply chain activities like those developed using a strategic planning tool called activity systems, described in Chapter 13. Components of the activity system included the following:

- *Conduct business with the customer through an "easy" customer interface.* Help the customer visualize the new office layout. Have the software configure the bill of material (BOM) for the order in real time.
- *Build to order.* Carry minimal amounts of raw material by paying only for what is used and having no raw material or finished goods inventory at all.
- *Deliver direct to the user's site.* Provide visibility on progress of the shipment to the dealer who would install the furniture. Have everything in the customer's order arrive in one shipment, helping the local dealer install the office quickly.

A key to Miller's achievement was its relationship with its suppliers. Just about every aspect of this relationship was redesigned. This required a dramatic reduction in the number of suppliers. A similar reduction was made in the number of parts, or SKUs (stockkeeping units), carried. Daily deliveries were also instituted. This was made possible by the closeness of suppliers to the SQA factories in the furniture-making center in southwest Michigan. The delivered stock of raw materials was on consignment, meaning it was paid for only after it was used for production.

Technology proved to be a vital enabler of new processes. Among the computer tools used were the following:

- An application called SupplyNet to track inventory at SQA and the suppliers, and to plan replenishment and production schedules.
- An order entry tool called SQA 1:1, plus a visualization tool for the new layouts called Z-Axis.
- An enterprise resource planning, (ERP) system to capture and maintain correct bills of material. Achieving bill of material accuracy was a major challenge.
- A manufacturing execution system, (MES) for maintaining material requirements and planning production.
- An internally developed tool called Expert Scheduling that checks for material availability and manufacturing capacity and automatically schedules about 50 percent of production. If automated scheduling were not possible, a human scheduler would intervene.

The following are typical measures of supply chain performance and indicate how much Miller SQA performance improved.

- Throughput, or capacity, up 25 percent with no additional investment
- On-time shipments: 99+ percent compared to an industry average of 75 percent
- Order lead time 2 days, when the industry standard was 5 weeks
- Inventory turns increased from 21 to over 100
- Staff productivity up 20 percent

The Herman Miller case is an important example of the opportunities to compete better at the retail level through improved supply chain management. It illustrates the impact of better processes enabled by technology. However, the work of conversion to the new supply chain was not just technology focused. It required accurate BOM, considerable collaboration with suppliers, process mapping across organizations, employer behavior change activities, and implementation of formal policies and procedures.

As a result, decision-making processes became more tightly orchestrated. Table 10.1 summarizes the "before" and "after" differences in the SQA supply chain design. The reader should note that the new processes fundamentally changed the nature of the decisions being made, automating many of them and tightening the timeframe in which the decisions were made.

Table 10.1   Herman Miller Changes in Decision Making

Decision Category	Before	After
Supplier selection	Many suppliers chosen on traditional criteria such as price	Fewer suppliers willing to collaborate in supporting new processes
Order configuration	Worked out by dealer Forwarded to plant	Translated into bill of materials as order developed. Electronically transmitted
Raw material replenishment	Forecast driven. Economic lot sizes ordered from suppliers	Demand-driven. Material pulled to staging areas as orders came in
Production scheduling	Manual. Based on availability of a wide range of materials. Sequential production. Order components gathered as completed	Much of it automated. Narrower number of SKUs. Staged material moved quickly to production. Simultaneous production of order components
Installation scheduling	Orders shipped to dealer sites. Installation separately scheduled by dealer	Orders shipped to installation site. Scheduled arrival determines installation timing

10.2 Proactive Decision Making

Information technology solution providers have answered the need for speed exemplified by Herman Miller. Supply chain and information technology worlds now evolve toward managing exceptions rather than pushing data at decision makers. Terms include *workflow, business rules* and *supply chain event management* (SCEM). *Workflow*, according to Wikipedia, is "the movement of documents and/or tasks through a work process." Workflow is enabled, but not dependent on, information technology. It must also be a by-product of task definition and assignment of responsibilities. These elements also define *business rules*, which define exceptional situations and predefined actions to respond. *SCEM*, according to the About Logistics Web site, is "an extension of process control" that defines a response to an unexpected event.[3] So, if the Herman Miller scheduling program, Expert Scheduling, couldn't schedule a particular order, a "proactive" system might automatically transfer it to the human scheduler.

What proactive systems add to conventional systems is a focus on decision-maker needs in those processes. Decision makers fulfill roles in the process based

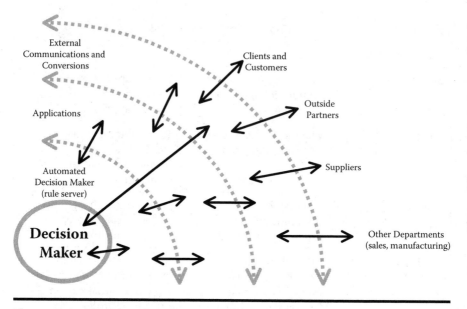

Figure 10.1 The proactive system model.

on the ultimate customer's needs expressed to the manufacturer through the retailers. Thus, where decisions are required, such as when the Herman Miller scheduler could not schedule a job, the proactive system uses the business rules to redirect the scheduling task for the proper human intervention.

In Figure 10.1, the decision maker is at the center. Extending the Herman Miller example, this decision maker is the production scheduler. Inputs from the external environment of suppliers, customers, and other departments either pass through existing applications such as the order entry system or go directly—by e-mail for example—to our decision maker. Inputs to the scheduler could come from any or all of the following:

- From the retailer or dealer at the customer's location with order changes
- From customers via retailers regarding convenient times to install their orders
- From transportation companies with shipping schedules to the point of installation
- From the Metering Center confirming the completeness of the BOM
- From suppliers notifying the scheduler of a delayed shipment
- From accounting reporting that the customer's check has bounced

The arrows symbolize the many potential data transactions within such a proactive system. What makes the environment "proactive" is the *rules server* that processes the inputs to our decision maker. The rules guide the information flow and the conditions that make the communication necessary. The delivery matches the needs of the individual decision maker and reflects the authority vested in that individual. Rules are a product of management practice on empowerment, continuous improvement, and organization philosophy. Values, philosophy of delegation, and decision analysis—not technology—dictate rules. These rules will be unique to any particular organization and, quite possibly, a source of competitive advantage from cheaper and faster processes. In many cases the critical examination of required decisions finds all sorts of alternative solutions that produce faster and better decisions. Individual practice, a result of training and habit, gives way to a "best practice" by design. It is important to remember that solutions are bounded by the needs of the customer and of the retail format that the manufacturer serves.

10.3 Applications for Information Technology

Information systems applications are on the market to support supply chain decision makers. Because most have met the test of serving a market need, the list of applications provides an overview of the solutions available for supply chain decision making. The Council of Supply Chain Management Professionals (CSCMP), formerly the Council of Logistics Management (CLM), maintains a software directory with capability listings from hundreds of software vendors. These include "best of breed" specialist tools as well as multifunction integrated applications. The list helps confused users find solutions to implement or upgrade their systems.

To demonstrate the types of decisions supported by technology, the nine General Functional Areas and 77 Specific Functionality categories in the directory are instructive. They are one way to frame the broad range of decision-making categories that are associated with SCM. Despite its size, the directory is incomplete with regard to applications that pertain to retail supply chains. To cover the entire range, one would have to add product development applications on the front end and retail store applications on the customer end.

Table 10.2 lists the General Functional Areas along with the number of functionalities for each. These are in alphabetical order—not in a supply chain-oriented sequence from raw material suppliers to customers. Table 10.3 describes each functional area briefly. This table has value as a checklist of 77 prescreened systems capabilities. These functionalities can assist any enterprise along the supply chain to assess whether it has capability gaps or unneeded software and associated processes. A company identifying a need while doing such an assessment does not necessarily have to fill that need with software from one of the vendors. It can resort to manual processes or less sophisticated tools if they meet the need. A company that is planning future software purchases can also use the list to develop and set priorities for requirements.

Note that the functionalities fall into two general categories—transaction support and planning. Transaction support applications handle day-to-day continuous operations such as placing orders and transporting merchandise. Planning functions vary by timeframe—intermediate (hours, days, or weeks) and long term

Table 10.2   CSCMP General Functional Areas

#	General Functional Areas	Number of Specific Functionalities
1.	Customer relationship management	10
2.	Forecasting	8
3.	Inventory planning/management	10
4.	Manufacturing	7
5.	Order processing	5
6.	Other advanced planning	7
7.	Procurement	8
8.	Transportation management	10
9.	Warehouse management	12
	Total:	77

(weeks, months, years). A "C" for continuous, an "I" for intermediate term, and an "L" for longer term show the likely timeframe for the functionality as it would be implemented in a company.

Figure 10.2, borrowed from William T. Walker, depicts the supply chain as zones.[4] This is a useful method because it recognizes that there are natural "breaks" as the product flows through the supply chain. This presentation is not unlike the U.S. Census classifications described in Chapter 3, Figure 3.1. Each resulting zone has individual issues that are not always shared with other zones. So, when we talk about procurement, manufacturing, distribution, and retailing, we are, in a sense, recognizing that these zones exist. The *upstream value-added transformation* zone produces raw materials and components. The *mid-stream value-added transformation* zone produces a finished product inventory ready for customization (final configuration, packaging, etc.) to retailer or customer requirements. Many in this zone are manufacturers producing products to a BOM with components from upstream trading partners. The *downstream value-added fulfillment zone* delivers products to end-users. A *reverse-stream value-added transformation* zone contains processes for repair, customer returns, recycling, or disposal. *Quality defect reverse streams* handle defects.

Within any zone there can be several echelons, each representing a step in the supply chain process. For example, product inventory in the OEM's warehouse may be a part of the *downstream value-added transformation* zone and include processing by multiple echelons such as a distributor, a retailer's distribution center, and a store before it reaches the end-user (Table 10.4).

Table 10.3   CSCMP Logistics Software Directory

Specific Functionalities by General Functional Area	Description of Functionality
Functional Area: Customer Relationship Management	
1. Broker/Agent/Distributor/Special Customer Interface "C"	Ability to tailor information exchanges with downstream trading partners.
2. Call Center Management "C"	Application for operating a center that receives customer inquiries/orders.
3. Content or Business Rules for Sales and Marketing "C"	A system with built-in automatic processing of related transactions.
4. Customer and Sales Data Warehousing & Analysis "L"	Capture of order histories for identifying trends and making marketing decisions.
5. Customer Self-Service "C"	Capability enabling customers to make purchases, usually over the Internet.
6. E-Commerce and Retail Storefront "C"	Systems capability to support Internet sales.
7. Field Sales Management "C"	Capability to support information needs of a field sales force.
8. Field Service Management "C"	Provision for the requirements of aftermarket service technicians and support.
9. Marketing Automation/ Email or Postal Mail Generation "I"	Sales communication automation for products & promotions.
10. Sales Force Automation "C"	Systems capability that automates processes for field sales.
Functional Area: Forecasting	
1. Adapts to Specific Events "I"	Can be updated based on occurrences of planned or unplanned "events."
2. Aggregation & Roll-up from Item Code through Family "C"	Can portray demand for any item from all the end products that require it.
3. Batch Processing "C"	Ability to forecast at the batch level representing an economic product quantity.
4. Best Fit from Several Statistical Models "I"	Capability of providing forecasts using multiple algorithms.
5. Collaborative Forecast Sharing "I"	Ability to share forecasts with trading partners according to agreements.
6. Graphical Output "C"	User friendly formats for information sharing.
7. Import & Export to Spreadsheet Software "C"	Ability to transfer data for analysis or incorporation into trading partner applications.
8. Sales & Marketing Adjustments "I"	Ability to modify forecasts to account for marketing plans.

Table 10.3 (continued)   CSCMP Logistics Software Directory

Specific Functionalities by General Functional Area	Description of Functionality
Functional Area: Inventory Planning/Management	
1. Collaborative Planning/Information Sharing "I"	An ability to provide multicompany supply chain partner information sharing.
2. Distribution Requirement Planning "I"	Capability to generate a plan for distribution resources based on orders or forecasts.
3. Dynamic Economic Order Quantity (EOQ) "I"	Applying rules to modify production lot sizes under changing conditions.
4. Dynamic Reorder Points "I"	Applying rules to change stock levels at which replenishment orders are generated.
5. Flexible Inventory Categorization "I"	A software capability to change inventory item categories (often volume/value based).
6. Material Requirement Planning (MRP) "I"	Core process to manage inputs and outputs of a manufacturing or other enterprise.
7. Multiple Item Codes with Cross References "I"	Ability to assign and track a common part with multiple product codes.
8. Multiple Stock Rotation Methods "I"	Flexibility to set different methods for stock rotation.
9. Multiple Units of Measure "C"	Ability to accommodate different units for individual markets.
10. Vendor Managed Inventory (VMI) "C"	Ability to stock replenishment services to a customer.
Functional Area: Manufacturing	
1. Discrete Manufacturing "C"	Common category of items with their own shape. Apparel, computers, and cars.
2. Manufacturing Execution Reporting "C"	Systems that load work centers and report work completed.
3. Manufacturing Resource Planning (MRP) "I"	A capability to manage manufacturing resources to meet order commitments.
4. Process Manufacturing "C"	Manufacture of items without a shape in flow lines. Liquids, lotions, and chemicals.
5. Repetitive Manufacturing "C"	High volume environment that emphasizes efficiency.
6. Shop Floor Management "C"	Large number of functions that control and track material movement through a factory.
7. Finite Capacity Planning "C"	Ongoing scheduling process designed to maintain a relatively even workload.

Functional Area: Order Processing

1. EDI Order Capture "C"	Applications for processing orders using electronic data exchange formats.
2. Internet Order Capture "C"	Applications for processing order using Internet formats.
3. Order Entry & Editing "C"	Automation of related processes for receiving and processing orders.
4. Order Tracking & Carrier Information "C"	Capability to capture order and report order status during production and transport.
5. Quotation "C"	Front-end activities to request vendor information that may lead to a purchase order.

Functional Area: Other Advanced Planning

1. Available to Promise (ATP) "I"	A capability measures current commitments against available capacity.
2. International Scope "C"	Ability to work across international borders.
3. Operation Simulation "L"	Ability to mimic operations in a computer to assess capacity and other features.
4. Strategy Modeling "L"	A capability to test logistics networks against longer term forecasts (1-5 years)
5. Supply Chain Optimization "L"	Capability to make tradeoffs between supply chain functions like capacity &inventory
6. Supply Chain Visibility "C"	Ability to process inputs from sensors along the chain to locate merchandise.
7. What-If Scenarios "L"	Capability to test various assumptions about the future.

Functional Area: Procurement

1. Blanket Orders "I"	Ability to generate longer-term agreement with suppliers that cover multiple purchases.
2. Contract Management "I"	Capability to automate functions related to specific contracts.
3. Internet "C"	Using the Internet to perform purchasing functions.
4. Marketplace "L"	Ability to capture information regarding suppliers by type or commodity group.
5. Purchase Forms & Approval "C"	Process for purchasing materials including requisitions and approvals.
6. Purchase Order Generation "C"	Capability to issue purchase order to suppliers.
7. Supplier Management "I"	Maintenance of status of suppliers for various goods and services.
8. Vendor Performance Tracking "I"	Provision for capturing cost, quality, and delivery information for suppliers' orders.

Table 10.3 (continued)   CSCMP Logistics Software Directory

Specific Functionalities by General Functional Area	Description of Functionality
Functional Area: Transportation Management	
1. Carrier Performance Tracking "C"	Provision for capturing carrier cost, quality, and delivery performance.
2. Dynamic Optimization "C"	Capability to manage transportation resources over a short time frame.
3. Freight Bill Audit "I"	Assuring that freight charges are proper in light of rate structure complexity.
4. Freight Bill Payment "C"	Providing for payment of freight bills.
5. Import Export Document Generation "C"	Generation of documents related to these functions.
6. Inbound Routing "C"	Planning and scheduling inbound shipments to manage workloads in the warehouse.
7. Load Planning "C"	Decision tools for assuring outbound load capacity is fully utilized.
8. Load Tendering/Carrier Communications "C"	Automated requests for services and related communications.
9. Pooled Distribution "C"	Working to combine shipments with others to reduce overall costs.
10. Reverse Logistics "C"	Handling of return goods.
Functional Area: Warehouse Management	
1. Bar Code Scanning "C"	Provides a capability to read barcodes and handle related information.
2. Batch/Lot Control "C"	Capability to group products or SKUs for tracking. Can apply to a picking list.
3. Cycle Counting "I"	Ability to select items and schedule periodic counts to verify inventory levels.
4. Dock Management "C"	Capability to schedule and plan inbound and outbound shipments.
5. Interleaving "C"	Managing assignments of multiple simultaneous warehouses.
6. Packing & Shipping Manifesting "C"	Preparation of the documents that document the orders in a shipment.
7. Productivity Reporting "I"	Tracking of activities in a warehouse and the resources that support them.
8. Progressive Storage "I"	Ability to store merchandise to reduce costs of storage and retrieval.
9. Radio Frequency "C"	The ability to manage information transmitted by radio in the warehouse.
10. Stock Rotation "C"	Minimization of losses due to expired use dates or shopworn conditions.
11. Value Added Services "C"	Capability to handle non-traditional warehouse services like labeling, assembly, etc.
12. Wave Management "C"	Providing a method to pick material so that its wait time for shipping is minimized.

Note: C—continuous, I—intermediate timeframe, L—longer-term timeframe.

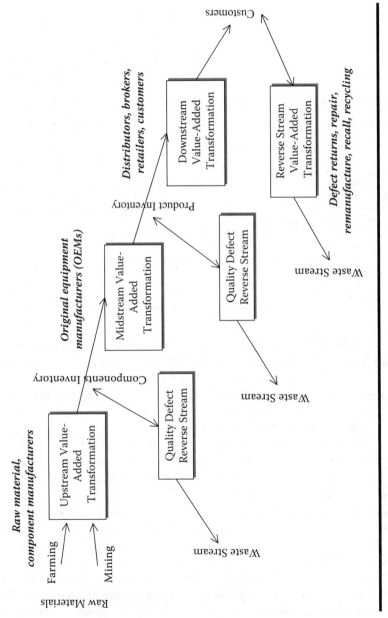

Figure 10.2 Supply chain zones.

Table 10.4   Functional Areas and Zones

#	General Functional Areas	Upstream Transformation	Midstream Manufacturing	Downstream Fulfillment	Reverse Streams
1.	Customer relationship management			•	
2.	Forecasting	•	•	•	
3.	Inventory planning/management		•	•	
4.	Manufacturing		•		
5.	Order processing		•	•	
6.	Other advanced planning	•	•		
7.	Procurement		•	•	
8.	Transportation management			•	
9.	Warehouse management			•	•

This framework is useful because each zone will call on different decision-making application types. For example, in Ford Motor Company's early years, Henry Ford ran a vertically integrated operation—from ore mining to steel production to manufacture and to delivery to the customer. Thus Ford operated in all the zones. Today, companies are increasingly dependent on trading partners; so they look to others to provide raw materials, products, and services.

To the degree that zones operate independently of each other in a particular supply chain, the more likely the zone bounds the enterprise's supply chain. This would be the case for a small manufacturer whose products are distributed by intermediaries (distributors) to a large number of retailers. The distance between that manufacturer and the end-user is great. For example, the produce in a grocery store has, in many cases, traveled quickly down a long channel of distribution. End-user loyalty in this case will likely accrue to the retailer. At the other end, an automobile manufacturer will be tightly linked with both its suppliers and dealers. End-user loyalty will likely be to the manufacturer, although dealer quality also plays a role in determining loyalty. A distributor like McKesson that caters to pharmacies, large and small, that takes on supply chain services, such as vendor managed inventory (VMI) for its retailer customers, will also need more systems capability. It can be seen as expanding the scope of its services back into the *midstream value-added transformation* zone.

Table 10.5 Assessing Information Requirements

| 1. Activity | 2. Process | 3. Type | As-Is | | | To-Be |
			4. Done/Not Done	5. How Done	6. Meets Needs	7. Future Vision
Make-to-order manufacturing	Raw materials ordering	Type II Two-way data exchange	Not done	Forecast replenishment	No	Demand-driven replenishment Type III

10.4 Assessing the Need for Information

With a major share of company expense consumed by or affected by information processors, reviewing information needs along the supply chain can pay handsome dividends. Table 10.5 outlines a method for assessing what information is needed and what can be done away with using methods in other chapters and the 77-item checklist here in Table 10.3. The purpose is to identify gaps and excesses in decision making. The methodology builds on tools and techniques from earlier chapters.

The columns in Table 10.5 are the following:

1. *Activity.* For the company using the Activity System methodology described in Chapter 13, identify the activity with which the information exchange is associated.
2. *Process.* Each activity consists of processes. Identify the process with which the information exchange is associated.
3. *Type.* List the information exchange type using the methodology described in Chapter 16, Section 16.1.2.
   a. One-way data exchange (transactional)
   b. Two-way data exchange (transactional/coordinative)
   c. Cooperative collaboration with simultaneous access to information
   d. Cognitive collaboration in cases of joint decision making where risk to both is high
4. *Done/Not Done.* State whether the information exchange is occurring or not.
5. *How Done.* If it is done, describe the method of exchange—data exchange, meetings, reports, etc.
6. *Meets Needs?* If done, is the current method satisfactory?
7. *Future Vision.* How should this exchange be done in the future? Solutions should not be limited to technology approaches.

Using this approach, a company can assess whether their information systems are aligned with their strategy, whether important information exchange tasks meet participant needs, wasteful activities, and needs for future information exchanges mechanisms. The purpose is to assure that money spent on developing and using information to aid decision-making is money well spent.

The example in Table 10.5 represents Herman Miller's desire to shift from forecast-driven to demand-driven replenishment of materials. The activity, in this case, was *make-to-order manufacturing* (Column 1). The process, which could be one of many for this activity, is *raw-material ordering* (Column 2). This was a traditional Type II collaboration with two-way data exchange (Column 3). Column 4 indicates that this is not done at the time the strategy was devised. Column 6 (*No*) indicates that the process must be changed. The future vision is for demand-driven replenishment, a Type III kind of collaboration.

10.5 Meeting Decision-Maker Needs—Summary

Changing supply chains, such as the effort undertaken by Herman Miller, will bring radical shifts in the roles of decision makers and their needs for information. Decision-making is not usually an item on the income statement, but it accounts for much of the cost and time incurred in executing processes. This chapter seeks to make that point and to guide the reader toward a methodology for achieving the benefits of improved "lean" decision making.

Endnotes

1. Information on the Herman Miller case is available at http://www.sternstewart.com/action/miller.php.
2. Bundy, Bill, Brown, Art, and Dean, Steve, Changing the rules of the game, Presentation Council of Logistics Management Annual Meeting, October 1999.
3. http://logistics.about.com/library/weekly/uc083002a.htm
4. Walker, William T., *Supply Chain Architecture: A Blueprint for Networking the Flow of Material, Information, and Cash*, Boca Raton, FL: CRC Press, 2005. p. 15.

RETAIL STRATEGY AND SUPPLY CHAINS

3

The four-chapter Part 3 describes how to formulate strategies for retail supply chain companies. Chapter 11 calls attention to the need to consider different kinds of product or services marketed by a single company. The implication is that, most companies, to be competitive, need more than one supply chain. The one-size-fits-all approach is insufficient. Chapter 12 describes how to "carve out" multiple supply chains from existing functional organizations. The chapter also describes the important role of enabling processes in supporting product-producing supply chains.

#	Name
11.	Product Types—Value to the Customer
12.	Businesses Inside the Business
13.	Activity Systems and Process Definition
14.	Supply Chain Management—Skills Required

The activity system tool from strategy guru Michael Porter, the subject of Chapter 13, is the first step toward supply chain change. Chapter 13 provides a framework for using the supply chain to support strategies for competing. Finally, in Chapter 14, the management skills for executing supply chain change are identified. A tool to assess the existence of such skills will aid in assuring that an organization has the human resources to do what it wants to do.

Chapter 11

Product Types—Value to the Customer

This chapter describes concepts and models that apply to products sold through retail channels. These concepts and models call attention to the fact that individual customers evaluate products differently and may place different values on one product over another. Chapter 2 introduced this concept when it described staple and fashion merchandise. Greater value for one product over another takes form in a higher profit margin somewhere in the supply chain—at the retailer, at an original equipment manufacturer (OEM), or perhaps at a supplier of a key component. Even though one partner may enjoy the premium margin, all trading partners benefit to the extent sales of the product are strong because sales represent increased demand at all levels. A key lesson is that supply chain design must be consistent with customer and end-user perceptions of product value.

Although Chapter 2 described processes used by retail and distribution organizations, this chapter focuses more on the producers of retail merchandise. These are the OEMs and their suppliers as shown Figure 1.1 in Chapter 1.

The strategy of adding more value to a product is the path of choice for manufacturers beset by the consequences of globalization. One example is what is called the *Nagoya boom*, reported in *The Wall Street Journal*.[1] The boom refers to a group of manufacturers supplying traditional "smokestack" industries such as steel that have moved production of their "staples" to low-cost regions and focused on high-value goods produced at home. Examples include research and development (R&D)-intensive products such as engines for hybrid cars and micro robots for industrial use.

Another industry on a distant side of the world reported a similar strategy. The privately owned Italian company, Finanziaria Arnoldo Caprai, has moved up the

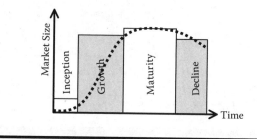

Figure 11.1 The product life cycle.

value curve for decades.[2] In the 1980s, the owner, Mr. Caprai, transformed his sweater line from lambs' wool to cashmere in response to competition from Hong Kong. He then shifted his sources for raw material and manufacturing to China but retained design control to protect his hard-to-copy products. Back in Italy, the company also found profitable niches in high-value linens, tablecloths, and lingerie.

An example of an invasion from the low side is the "two buck chuck," a popular product from Bronco Wine Company. Varietals under the Charles Shaw brand are priced at $2 retail in California and only slightly higher in states having higher liquor taxes. Having mastered the art of cost cutting, according to the *Los Angeles Times,* Bronco has been "driving down costs and prices in a way that is shaking up the entire (wine) industry."[3] Bronco's partner, retailer Trader Joe's, has successfully exploited the Charles Shaw brand as a traffic builder for its globally sourced, successful grocery stores.

A principle of this book is that supply chain design must reflect the value of the product to end-users. That is, a supply chain for a low-value product should be different from one for a high-value product. This difference is ignored in many companies that employ a one-size-fits-all supply chain for all their products. Bronco Wine Company carved a low-end niche by taking a cost-cutting knife to the wine supply chain.

To capture more value, some business models use vertically integrated supply chains. In this way, the retailer maintains control of product design and manufacture. Like the Caprai company discussed earlier, retailers Zara (latest fashion clothing) and IKEA (knockdown furniture) retain design control over their products, communicating the brands' understanding of their customers' taste and capturing the value customers place on those designs. Au Bon Pan and Jack in the Box, who run fast-food stores, push new sandwiches and other menu items to entice their customers to return. Software companies, motion picture, and music producers survive on a steady flow of new products.

Other retailers market diverse sets of products designed and made by others. These retailers sift through the offerings of many designers and manufacturers to find the high-value "gems." Department stores, discount stores, grocers, and most small retailers fit this model. Wal-Mart displays its lowest priced item in its stores and keeps higher-priced (and profit) alternatives near by. Wherever a company is located in the supply chain—as a retailer, a distributor, or as a supplier—supply chain designers should be aware of the concepts described in the following sections.

11.1 The Product Life Cycle

An important concept for supply chain designers is one long used by marketers, called the *product life cycle*. Figure 11.1 illustrates the product life cycle showing four stages in the life of a product—inception (also called the introductory stage), growth, maturity, and decline. The model is helpful in defining the role of supply chain management (SCM) at different stages in the life cycle. This becomes complicated in supply chains where there are many different products in the chain at different stages in the life cycle. The consequence, to the harm of many companies serving retail markets, is the one-size-fits-all supply chains many should avoid, not ones tailored to products at different stages in the life cycle.

Another complication related to the retail industry is the concept of a "product." Retailers often think of *categories* rather than individual products. Categories, according to Levy and Weitz, can be any grouping that makes sense to the retailer.[4] Each category will have many individual products and many more stockkeeping units (SKUs), as discussed in the merchandise budgeting sections, 2.2 and 2.3, in Chapter 2. So, *product*, in a discussion of the product life cycle concept, also applies to product categories.

In retailing, a category consists of items that are substitutable for each other. An apparel retailer might have categories for men's sportswear or girls' swimwear. An automobile dealer may use categories such as sport utility vehicles (SUVs), sedans, or minivans. For maximum effectiveness, supply chain trading partners must agree on category definitions and respond to the needs of the customer by providing the products that match their choice criteria.

Levy and Weitz identify four types of "category life cycle" in terms of the longevity of the category product line:

1. Fad—a one-shot wonder with a very short life cycle, perhaps one season.
2. Fashion—a multiseason product with many individual products and SKUs during its life cycle.
3. Staple—a basic product that achieves considerable longevity but eventually goes into decline.
4. Seasonal—a product whose sales fluctuate over the course of a year. This type includes both fashion and staple items.

The authors note that "forecasting and inventory management systems used for fads and fashion merchandise are very different than those used for staples."[5] One of these differences is the merchandise budgeting approach to planning inventories described in Chapter 2, Section 2.3.

In the inception stage, the product or category is at center stage. If the product is not a new version of an existing product line (such as a new movie, CD, software program, apparel style, sandwich, or automobile), a new supply chain will be needed. Often, even when it is needed, supply chain design is a secondary priority in the inception stage. This is definitely the case in many high-tech companies in electronics or software industries with hot new products. Ideally, these companies should start early to line up customers and suppliers—that is to say, a supply chain—in the event the product is successful and moves into the growth stage.

Growth products—whether they are fad, fashion, or new technology—in the next stage are climbing to the top of the sales curve. The products become profitable for the industry leaders; improved versions of the product better match customer needs, and supply chain trading partners enjoy profits from high margins and high volume. Supply chain processes are geared to keep up with demand, which is ample for all but the worst competitors.

The maturity stage represents the products we buy day to day, or the "staples." These are also known as *frequently purchased consumer goods* or FPCGs. Some would say the growth product has been "commoditized." Competition stiffens; the supply chain mission moves toward cost reduction as higher-cost industry participants are squeezed out of the market. Competitors target segments with extended product features to maintain their volume. Although mature products must have efficient supply chains, the base products themselves are no longer exceptional when compared to competitors. Extended product features such as service, financing, and a reputation for reliability, play an increased role. An example of a product in maturity is the TV show or movie repackaged as a DVD.

Products in decline, former staples, hang on for dear life. Unless they move backward to another phase by rejuvenating their product or supply chain, they won't survive. For example, Arm and Hammer successfully revived their product by finding numerous new applications for baking soda, combining it with other products or brands (toothpaste, laundry detergent, and various types of deodorizers). In many cases, the supply chain task is to identify and winnow out products in the decline stage from the portfolio before they become unprofitable. Fad products with short product life cycles die quickly and are more easily extinguished than staple merchandise.

Long-lived legacy products must be supported after they are no longer sold. Capital goods such as automobiles, computers, and appliances are examples. Maintaining long-term commitments requires moving the product support function into a different supply chain altogether. One can argue that, for the long-lived product, aftermarket support regenerates the product or its components as fashion or staple merchandise. An example is the vintage car collection. New challenges arise, e.g., finding parts, warranty and nonwarranty service and repairs, software maintenance, providing manuals and parts lists, and call-in technical support.

A shortfall in some retail trading partner strategies is treating the aftermarket as an afterthought. Other industries such as cell phones and computer printers actually focus on the aftermarket as part of their basic strategy, realizing that phone minutes and ink cartridges will generate far more profit over the life of the original base product than the phone or the computer printer did at the time of purchase. Thus, many companies use a penetration pricing strategy for the original product when they have a sense that there will be a very strong aftermarket.

Often, there are opportunities to convert owners of long-lived legacy products to new offerings. For example, GE Appliances has employed a "repair or replace" calculator to guide customers in making a replacement decision for appliances like refrigerators. Just type in the make and model year, and the calculator would advise you. At any rate, for the long-life product, ultimate profitability may not be determined until long after the initial product sales cease.

11.2 Innovative and Functional Products

Marshall Fisher describes a similar framework for ensuring that supply chain design is appropriate for two different product types.[6] His two types, *functional* and *innovative,* are different by virtue of the nature of product demand. Functional products, as the name implies, are the staples described above. Competition is fierce for these products, and margins along the supply chain are thin, but the demand is constant and relatively easy to forecast. In the life-cycle model, these products would be in the mature or decline phases.

Innovative products are differentiated in the market; they are fads or fashions and are likely in the inception and growth stages in the product life cycle. Seasonal products also fit this model. Innovative products have advanced technological features or styling, or both. They carry higher margins, but demand can be hard to forecast, and their life cycles are likely to be short.

Fisher characterizes the features of each type of supply chain summarized in Table 11.1. Functional products generally will have longer lives than innovative products. Their demand will be easier to forecast with corresponding lower chances of stockouts or markdowns. Lead times should be determined by cost trade-offs that take into account production and distribution economics, the cost of inventory, and other such factors. Innovative products have short lives. The benefits of high profitability are offset by market risks that take the form of higher forecast errors and corresponding markdown threats from overproduction or overpurchasing. Ideally, lead time would be the result of a supply chain design that maximizes flexibility within forecast ranges of market demand.

Fisher, like Levy and Weitz, asserts that these two product types require fundamentally different supply chains. Functional products require an *efficient* supply chain; innovative products require *responsive* supply chains. For example, American Apparel, before its recent acquisition, could take a design idea from a customer, scribble it on a napkin, fax it to the factory, and have it in the product line in a matter of hours.[7] Again, the presence of both types of products or product categories will challenge the company that employs a one-size-fits-all supply chain.

Table 11.1   Differences between Innovative and Functional Products

	Functional Products (Staples)	*Innovative Products (Fads, Fashions)*
Length of product life cycle	Long	Short
Profitability per unit	Low	High
Forecast errors	Low	High
Stockout rates	Low risk	High risk
Markdown	Unlikely	Likely for excess merchandise
Lead time	Set by economics/ competition	Set by supply chain flexibility

Source: From Ayers, James B., *Handbook of Supply Chain Management,* 2nd ed., Boca Raton: CRC Press, 2006.

11.3 Market Mediation Costs

Fisher also advises recognition of what he calls "market mediation" costs. This is quite rare in current management practice, however. The mission of the supply chain is to match supply and demand, resulting in the satisfaction of marketplace needs. Fisher recommends understanding and measuring market mediation costs in designing and operating supply chains. These market mediation costs result from mismatches in demand and supply, essentially failing in the basic SCM mission. This is particularly difficult because forecasting demand for innovative products is complex and is often less than accurate.

Disconnects between supply and demand result in market mediation costs. If there is too much product, the price must be marked down. If there is too little product, the company incurs the opportunity cost from lost sales. These include the revenue and profits from the sale as well as customer disappointment. In some cases, prices can be raised in times of short supply but, more generally, only in markets that are relatively inelastic in terms of supply and demand. It is hard to get far away from the consumer's reference price. When market mediation costs are taken into account, the added cost of an inflexible supply chain can be substantial compared to the budgeted logistics costs of getting the product to market. Most measurement systems ignore this reality.

For many products such as automobiles, both functional and innovative products can be assembled on the same production line. Fisher notes that a functional car like a four-door sedan should use an efficient supply chain with as much cost squeezed out as possible. But a high-margin convertible or hybrid that's popular with customers could earn more profit with a flexible supply chain that's responsive to demand. This point is important because some managers may think that a tailored supply chain will involve duplicate facilities. Note that this can be done without changing the physical process flows for the base product involving assembly and distribution but by modifying the business rules for production scheduling, finished goods, and work-in-process inventory levels. So, the convertible and the sedan could be assembled on the same production line, but the line's scheduling is governed by different parameters.

Applying Fisher's model, supply chain design has two branches. For the functional product, it means advances that reduce the cost of sourcing, manufacturing, inventory, distribution, and sales. For the innovative product, it means reducing the physical costs of the product where appropriate, while recognizing potential market mediation costs. This is a more complex equation because most companies do not, and in fact, cannot track these costs with precision. However, any attempt to reduce lost sales will certainly require as much flexibility in the supply chain design as possible and argues for applying the SCM postponement strategy when possible. This supports the *flexibility imperative* driver of supply chain change described in Chapter 6, Section 6.5. Too few organizations pursue this goal, seeking instead to focus on cost reduction when designing supply chain processes.

Table 11.2 illustrates the two types of market mediation costs—the situation when actual demand falls short of forecast and when actual demand exceeds the forecast. The table assumes that the company produces or orders the forecast number of units (100,000). It also assumes that the supply chain lead time and flexibility makes it impossible to adjust as it becomes apparent what the actual sales will be.

The left-hand column calculates the market mediation cost from a shortfall in demand. The company is paid full price ($100) for 70,000 units, whereas 30,000 must be sold at a discount ($30). Because the unit cost is $40, the result is a loss of $10 on each discounted unit. The total market mediation cost would be $300,000. The right-hand column calculates market mediation cost in the case of lost sales of 30,000. In this case the market mediation cost is the gross margin ($60) times the number of units of lost sales (30,000), or $1,800,000.

Two obstacles retard putting this concept to work in the retail industry. First, accounting systems do a fair job of capturing the markdowns that go with shortfalls in demand, but altogether ignore the lost opportunities from underforecasting demand. So, extra analysis based on estimates of lost sales must be done. This is extra work and may not seem justified. The second obstacle is the paradigm that supply chains represent only cost and need to be measured on cost alone. Actions that increase flexibility but add cost are discouraged. Examples include extra capacity, buffer inventories, and airfreight over ocean freight.

Table 11.2 Illustration of Market Mediation Costs

	Forecast ($)		
Forecast (units)	100,000		
Unit price	100		
Unit cost	40		
Gross margin	60		
Sales Less Than Forecast			*Sales More Than Forecast*	
Actual sales (units)	70,000		Actual demand	130,000
# Units marked down	30,000	*Forecast Error (units)*	Lost sales (units)	30,000
Markdown price	$ 30			
Loss per unit	$ (10)		Gross margin per unit	$ 60
Markdown cost	$(300,000)	*Market Mediation Cost*	Lost profit	$1,800,000

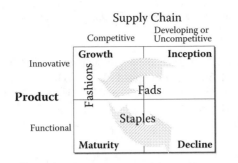

Figure 11.2   Product life-cycle grid.

11.4 Customer Value and Product Types—Summary

Figure 11.2 summarizes the concepts described in this chapter in a product life-cycle "grid." The grid shows the inception, or introductory, stage in the upper right-hand corner. The supply chain challenge, for an entirely new product, is to develop trading partners in advance of higher levels of production. This could be the domain of the fad products that are "here today and gone tomorrow." The supply chain should maximize profit over the brief product life.

The next quadrant (upper left) is the growth stage. It contains longer-lived fad products and fashion-type products that have higher profit margins. The supply chain challenge is meeting the demand. The maturity stage is at the lower left-hand quadrant. This is the home of staples requiring efficient supply chains. Some of these staples may be moving into the decline stage. Products in the decline stage are candidates either for aftermarket innovations or elimination.

This chapter has presented the case that retail supply chains must be designed with the perception of customer value and product competition in mind. This will maximize returns to the retailer and its trading partners in terms of customer loyalty and profit, and to the customer in terms of met needs. The implications are important to the retail enterprise and the manufacturers and distributors that support them. Creativity and collaboration by trading partners is the surest route to achieving winning supply chain designs. The next two chapters describe how they might go about the task.

Endnotes

1. Sapsford, Jathon, "Japan's Economy Gains Steam from Manufacturing Heartland," *The Wall Street Journal,* October 11, 2005, p. A1.
2. Di Leo, Luca and Stock, Jenny, "Trying to Stay a Cut above Chinese Textiles," *The Wall Street Journal,* July 25, 2005, p. A13.
3. Hirsch, Jerry, "Wal-Mart of Wine," *Los Angeles Times,* April 30, 2006, p. C1.

4. Levy, Michael and Weitz, Barton A., *Retailing Management,* 5th ed., New Delhi: Tata McGraw-Hill, 2004, chap. 12.
5. Ibid. p. 380.
6. Fisher, Marshall L., "What Is the Right Supply Chain for Your Product?" *Harvard Business Review,* (75/2), March–April 1997, 105–116.
7. Dean, Josh, "Dov Charney, Like It or Not," www.inc.com/magazine/20050901/american-apparel, pp. 1–9.

Chapter 12

Businesses Inside the Business

This chapter extends the discussion of product types and customer value described in Chapter 11. Specifically, the discussion here builds on the argument that adding value to retail customers and end-users can best be done with supply chains tailored to specific market needs. This means that a retailer, distributor, or manufacturer may need more than one supply chain. Although having multiple supply chains is not the case in most companies now, the authors predict that multiple supply chains will become the norm for all but the simplest of businesses. For any trading partner—retail store chain, distributor, manufacturer, service provider, or parts supplier—there is likely to be a need for parallel processes for physical, information, or financial flows. Some will say that this is what distribution "channels" are, but the concept we discuss goes beyond channels. As described later, multiple supply chains do not necessarily require costly duplication of physical plant, working capital, or workers.

There is ample evidence of the move toward this concept; the often-used example of Wal-Mart is one. In mid-2006, Wal-Mart decided to drop their one-size-fits-all approach to store design and stocking.[1] Its new approach created six store "models" with different merchandise, staff, and logistics support. The company admitted that by serving all customers with the same store type they were also underserving everyone. The Wal-Mart models include the following: affluent, African Americans, empty nesters, Hispanics, suburbanites, and rural markets.

12.1 The Conventional Chain

Standing in the way of multiple customer-serving supply chains is the conventional functional organization present in most enterprises. This setup consists of specialized departments focused on a narrow mission and measured on how that mission is accomplished. The functions of a manufacturer serving retail customers include purchasing, manufacturing, marketing, distribution, design engineering, finance, and human resources. Distributors and retailers may also be organized in a similar way, creating internal walls, often called "silos," which results in internal organization barriers that impede the flow of products and information. Also, department-level measures of success will produce unintended consequences. For example, a transportation manager of a retailer or distributor might refuse to use expensive airfreight to rush a delivery to highly valued customer because that individual is measured on the cost of transportation. The driver of supply chain change, process-centered management, described in Chapter 6, Section 6.6, is the antidote. This alternative view is one of end-to-end processes, not collections of individual departments.

Before embarking on an end-to-end supply chain design effort, there's a need to define the boundaries of that supply chain. In effect, the supply chain will be "carved out" of the overall operation, creating "businesses inside the business." This helps knock down barriers and leads to ways to increase value to customers. The method described here builds on the principle of market segmentation used in the retail industry. Tailored supply chains support and cater to profitable segments and encourage participants at all echelons to work together.

12.2 Market Segments

The supply chain model in Chapter 1 (Figure 1.1) showed end-users as the consumers of retail goods and services. Unlike the depiction in Figure 1.1, these end-users are not monolithic; that is, they do fall into groups based on purchasing proclivities and can be described by any number of factors. Figure 7.1 is the "supply chain reality." Marketers define these groups as segments and tailor their marketing strategies to the needs of these segments. These needs are explicitly identified through company experience, sales analysis, or market research.

Levy and Weitz, in *Retailing Management*, identify the three components of a successful retail strategy: the target market (segment or segments served), the nature of the retail offering, and the nature of the competitive advantage.[2] For example, Nordstrom targets middle- to upper-income customers using a fashion specialty department store format and is best known for its superior customer service. An appropriate supply chain design will support all three market strategy components.

Segmentation of a market can be based on a number of factors including the following:

Geography or location

Income level

Demographics such as age and gender

Frequency of usage

Benefits of value to the customer or end-user, such as convenience, cost, and
prestige

Preference for distribution channels

Family life-cycle stage

Although useful for designing retail strategies, this type of segmentation may or
may not be helpful in designing the supply chain to serve the segment. In fact, different supply chains may not be needed for different customer segments. A different
approach, beyond market segmentation, is needed to aid those identifying the need
for and designing supply chain processes.

12.3 Spheres—Modules for Supply Chain Design

The recommended tool to identify the boundaries of supply chains is a *sphere*, introduced in a previous book in this series, the *Handbook of Supply Chain Management*,
First Edition.[3] A sphere is defined as a *market–product–operation* combination
that provides a way to "divide and conquer" in developing and implementing supply chain processes. The term *sphere* comes from the three dimensions—markets,
products, and operations—summarized in Table 12.1. Identifying spheres draws
boundaries around the supply chain, helps decide what organization model to follow, and enables identification of requirements for and development of customer
serving processes. All three of these elements are vital to successful supply chain
management (SCM) that supports retail strategies for competing.

The dimensions, in the left-hand column in Table 12.1, are markets, products,
and operations. The *market* portion of the sphere definition can include multiple
segments as long as a common supply chain can serve those segments. This definition does not have to follow segmentation for marketing or advertising strategies,
which may be of limited use for designing operating processes.

Products are those sold to the identified retail market. They can be expressed as
categories or as other groupings used in that particular retail business. This section
describes the Wal-Mart "Remix" program that set up a supply chain for high-volume products. For a complex product with many components, the "products" could
be major component groups such as high-value custom components or low-value
commodity components. The product includes not only the base physical product
but also extended product features that are part of the supply chain processes. For
example, this would include the dealer network for automobiles because the dealer
makes the initial sale and provides after-sales service.

Table 12.1 Sphere Dimensions

Dimension	Definition
Markets	Defined by customer groups or segments where end-users have common characteristics and buying behavior. Does not have to match segments identified for marketing strategies
Products	Includes the physical, or base, product, major components, or extended product features such as customer service, inventory and scheduling policies, warranties and aftermarket support, financing, technical support, and other features
Operations	Suppliers, manufacturing/production capabilities, distribution organizations/channels, equipment, and facilities. Can be either inside the company or at upstream or downstream external trading partner operations

Operations are the supply chain "machinery" used to source, make, and deliver the products to the customers. These include hard assets such as the supplier base, manufacturing, distribution networks, vehicles and equipment, and facilities of all types. Operations can also include soft assets and capabilities that support the sphere, such as information systems, a customer service center, a sourcing organization, vendor agreements, and so forth.

Figure 12.1 is a supply chain model that provides examples of the sphere concept. The end-users are on the right; the different patterns in the vertical bar represent different customer groups—#1, #2, and #3. An option is to have *market-centric* supply chains serving each of the three groups. This is appropriate if there needs to be separate supply chains based on different customer/end-user requirements.

Moving to the middle of Figure 12.1, there are three products, A, B, and C. Each of the three products might also justify a separate focused supply chain. These would be *product-centric* supply chains. Often, capital intensiveness or the need for specialized production or distribution capabilities will dictate product-centric supply chains. Car companies might use this approach, with the products being the platforms producing similar cars under different brand names.

There are also *operations-centric* supply chains where some operating capabilities are important to all products and markets. In these cases, competitive advantage comes from supply chain processes that are within a company or are shared among trading partners. These are also referred to as "enabling" processes. Examples include transportation networks, information systems, performance measures, and research and development capability.

Defining spheres is an intuitive right-brained exercise that should build on the company's strategic planning process and, ideally, would be part of that process. The syntax for defining a sphere simply puts the market/product/operations combination together with a "divider" between each part of the definition. Table 12.2

Figure 12.1 Sphere concept.

Table 12.2 Sphere Examples

#	Type	Markets	Products	Operations
1.	Market-centric	Market 1	All (A, B, and C)	All
2.	Product-centric	All markets (1, 2, and 3)	Product C	All
3.	Operations-centric (enabling)	All markets	All Products	Sourcing, buying, quality assurance

lists examples based on the supply chains shown in Figure 12.1 and displayed in Figure 12.2.

Sphere #1, shown as a slanted rectangle in Figure 12.2, is market-centric. It focuses on delivering all company products to one market, Market 1. Operations in this sphere would include those needed to deliver all three products to that market. For example, Market 1 might carve out the Internet sales channel, the products to be sold there, and the operations to support that channel. So, all the operations needed just for Internet sales would be included in the sphere.

Another market-centric example would focus on tailored services for high net-worth individuals by a financial services firm. The sphere would provide specialized products (investments, loans, etc.) just for this group. Operations could include account executives, investment advice, and special reports on investments, travel services, and easy access to account data.

Sphere #2 is product-centric—built around product C—and is shown as a large shaded area in Figure 12.2. With this concept, separate self-contained spheres

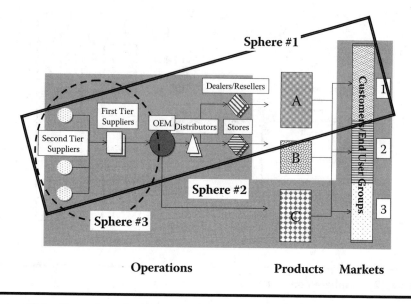

Operations   **Products**   **Markets**

Figure 12.2   Examples of spheres.

(one each for products A, B, and C) handle their assigned products. All the operations needed to produce Product C are included in the sphere. The U.S. automaker Chrysler Group employs this concept with platform teams that design and produce the various brands that make up the platform. The company is being separated from Daimler, but will likely keep its identity as "Chrysler." Chrysler platforms include large car, small car, Jeep, truck, and minivans. Each platform team serves dealers who likely market products from several of the platform groups and even from other manufacturers.

In another product-centric example, Wal-Mart has separated its products into fast selling and regular as part of a program called "Remix." The purpose is to move high-volume products direct to store shelves to limit stockouts.[4] The effort in its 117 distribution centers, averaging 600,000 cases daily, separates selling merchandise (paper towels, toilet paper, seasonal items, and some foods) from regular deliveries. This saves time when the goods arrive at the store, where employees no longer need to sift through the incoming shipment to find the fast movers. To make sure no shelves are empty, selected warehouses are designated for "high-velocity" handling. They are designed accordingly to save time at the store and increase sales per square foot by preventing stockouts. With the sphere idea applied to Wal-Mart's Remix program, the new product-centric sphere could be defined as follows: all markets/fast-moving products/selected high-velocity warehouses and supporting processes.

The operations piece of the sphere would include facilities, equipment, and transportation resources needed to keep fast movers rolling off the shelves quickly.

Component candidates are purchasing, cross-docking, supplier collaboration, and special arrangements with transportation companies.

Sphere #3, shown on the left in Figure 12.2 as an oval, is operations-centric. Such spheres are *enabling spheres,* whereas market-centric and product-centric spheres are *product-producing* spheres. The Wal-Mart buying organization that finds sources (meaning it approves suppliers but does not make purchases) for both high-speed and low-speed products for all stores, could be such a sphere (all markets/all products/sourcing organization). If the high-speed and low-speed spheres do the actual buying, the buying organization would be included in those spheres—enabled by the sourcing organization that finds the vendors they buy from.

Chrysler, mentioned earlier, also has an enabling platform operation for power train components (engines, transmissions). This capability serves all the platform teams (all products, all markets, power train design and manufacture). Applying the sphere taxonomy to one of the six Wal-Mart tailored format stores would produce a definition such as affluent customers/tailored merchandise categories/designated stores. In this example, the Wal-Mart purchasing and distribution capability would be an enabling capability for all six market-centric spheres.

The sphere approach puts forward a method to align the supply chain to the needs of customers and end-users. The choice of spheres will lead to process design, the organizations needed to run them, the systems needed to support the processes, and the metrics to manage the supply chain. Chapter 13 describes the next step in this process after spheres have been defined.

12.4 Summary—Businesses Inside the Business

Focused supply chain designs produce competitive advantage, adding more value to customers and end-users. The company that views the supply chain as a strategic asset needs a way to begin the design process. Spheres are the way.

Endnotes

1. Zimmerman, Ann, "Thinking Local: To Boost Sales, Wal-Mart Drops One-Size-Fits-All Approach," *The Wall Street Journal,* September 7, 2006, p. A1.
2. Levy, Michael and Weitz, Barton A., Retailing Management, 5th ed., New Delhi: Tata McGraw-Hill, 2004, chap. 12.
3. Ayers, James B., *Handbook of Supply Chain Management,* 2nd ed., Boca Raton: CRC Press, 2006, chap. 18.
4. Hudson, Kris, "Wal-Mart's Need for Speed," *The Wall Street Journal,* September 26, 2005, p. B4.

Chapter 13

Activity Systems and Process Definition

This chapter describes the application of spheres, or "businesses inside the business," discussed in Chapter 12. The path described here is from sphere definition to supply chain processes that add value for customers or end-users and erect barriers to competitors. This would be the case for companies seeking a "blue ocean strategy."[1] Such strategies seek monopolies in uncontested market "space."

The recommended tool for process development is the *activity system*, an approach developed by Michael Porter of the Harvard Business School. Dr. Porter has authored 17 books and over 100 articles on strategy. In 2001, Harvard University and the Harvard Business School created the Institute for Strategy and Competitiveness to further Professor Porter's work. Activity systems apply no matter where a company is located in the retail supply chain—retailer, distributor, original equipment manufacturer (OEM), or supplier to an OEM.

The authors' experiences with clients demonstrate the value of activity systems. The approach fits well with facilitated team sessions. Company managers serving on design teams readily grasp the process, and subsequent use increases understanding and willingness to think strategically.

This chapter turns to retailer Inter IKEA Systems B.V., the Swedish knockdown furniture retailer, as an illustration of activity systems. Dr. Porter employed this company in an article describing the activity system methodology.[2] The case study here contains insights from that article and additions based on IKEA's Web site, other articles, and information about the company. Another example later in this chapter will recall the Wal-Mart Remix effort described in Chapter 12.

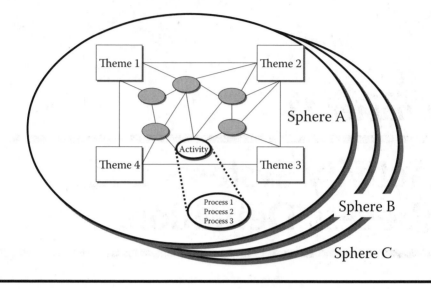

Figure 13.1   Spheres, themes, activities, and processes.

Figure 13.1 depicts the relationship between components in the supply chain planning process. The figure assumes that the planning task described in Chapter 12 has identified spheres that are businesses within the business. These "carved-out" supply chains are suitable for focused strategies leading to custom supply chains. In Figure 13.1, the spheres are labeled sphere A, sphere B, and sphere C. Inside sphere A, there's a picture of an activity system with strategic "themes" anchoring the activity system. Smaller, shaded "activities" support the themes. Within each activity, there are implementing processes.

The case study company, IKEA, built its business model over a long period beginning in the late 1940s. Over time it has become a leader in its niche by the choices made in that process. Activity systems are a more recent planning innovation, so IKEA didn't employ the tool while building the business. Nevertheless, the IKEA uniqueness presents a formidable barrier to competitors—one that supply chain planners can look to in creating their own business models.

13.1 Activity System—the IKEA Example

IKEA uses low-cost methods to make purchases of home furnishings, mostly furniture, available to the widest possible market. IKEA began to design its own furniture in 1955 and opened its first store in Sweden in 1958. In 1959 it began to produce self-assembly furniture to lower freight charges and other costs to retail customers. This approach continues today. IKEA now has over 200 stores in 30 countries. Each store has about 9500 items for sale. Its 2005 sales are over €15 billion (over $20 billion).

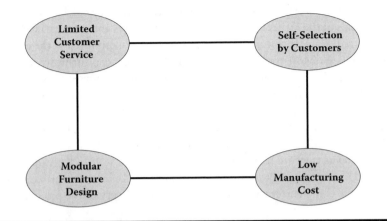

Figure 13.2   Strategic themes for IKEA.

The "IKEA concept" guides the company. This concept is to make "well-designed, functional home furnishing products" at low, affordable prices. In fact, the design process for a new product begins by setting the retail price. It then proceeds to design production processes that meet the cost objective. Finally, the product is designed to IKEA's style standard. This standard omits cost-adding frills that add no value in terms of functionality. The following sections use IKEA describe the process of creating an activity system.

13.1.1 Make Choices, Develop Themes

A first step in developing an activity system is to make choices based on trade-offs between strategic options. According to Porter, there is no strategy if choices aren't made. It is choices that lead to a unique strategy capable of repelling competitive assaults. In particular, operating effectiveness, or low-cost production, is not a strategy. Any competitor can probably copy cost-cutting strategies.

The strategic choices, also called "themes," anchor the strategy as shown in Figure 13.2. The themes reflect the thrifty philosophy of IKEA founder Ingvar Kamprad, who came from a region of Sweden where people, mostly farmers, worked hard to support themselves. These customers wanted value for their money. In applying the process to IKEA, Porter identifies four themes to illustrate the power of activity systems:

1. Low manufacturing cost—for control of cost and style
2. Modular furniture design—for minimizing shipping and storage cost
3. Limited customer service—to secure store labor efficiency
4. Self-selection by customers—to involve the customer and further reduce cost

Themes are shown as large shaded ovals in Figure 13.2. They can be viewed as "features" or goals of the IKEA interaction between its stores and customers. When one pictures a traditional furniture store, what may come to mind is just the opposite of the IKEA model. Most traditional stores will have high-end furniture, ample sales staff, and long lead times for delivery unless the customer buys store stock.

Chapter 12 introduced the idea of functional and innovative products. IKEA blends the virtues of both types. It stresses low cost by purging design frills and supply chain steps out of its processes. This is the characteristic of functional products. On the other hand, it offers modern product designs that satisfy even high-end buyers as long as they are handy with a screwdriver and seek IKEA value. The best choice for IKEA products is to call them "innovative" in terms of the base, physical product while being extremely "functional" in the delivery of the product.

13.1.2 Define Activities

The next step makes the activity system approach valuable to supply chain planning. It requires definition of the activities that are needed to support the strategic choices. These activities constitute enterprise operations, high-level strategy to day-to-day working processes. Figure 13.3 shows some of the activities needed to implement IKEA's themes.

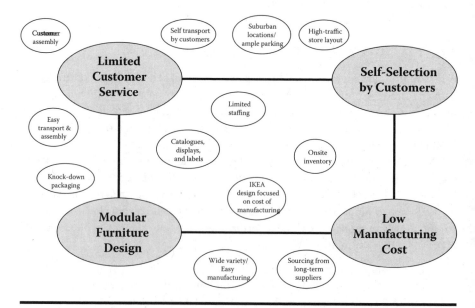

Figure 13.3 Strategic activities.

The activities support the low-cost theme by using modular furniture that is packaged in "knockdown" form, that is, unassembled. This minimizes shipping cost and storage space at warehouse-like stores sized to hold inventory. To facilitate transactions, stores are located where there is ample parking. This enables transport by customers for bulky merchandise. The low-cost theme also applies to the store sales staff. IKEA calls this "customer involvement" in the sales process. This includes picking out merchandise (IKEA provides tape measures), transporting them home, and assembly. For those who can't or won't perform these tasks, IKEA will do it for a fee.

13.1.3 Draw Links

The final step shows how activities support each of the themes and other activities. Figure 13.4 shows these linkages. IKEA suppliers have long-term relationships with the company. They work with product designers to ensure that the retail price target for the product is achievable. The activity *catalogs, displays, and labels* supports the themes *limited customer service* and *self-selection by customers*. It also supports the *limited staffing* activity, replacing personal with printed customer assistance.

Porter holds that the links between activities and choices lead to strategic "fit." This fit creates and sustains competitive advantage. Consistency between numerous complementary activities is harder to duplicate than a single activity, making competitive copies difficult to implement.

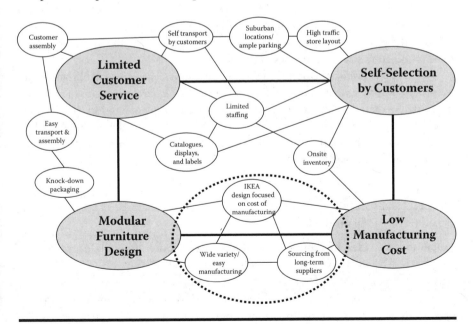

Figure 13.4   Activities and links.

There are three types of fit. First-order strategic fit means direct support or "simple consistency." Eliminating design frills is an example of first-order fit in meeting IKEA's cost objectives. Strategic fit of the second order is demonstrated when activities reinforce each other. *Suburban locations/ample parking* supports *high traffic store layout* and *self transport by customers* because both of these activities require ample parking space. IKEA's low costs draw many customers; they will require parking spaces while shopping. Besides, of course, the same customers use their own vehicles to haul away their purchases.

Third-order fit is what Porter calls "optimization of effort." Establishing long-term relationships with manufacturing suppliers is an example. With the building of a "relationship," IKEA creates the environment for collaboration needed to make product functionality and design trade-offs. This harmonizes the product and manufacturing strategies along the supply chain and results in the best-designed products for the customer at retail. Achieving this third-order fit is particularly important to supply chain designers because optimization of effort among trading partners is an ultimate supply chain management (SCM) goal.

13.2 Enabling Spheres and Supply Chain Processes

This section extends the activity system methodology to the implementation of support processes needed to implement company goals at the retail level. Figure 13.1 shows that the activity system should be supported by needed processes under each activity. These will likely exist in a mature company but need to be created in a startup. The processes may be perfectly fine as they exist. More likely, they will have to be modified to suit the purposes of the new strategy.

At this point, it may be useful to set up operations-centric, or enabling, spheres for process improvement. A dotted line in Figure 13.4 encircles a group of activities in the IKEA activity system suitable for combined implementation. This sphere would be especially important as a multicompany effort involving IKEA and its suppliers. Using the market–product–operations taxonomy from Chapter 12, the sphere could be defined as follows:

Markets	All markets
Products	All products
Operations	IKEA marketing, new product design, procurement, product cost accounting; supplier representatives

For the wide variety of home furnishing it sells, IKEA has an option of multiple operations-focused spheres for different product categories, such as storage items, kitchenware, or furniture collection. Processes that could fall under the purview of a design team for this sphere could include the following:

1. Develop new product ideas.
2. Prepare new product designs.
3. Perform market research.
4. Source materials from suppliers.
5. Gather process costs from suppliers.
6. Prepare design templates for product categories.
7. Work with suppliers to implement new production processes.
8. Coordinate packaging development.
9. Prepare catalog, display, and label information.
10. Forecast sales; suggest inventory levels.

Note that this would be a cross-functional team, one designed to speed new product introductions to retail markets. Should this construct take on a "category manager" flavor, the product portion of the sphere definition would be one of the categories. For furniture maker IKEA, one product-centric sphere definition scheme could be living room, bedroom, kitchen, and so forth. Another could be table, chairs, desks, utensils, and so forth, or the types of categories previously cited.

13.3 Defining Processes

To define processes in a traditional supply chain setting, we return to the Wal-Mart example in Chapter 12. That example is the Remix program that splits Wal-Mart distribution between warehouses for standard fare and those for fast-moving items. The purpose is to ensure that fast-moving products are always on store shelves, reduce stockouts, and avoid wasted time of store workers who must sort through all merchandise types (fast-moving and slow-moving) as shipments arrive. This product-centric sphere was defined in Chapter 12 as follows: all markets/fast-moving products/selected high-velocity warehouses and supporting organization, systems, and processes.

Creating this sphere reflects the fact that Wal-Mart, and other retailers no doubt, must handle at least two types of products, if not more. The first business handles the routine medium- and low-volume products. Legacy processes probably are built to satisfy the needs of the "average" product—an example of a one-size-fits-all supply chain. However, such supply chains are probably too slow for fast-moving products, as Wal-Mart understood. Its reaction wasn't to "tinker" with existing "slow" process but supplant that process entirely for its high-volume products.

Note that Remix is not only for high-value items. Many of these products may indeed be low-price, low-margin items, but customers buy them in large quantities. Toilet paper, detergent, and paper towels are examples; customers buy one or more of these items every time they go to the store. The absence of these items from shelves causes shoppers who want these items to go to competitors for satisfaction of these needs, taking their other business with them. Therefore, avoiding stockouts in these high volume categories is exceedingly important.

Figure 13.5 depicts a possible Remix activity system. This example could apply to Wal-Mart or others seeking to develop a sphere for high-velocity retail products. In fact, the fundamental choice is to abandon the one-size-fits-all approach in favor of one that addresses distribution for the high-volume product group in a fundamentally different way. This activity system also employs four choices, or themes:

1. Dedicated warehouses (distribution centers or DCs)—for a selected subset of high-volume products that need to be in stock at all times.
2. Frequent replenishment—to ensure cost-effective supply. This requires OEM suppliers to deliver frequently to lower inventory, quickly adjust to demand fluctuations, ensure supply, and facilitate cross-dock handling. It also encompasses frequent store replenishment through "milk-run" type fixed interval replenishment schedules.
3. Coordinated delivery scheduling—to synchronize store, DC, and transportation schedules so that high-volume items arrive at stores at the most convenient feasible time.
4. Expedited shelf stocking—by removing the work required to handle selected stockkeeping units (SKUs) and separate delivery of high-volume items.

Figure 13.5 shows 11 supporting activities. Table 13.1 groups these, identifies the fit order (1st, 2nd, 3rd) of the activity, and provides descriptions or processes associated with each activity. Table 13.1 grouping points to the multifunction nature of activities in this sphere. Not only must several internal departments be involved, but also the contracting activity, in particular, must draw in OEM and transportation providers to collaborate on implementation. In Wal-Mart's case, transportation providers can include Wal-Mart's own fleet as well as those of contracted companies.

Table 13.1 Wal-Mart Remix Activities and Processes

#	Activity	Fit Order[a]	Description/Processes
Contracting Functions			
1.	OEM contracting	3rd	Write contracts to coordinate operations. Provide RFID tags at item, pallet, or container level. Establish transportation interface. Purchase high-volume items from OEM suppliers.
2.	Transportation contracting	3rd	Contract for frequency/cost of deliveries. Establish scheduling methods for store delivery that minimizes disruptions.

Table 13.1 (continued)   Wal-Mart Remix Activities and Processes

#	*Activity*	*Fit Order[a]*	*Description/Processes*
Product Selection Functions			
3.	Industrial engineering support	3rd	Minimize total cost. Adjust product eligibility criteria. Perform warehousing, transportation network design.
4.	Fast-product criteria	1st	Provide yardsticks/tests for selecting SKUs for fast-track inclusion.
5.	Product eligibility methodology	2nd	Maintain product list by store. Include assignment of store–SKU combinations to selected high-volume DCs.
Operating Functions			
6.	DC material-handling systems	2nd	Design and equip DCs with racks, conveyors, docks, and equipment to move stock quickly.
7.	DC product preparation	1st	Get agreement on SKU-specific configurations for products to be delivered to stores.
8.	RFID tagging	1st	Define SKU-specific requirements for RFID to speed processing along the supply chain.
9.	Transportation scheduling system	3rd	Coordinate OEM, DC, and store schedules. Optimize to the extent possible.
Control Functions			
10.	Stockout tracking	2nd	Flag candidate SKUs. Test criteria; maintain list of high-volume items.
11.	Store measurements	1st	Design and measure parameters that confirm effectiveness such as store profitability, market share, stockout history, and sales of high-volume SKUs.

Note: OEM = original equipment manufacturer, RFID = radio frequency identification, SKU = stockkeeping unit, DC = distribution center.

[a] 1st-order fit is *simple consistence*, 2nd-order fit is *reinforcing* other activities, and 3rd-order fit is *optimization of effort*.

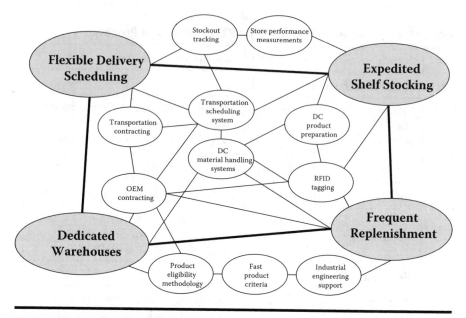

Figure 13.5   Wal-Mart Remix activity system.

The fit column indicates the nature of the fit: 1st order is simple consistency; 2nd order is reinforcing of other activities, and 3rd order is overall optimization of effort. Certainly, both contracting activities (#1 and #2 in Table 13.1) seek to set ground rules for trading-partner coordination. Industrial engineering support (#3) is a service for all the processes. Its most visible impact is felt in determining which SKU–store combinations should be included in the Remix program. The transportation scheduling system (#9) orchestrates the activities of the various parties (DC, store, and transportation provider).

13.4 Activity Systems and Process Definition—Summary

Many supply chain improvement projects fall short of expectations because participants have no roadmap. Such a roadmap will identify the need and set criteria for operating processes. The activity system provides such a roadmap. It improves the chances that the linkages between strategy and operations are strong, with no needed supply chain process omitted from the design.

Endnotes

1. W. Chan Kim and Renée Mauborgne, *Blue Ocean Strategy,* Boston: Harvard Business School Press, 2005.
2. Porter, Michael E., "What is Strategy?" *Harvard Business Review,* (74/6) November–December, 1996. pp. 61–78.

Chapter 14

Retail Supply Chain Management—Skills Required

Management skills are the key to implementing changes to retail supply chains. Effective retail supply chain management (SCM) requires broad skills everywhere from strategy-making to improvement of operating processes. This is counter to the mindset in many organizations. The conventional mindset holds that retail SCM is limited in scope, confined either to procurement or physical distribution. In other words, it has a role in controlling costs but no role in improving strategic position. Company's merchants and store management implement strategy.

The examples in Chapters 12 and 13 illustrate the challenge. For example, IKEA built its current business model over decades and, in so doing, refined its supply chain operations, but companies in today's fast-moving competitive environments do not have that luxury. Competitive forces and the globalization of markets make strategic change a constant necessity.

Defining and building activity systems requires the management capabilities described in this chapter. These broad skills call for both "right brain," or aesthetic, intuitive capabilities, and "left brain," or logical, analytical capabilities. Right-brain skills are brought to bear in merchandise selection, store decoration, advertising, and the sales process. Left-brain skills are needed in the back office—to move the product around, locate stores, stock the shelves, and track money. In developing and implementing retail supply chain strategies, both are needed.

According to *The Wall Street Journal*, the retail industry has been long on the right-brain skills, coming up short on the left-brain side.[1] The article notes that many retail executives have made decisions based on instinct rather than analysis. The advent of computers has brought about significant movement toward analytical management. A solution for companies such as Coach and Limited Brands, Ltd., and others has been to look for those with highly developed analytical skills in business schools.

The trend is echoed by an effort sponsored by the Retail Industry Leaders Association (RILA) to enroll retail employees in its Retail Supply Chain Certification Program. The aim is to increase skills and consistency in management practices along the retail supply chain. Topics studied include statistics, supply chain fundamentals, inventory management, metrics, and process integration.

14.1 Five Tasks for SCM Excellence

Although the need for new skills is recognized, the right- and the left-brain perspectives are often in conflict. There is a need for tools and processes to bring them together, such as those described in this book. The work of implementing effective supply chain change is carried out by way of five management tasks. Table 14.1 defines the five tasks and lists retail supply chain functions involved in each.

No matter where a company is along the supply chain, a strategy to compete is needed whether it be for retailers that sell to consumers, distributors, service providers, original equipment manufacturers (OEMs), or second-tier suppliers. Each of these supply chain players must have access to strategy-making skills to remain competitive. Figure 14.1 shows the relationships between the retail SCM tasks. The format is a phased-project Gantt chart displaying the sequence in which the tasks are performed. Task 1 strategy development begins the process in Phase 1. Deliverables include sphere definitions and activity systems for each sphere as described in Chapters 12 and 13. These also produce the requirements for collaboration for internal alignment and partnerships with trading partners.

Phases 2 and 3 bring internal alignment (Task 2) followed by alignment with trading partners (Task 3). Tasks 4 and 5 address process development or improvements to existing processes. These tasks rely on new information technology (Task 4) and other process development approaches (Task 5). An important goal is to achieve the benefits of the demand-driven supply chain. Tasks 4 and 5 must be tied together to avoid implementing technology for its own sake. Investments in technology must be justified in terms of process changes that result in better customer service or a greater return on investment or both. Once a strategy is in place, the feedback loops shown in Figure 14.1 trigger continuous improvement to upgrade the strategy and the processes.

14.2 Assessing Retail SCM Skills

Before embarking on the design and implementation of a supply chain strategy, a management team should understand its capabilities with regard to

Table 14.1 Five Retail SCM Tasks

	Task	Description	Retail Functions Involved
1.	Designing supply chains for strategic advantage	Competitive success requires supply chain innovation. Supply chain designs must support company strategies for competing	Senior management functions, merchandise management groups, marketing, sales, category managers, senior financial executives
2.	Implementing collaborative relationships	Internal organization form, responsibilities, and measures enable supply chain innovation. The task covers relationships and communication inside the organization needed to implement processes that cross department boundaries	Functional managers from operations, marketing, and sales, direct reports to chief executive, financial management, information systems
3.	Forging supply chain partnerships	Outside partners are needed to be successful. Old paradigms must be discarded. Implementation requires an organized, multicompany project approach	Merchandising, procurement, sourcing, and operations
4.	Managing supply chain information	Opportunities to succeed wildly or fail miserably abound. Information systems must support the supply chain processes that are embedded in activity systems	Process teams from affected departments, information technology, finance staff
5.	Removing cost from the supply chain	Effective change to improve service and reduce cost requires understanding and managing root causes of cost in supply chain processes	

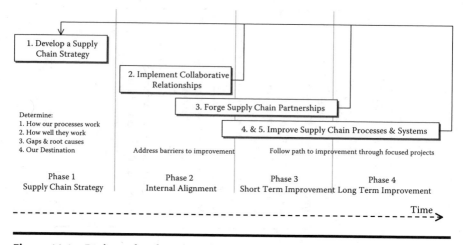

Figure 14.1   Project plan for executing retail SCM tasks.

performing the five SCM tasks. Because retailers stand at the end of the supply chain, it is particularly important that they take a look at not only company abilities but also those of its supply chain partners. The maturity matrix in Table 14.2 describes a tool for this purpose. It shows levels of management capability with respect to the five tasks. The team can readily identify a position on the matrix from the descriptions in each cell.

The assessment using the matrix should be a two-step process. First, it should address the current state of practice in the company. This answers the question whether current supply chain processes support existing strategies. It can be called the "as-is" level of maturity. The assessment may also show that little in the way of SCM practice even exists.

Second, the matrix can also assess company capability. Dimensions of capability include the capabilities of management team members, the willingness to change, the urgency for action, and the presence of resources needed to change. The latter include capital and the time required to make changes. For example, current practice for *Task 1: designing supply chains for strategic advantage* may be Level I: dysfunctional. But a newly hired management team may be capable of Level III or IV practice.

Chapter 13 developed two activity systems—one for IKEA and the other for the Wal-Mart Remix program. Table 14.3 illustrates the importance of having a "full quiver" of capabilities in implementing a new, or refining an existing, activity system. The table lists some of the elements of the IKEA and Remix activity systems and their requirements for retail SCM skills. The table also describes barriers to success that might be encountered during implementation. Skill at the retail SCM task will help navigate the barriers.

Table 14.2 Levels of Retail SCM Capability

Task	Name	I. Dysfunctional	II. Infrastructure	III. Cost reduction	IV. Collaboration	V. Strategic Contribution
				Stages of Retail SCM Capability		
1.	Designing supply chains for strategic advantage	No strategy exists around which to create supply chain designs	Some supply chain awareness. Managers view the company as standalone	Supply chain processes viewed as a nonstrategic, one-size-fits-all supply chain	Joint initiatives are pursued on a limited basis with trading partners	Activity systems are implemented for strategic advantage
2.	Implementing collaborative relationships	Internal department measures, goals, and objectives conflict with supply chain excellence	Organization is functionally focused. Initiatives are departmental	Internal cross-functional initiatives that focus on cost reduction are chartered	Supply chain has moved into a single function that manages multicompany relationships	The organization has established multicompany infrastructure for important chains
3.	Forging supply chain partnerships	Relationships with suppliers and customers are arm's length at best, antagonistic at worst	Collaboration up and down the supply chain is limited to transaction data	Efforts are limited to supplier initiatives focused on cost reduction, not revenue increases	Partners collaborate, but roles are static. Partners pursue strategies based on activity systems	Trading partners alter their value contributions through transfers of responsibility

Table 14.2 (continued)   Levels of Retail SCM Capability

Task	Name	I. Dysfunctional	II. Infrastructure	III. Cost reduction	IV. Collaboration	V. Strategic Contribution
				Stages of Retail SCM Capability		
4.	Managing supply chain information	Basic information needed for decision making is missing, not timely, or inaccurate	Technology improvements focus on individual departments and maintenance	Systems efforts support cost reduction within the organization. Probably not process justified	Two-way information exchange supports transactions and mutual decision making	Appropriate level of technology is integrated into supply chain activity systems and processes
5.	Removing cost from the supply chain	Cost reduction and process improvement is a "hit-and-miss" affair. Efforts often hurt more than they help	Reductions are internal and tracked by department budgets. Customer service not considered	Cost reduction efforts cross departments but are limited to internal efforts	Cost reduction is limited to logistics, purchasing, and other operating costs at the multicompany level	Cost reduction across the supply chain is the target. Benefits are shared among partners

Table 14.3   Implementing Case Study Activity Systems—Retail SCM Skills Required

	Retail SCM Management Tasks
1.	Designing supply chains for strategic advantage
2.	Implementing collaborative relationships
3.	Forging supply chain partnerships
4.	Managing supply chain information
5.	Removing cost from the supply chain

Activities Requiring Retail SCM Skills	1	2	3	4	5	Likely Barriers
IKEA Activity System						
IKEA design focused on cost of manufacturing	•	•	•		•	Trade-offs between design and cost. Need to cooperate with suppliers
Sourcing from long-term suppliers	•		•			Developing and maintaining lasting relationships. Building trust
On-site inventory					•	Forecasting correct amounts. Providing timely replenishment
Knockdown packaging			•		•	Product configuration and packaging design
Suburban locations/ample parking		•				Agreement on attractive sites
Limited staffing					•	Developing substitutes for staff while providing adequate service
Wal-Mart Remix Activity System						
Industrial engineering support	•			•	•	Finding skilled people to execute strategy who understand operations
Product eligibility methodology		•			•	Agreeing to criteria/items selected for high-volume distribution process
OEM contracting			•		•	Coordinating deliveries and format with suppliers

Table 14.3 (continued)   Implementing Case Study Activity Systems—Retail SCM Skills Required

Activities Requiring Retail SCM Skills	1	2	3	4	5	Likely Barriers
Transportation contracting			•		•	Coordinating operations and making trade-offs with transporters
Transportation scheduling system				•	•	Developing and maintaining system. Contingency planning
DC material handling system				•	•	Equipment decisions. Technical design. Use of technology
RFID tagging				•	•	Cost to suppliers. Benefit identification. How deployed– item, pallet, etc
Stockout tracking				•		Definitions. Accuracy of information
Store performance measurements		•		•	•	Store/management agreement. Data collection and presentation

Retail enterprise planners should weigh their strategic plans by listing the barriers to implementation. This could also lead to an introspective review of enterprise talents. Hiring people with new skills or commissioning consultants can fill any gaps. However, a strategy that rests on unfamiliar technologies, for example, might better be changed.

14.3 Summary—SCM Skills

This chapter is meant to link supply chain design with the need for skills to implement the design. Too often, supply chain functions are relegated to narrow functions—procurement, merchandising, and distribution come to mind. But the retail SCM discipline is broader than that exemplified by this practice. The real success stories in retail SCM can be traced to unique hard-to-copy processes that are well designed and executed. This is no simple task in the competitive retail market place; new skills are needed.

Endnotes

1. Clark, "Monica, More Retailers Shop Business Schools for Talent," *The Wall Street Journal*, September 18, 2006, p. B4.

RETAIL SUPPLY CHAIN PROCESS IMPROVEMENT

Part 4 describes initiatives to improve supply chain processes. Topics range from right-brain organization to left-brain application of new technology for tracking products along the chain.

#	Name
15.	Organizing to Improve Supply Chain Performance
16.	Collaboration with Supply Chain Partners
17.	The Demand-Driven Supply Chain
18.	Product Tracking Along Retail Supply Chains

The West Marine case in Chapter 15 describes one retailer's efforts at collaborating with its trading partners. The process relied on CPFR, an industry blueprint for collaboration. The chapter describes CPFR and other models for collaboration.

Chapter 16 illustrates trends toward "fewer but better" trading partners along the chain. One step in this direction is classifying partnership types—whether the combination takes the form of an informal agreement or an outright merger. Core competencies are another topic because the decision to partner requires some definition what competencies really need to be protected to survive.

One of the most important topics in retail is the demand-driven supply chain, often referred to as "pull." Chapter 17 presents a process for converting a supply chain to demand-driven decision making. This means actual demand is the basis for replenishment decisions, not forecasts.

Technology is transforming retail supply chains. An important component is technology such as advanced bar codes and RFID to track product movements. This is the subject of Chapter 18.

Chapter 15

Organizing to Improve Retail Supply Chain Performance

Chapter 14 described the implications of activity system design for acquiring management skills to improve competitive position. The current chapter describes the issues faced in aligning those skills to design and implement needed changes in a retailer's supply chain. Many of the activities described in this chapter will occur in phase 2 (internal alignment) of our project management timeline shown in Figure 14.1. These activities call for skills in task 2 of our SCM skill set (implement collaborative relationships.) The collaborative relationships discussed here are those inside the organization—particularly across departments. Chapter 16 describes issues related to extending the strategy *across* company boundaries to trading partners. Trading partners in the retail supply chain include retailers themselves, distributors, transportation and other service companies, product manufacturers, or original equipment manufacturers (OEMs), and the OEMs' second-tier manufacturing suppliers.

Figure 15.1 is a framework for designing a supply chain strategy as part of phase 1 (develop a supply chain strategy) of Figure 14.1. The model starts with the *as-is* in the lower left-hand corner. Once the as-is documentation is complete, an improvement team can produce an evaluation of the as-is and develop a vision for the future, the *to-be* destination. *Barriers* are inevitable along the *pathway* to the destination. Pathway projects, in circles, are of two types—internal (gray circles)

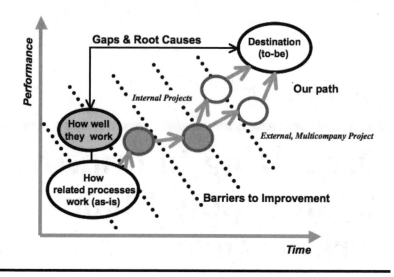

Figure 15.1   Model for implementing supply chain change.

and external (white circles). Internal projects are those the company undertakes independently; the external projects are those requiring the cooperation of trading partners. Performing such an analysis is an important step in achieving internal alignment for implementing change.

Some reengineering practitioners may reject the idea of working from the as-is. This philosophy rejects the as-is-existing situation in favor of a "start-from-scratch" approach. The authors and others argue for documenting the as-is for many reasons. One article, in describing tools for lean manufacturing, states the case well.[1]

- You will understand not only "what" but also "why"—the root causes—processes need improving. Documenting only the results of the current situation does not provide these insights.
- Mapping processes collectively leads to shared insights.
- Direct observation is a valuable skill that is embellished by the process.
- The current state is a "gold mine" in terms of insights about past experiments and failures.
- You identify and gain understanding of mistakes you are currently making.
- You must be doing something right, or you wouldn't be in business. You'll want to retain process features that are working.
- You need an understanding of the existing situation to create the necessary "tension" to move the change process forward.

This list should be kept in mind if there is a temptation to shortcut the processes recommended in Figure 15.1 by passing the as-is step.

		1975	1980	1985	1990	1995	2000	2005	
					Case Study Period 1996 -2002				
No. Stores*		1	3	13	19	72	233	404	
Sales ($millions)*					$75	$224	$508	$692	
*Approximate figures									
Acquisitions/mergers:			◆ 1978 West Products -- mail order business						
				◆ 1983 Newport Supply - 5 stores					
					◆ 1986 Cal Marine Chain - 3 stores				
							◆ 1996 E&B Marine -- 150 stores		
						2003 BoatU.S. -- 62 stores		◆	

Figure 15.2   West Marine history.

15.1 West Marine Case

This chapter relies on a case study of retailer West Marine to illustrate approaches to working with trading partners and achieving internal alignments.[2] This is one of the companies that illustrates the range of retailer types in Chapter 3. The use of the case here is not intended to promote the West Marine solution for every retailer. Even though the case describes a retailer's perspective, it will help manufacturers, distributors, and third-party service providers understand issues faced by their retail customers. Other retailers are likely to take steps similar to those adopted by West Marine. Also, many retailers, including West Marine, are in a strong position with regard to their suppliers and can effectively dictate the direction suppliers must take if they want to retain the retailer's business.

Business schools work with companies in developing case studies for teaching purposes. Lyn Denend authored the West Marine case, published in April 2005, under the supervision of Dr. Hau Lee of the Stanford Business School. Dr. Lee is an authority on supply chain management. The case illustrates challenges in a marine supply retail business and describes one retailer's path toward solving these problems. Through Larry Smith, Senior Vice President, Planning and Replenishment, West Marine has also been active in the VICS CPFR (Collaborative Planning, Forecasting, and Replenishment) Committee, which sponsors the CPFR®[3] initiative. West Marine implemented CPFR as part of its solution. Smith also updated the West Marine story in a related article, which was also a source for this chapter.[4]

Figure 15.2 is a West Marine timeline annotated with data available from the case and the company. West Marine was founded in 1968 with a narrow product line and first-year sales by mail order of $32,000; it went public with sales of $123 million in 1993. The company has marketed its products through its stores, via the Internet and catalogs, and through wholesale channels. According to the study, West Marine considered itself a "specialty retailer" and benchmarked itself against companies such as Brookstone and Cost Plus.

The company grew steadily until it acquired a rival, E&B Marine, in 1996—the starting date for our case period (1996—2002) as shown on the timeline. Just prior to the acquisition, West Marine had about $224 million in sales and about 50,000 products. Acquiring E&B, a financially troubled retailer with 63 stores, opened a new market in the powerboat segment. West Marine, with 161 stores, was better known in the sailboat segment.

West Marine runs three types of stores: *standard*, or traditional, stores (8000 sq. ft., 8000–10,000 SKUs [stock keeping units], about $1.5 million in annual sales), *express* stores (2800 sq. ft., 2500 SKUs, $600,000–$800,000), and *megastores* (24,000–30,000 sq. ft., 30,000 SKUs, $10–$15 million). West Marine relies on its own distribution network to stock its stores. Its 250,000-sq.-ft. western distribution center is in Hollister, California, and was opened in 1996. The 472,000-sq.-ft. Rock Hill, South Carolina, facility was opened in 1998. Today, most merchandise flows through distribution centres (DCs), although the company seeks to increase direct-to-store shipments from its suppliers.

After the 1996 merger, the company stumbled badly, and a turnaround began in 1998 with the hiring of a new CEO, who pursued a strategy that relied heavily on changes to the supply chain. The sections that follow organize data from the case, company reports, and an interview with vice president Larry Smith into tables illustrating the steps in the Figure 15.1 model for implementing change.

15.1.1 West Marine As-Is

Table 15.1 describes the supply chain situation that, although not readily apparent at the time of the merger, contributed to West Marine's troubles. These factors were the result of many forces. Industry consolidation, with West Marine fast becoming the leading player, was a symptom of a mature or even declining market. The E&B powerboat business brought new products, suppliers, and customer buying behaviors into the West Marine environment. In particular, the powerboat customer was more price sensitive than the sailing customer. Also, West Marine practices gave customers what they wanted when and where they wanted it, with little sensitivity to the costs of that service. Management mindset reinforced this attitude, and lack of supply chain awareness dulled management senses to the coming crisis.

The last six items (#7 to 12) on the as-is list are symptomatic of operations on the point of breakdown. Many companies in retail supply chains take operations for granted. But when they break for any reason, the penalties are serious. West Marine wanted top-level service and was willing to pay the price in terms of low inventory turnover. So, it was particularly painful when stock availability suffered and lost sales penalties occurred in spite of high inventories. The growth before the E&B merger had been small enough to be manageable. The size of the E&B operation was more than West Marine could absorb.

In many new companies, the management team comes out of the industry. In the West Marine case, the company served a recreation industry in which many on the management team were active boating enthusiasts and drew their experience from their market space. However, they lacked broader skills. At a larger size, such enthusiasm is not sufficient to efficiently manage the myriad transactions necessary to serve customers efficiently. The introduction to Chapter 14 describes recent efforts to build managerial skills in retail companies.

15.1.2 Evaluation of the As-Is

The evaluation process for the as-is situation of a retailer should use data analysis, benchmarking comparisons, and team sessions to draw conclusions about the current situation. Such conclusions should call attention to the needs for change that should be addressed in designing the to-be destination. One way to format this evaluation is around processes, organization, and systems as shown in Table 15.2. Note that the evaluation points to problems in each of the three areas, and some evaluations could apply to more than one category. For example, inbound processing (#4) could be interpreted as a process problem as shown or as an organization problem with a gap in internal communications. It would be an organization problem to the extent that performance measures for purchasing encourage overbuying. It is a process problem if the DCs aren't prepared to receive the merchandise.

Some assessments are broad, such as leadership (#5). The evaluation calls for a wide-ranging change in management team skills. On the other hand, internal collaboration (#6) is more specific. It calls for the need for better forecasting methods. In addition, the implication is that, when the forecasts could be improved, they should be shared with the suppliers who need to act on them (#8). Such forecast sharing could improve merchandise availability and lower the supplier's cost by reducing "surprises." The systems group notes the general lack of ability, not of software, to make it work properly (#9 and 10). This gap includes data accuracy and technical capabilities.

15.1.3 Destination (To-Be)

The West Marine *strategic framework*, or "to-be," included three important components: a vision, strategic performance indicators, and critical success factors. Chief features of the to-be, listed in Table 15.3, provide high-level direction toward improvement. These begin (#1, #2, and #3) with goals setting and establishing accountability for supply chain results. These three reflect a need to restrain West Marine growth to stem the effect of lost sales that had cut profits from $15 million to $1 million.

The direction relied on processes from the CPFR® initiative, described later in this chapter. Smith of West Marine had become familiar with CPFR while at Kmart, and turned to the model to help West Marine. At the time of the case, CPFR encompassed nine model processes shown in Table 15.4. These processes guided CPFR users in redesigning their operations. Today's CPFR model, summarized in Figure 15.4, is a circular process that depicts a continuum of processes

Table 15.1   West Marine As-Is

	Supply Chain Features	As-Is Situation Post Merger (1996)
1.	Industry trends	Its growth had made West Marine an industry leader. Consolidation was ongoing in the industry, which was also shrinking as boaters left the sport. Among other factors, supply chain problems (cost and availability of supplies) contributed to the decline in boaters.
2.	Customer linkages	The most profitable customers used multiple channels (store, Internet, catalog) to purchase West Marine products.
3.	Service philosophy	West Marine adhered to a high customer service philosophy requiring higher inventories than other retailers.
4.	Seasonality	Large seasonal swings in business levels and product mix were common. West Marine used tailored mailings for warm and cold climates and each customer segment.
5.	Management mindset	At the time of the E&B acquisition, West Marine managers thought of themselves as "boaters first and businessmen second." The consequence was "chaos" and poor financial performance.
6.	Supply chain awareness	There were many supply chain problems, but few managers were aware of the impact of their operating practices on the business. This created a reactive fire-fighting environment. The E&B acquisition aggravated the situation when the number of suppliers increased from 1000 to 1400.
7.	Supplier base	The supplier base was fragmented. Most suppliers were not sophisticated or well capitalized. For example, there were often multiple deliveries for one order, doubling or tripling the handling involved.
8.	Merger impact	The 1996 merger with E&B Marine went smoothly financially. However, infrastructure implementation was rocky. Systems and processes were inadequate to keep all stores stocked. The results were "disastrous" with an 8 percent sales drop in the first year after the acquisition.

Table 15.1 (continued)   West Marine As-Is

	Supply Chain Features	As-Is Situation Post Merger (1996)
9.	Data infrastructure	After the E&B acquisition, data integrity was suspect. Back-end databases were not interfaced between the companies. There was no way to gain an accurate end-to-end understanding of supply chain performance.
10.	Distribution center changes	At about the same time as the acquisition, West Marine shifted from a 70,000-sq.-ft. distribution center (DC) to the nearby, automated 500,000-sq.-ft. facility at Rock Hill to serve its Eastern customers. Employees didn't have the skills to operate the technically advanced facility.
11.	Staff turnover	Turnover at Rock Hill increased to where 1200 people were hired to fill 280 peak-season positions.
12.	Supply chain bottlenecks	Sales levels were increasing at the time of the acquisition. Distribution bottlenecks occurred as incoming and outgoing volumes overwhelmed employees at the Rock Hill DC. Peak season out-of-stocks reached 25 percent.

Table 15.2   West Marine Evaluation

	Supply Chain Success Factor	As-Is Assessments and Conclusions
Processes		
1.	Supply chain processes	The company had outgrown its infrastructure. No formal processes existed. New supply chain processes were needed.
2.	Operations planning	The merger was botched from a customer-service viewpoint. West Marine overlooked the advantages of preserving the E&B brand by changing the storefronts.
3.	Supply base	The supply chain was "complex, difficult, and broken" and needed fixing. There were too many vendors for a company with seasonal influx of inventory. Some boating industry vendors in larger companies were "second-class" citizens due to the industry's lower priority.

Table 15.2 (continued)   West Marine Evaluation

	Supply Chain Success Factor	*As-Is Assessments and Conclusions*
4.	Inbound processing	Merchandising did not consider supply chain issues in deal-buys with suppliers. This caused unexpected surprises at DCs and disrupted in-process replenishment activities.
Organization		
5.	Leadership	A need existed for more business experience on the management team. Going to the next level—from $500 million to $1 billion in sales—required new skills.
6.	Internal collaboration	Supply chain planning and replenishment were disconnected in the merchandising team. Forecasts were considered inaccurate and generally useless.
7.	Cost consciousness	West Marine needed to address culture. Some would "take care of the customer" at any cost. No rules/guidelines existed for day-to-day decision making to implement the principle.
8.	Supplier communications	There was substandard communication and collaboration with suppliers. Relationships were conducted on a purchase-order-to-purchase-order basis. For example, a product would be added to West Marine's assortment, but no quantity forecasts were given to the supplier, causing shortages, including those associated with promotions.
Systems		
9.	Information systems	Although information systems were modern by most standards, they were not being utilized properly, nor could they be reliable without accurate data.
10.	Technical capabilities	West Marine had a "Ferrari" of SCM software but no one who could drive it. Software complexity was beyond organizational capabilities.

Table 15.3　West Marine Destination (To-Be)

	Category	To-Be Features
1.	Supply chain objectives	Goals, defined by "strategic performance indicators," were set for return on equity (ROE), cash flow, comparative year-to-year sales, earnings, service levels, market share, customer satisfaction, and employee satisfaction.
2.	Critical success factors (CSF)	CSF emphasized efficient execution, best of class SCM, right product assortments at the right place at the right time, strong customer relationship culture to maximize sales and profits, effective marketing strategy, and motivated professional associates.
3.	Responsibilities	Individual leaders defined tactics for their functions to deliver the results. Formal reports tracked progress toward goals.
4.	Phased growth	To avert crisis, West Marine halted store expansion in order to stabilize the supply chain.
5.	Visibility	To get relief from firefighting, the company focused on achieving end-to-end visibility and increased collaboration between inside functions and with suppliers.
6.	Shared forecast role	West Marine adopted CPFR processes to align internally and with suppliers. The heart of CPFR was the shared forecast. Features included exception management, performance measures, monetized risk, and incentives to collaborate.
7.	Supply chain synchronization	West Marine synchronized its purchasing cycle with the manufacturers' production cycles. This enabled "make-to-demand" or demand-driven decision making. It also reduced the need for manufacturer finished goods inventories.

that build on each other. Process categories include strategy and planning, demand and supply management, execution, and analysis. For additional information, see http://www.vics.org/committees/cpfr/.

One emphasis during this time at West Marine was on improving forecasts. This included defining responsibility for the forecasts, improving their accuracy

Table 15.4   CPFR Processes (at time of case)

Planning	Develop front-end agreements
	Create joint business plan
Forecasting	Create sales forecast
	Identify exceptions for sales forecast
	Resolve/collaborate on exception items
	Create order forecast
	Identify exceptions for order forecast
	Resolve/collaborate on exception items
Replenishment	Generate orders

and relevance, and making the commitment to act upon them. An early West Marine decision was to assume sole and independent responsibility for forecasts and replenishment at the retail level rather than sharing that responsibility with suppliers. In CPFR terms, this is referred to as conventional order management. Other options include sharing the responsibility for order planning/forecasting and order generation with suppliers. The conventional choice was based on the belief that the buyer was best suited to generate and own the forecast.[5]

15.1.4 Barriers to Success

Realism about barriers and addressing them improves the chances of success. *Barriers* are defined in this book as environmental factors. A *constraint* is a limitation on actions that can be taken. An example of a constraint could be a decision to stay in a location because of a long-term lease or a limit on money available to implement a plan. For example, one constraint enacted by West Marine management was that internal transfers of personnel should satisfy new organization roles, not headcount increases.

As West Marine progressed, it encountered barriers. Table 15.5 lists several. The first three are internal to the firm and are likely to exist in any organization. They are defensiveness, cross-department cooperation, and internal opposition. West Marine was challenged to restore its financial vitality, and the pressures that arose caused the team to collaborate less when the need existed to collaborate more. This could have been the result of increased requirements for accountability and the accompanying performance measures that were implemented.

Success also depended on the cooperation of four departments that needed to cooperate—merchandising, planning and replenishment, distribution, and

Table 15.5   Barriers to Success

	Barrier Type	Barrier Description
1.	Defensiveness	As West Marine struggled, improvement teams were less inclined to share issues, challenges, and needs across organizational boundaries
2.	Cross-department cooperation	The changes required four executives to collaborate to make improvements, including merchandising, planning and replenishment, distribution, and information systems
3.	Internal opposition	A CPFR pilot met with mixed enthusiasm internally. Results won many over, but others chafed at the rules and structure
4.	Supplier reluctance	West Marine had to continuously sell CPFR to suppliers. Many suppliers didn't believe the benefits were worth the price. Some vendors argued over performance metric relevancy and accuracy

information systems. Coordination was an obstacle to success. Because applying CPFR processes changed the way people had to work, "push back" occurred in the early stages. However, successes begat enthusiasm among those who could see the results.

The last barrier listed (#4) was supplier reluctance to collaborate with West Marine. The CPFR processes included regular communications and updates between entities. Also, information technology solutions encouraged suppliers to make their systems compatible with the West Marine forecast formats. As with any measurements, those being measured disputed the relevancy and accuracy of the metrics, resulting in additional communications challenges.

15.1.5 Pathway to Change

Table 15.6 details important components of the West Marine solution to the situation generated by the E&B merger. Larry Smith summarized the collective impact of the changes.

- The West Marine supply chain was converted from supplier-driven push to demand-driven pull.
- Forecast accuracy increased to 85 percent; on-time shipments to 80 percent.
- CPFR has extended to 200 suppliers and 20,000 items, representing 90 percent of the procurement spend.

Table 15.6 Pathway

	Project Type	Implementation Subprojects
Internally Focused Changes		
1.	Departmental alignment	The CEO addressed multidepartment processes to plan the transition and demanded joint accountability. He did not tolerate silo mentalities.
2.	Culture change	West Marine brought in an expert in culture change who redefined roles and refocused employees on their jobs.
3.	Communication	The company sought to open lines of communication with cross-functional meetings and project teams. It encouraged mutual responsibility among departments for cross-functional metrics.
4.	Supply chain role	West Marine assumed responsibility for the forecasting process, including order planning and order generating. It also committed to buy any order they forecasted seeking to eliminate bullwhips along the supply chain. The initiative required one scalable systems platform, not multiple incompatible ones.
5.	Technology choices	West Marine adopted a suite of applications from JDA Software Group Ltd.—Merchandise Management System, POS, and Warehouse Management System.
6.	Integration	The company started to codevelop a multi-echelon solution with JDA that integrated store and warehouse replenishment. This would free time to work with suppliers rather than reconciling data. The company ended up developing a custom solution. It claims it is one of the first in the retail industry.
7.	Forecast methodology	West Marine forecast components included base annual forecasts, seasonal selling curves (profiles), ranking or service level for items by importance, and demand from DCs for items that West Marine did not stock. These changes enabled accurate 52-week forecasts of supplier orders with little manual intervention. Other factors were seasonal geographic profiles, product rank, and scheduled promotions. The forecasts were updated every 24 hours as timeliness was a key to accuracy.

Table 15.6 (continued) Pathway

	Project Type	Implementation Subprojects
8.	Data integrity and consistency	Data cleanup effort included shipping quantities, case pack quantities, and other data needed for reducing errors. The effort matched store quantities with DC quantities and set rules on authorizing changes.
9.	Merchandising, planning, and replenishment	Organization changes included reorganization and definition of roles of between merchandising and planning and replenishment. The company deployed a category management approach for 24 distinct product clusters. There is a category manager (CM) and assistant category manager for each. A collocated merchandise planner and a replenishment analyst were added to each team. CMs decided what to sell in which channels and negotiated vendor agreements. Merchandise planners acted as "supply chain captains" cutting POs, monitoring shipments and fill rates, and coordinating from the supplier to the DC. The replenishment analyst worked to get the merchandise from the DC to the store—monitoring forecasts, insuring stores-received products, and managing special requests.
10.	Store operations	Teams worked with assortment planning (part of the planning and replenishment department), visual merchandising, and marketing. Assortment planning assured that each store had the right mix. Visual Merchandising used planograms to locate each store's assortment and provide consistency between stores.
11.	DC labor	West Marine developed work standards in the warehouse to improve labor productivity.
12.	Space and shipping efficiencies	The warehouses used technology to document the dimensions and weight to manage storage space in the warehouse. This also enabled filling cartons to fully utilize shipping space through standard packaging.

Table 15.6 (continued)   Pathway

	Project Type	Implementation Subprojects
Externally Focused Changes		
13.	EDI (electronic data interchange)	West Marine implemented EDI to standardize electronic transfer of information. EDI coverage included purchase orders, invoices, and shipment notifications. Use of EDI by suppliers was requested, not demanded. The EDI increased visibility of inbound inventory liability and suppliers' performance.
14.	CPFR pilot test	The company initiated CPFR pilot following structural, process, and information system changes, picking 12 suppliers. West Marine spelled out goals and expected performance levels and required no investments by the vendors. Each had to designate someone in the organization to deal with supply chain captains.
15.	Supply base deployment	The deployment consisted of weekly forecast sharing. It also required vendors to provide weekly performance updates and participate in monthly status meetings with team and vendor representative.
16.	Commitment to orders	West Marine guaranteed no hassle to suppliers and promised to commit to purchase 100 percent of forecast orders. West Marine became responsible for any mistakes.
17.	Inbound transportation	West Marine picked up shipments from vendors to decrease freight costs and control the flow of material into the DCs.

■ West Marine was able to effectively incorporate another purchase—of rival BoatU.S.—in 2003. The BoatU.S. distribution center was integrated in 30 days, and in-store systems in 60 days.

Internal collaboration, the subject of this chapter, was the key to West Marine's successful recovery. Figure 15.3 displays departmental accountabilities that resulted from the implementation (#9 in Table 15.6). The figure is an example of a tool for presenting as-is and to-be organization responsibilities. Across the top are the supply chain processes West Marine relies on. Down the left are the positions that participate in each process. One enhancement is, when applicable, to show how, not just

Positions/Entities	Department	Concept				Plan						Action					
		Source Product	Negotiate Vendor Agreement	Determine Pricing & Margin	Determine Promotability	Define Assortment	Formalize Pricing	Incorporate into Planograms	Create Initial Forecast	Prepare for Rollout	Plan Specific Promotions	Lead Forecasts	Share Forecast with Vendor	Purchase Initial Fill	Implement Product Roll-Outs	Execute Collaborative Processes	Execute Scheduled Promotions
Category Management	Merch	●	●	●	●	●	●	●	●	●	●					●	●
Assortment Planning	P&R					●		●				●					
Merchandise Planning	P&R								●		●		●	●		●	●
Replenishment Analysis	P&R									●		●		●			●
Marketing	Mrktg										●						●
Visual Merchandising	Merch							●									
Stores																●	●
Vendors			●		●	●			●	●							

Merch	Merchandising	
P&R	Planning & Replenishment	
Mrktg	Marketing	

Figure 15.3 Functional responsibilities (to-be).

whether, the position participates in the process. Common modes of participation include *accountable* (has decision-making authority), *responsible* (completes certain processes), *consulted* (provides input), and *informed* (receives progress reports).

Chapter 17 describes the migration from the forecast-driven to the demand-driven supply chain. In the demand-driven supply chain, decisions are based on actual end-user demand rather than forecasts. West Marine claims to have displaced its push methods with pull. But it still relies on what it calls "forecasts." There is no inconsistency here for the following reasons:

- West Marine updates its forecasts daily (#7). So, what it calls forecasts are in reality tracking actual demand.
- West Marine has synchronized its ordering and promotions in collaboration with its suppliers, recognizing that each supplier has a different lead time depending on its products.
- West Marine has also created multi-echelon systems (#6) so that there are no disconnects between transferring the data on customer purchases and how replacement merchandise is planned by stores and DCs.

15.2 Continuous Improvement Cycles

Once a strategy is in place, such as the one West Marine developed in a period of distress, a company needs to continuously improve its processes. This process is often presented as a continuous cycle. The total quality, or TQM, approach calls for the Shewhart, or Deming, cycle: Plan-Do-Check-Act (PDCA). Six Sigma adds a step to reach DMAIC: Define, Measure, Analyze, Improve, Control. CPFR, as mentioned earlier, has adopted a more complex cycle that also depicts a continuous process for improvement. In fact, West Marine used that approach in moving beyond its short-term turnaround objectives described earlier in the case study.

Although continuous improvement cycles are deceptively simple, they are often hard to maintain. This is not true in "crisis" situations similar to that faced by West Marine where adversity produced urgency. However, continuous improvement is probably the best insurance against falling into a situation that requires crisis management. Of these methods, only CPFR focuses on multicompany efforts. However, PDCA and DMAIC can be applied at the multicompany level.

15.2.1 PDCA in a Retail Supply Chain

The *Plan* step requires an overall strategy for the organization along with a list of priorities for process improvements. In addition to supply chain considerations, this could include a vision for future processes, financial objectives, and product development plans. The plan can identify ways a reconstituted supply chain should support the firm's retail strategy. A plan might also divide the supply chain into processes. Examples include order fulfillment, payments, inbound material, physical distribution, production control, and new product introduction. The planning often includes a definition of the new method that is to be tried. The activity system tool described in Chapter 13 can fill this role.

The *Do* step includes further design of the proposed change in organization and its implementation. It tests a wider range of solutions in pilot implementations. The *Do* step should also implement the organizational structure and measurements. It also implements facility and information technology modifications to support the redesigned processes.

In the *Check* step, a management team might change the solution based on objectives for improvement. This is done in an appropriate amount of time, depending on the changes being made. *Act* evaluates the change and confirms that it is to be retained or it is to be discarded. *Act* also extends proven solutions as appropriate, thereby restarting the *Plan* step.

15.2.2 DMAIC

DMAIC is also a cyclical process like PDCA. *Define* encompasses retail customer definition, critical issues, and processes to be covered. *Measure* collects data relevant

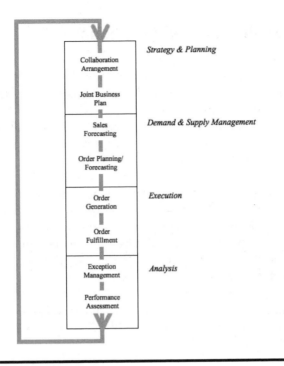

Figure 15.4   Current CPFR model.

to the processes from available sources. This includes information from external and internal customers of the processes. Because processes are there to benefit customers, this information should point to areas for improvement.

Analyze dissects the data and often creates what are called process or value stream maps. Their purpose is to understand reasons for the shortfalls as seen by customers. *Improve* means implementing solutions, and is a creative process. *Control* means locking in the changes. This includes implementing supporting systems and facilities. It also requires monitoring to avoid backsliding.

15.2.3 CPFR Model

The updated CPFR model as published by VICS is complex. Figure 15.4 is a simplified version. The CPFR model also displays the processes as a cycle that is continuously upgraded. Within it are eight core supply chain processes that are jointly executed between retailers and the manufacturers that supply them. Figure 15.4 shows the eight processes in four groups, reflecting different phases of a continuous improvement process. An examination of the CPFR model correlates strongly with the PDCA and DMAIC processes. However, the principal difference is that CPFR processes require an ongoing collaboration between trading partners: retailers, distributors, suppliers and, ideally, raw material producers.

15.3 S&OP Process and Functional Roles

One of the barriers West Marine had to overcome was the need for internal departments to collaborate through information exchange and cross-department process design. Perhaps this is because the goals and measures of the departments were different. Operations departments seek from sales or, in a retail setting, the merchandising function, "iron clad" forecasts around which to build production and purchasing schedules. However, in many industries, accurate forecasts are hard to come by. In other words, the forecast is either wrong or, in the rare incidents when it is correct, it was just plain lucky. This was the as-is situation at West Marine and led to calls for a sales and operations planning process, also called S&OP. As the name implies, S&OP calls for collaboration between the sales and operations functions and is increasingly common in manufacturing companies.

Defining S&OP is difficult because it has different meanings in different companies and industries. The APICS dictionary, an authority on related terminology, defines S&OP as the following:

> A planning process with a 2-5 year horizon that develops tactical plans to support the organization's business plan. The objective is to balance supply and demand.[6]

According to APICS, the input is a 5 to 10-year business plan; the output is a 12 to 18-month master production schedule. The product of the S&OP process produces "tactical plans to balance supply and demand." S&OP is not necessarily conducted with trading partners. However, corresponding CPFR processes certainly are.

Benefits of the S&OP process include a common set of numbers and assumptions, added business visibility for both departments, and team building. The process of getting the merchandising and operations departments together is complicated. In a large organization, there may be a "many-to-many" relationship between merchandising organization and the functions that serve them. This means there are a lot of products and entities contributing to forecasts. To address this problem, West Marine collocated its merchandising and replenishment functions into category teams. It also orchestrated a disciplined schedule of meetings with other functions and suppliers.

Table 15.7 lists topics for the S&OP dialog. Each company will differ in terms of the forum for the dialog. Simpler organizations where the functions are colocated have an easier job than the global organization with the many-to-many relationship between functions.

The table contains two categories for the S&OP agenda: general requirements and supply chain requirements. The former apply to all products, whereas the latter apply to individual products or product categories. A general requirement deals with

Table 15.7 S&OP Functional Contributions

	Merchandising/Sales Contributions	Operations Contributions
General Requirements	Market trends Sales plan by product category Customer segments and corresponding needs Pricing, profit and cost objectives Competitive response times New product plans and requirements Metrics for customer service Metrics for supply chain performance	Production locations and third-party sources Capacity constraints and plans for addressing them Inventory policies Supply chain problems (raw materials, manufacturing, distribution) Methods for information exchange Plans to ensure data integrity Metrics for supply chain performance
Supply chain Requirements	Desired paths to end-users Seasonal patterns Promotions Price increases Direct shipment to customers Favored configurations (size, dosages, packaging) Plans for adding/dropping SKUs, new products	Cost reductions leading to better margins and lower prices Past consumption, trends, forecasts Replenishment policy Supplier lead times Direct shipment selections Stocking strategy by echelon Resource requirement plans New product supply chain setup

Note: S&OP = sales and operations planning, SKM = stockkeeping unit.

responsibility for supply chain performance metrics. This can be a "hot potato." If operations stocks to a merchandising forecast, can it be responsible if inventory is too high? Is anyone going to call a high-producing salesperson on the carpet for a faulty forecast? This is doubtful. Is an accurate forecast even possible? Sometimes they are, and sometimes they are not. Can supply chain design immunize against the consequences of poor forecasts? Tools for the demand-driven supply chain described in Chapter 17 will help. Our case in this chapter showed how West Marine made its supply chain more demand-driven through a variety of measures.

15.5 Organizing to Improve Performance—Summary

This chapter has focused on achieving internal alignment to execute a supply chain strategy. The West Marine case describes how a company team might document the problems and opportunities and prepare a plan for implementation. Retailers and their manufacturing suppliers are mutually dependent. So, their support must be forthcoming. Chapter 16 returns to the West Marine case to further discuss issues related to this kind of collaboration.

Endnotes

1. Pawley, Dennis and Flinchbaugh, Jamie, The current state: progress starts here, *Manufacturing Engineering*, October 2006, pp. 71–81.
2. Denend, Lyn, West Marine: Driving Growth through Shipshape Supply Chain management, Stanford Graduate School of Business Case Study GS-34, 2005.
3. CPFR (Collaborative Planning, Forecasting, and Replenishment) is the registered trademark of the Voluntary Interindustry Commerce Solutions Association, or VICS.
4. Smith, Larry, "A CPFR Success Story," *Supply Chain Management Review*, March 2006, pp. 29–36.
5. Ibid.
6. Leimanis, Eriks, *APICS Illustrated Dictionary*, 11th edition, APICS—The Educational Society for Resource Management, 2004.

Chapter 16

Collaboration with Supply Chain Partners

Chapter 15 focused on alignment of a supply chain strategy among functions within a company. This chapter describes issues related to multicompany efforts, those that take place between trading partners. West Marine, the case discussed in Chapter 15, describes how that company sought to improve its supplier-related processes. Examples listed in Table 15.6 included electronic data interchange (EDI), collaborative planning, forecasting, and replenishment (CPFR), forecast sharing under West Marine control, and pickup of orders at supplier locations. To make life easier for its suppliers, West Marine accommodated the inevitable varying lead times of suppliers due to product manufacturing and delivery differences. To "synchronize" their replenishments, they accommodated needs of suppliers to be productive. West Marine also agreed, in order to show that it backed its forecasts, to commit to buy any order it had forecast. Indeed, data provided to suppliers was in an "order format," not just expected quantities for different stockkeeping units (SKUs).

West Marine operates in a consolidating industry, having grown through acquisitions of other large players. The result is that suppliers to the marine industry are in a weak position in terms of bargaining power. Without West Marine, most would have significantly lower sales, giving the retailer considerable power in the supply chain. This is a compelling motivation to "play ball" by adapting one's systems, attending frequent meetings, and cooperating in continuous improvement initiatives as directed by the large retailer. Chapter 21 returns to the topic as it applies to cost reduction.

This chapter describes trends and issues faced by trading partners seeking to change the basis for doing business through more organized partnerships. In our case study, West Marine went from a purchase-order-to-purchase-order relationship with its suppliers to being an active collaborator over the longer term. Survival as manufacturers and retailers will necessitate similar partnerships in the future, with the sharing of data and decision making being an important foundation of these new relationships.

However, caution about collaboration should be exercised, as demonstrated by several documented lawsuits. Here are some anecdotes reflecting the opportunities and problems that go with multicompany retail supply chain efforts:

- An apparel manufacturer, Global Vision, sued Wal-Mart over deducting the cost of returned merchandise. Contracts did not specify loss sharing on slow-selling merchandise.[1]
- Old Mail Boxes Etc. stores have had their profits squeezed after being acquired by UPS shipping—in spite of earlier assurances of increased business.[2] Cited reasons include opening new UPS stores nearby and extracting higher fees.
- Toys 'R' Us sued Amazon for displaying multiple toy retailers on its Web site.[3] Issues included exclusivity for Toys 'R' Us and lack of product breadth for Amazon. The heart of the issue was Amazon's reliance on other retailers for an increasing share of its profits.

16.1 Supply Chain Roles

The term supply *chain* implies an increase in external partnerships as companies link their operations. A single manufacturing company that delivers retail merchandise will have an upstream supply chain for the raw materials and will serve a downstream supply chain to customers and end-users via multiple retailers. However, it does not necessarily have to have partnerships with either the upstream or downstream trading partners. Retailers also may operate from purchase order to purchase order rather than in collaboration with its suppliers—as West Marine did before its crisis.

16.1.1 Fewer but Broader

Figure 16.1 models the traditional relationship between suppliers, their customers, and end-users. The model reflects a transaction-based relationship similar to what West Marine had before its changes. In this model, the buyer–seller linkage is driven by price and other conditions such as quality and delivery. Customers and ultimate end-users, on the right, also have their choices of supplier. In logistics circles, these supply chain levels are called *echelons*, a term also used here.

Procurement policies and practices perpetuate the traditional model by requiring several suppliers for each material category, as shown by multiple participants

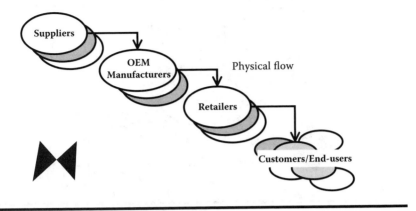

Figure 16.1   Traditional partnership model.

at the retailer and manufacturing echelons. For example, West Marine may carry life jackets from a number of different suppliers. This ensures that the company will be protected from stockouts or dependence on a manufacturer whose quality suddenly deteriorates. Also, certain West Marine customers will favor one product over the other. The figure also shows spaces between the players, reflecting the "arm's length" nature of the relationships. There is little sharing in terms of technology, data, capital spending, promotion plans, or facilities. Some use the "bow tie" figure in the box to represent this "single point of contact" model.

Managers with traditional logistics and procurement mindsets find comfort in this arrangement. Having multiple suppliers, they feel, provides the "best value" often equated to the lowest price. In fact, decisions over source selection are simplified by having fewer factors to consider beyond price. Having multiple suppliers also is seen to assure reliable supplies. If one vendor has a problem, another will cover the shortfall, often a necessity if a firm does business with shaky suppliers who owe their position to low prices. Traditional managers also equate low price with the most cost-effective solution. Indeed, their performance measures often support that paradigm.

In traditional companies, the procurement function processes the transactions necessary to buy and stock needed material. Most procurement functions have skill levels sufficient to execute this task. Unfortunately, there is too little talent available for strategic thinking and for managing partnerships. The lack of skill and resistance to change are bottlenecks for partnering in supply chains.

As demonstrated by the West Marine case, an alternative model is emerging. This is represented in Figure 16.2. The figure shows there are fewer echelons, a result of simplifying the supply chain. It also shows that manufacturers and retailers have expanded their roles—symbolized by overlapping circles. There is more communications between the companies, symbolized by the "diamond" shown in the box.

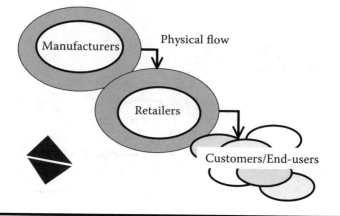

Figure 16.2 Emerging partnership model.

Ford Motor Co., the large but recently struggling automaker, is rethinking its relationships with suppliers.[4] The result will be fewer suppliers, each supplying more of the company's $70 billion annual material requirements. Savings are expected in direct materials, warranty costs, and services, and have the largest potential return in Ford's return to profitability.

Another example of the expanding role players along the retail supply chain is Amazon's leveraging of its knowledge of reading preferences to alert each customer to related new works. In this way, Amazon moves beyond being a bookseller, a traditional supply chain role, to a builder of libraries, an emerging supply chain role. West Marine conducted breakthrough sessions with its largest suppliers. According to ITT Industries' Jabsco division's president, his company was missing the "voice of the customer" in its lean and Six Sigma efforts. Chapter 7, Section 7.5 describes quality function deployment (QFD), a tool to capture this voice. At meetings with West Marine, a pump manufacturer, the Jabsco executive had to "commit to breakthrough results for us and West Marine."[5]

West Marine also reached back to its suppliers by taking over the transportation of merchandise into its distribution centers. This gave the company greater control over schedules and transportation costs. It also encouraged its manufacturers to bypass its distribution centers with direct shipments to West Marine's stores. This kind of creativity is needed for supply chain partners to fill in the open space between trading partners. One fruitful area is trying to establish higher forms of collaboration described in the model that follows.

16.1.2 Collaboration Landscape

In the 2000–2003 timeframe, the Supply Chain Council commissioned a team from member companies to explore the theme of collaboration. The effort identified a collaboration spectrum with four levels of activity between trading partners. The following descriptions range from lower to higher levels of collaboration:

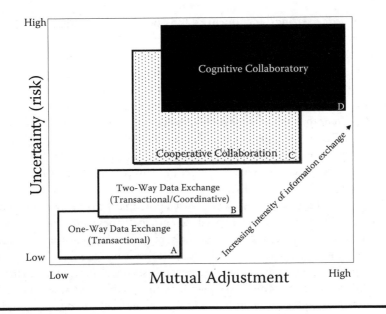

Figure 16.3 Collaboration levels.

- *Data exchange, collaboration* where partners exchange information as required, principally to complete day-to-day transactions. Data exchange can have two forms: one-way or two-way.
- *Cooperative collaboration,* where partners share systems and tools so each partner has simultaneous access to information needed for decision making. However, the decisions made are independent. Examples range from sales and forecasting data to personal interactions for planning.
- *Cognitive collaboration,* involving "joint, concurrent intellectual and cognitive activity between partners." This level embraces information sharing to jointly gain and weigh knowledge on the way to joint decisions. This collaboration level includes "knowledge" exchanges included in our definition of supply chain flows in Chapter 1, Section 1.2.

Figure 16.3 describes the landscape for collaboration types using this model. On the vertical axis is uncertainty, or exposure to risk. The horizontal axis measures "mutual adjustment." Low levels mean that, whatever the consequences, outcomes will bring little disruption to either party's operation. Business will "go on as usual." Higher levels of mutual adjustment bring the need for more collaboration because outcomes have major implications for both parties. The volume, frequency, and complexity are factors in the "intensity of information exchange," shown by a sloping arrow on the right. As mutual adjustment and uncertainty increase, so does the need for increasing the intensity of information exchange.

In *transaction* settings, low intensity is associated with readily available commodity products at widely known market prices. It is likely such a transaction can be completed by a simple one-way information transaction—box A in Figure 16.3. For example, a buyer goes to a retail bookstore, Barnes and Noble, to buy a book for its marked price. The book is in stock; the buyer buys the book and leaves the store. Communication is *one-way* from the book buyer to the bookstore.

To the extent that any of these three conditions grows more uncertain, the need for communication increases. In box B, the book buyer goes online and orders a book from Amazon or another seller. The seller confirms the order by e-mail and notifies the buyer when the book is shipped. In this setting, there is *two-way* communication between buyer and seller.

High levels of mutual adjustment go with potentially disruptive outcomes. So, the *cognitive collaboratory* in box D needs to anticipate these outcomes and possible reactions. As an example, the auto assembly plant receiving just-in-time components shuts down if a single part is missing. The resulting "cognitive collaboratory" assures capacity at the supplier, qualifies new parts, constructs supplier plants close to assembly plants (or even inside the plant), requires buffer stocks, sets up real-time communications, and continuously monitors the financial and operating health of the supplier.

Box C, cooperative collaboration, holds an interesting position in the collaboration spectrum. Examples include insurance agents selling a range of policies that vary by individual need, real-estate agents providing buyers information on houses and prices, companies that must configure their products—think car dealers or computer merchants such as Dell—and anyone who provides sales or customer service along the supply chain. West Marine employs technically capable salespeople to counsel customers on expensive purchases. Amazon's communication of new offerings on topics of interest is another example. The "Geek Squad" that advises customers at retailer Best Buy plays a similar role.

One problem occurs when categorizing a buyer–seller relationship as a "B" when it is really a "C." In fact, the "clicks and bricks" movement allows the buyer to choose whether he or she wants to deal in a B or C environment. As another example, in the dot-com era and more recently, companies have tried to establish "markets" for goods and services through brokerage sites and reverse auctions. Sometimes these work, providing execution in a B environment. At other times, especially for complicated, technical goods and services, a box C interaction is appropriate. Companies can define supply chains for customers wanting different levels of collaboration in making decisions on purchases. West Marine's most profitable customers, for example, used three of its supply chains—its stores, its catalog, and the Internet—to fulfill their needs.

Table 16.1 uses the model to characterize other West Marine interactions with its suppliers. Note that EDI and CPFR are characterized as data exchanges. Picking up supplier merchandise is seen, once the mechanisms are in place, as a two-way exchange to arrange the pickups. Higher levels of collaboration characterize

Table 16.1   West Marine Supplier Collaboration Types

External Focused Changes	A One-Way Data Exchange	B Two-way Data Exchange	C Cooperative Collaboration	D Cognitive Collaboration
EDI		•		
CPFR	•	•		
Supply base deployment			•	
Commitment to orders			•	
Inbound transportation		•		
"Breakthroughs"				•
Promotion planning				•

Note: EDI = electronic data interchange, CPFR = Collaborative Planning, Forecasting, and Replenishment.

deployment of forecasts to the supplier base, the West Marine commitment to buy its forecast regardless of actual demand, and its breakthroughs and the promotion planning that consisted of one-on-one collaborations with individual suppliers.

16.2 Core Competency

Another motivator for partnerships, and a deeper strategic one, is the need to focus on "core competencies." In other words, "We do what we do best; partners do the rest." Assumptions about core competency underlie many decisions about partnerships. A decision to perform or not perform an activity or produce or not produce some component of a good or service is a strategic decision. In fact, the emerging model in Figure 16.2 implies shuffling of tasks up and down the supply chain. West Marine's taking over inbound merchandise transportation is an example. In this case, it was "insourcing" rather than outsourcing. The net result will often be fewer echelons and individual participants adding value to the chain. Deciding which capabilities to retain and cultivate and finding the right partners can be daunting. Typical candidates for outsourcing noncompetencies include manufacturing, facilities management, information systems, transportation, and inventory management. For many retailers with strong private label lines, various parts of the supply chain activities are outsourced, including the actual manufacture of goods. Retailers included in this group are Gap, Macy's, and Target, among many others.

Figure 16.4   Competencies: the roots of competitiveness.

Gary Hamel and C.K. Prahalad introduced the concept of core competencies.[6] The concept holds that competitive success requires the nurturing of distinctive skills, or "competencies." Other activity may contribute little to competitive position. In the worst case, "noncore" activity diverts management attention from activities that create real value. Hamel and Prahalad define competitiveness on three levels. These are (1) core competence, (2) core products, and (3) end products. Their analogy is a tree, as shown in Figure 16.4, with core competencies as the roots, and end products as leaves.

In the figure, one or more competencies support a "core product." These core products are the heart of many products that go to market. So Honda's core products, engines and power trains, produce multiple motorized products including automobiles, all-terrain vehicles, outboard motors, personal watercraft, generators, and engines. The "businesses" promote and sell end products that have their roots as core products based on core competencies.

The authors illustrate the point with Canon, a manufacturer of high-technology products. Canon has three core competencies—in precision mechanics, fine optics, and microelectronics. Similar to Honda, Canon applies combinations of these to a score of products ranging from cameras to copiers.

In their article, Hamel and Prahalad point to the important role of partnerships in nurturing core competencies. They believe partnerships are an inexpensive way to advance a competence. They also decry the tendency of many companies to organize around strategic business units (SBUs) at the business level (the leaves), arguably the least important level in the long run. For example, Gap focuses on the relative performances of their major SBUs: Gap, Old Navy, and Banana Republic. SBU performance measures are immediate, focusing on profits generated from the sale of end products. Unfortunately, no single SBU is a custodian of core competencies or perhaps even core products. The "roots," or competencies, which should be nurtured across SBU boundaries, can wither because of management focus on SBU performance.

Because core products rely on multiple competencies, a competence can also be integration of diverse technologies. This integration requires movement of technology across SBUs and partnership companies. Another competency might also be found in building partnerships. If partnerships become vital to success in the business, it's not unreasonable to treat partnership-building skills as competencies. West Marine would be a good example of a retail chain that decided to cultivate this competency.

The shaded competence on the lower right in Figure 16.4 represents a competency in the five tasks that constitute SCM. One would certainly agree that Wal-Mart and Dell have demonstrated potent SCM core competencies. One could also argue that any successful retailer needs to cultivate similar competencies, and any manufacturer of retail merchandise would also do so if it wants to profitably serve retailers.

16.3 Partnerships Vocabulary

A structured classification scheme will help identify and describe partnership opportunities. The need is particularly pertinent to businesses for which partnering is a novelty. Many have muddled along for years doing everything themselves, bargaining at arm's length with trading partners and, in many cases, cultivating a "not invented here" syndrome. The recommended classification has three dimensions. These are *purpose, direction,* and *choice.* If you describe your need for a partner in each of these dimensions, you are off to a good start in making the right choice of partnership alternatives and even specific partners.

16.3.1 Partnership Purpose

This classification category goes to the fundamental reason for the partnership. The most important factor is whether the partnership will create new "space" along the supply chain. Creating space does not necessarily create cost reductions, which has been the prime motivator of many partnerships and mergers. Creating new space is similar to the concept behind the Blue Ocean strategy. In this approach, a company gains in a monopoly in an unserved marketplace.[7]

With respect to mergers, consultants from McKinsey & Co. have documented what they call the "habits" of the busiest acquirers.[8] The authors note that mergers and acquisitions (M&A) should be a tool, not a strategy in and of itself. Companies trying to promote their top lines have often tried to use acquisition as a strategy for growth. In the 1980s, many large conglomerates acquired retailers to "grow" their organizations and to increase their markets. However, there was no real strategic base for these acquisitions, and because these conglomerates did not

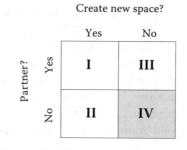

Figure 16.5 Potential for new supply chain space.

understand the retail business, divestitures and bankruptcies occurred with regularity. Later research found that investment bankers and lawyers brought no competitive advantage to acquirers. The best acquirers sought to fill a "hole" or, as we describe it, "space," in their strategy that could not be filled inside.

Of course, creating new space is more complex than refining existing roles. Most partnerships are intended to refine current positions with lower cost or better service rather than to define new space. In many cases, the potential to define new space is not even considered. In Figure 16.2, the expanded shaded circles around those of the manufacturers and retailers symbolize new space.

West Marine, as described in Chapter 15, ran into trouble when it merged with a large competitor, E&B Marine. West Marine had focused on the sailing segment, and E&B on power boaters. This example did not create new space. In fact, when West Marine started converting E&B stores to its own brand, assortment, and pricing, it lost customers and destroyed value.

Figure 16.5 shows the options for defining partnership purpose in terms of creating space. The shaded square (quadrant IV) represents the as-is situation with respect to partnering. The decision process includes two steps: first, identifying whether new space is created, and second, deciding how to fill that space in the supply chain—either organically (internally) or by merger. Moves from quadrant IV to either quadrant I or quadrant II positions represent this decision. The second decision is whether a company can do this on its own (quadrant II) or it can choose to partner (quadrant I). Few partnerships create new space. At least initially, the West Marine merger with E&B was a quadrant III transaction.

Good examples of creating space occur in technology products when each partner brings a critical technical capability not possessed by the other partner. Pharmaceutical distributor McKesson follows this model with its large and small retail customers—as described in Chapter 3, Section 3.3. Li and Fung, also discussed in Section 3.3, fills holes in the supply chain also. Distributors and third-party logistics providers create space when they take responsibility for stocking or customizing merchandise. Another example is manufacturers making merchandise floor-ready by providing it pre-tagged and on hangers, moving that preparation function out of the store.

Figure 16.6   Partnership directions.

16.3.2 Partnership Direction

Direction, the second classification category, is the term we give to the relative positions of the partnering companies along the supply chain. Figure 16.6 shows different directions. A "horizontal" combination, similar to the retailer combination between West Marine and E&B, means each partner is at the same echelon, and partner activity systems, as described in Chapter 13, will overlap. Another example is two wholesale distributors partnering to offer increased geographical coverage. Code sharing by airlines is another. Hewlett-Packard and Compaq as well as Daimler-Benz and Chrysler Group are also examples of horizontal partnerships.

Partners in different echelons, whose capabilities do not overlap, represent a "vertical" partnership. An example is Wal-Mart, a retailer, providing point-of-sale information to McKesson to establish vendor-managed inventory. McKesson, as an upstream partner in the supply chain, is then able to provide timely delivery direct to Wal-Mart stores. McKesson's new "space" is the vendor-managed inventory service.

Figure 16.6 illustrates horizontal and vertical partnerships. Vertical partnerships reflect the trend toward supply chain consolidation for process simplification, reduced handling and transportation, and increased flexibility. For example, Chapter 17, Subsection 17.1.4, describes "disintermediation" of a distributor to simplify a supply chain. The emerging model of the supply chain described in Figure 16.2 forecasts growth of partnerships in the vertical direction. In these cases, fewer players perform more supply chain functions, capturing a greater share of supply chain value.

16.3.3 Partnership Choice

This category captures the relative strength of each partner. It is called "choice" because it reflects the availability of options for partnering. High choice means there are many options for partnering and trading partners; low choice means there are few options. Manufacturers of functional products have few choices when it comes to supplying a channel master such as Wal-Mart. If they want to sell to the largest retailer, they must follow Wal-Mart's rules. West Marine in fact has become the Wal-Mart of the marine aftermarket industry. Its suppliers have low choice of "whether" and "who" when it comes to partnering. On the other hand, in less concentrated industries and with growing innovative products, there are many choices for partnering. Current consolidation and the growth of very large chains such as Target and Best Buy have either reduced partnership opportunities for manufacturers or made them more of a necessity.

To establish a classification representing choice, we rely on a data management paradigm. Table 16.2 explains forms of partnership relationships. In the relationship characterization in column one, your company is first. The options you have are second. For example, in retail, Wal-Mart would be a "one-to-many" company. It is the largest customer for most of the products it buys. Presumably, Wal-Mart, as a channel master, has many partners/suppliers eager for its business from whom to choose. Likewise, a supplier to Wal-Mart would be a "many-to-one" if there were several choices for Wal-Mart for the product it sells. A manufacturing company or a distributor in a "many-to-one" situation may have a tough time standing out from the crowd. However, Chapters 12 and 13 describe how to structure oneself to be a viable partner to a channel master. The rewards could be worth it. Having a distinctive ability could enable a leader to consolidate an industry, acquiring its former competitors, or gain market share from those who fail to recognize or are much less ready to make needed changes.

16.4 Organizing a Partnership

Organization design is an art form. New contributions occur frequently, but the topic of multicompany structures has barely been touched. Perhaps there are good reasons for this, because it is hard to impose conditions on trading partners. On the other hand, those entrusted with establishing partnerships should consider what kind of structure is needed. Table 16.3 outlines components of a partnership agreement.[9]

Surprisingly, companies overlook the role of contract incentives in motivating improvements. Consultants from McKinsey & Company documented this lapse in a study of 12 European food and consumer products manufacturers.[10] In retail industries in major European countries, most of which were consolidating, the researchers found that there are few manufacturers offering "bracket prices." Such prices provide unit price discounts for ordering larger volumes. For example, it becomes cheaper for the retailer to order truckloads of a product rather than single pallets.

Table 16.2 Partnership Relationships Permission

Relationship	Description	Application
Many to many	Your company, one of many serving your market, has many partner candidates from which to choose. Neither partner is currently a dominant company	Two companies form a partnership to separate themselves from the crowd. They may do so to target a particular segment neither could approach alone. An industry "rollup" or consolidation is an example in which a dominant company buys others offering similar services. In the marine aftermarket, West Marine played the consolidator role
One to many	Your company is large and you have many options for selecting partners	You select the "best of breed" for partnering or, working alone, you develop capabilities appealing to many customers. Dell is a vertical example partnering with its suppliers
Many to one	Your company has a low market share and must compete with others for the business of the strong partner	You develop strategies for distinguishing yourself so you become the chosen one. You may ignore other segments to focus on the needs of the targeted strong partner. Successful West Marine suppliers of commodity-type products could do this by participating in the CPFR initiative
One to one	This is a peer arrangement with dominant partners on each side. There is little choice in partner selection	Because the size of the market and the scale of operations required, there are few choices. The Wal-Mart/McKesson VMI effort was a vertical example

Note: CPFR = Collaborative Planning, Forecasting, and Replenishment; vmi = vendor-managed inventory.

The authors note that the logistics costs are from 5 to 20 percent of net sales. So they believe that having such discounts could reduce retailer costs by 2 to 3 percent of retail price. They also point out that salespeople have little experience or expertise in negotiating cost-efficient terms. They also note that lowering barriers in the United States is increasing the use of pricing that recognizes supply chain efficiencies.

Table 16.3 Partnership Agreement Articles (permission required from CRC)

Partnership Article	Description
Purpose	Establishes the need for the partnership.
Parties to the agreement	Provides the legal names involved in the partnership. This is important because larger companies have many legal entities
Basis of the agreement	The shared value proposition. Partnership expectations
Organizational process boundaries	Areas of primary supply chain process responsibility
Interface response time	Response expectations over time and space (geography)
Decision escalation	Hierarchy of individuals or positions on both sides of the partnership who will resolve issues
Face-to-face meetings	The parties involved in the meetings (including senior management) and the frequency
Performance measurement	Shared performance measures with which to track the effectiveness of the partnership
Intellectual property	Each partner's rights to trade secrets, trademarks, copyrights, and patents arising from the partnership
Investment decision making	Expectations for each party's share of investments and returns
Mediation and conflict resolution	Defined process for conflict resolution
Non-Exclusive Provision	Acknowledgement of the right of either party to participate in other supply chain networks, even if they compete
Renewal	Term of the partnership. Whether renewal is automatic or not
Signatures	Senior executive commitment from each organization

Once agreements are in place, overseeing a complicated effort requires new ways to organize and control the effort. A previous article describes "stage-3" SCM, referring to the participation of multiple companies.[11] Chapter 6, Subsection 6.7.2 introduced the structure of a stage-3 SCM effort. In this model, stage 1 is the department level; stage 2 is the company or business-unit level. West Marine was at stage 1 or 2 when it was purchasing merchandise on an order-by-order basis. New stage-3 practices produce a cooperative effort such as CPFR that includes trading partners in supply chain improvement. The following features will characterize stage-3 supply chain improvement and should be considered in implementing each partnership:

- A focused and measurable goal for the effort with objectives such as strategic positioning, market share increase, and financial improvement. The West Marine program described these as "breakthroughs." Ideally, these initiatives should consider the partnership as the enterprise, rather than as individual companies.
- Multicompany funding and staffing—Joint projects reflect a commitment to effective supply chain design. Such participation will shorten implementation lead time. A challenge will be to balance contributions among partners through win-win contracting.
- As necessary, a third-party "honest broker" to facilitate the effort and provide an outside, neutral perspective. The third party can be a team member or consultant jointly funded by the partners.
- A CEO steering committee from partner enterprises. The steering committee should meet frequently while establishing the partnership, and as necessary during its operation.
- Multiyear projects with self-funding short-term wins. The model for implementing supply chain change described in Chapters 15 and 17 is useful for structuring this effort. This allows the program to be sustained by its own cash-flow benefits.
- Process integration—This means deployment of appropriate technology solutions. A plan for systems to share information should accompany the design of partnership processes.

The initiative for supply chain improvement will come from a *sponsor's* firm. The sponsor is an executive who champions the effort. The sponsor's firm may be a dominant player in the supply chain or one with a major stake in the project's success. The sponsor should have completed the partnership preparation steps described earlier in this chapter and will likely be somewhere in the process of developing and implementing its supply chain strategy. A project timeline similar to that introduced as Figure 14.1 is appropriate. Indeed, the sponsor's firm may have already completed internal restructuring tasks.

16.5 Partner Collaboration—Summary

The emerging model of collaboration calls for new capabilities in building partnerships. These capabilities include developing partnership strategies during the planning processes, deciding what types of partnerships should be pursued, and implementing the partnerships through multicompany projects.

Endnotes

1. Zimmerman, Ann, "Working Things Out with a Giant Customer," *The Wall Street Journal,* October 17, 2006, p. B4.
2. Gibson, Richard, "Package Deal," *The Wall Street Journal,* May 8, 2006, p. R13.
3. Mangalindan, Mylene, "How Amazon's Dream Alliance with Toys 'R' Us Went So Sour," *The Wall Street Journal,* January 23, 2006, p. A1.
4. McCracken, Jeffrey, "Ford Seeks Big Savings by Overhauling Supply System," *The Wall Street Journal,* September 29, 2005, page A1.
5. Smith, Larry, "A CPFR Success Story," *Supply Chain Management Review,* March 2006, page 35.
6. Hamel, Gary and Prahalad, C.K., "The Core Competency of the Corporation," *Harvard Business Review,* (68/3) May–June, 1990, pp. 79–90.
7. For more reading, see the following: W. Chan Kim and Renée Mauborgne, *Blue Ocean Strategy,* Boston: Harvard Business School Press, 2005.
8. Palter, Robert N. and Srinivasan, Dev, "Habits of the Busiest Acquirers," *The McKinsey Quarterly: the Online Journal of McKinsey & Co.,* July 2006.
9. Walker, William T., *Supply Chain Architecture: A Blueprint for Networking the Flow of Material, Information, and Cash,* Boca Raton: CRC Press, 2005.
10. Sänger, Frank and Tochtermann, Thomas C.A., "Better Logistics in European Consumer Goods," *The McKinsey Quarterly: Web exclusive,* January 2007.
11. Ayers, James B., Gustin, Craig and Stephens, Scott, "Reengineering the supply chain," *Information Strategy: the Executive's Journal,* Fall, 1997 (14/1), pp. 13–18.

Chapter 17

The Demand-Driven
Supply Chain

Chapters 15 and 16 described how to enlist internal departments and trading partners in collaborative improvement efforts. This chapter focuses on what these improved relationships might seek to accomplish. As in the West Marine case, the most ambitious of these efforts should be pursuit of the demand-driven supply chain. In this vision, actual *demand* displaces *forecasts* as the basis for replenishment decisions. This is not an overnight process but one that involves continuous improvement.

The chapter begins by defining what it means to be demand-driven, and tools for achieving the demand-driven goal follow. Finally, the chapter addresses the subject of sponsorship—what players in the supply chain—retailers, distributors, or original equipment manufacturers (OEMs)—might logically lead the transition to the demand-driven supply chain.

17.1 Vision for the Demand-Driven Supply Chain

Most supply chain practitioners are aware of the virtues of being "demand-driven." In fact, the quest to be demand-driven is behind many of today's innovations in SCM. One example is RFID mandates such as those described later in Chapter 18. RFID stands for radio frequency identification. RFID technology is not instituted for its own sake but as a means to achieve increased visibility. Visibility, in turn, enables the efficiencies and customer service improvements that go with being demand driven, with RFID-tracked merchandise providing accurate location information required for better decisions.

Another motivating trend is the growth of "scan-based trading." With this practice, the manufacturer or distributor retains ownership of merchandise until it is purchased (scanned). This shifts inventory costs upstream in the supply chain. On the other hand, it can, in some cases, provide a competitive advantage to the seller as well as tighter information links with customers that increase visibility over final demand. This information can be put to work in developing a demand-driven supply chain.

Just what the term *demand-driven* means is less widely accepted. In this chapter, we define it as follows:

Basing supply chain decisions on actual end-user consumption rather than forecasts.

Decisions, in this definition, are those required to plan and schedule operations along the chain. They are driven by the need to replenish stocks as customer demand "pulls" merchandise out of the supply chain. These operating decisions turn factories on and off, approve accumulation or burn-off of inventory, introduce new products, generate markdowns when necessary, and plan capacity at various links.

Longer-term decisions such as how much capacity to have will always depend to some extent, on forecasts; they are not included in this definition. Note also that the demand-driven supply chain will be driven by *end-user consumption*. This might not be the same as actual *sales* because a purchase may not coincide with consumption, particularly far upstream in supply chains with long lead times. Another supply chain classification, *push* or *pull*, may be familiar to readers. Forecasts are associated with *push* strategies that force merchandise to the next-in-line participant in the supply chain without understanding what the end-user is consuming. *Pull* approaches utilize end-user demand for products from retailers for making decisions, thereby "pulling" merchandise through the supply chain. In summary, practitioners refer to the *forecast-driven* supply chain environment as "push," and the *demand-driven* environment as "pull."

Why is becoming demand-driven important? Basically, forecasts for many products are unreliable. Cynics say forecasts are either "wrong or lucky." Even though companies automate the forecasting process and continuously search for better algorithms, the time and effort required to produce and apply forecasts often create paperwork and teeth gnashing. Behavior also plays an important role. What if the production forecast falls below sales commitments? The forecast gets boosted whether the business is there or not. Another problem is that sales departments sometimes provide forecasts in currency terms or product categories. These don't align with the needed operating decisions on what stockkeeping unit (SKU) to make, in what quantities, and when to make it.

The result is the unfortunate reality of inventory accumulation, as described in Chapter 7, Section 7.4, along the chain, and "bullwhips," wide fluctuations in production without commensurate changes in end-user consumption. These inventories stretch the "cash-to-cash" cycle, requiring more working capital to support the business. Dell's direct or "build-to-order" (BTO) model is a frequently cited example of shortening this cycle. Dell's business assembles final products from vendor parts after orders are received and paid for. Its cash-to-cash cycle is thus negative—the customer pays Dell before Dell pays the suppliers. The Toyota Production System, the foundation of "lean" approaches, also has a "make one move one" philosophy. West Marine, described in Chapters 15 and 16, approached this ideal with its daily updates and multiechelon planning systems in which each user had the same data.

Many other retailers and their suppliers would like a similar model. Although this is not always possible, companies can move in the Toyota and Dell direction if they try. There are many examples of retailers exploiting demand-driven techniques. The retail or grocery store is one. The store merely captures what merchandise is popular with customers who register their votes at the checkout line. The empty shelf signals a need for replenishment, a "visual" signal. The shelf may be filled, in the case of the retail store, by an order to the distribution center or manufacturer. The "Breadman" or jobber may do the same for the grocery store on frequent fixed-schedule visits, an arrangement called *vendor-managed inventory,* or VMI. In these cases, demand "pulls" the product along the supply chain as consumption occurs. The advent of scanners in the late 1970s and early 1980s has further streamlined the process and has made possible electronic replenishment systems for many items.

Benetton, whose brand is "United Colors of Benetton," has delayed dyeing its sweaters until the market signaled the current season's most popular colors, using the technique called *postponement,* discussed later. Once consumers register their preferences, Benetton can plan its color assortment to minimize dead stock and write-downs. Another example is in-store paint matching using spectrometers that blend a few basic colors into an infinite number of combinations. Pharmacists also employ a demand-driven process when they dispense labeled prescriptions of 10 or 20 tablets from larger containers.

Weighing against becoming demand-driven are complications inherent in retail marketing strategies. These strategies rely on fashion items, seasonal product sales, and frequent product promotions. This book does not contend that forecasts should or can be abolished, especially in these categories. However, increasing the role of actual demand in supply chain decisions, for all categories of goods, will improve both financial performance and customer service.

As a general principle, retail supply chains, as they operate today, can be *more* demand-driven, if not totally so. This includes the supply chains for fashion, seasonal and promotional sales. So, the property we call demand driven is not absolute. Its pursuit can be approached using continuous improvement models described in Chapter 15, Section 15.2, taken as far as possible within constraints imposed by the products sold and the markets served. This chapter describes how to undertake such a journey.

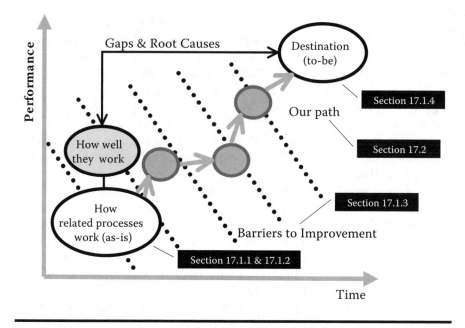

Figure 17.1   Model for implementing supply chain change.

Figure 17.1 repeats our model for supply chain change and the elements of the model addressed in this chapter, which is quite lengthy. The figure shows which chapter sections describe each element in the model. At the lower left is the "as-is" representing the existing processes for decision making in the supply chain. A separate evaluation of those processes (how well they work) utilizes benchmarks, analysis, the perception of employees and participants, and inputs from trading partners. This evaluation takes into account product types, barriers, and business goals. This part of the model is the subject of Subsections 17.1.1 and 17.1.2.

Constraints that cannot be changed may limit what can be done in terms of the destination. An example is a decision to use an existing system or to produce merchandise in a particular plant. *Barriers* must be navigated to arrive at the destination. The "path" is shown in the form of sequenced "projects" (in smaller circles) designed to close the gaps between the as-is and to-be. Some of these are likely to be multicompany projects. This topic is covered in Subsection 17.1.3.

A destination (upper right) for becoming demand-driven is defined next. This enables identification of gaps between the as-is and to-be. The gap analysis includes metrics, benchmarks, process design, governance along the supply chain, organizational structure, measurements, and systems. Subsection 17.1.4 covers this part of the model. Section 17.2 describes the pathway to the demand-driven supply chain.

This section uses the model in Figure 17.1 to describe how a company might develop a vision and project a plan for implementing the demand-driven supply

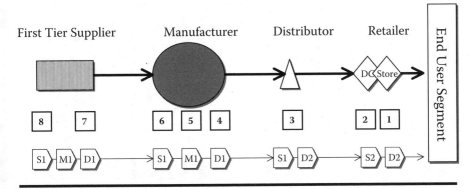

Figure 17.2   Decision making along a supply chain.

chain. It begins with understanding the starting environment. Chapter 15 used the West Marine case as an example of the types of findings and conclusions that could result from applying the process. See Chapter 15, Tables 15.1 through 15.6, for details of the case.

17.1.1 Documenting the Current Situation

To establish a vision for a demand-driven supply chain of the future, one should start with the current situation. Figure 17.2 illustrates a simple supply chain delivering a product to an end-user market segment. Supply chain decision points are shown as numbers along the bottom of Figure 17.2 beginning at level 1 (the retailer) and extend back to level 8 (a first-tier supplier). Table 17.1 documents each of the decisions. Data for Table 17.1 comes from industry knowledge, direct from the trading partners, or as educated guesses.

The figure and table (column 2) also show the entities in the supply chain and describe the steps they take to order material/merchandise or produce that merchandise (column 3). The action or decision required (column 4) and their frequencies (column 5) are also shown in the table. Column 6 shows the lead time to complete each step, capturing the output of an important process called time mapping. Note that this example requires 21 weeks of lead time from the point an item is purchased until that signal is recorded with the manufacturer's supplier. The last three columns describe tools and data used in each decision (column 7), responsible parties (column 8), and whether the decision is forecast driven or demand driven (column 9). Out of eight decisions in this example, only two are demand driven. One way to characterize the supply chain is to measure the percentage of decisions that are demand driven. In this case, it is 25 percent (two out of eight decisions).

At the bottom of Figure 17.2 are a series of large arrows. These are a representation of the decisions using the configuration model from SCOR, which stands for

Table 17.1 Documenting As-Is Supply Chain Decisions

#	2 Entities	3 Step	4 Decision/ Action Required	5 Frequency	6 Lead Time (weeks)	7 Basis of Decision	8 Responsibility	9 Forecast or Demand Driven
1.	Retail chain	Order: store-level replenishment	Refill stock to target levels	Daily	1	Point-of-sale system data	Automatic. Set by chain replenishment system	Demand driven
2.		Order: chain distribution center replenishment	Reorder predetermined batch quantity	Weekly	2	Reorder point set in system by SKU	Automated system. Buyer reviews by exception	Demand driven
3.	Distributor	Order: manufacturer warehouse replenishment	Order predetermined batch quantity	Biweekly	4	Reorder point and forecast	Demand manager using forecast. Review by exceptions	Forecast driven

#		Activity	Batch/order basis	Frequency		Driver	Responsible	Type
4.	Manufacturer (OEM)	Produce: manufacturer	To make or not to make a batch on fixed schedule	Monthly	2	Orders from warehouse	Factory production planner; Manufacturing manager	Forecast driven
5.		Order: manufacturer raw material	Order predetermined batch quantity	Quarterly	4	Sales forecast	Commodity manager/buyer; Sales department	Forecast driven
6.	Manufacturer's supplier	Order: supplier warehouse replenishment	Batch size based on forecast	Quarterly	4	Manufacturer forecast	Commodity planner	Forecast driven
7.		Produce: supplier	Batch size based on forecast	Quarterly	1	Sales forecast and production plan	Factory production planner; Manufacturing manager	Forecast driven
8.		Order: supplier material replenishment	Batch size based on forecast	Quarterly	3	Sales forecast	Commodity manager	Forecast driven

Note: OEM = original equipment manufacturer, SKU = stockkeeping unit.

Supply Chain Operations Reference Model, maintained by member companies in the Supply Chain Council. The threads provide a user-friendly overview of a supply chain. The letters "S, M, D" stand for source, make, deliver, high-level supply chain processes in SCOR. The "1," and "2" designate whether the action is "to stock" or to "order"—essentially whether it is forecast driven or demand driven. A "3" covers engineer-to-order links in other chains but not in this one. The tool is meant to capture configurations of larger supply chains that may spread over many companies.

Creating a vision for such a supply chain would assess whether any of these decisions can be converted from forecast driven to demand driven. This analysis, particularly when aided by internal functions and trading partners, leads to goals for improvement and identifies good places to start. These are often the points where the lead time is the greatest. The West Marine case in Chapter 15 sought to make decisions demand driven by using common data at levels 1 and 2 and frequent sharing of up-to-date information with at least levels 3 through 5.

A question that is fair to ask is, "Can one part of the supply chain be forecast driven and another demand driven?" Of particular concern is when a demand-driven step is further upstream, feeding forecast-driven processes. The answer is, "Yes," and the situation occurs frequently. For example, a manufacturer may consider the distributor as its "ultimate" customer. Yet the distributor orders from the manufacturer according to its own or retailer forecasts, while the manufacturer produces to the distributor's pull signals. So, the distributor is forecast driven, whereas the manufacturer is demand driven. This chapter next describes the implications of product types, how to address barriers, and the path from forecast-driven to demand-driven processes.

17.1.2 Product Types

Becoming more demand driven will, in many cases, require both process and product changes. This section addresses the product design characteristics that support increasing the chain's demand-driven percentage. The most important product quality is commonality in components. Benetton sweaters in white all look alike, except for size. It is the color that makes them different. Delaying dyeing of the sweaters until the market has signaled demand levels for each color is an example of *postponement*. This is because the final decision on configuration is made later (is postponed) in the supply chain process. Commonality, incidentally, also applies to services and software. Standardized procedures, such as producing a will or trust, or software modules that developers can transport to new applications, speed delivery to customers by not reinventing the wheel. This approach to software application development is called Service-Oriented Architecture, or SOA.[1]

The demand-driven supply chain design must also consider product structures. The Theory of Constraints (TOC), developed by Eliyahu M. Goldratt and his colleagues, defines basic product structures and uses the letters V-A-T to distinguish them. A "V" product example is the Honda engine that goes to end-user markets in autos, watercraft, and snowmobiles. The core of each product is the Honda engine, and the products are built around it. The V product also applies to many consumer goods such as food, consumer package goods, and pharmaceuticals. A food example is the orange, which goes to market as produce, juice, marmalade, sherbet, and other products. Consumer package goods and pharmaceuticals often originate in a single chemical formulation. In these cases, the formulation serves as a base for multiple products that differ in form (liquid, tablets, gels, lotions, etc.), dosages, size and quantity, and packaging. Packaging variations occur by virtue of several brands for consumer package goods, local legal requirements such as those for pharmaceuticals, or languages for markets around the world. Later in this chapter we'll apply a demand-driven technique to such a product.

An "A" structure product such as automobiles has many components that go into a single delivered product. Dell's personal computer supply chain matches an A structure. The demand signal to Dell's component makers comes at final assembly after the customer orders a computer. Components are pulled up to Dell assembly lines as outgoing configured computers deplete the stock of supplier items. To support their model, Dell provides supplier visibility for these stock levels to better assure timely replenishment.

A "T" structure is also common in the consumer packaged goods, chemical, and pharmaceutical industries. Mix-to-order paint in the hardware store is an example. A few paint colors make a virtually infinite variety of colors and are configured at the point of sale. The ultimate product of a grocery store is the market basket. Each basket is a unique mix of individual products, with combinations that could never be forecast. The customer herself configures each basket from store shelves using a grocery list.

17.1.3 Barriers to the Demand-Driven Supply Chain

Given the variety of products and product types, there are many reasons why retail supply chains rely so heavily on forecasts. We call these barriers rather than constraints because they can be managed, meaning we can adapt our demand-driven approach to accommodate the barrier. A "constraint," on the other hand, cannot be managed. Before embarking on a quest to become more demand-driven, a retailer, distributor, or manufacturer should understand and plan for constraints and barriers. Here are some of the common barriers, several of which were present in the West Marine case:

1. *Unwillingness or unawareness of the value of operations.* Top management does not perceive operations as a source of strategic advantage. Like West Marine, the founding management team has little awareness of supply chain issues. Only in the last ten or fifteen years have retailers focused on SCM as a source of competitive advantage.

2. *Organizational boundaries.* There are internal boundaries between functions, particularly sales and operations and, often, marketing and sales, where collaboration is needed for the retailer and its supply chain partners to become demand-driven.

3. *Training.* Many merchandise and production planners have been trained to use methods that utilize forecasts based on lead times. These processes are embedded in enterprise resource planning (ERP) systems.

4. *Lack of skills.* As described later, multiple disciplines are required for the transition to the demand-driven supply chain. Many companies do not have the knowhow to reform their processes. A mission of this book is to address this situation.

5. *Inability to collaborate.* A consensus to proceed has to exist among supply chain partners, or one of the partners has to be strong enough to lead the others down the path to becoming a demand-driven supply chain. The fact that a manufacturer sells to multiple retailers can also hamper collaboration because the manufacturer is serving "masters" with different supply chain agendas.

6. *Choppy product flow.* Contributing factors include items mentioned earlier, such as seasonal sales with long lead times, sporadic promotions, short product life cycles, and fashion items with little sales history. Also included in this category are differences in replenishment cycle frequencies, too many participating companies, and component lead times throughout the chain.

A company or a group of trading partners must identify and plan for these barriers. A next step on the path is to understand the potential to be demand driven, taking these barriers into account.

17.1.4 The To-Be and Potential To-Be Demand Driven

The physical structure of the product and the existence of barriers will affect how demand-driven a supply chain can be. Certainly, the decision of any one company to make change is constrained by its influence in the chain. Wal-Mart, a customer with a lot of clout for many manufacturers, is taking the lead when it requires its suppliers to put RFID tags on products shipped to them. Earlier, companies such as McKesson, a distributor, and P&G, a manufacturer, led in implementing VMI with big companies such as Wal-Mart. Both VMI examples were steps on the path to the demand-driven supply chain.

Measuring the potential to be demand driven means assessing the potential to convert decisions from forecast driven to demand driven. This transition could be developed as a collaborative effort between a retailer and one of its larger manufacturing suppliers. Table 17.2 uses the Table 17.1 format to display one such vision. Changes between the as-is in Table 17.1 and to-be in Table 17.2 are shown by text in italics in Table 17.2. The following is a summary of the principal changes:

- The to-be vision shows that the distributor is removed from the supply chain process for at least a portion of the product flow, an example of *disintermediation*. This cuts lead time and simplifies the chain.
- The vision also synchronizes the factory with the weekly cycle at the retailer's distribution center (DC). This has the effect of converting steps 4 and 5 from forecast driven to demand driven. Once implemented, this would increase the demand-driven percentage in the supply chain from 25 to 57. Also, lead time from the manufacturer to the end-user sale is reduced from thirteen weeks to six. This change may face opposition from the distribution department that wants to fill trucks as full as possible, and from the manufacturing department that wants larger batches.

Note that the two principal changes are of different types, and both types are necessary to become more demand driven. The first, disintermediation, removing an echelon from the supply chain, requires a multifunctional decision that includes senior management, distribution, sales and marketing, and operations. It is a "management improvement" requiring an executive decision. The second, an "operating improvement," is more in line with traditional process-improvement approaches.

The OEM's vision does not touch the processes for its own supplier. There could be a number of reasons. First, the manufacturer's business might not be significant enough to influence the supplier of input materials. The decision could also be a question of priorities, and there might be insufficient benefits from inventory reduction and other savings to justify the effort. Another factor will be the supply-demand situation for the supplier's product. If the supplier's product is in short supply, bargaining power may be limited. Large batches must be purchased to obtain access to the materials at a reasonable price. On the other hand, perhaps this effort to become more demand driven could proceed in the future. That effort could establish a similar partnership with the supplier or could shift business to another, more flexible supplier or distributor.

Sometimes a supply chain needs to add a distributor, the reverse of disintermediation. This was the case in the United States with Toyota's aftermarket parts supply chain.[2] North American Parts Operations (NAPO) coordinates 250,000 service parts and accessories to keep 20 million Toyota, Lexus, and Scion automobiles on the road. Toyota, before implementing a lean service parts chain, had over 500 suppliers shipping directly to 11 parts distribution centers (PDC). These PDCs serviced dealerships at the retail level. This situation led to a proliferation of small shipments, averaging 15 daily, into each PDC from each supplier. The many deliveries disrupted PDC operations that needed to focus on serving dealers. This was also costly for manufacturers because they were shipping all over the country to the 11 PDCs throughout the month. The NAPO response was to establish two parts centers, one in California (western United States) and the other in Kentucky (eastern United States), to take these shipments. These in turn serviced the 11 PDCs in

Table 17.2 Vision for To-Be Supply Chain Decisions

1 Level	2 Entities	3 Step	4 Decision/Action Required	5 Frequency	6 Lead Time (weeks)	7 Basis of Decision	8 Responsibility	9 Forecast or Demand Driven
1	Retail chain	Order: store-level replenishment	Refill stock to target levels	Daily	1	Point-of-sale (POS) system data	Automatic. Set by chain replenishment system	Demand driven
2		Order: chain distribution center replenishment	Reorder predetermined batch quantity	Weekly	1	Reorder point set in system by SKU	Automated system. Buyer reviews by exception	Demand driven
3	Distributor	Remove the distributor from the supply chain. Institute direct delivery to the retail distribution center by the manufacturer						

#		Activity	Rule	Frequency		Input	Role	Driver
4	Manufacturer	Produce: manufacturer	To make or not to make a batch on fixed schedule	Weekly	2	POS data from the retail chain	Factory production planner	Demand driven
5	Manufacturer	Order: manufacturer raw material	Order predetermined batch quantity	Weekly	2	Factory consumption	Factory production planner	Demand driven
6	Manufacturer's supplier	Order: supplier warehouse replenishment	Batch size based on forecast	Quarterly	4	Manufacturer forecast	Commodity planner	Forecast driven
7	Manufacturer's supplier	Produce: supplier	Batch size based on forecast	Quarterly	1	Sales forecast and production plan	Factory production planner Manufacturing manage	Forecast driven
8	Manufacturer's supplier	Order: supplier material replenishment	Batch size based on forecast	Quarterly	3	Sales forecast	Commodity manager	Forecast driven

a more coordinated way, enabling *heijunka* (demand-driven smooth flow) through-out the supply chain. It also represents a form of postponement by more closely timing quantities from the parts centers to the PDCs, enabling demand-driven decisions at the PDC rather than forecast-driven ones.

17.2 The Path from Forecast-Driven to Demand-Driven Supply Chain

This section describes the path to the demand-driven supply chain and identifies tools to use on the journey. These include those from several approaches: lean, Theory of Constraints, Six Sigma, and RFID. Often these tools are applied to reduce inventory and operating costs; but their potency in creating a demand-driven supply chain should not be overlooked, and companies should add this goal to their mission. As an example from Chapter 16, one of West Marine's pump suppliers, the Jabsco division of ITT Industries, found that they could leverage their Six-Sigma effort to meet West Marine's demands.[3]

17.2.1 Continuous Improvement Model for the Demand-Driven Supply Chain

Figure 17.3 describes a cyclical continuous improvement process for applying tools to create a demand-driven supply chain. This process will take time to complete; it is not one that happens quickly by fiat. At the core of the process is time mapping, a

Figure 17.3   Achieving the demand-driven supply chain.

careful documentation of lead times throughout the supply chain as demonstrated in Table 17.1. Cutting lead time and cycle times will aid the journey to the demand-driven goal. By shortening these times, fewer inventories are required in the cycle getting the retailer's order fulfillment much closer to the time of the consumer's product acquisition.

Two important methodologies for becoming demand driven rely on the virtues of *Commonality* discussed earlier. These are *postponement* and the *3C Alternative to MRPII*, shown at the top of the cycle in Figure 17.3. Examples of postponement include companies already noted in this chapter. Dell's build-to-order model for its A-type products, "postpones" commitment of final product configurations until the order arrives. Mix-to-order paint technology at the point of sale enables blending colors to match other colors or paint chips provided by the customer. Apparel companies such as American Apparel and United Colors of Benetton delay dying garments until consumer demand for specific colors is determined by market performance, thereby avoiding costly errors.

A company implementing a demand-driven supply chain could start immediately to convert its decisions from forecast driven to demand driven. This should trigger efforts employing both operational and management tools to help cut both cycle time and lead time in the supply chain.

17.2.2 The 3C Alternative to MRPII

The 3C Alternative to MRPII deserves particular attention.[4] Although there are many ways to reach a demand-driven supply chain, this methodology has the elements one must address on such a journey. Similar to postponement, 3C capitalizes on the *Commonality* (one of the Cs) inherent in product structures. It is especially appropriate in products and market combinations where achieving forecast accuracy is difficult. This is likely in V and T products where products with a common base are sold in many forms and outlets. The fact that A products are sold through fewer channels means there are fewer sources for forecast data on which to base decisions. However, A products built on common modules such as Honda engines, could also consider 3C.

The other Cs in 3C are *Consumption* and *Capacity*. Consumption comes from the demand-driven property in 3C wherein end-user consumption drives decisions along the chain. This is achieved by identifying "consumption centers" between each link in the chain. The consumption centers trigger replenishment orders from upstream sources. This feature addresses the common problem of lag due to differing replenishment lead times and serves to synchronize the chain.

Another example of a supply chain, shown in Figure 17.4 helps explain 3C. This is a V-type product example because it begins with a simple formulation that is reshaped into different configurations based on packaging and labels. Similar to the example in Figure 17.2, only retailers (1) and distributors (2) closest to the end-user

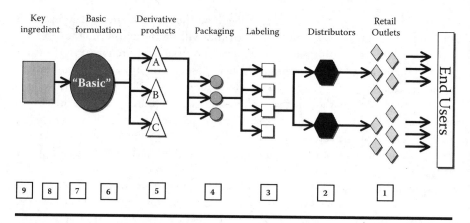

Figure 17.4 Example supply chain for 3C application.

have visibility over actual consumption. If they base their decisions on demand, the percentage demand-driven for the supply chain is 22 (2/9). With consumption centers further back in the chain (3 upward), replenishment will be by demand rather than forecast, increasing the percentage of decisions that are demand driven. For V-type products as in this example, the percentage should ultimately be high—90 to 100 percent.

Capacity, the last C, sets 3C replenishment rules. This is how much to replenish when the signal comes. These replenishments are on fixed intervals called the "time between pulls (or purchases)," or TBP. Note that 3C employs a fixed interval, variable quantity reordering cycle, rather than a fixed quantity, variable interval one used by many who rely on economic order quantity (EOQ) formulations. This ensures regular flow; one knows that product will move at every interval as long as there is consumption. If there is no end-user consumption, no production will occur, limiting inventory buildup without the corresponding end-user demand. Also, by setting rules based on capacity, there can never—at least theoretically—be an out-of-stock condition.

The data in Table 17.3 illustrates how to derive a replenishment rule for manufacturing the Basic formulation (level 6)—labeled "Basic" in Figure 17.4. This is the raw material for the three derivative products in Figure 17.4, products A, B, and C. With data from the bill of materials, or BOM, Table 17.3 shows how much Basic is required for each derivative product—4 units for each unit of product A, 10 units for product B, and 2 units for product C.

Conventional practice would have us forecasting all the end items for A, B, and C to decide how much Basic to produce. However, 3C takes a simpler approach. The rule is based on the frequency that Basic will be produced (the TBP), which is weekly in the example. The Capacity feature of 3C requires us to determine how much Basic could ever conceivably be consumed in the TBP period (a week). This capacity would assume that the largest user of Basic is 100 percent of product

Table 17.3 3C Alternative Method for Replenishment

	Product A	Product B	Product C	Target for Basic
"Basic" required per unit	4 units	10 units	2 units	4000a
Capacity per week	1000	50	500	

a 4 Units A × 1000.

demand. In this case, this is product A that would require 4000 units. If nothing but product A were sold, 4000 units of Basic would be required. For product B this figure is 500 units, for product C it is 1000 units. This assumption is conservative because products B and C will likely also be sold in any given week.

So, the business rule is that Basic replenishment be sufficient to reach the target inventory of 4000 units. If downstream demand has "pulled," or consumed, 1500 units of Basic in the past week, then 1500 units would be ordered. If none were pulled, zero units would be ordered. No rule could be simpler. Note that the 3C method also builds in reserve stock of Basic to populate the chain with initial inventory and to account for Basic's lead time. But, essentially, the amount consumed equals the amount reordered, and the customer demand is satisfied.

One reaction might be that targeting so conservatively will result in excess Basic inventory. The reality is that Basic will be consumed as it is produced, so that actual cycling inventory levels will never reach 4000 units. Also, the methodology allows for cutting back on the target inventory since the 100 percent assumption is highly unlikely, and the peak consumption of product B and C is far below that of Product A.

How does one determine the "capacity per week" for each product? If there were a manufacturing constraint, it could be in Basic production or even that of the key ingredient supplier (level 8). If supply chain capacity is not limited by physical constraints, then the constraint is the maximum sales rate of all the products that use Basic. For most T- and V-type products, internal constraints are unlikely in downstream processes such as assembly, packaging, and labeling.

For a T-type product, the chief consumption center will be at the very end of the chain closest to the end-user. A T-type product supplier seeking to provide VMI services to retailers with a broad customer base could use 3C to assure that enough inventory is on hand. For example, in Figure 17.4, the key ingredient supplier who serves many customers could manage its finished goods with 3C.

The supplier of a component to A-type assembly manufacturers such as Dell or General Motors could provide reliable, responsive VMI services to customers using 3C. Forecasts from the suppliers would establish initial inventories and be the basis for target inventories, providing a competitive advantage in selling to these customers.

Perhaps the greatest value of 3C is to V-type supply chains as in our example in Figure 17.4. Forecasting is really difficult because there are so many final product SKUs. Here, 3C offers an attractive alternative to synchronize the supply chain in the face of variable lead time and replenishment cycles, preventing inventory buildup and lost sales due to outages. Reducing lost sales addresses market mediation costs that arise from mismatches in supply and demand. These costs were the subject of Chapter 11, Section 11.3.

Mentioned earlier was the fact that retail supply chains must respond to goods in different parts of their life cycle, especially hard-to-predict fashion products. Some products may be "mature" or near the end of their economic lives; others may be "growth" products in great demand because of their novelty. Other special situations arise from promotions and sales, and seasonal goods. All these factors are arguments for moving from a forecast-driven planning method to a demand-driven one that offers more flexibility. The next section describes process improvement tools that complement postponement and 3C and make retail supply chains better able to handle seasonal and other special circumstances.

17.3 Demand-Driven Tools and Techniques

The Figure 17.3 toolkit for initiatives that support the transition to the demand-driven supply chain shows both operations and management improvements. As we saw in Table 17.2, both types of improvement are required. The groups differ in the talents they call upon. Operating improvements require industrial and manufacturing engineering type skills. Management improvements are business-related actions, such as pruning products, reducing suppliers, and collaborating with trading partners.

Achievements in these efforts will show up in time mapping that reflects lead time and cycle time. Because there is some variability in how these terms are defined, the authors here provide working definitions for them. *Lead time* is defined as industry expectation, set by market forces, for the time required from order entry to delivery of the product. It can also include the time to totally close the transaction, including inspecting the product and making payment. *Cycle time* is the amount of time it takes to produce the product if the velocity were 100 percent and there were no pauses or queues in the operation. That is, the product moves quickly from one step to another through the process. If a seller maintains a finished-goods inventory, the lead time will likely be less than the cycle time. Dell has prospered because it, not necessarily its suppliers, has a cycle time that is less than the industry standard lead time for custom computers. For a major build-to-order purchase, for example an aircraft, the cycle time is less than the lead time because the customer is reserving a place in a future production schedule that could be years away.

Being able to claim the shortest lead time among competitors is a customer service advantage. Reducing cycle time to support the demand-driven supply chain also leads to competitive advantages in the marketplace through lower costs and better responses to market changes. This is possible because velocities—the percentage of lead time required by cycle time—in many supply chains are less than 5 percent.

17.3.1 Operating Improvements

Many of the operating improvements listed here have been or are being adopted by companies. There will be few readers who will not have heard of "lean" or "Six Sigma," for example. This section links them with the implementation of the demand-driven supply chain. Too often, they are only pursued for their own sake, not as part of an overall strategy to become demand driven. Companies can enjoy higher returns if they blend these solutions. The obstacle to this is the reality that certain techniques come into fashion from time to time even though their underpinnings are not really new. Despite short-term hype, their pursuit in a competent way will add value to most companies, particularly if the company increases its expectations in terms of becoming more demand driven.

17.3.1.1 Lean Supply Chain Approaches

There are many techniques that arise from the Toyota Production System (TPS) that are collectively referred to as lean manufacturing or, more recently, lean supply chain. The two "pillars" of TPS are the following[5]:

- *Just-in-time* (JIT). This refers to the goal of producing the right products in the needed quantities at the right time, or being demand driven. JIT in the TPS infiltrates the production process. JIT is also a goal of postponement and 3C.
- *Autonomation.* This is "autonomous defect control." This term refers to preventing the passing of defective units from one step to another, avoiding disruption.

Popular lean approaches under the umbrella of these pillars include the following:

Kanban systems to pull product through the factory and supply chain. These systems link operations and use signals to notify upstream operations when to deliver and make more production units. The tool supports the demand-driven supply chain at the factory and work-center levels. Kanban is a fixed-quantity, variable-interval approach, and can be used at intermediate processes between 3C variable-quantity, fixed-interval consumption centers. There are some operations that may require a minimum batch size to make production or shipping economical. If this is the case, 3C replenishment quantities should be expressed in "batches" rather than "units."

Production smoothing (heijunka). This is load leveling that establishes an operating band that avoids too rapid fluctuations in production. A major waste is uneven production for example, where most of the production is at the end of fiscal periods, usually months or quarters. In 3C-regulated production, smoothing would assure that each item has a slot in production/shipping schedules during the time between pulls. Production leveling includes the idea of "takt" time, also called the "drumbeat" TOC. Takt time can be long or short depending on the type of product. Boeing might produce seven aircraft a month, whereas GE produces 700 light bulbs a minute. The takt time in the first case is 4.2 days, in the latter it is 0.086 seconds.

Standardized operations/standard work. Documentation of individual operations as well as factorywide expectations for a process ensures that best practices will be employed. The standard way includes cycle time, the operations routine, work methods, skill definitions, and quantity of work in process.

Setup reduction. These efforts, referred to as SMED for *single minute exchange of dies*, involve advanced preparation of equipment needed for production in factories. The preparation enables a fast changeover from one operation to another. This is a foundation for attacking the batch mentality that squeezes as much production as possible out of a single setup. The result of SMED efforts is better utilization of capacity and fewer interruptions in the flow of product through the chain.

Cells with improved layouts and flexible workers. In manufacturing and distribution centers, a worker can operate several types of machines and is cross trained in different operations. Multifunctional workers also enable the operation to work with fewer workers. All the resources needed to fulfill a customer need are clustered together in a cell. Increasingly, this includes not only production capabilities but also customer service, quality, engineering, and finance staff.

Small group improvement efforts. These efforts keep moving the organization toward continuous improvement in operations. *Kaizen* in Japanese means continuous improvement. Other sources of improvement are very intense projects that produce more radical, innovative change. In lean circles, these are called *kaikaku.* Chapter 15 described several continuous improvement kaizen models. These included PDCA (Plan-Do-Check-Act) and Six Sigma's DMAIC (Define–measure–analyze–improve–control). Undertaking the development of a supply chain strategy, using the model for change, is a kaikaku-type undertaking. Sometimes, such efforts seek to uncover "obstacles in the river." This is done by deliberately moving resources such as staff and inventory from a smoothly running process. When problems emerge, such as a rock or sandbar in the river, the company knows what to work on to improve the process.

Visual controls. These are easy-to-see displays of what is happening in operations. An example is prominent display of any conditions causing an interruption of flow so there is immediate awareness and understanding of deviations from normal processes. A worker can stop a production line if defects are being produced, thereby encouraging quick correction of the situation. With 3C, the tasks of monitoring consumption centers for shortfalls or excess inventory and calculating replenishment quantities are simplified.

17.3.1.2 Constraint Management

Figures 17.2 and 17.4 depict flow in the supply chain. TOC, referred to previously, observes that each process has a constraint and that these constraints need to be well managed. TOC calls the constraint the capacity constraint resource, or CCR. The CCR could be the same capacity constraint employed in setting replenishment levels with 3C. In our example in subsection 17.2.2, the constraint was the sales rate, not a physical constraint. In Table 17.1, the four-week lead time for the supplier finished goods replenishment (#6) might indicate a physical constraint in the supplier's production processes.

TOC calls for recognizing the constraint and adjusting inputs to the manufacturing enterprise or the supply chain so as not to exceed capacity at the constraint. Some companies, through lack of awareness of the constraint, may attempt to push too much product into the front end of their pipelines. This may be in response to previously mentioned new product introductions, sales campaigns, or promotions. It could also be from attempts to "stuff" channels with inventory to improve reported financial results.

TOC makes two other recommendations with regard to constraints. These are the following:

1. In seeking out investments to reduce costs, look for the CCR. Improvements there will return greater benefits because they improve the throughput, or capacity, of the entire supply chain. Savings at nonconstraints are minimal.
2. Use inventory to protect the CCR from upstream interruptions. So, in the event a nonconstraint operation ahead of the CCR is unavailable for a time, additional inventory will keep the CCR going until flow is restored. This is accommodated in the 3C methodology by considering upstream lead time when setting up initial inventories.

17.3.1.3 Quality Improvements

Quality improvements emphasize improving process capabilities to minimize product variation. These occur at the "hands-on" operations that create value for the customer. These take the form of Six Sigma initiatives in many companies. Six Sigma initiatives often travel alongside lean and TOC implementations as managers grope for improvements.

Reducing process variability is even more critical as partners become more tightly bound by JIT replenishments in demand-driven supply chains. As this trend continues, slip-ups by partners are magnified several times. We address this in this section because poor processes lead to bad parts or no parts as downstream operations dry up, creating a scramble along the chain to fill in the gap. Indeed, many expeditors, purchasing people, ERP systems, and inventory-tracking methods are needed to react to foul-ups. At the retail level, the result can be costly stockouts. Take away the quality deficiencies, then costs drop and revenues increase.

Process capability measures how well a process can perform to the specification set for it. The metrics of process capability are statistical and measure how well a process conforms to these specifications. The specification in whatever form is an important part of the buyer–seller relationship. Too tight a specification means the seller must go to extraordinary means to meet the specification. It could also lead to scrap, lost sales, and profit erosion. Sometimes, specifications are set without consideration of the capabilities of the manufacturing or distribution processes. Too loose a specification, on the other hand, spells trouble when the seller's components go into the buyer's product, potentially resulting in poor quality products and a negative reaction at the end-user level that creates a backlash aimed at the retailer. Any of these conditions will gum up a demand-driven supply chain.

The statistics for quality have been around for a long time. Common performance measures include P_p, P_{pk}, C_p, C_{pk}, first-time capability (FTC), line speed, and defective parts per million (ppm). This section provides an overview of common process capability terms and addresses their importance in the demand-driven supply chain.

The capability measures assume that outcomes of most processes will follow a normal distribution, known as the bell-shaped curve. Each normal distribution is specified by a *mean* (called X-bar) and a *standard deviation* symbolized by the Greek letter sigma, σ. The mean is the average of all the process outcomes; the standard deviation is a measure of the variation from the mean.

Both means and standard deviations can be calculated with spreadsheet programs. Adding all the outcomes and dividing by the number of observations gives the mean. For example, the mean of 1, 2, and 3 is (1 + 2 + 3)/3 = 2. The standard deviation takes the difference between each observation and the observation mean, squares it to remove plus and minus values, then divides by the number of observations, and finally takes the square root of the result. In the normal distribution, 68.3 percent of all outcomes are in one standard deviation, 95.4 percent are within two, and 99.7 percent are within three.

The three normal distributions in Figure 17.5 have the same mean but different standard deviations. "A" at the bottom has the highest standard deviation because it is the "fattest." "C" has the lowest because it is the narrowest. Because predictability is good when it comes to processes, a smaller sigma signals low variation from the specification, the sign of a reliable process.

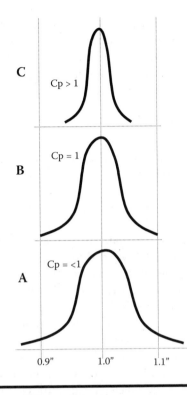

Figure 17.5   Process capability terminology.

However, reliability such as that in distributions A and B is not enough when you consider that there may be many processes required to produce a product. Even a "three sigma" process capability will produce 3000 defects in a million tries. With many processes required to make a product, at three-sigma levels there will be many defective products unless expensive inspection steps are added to the process. A Six-Sigma capability close to what we see in B and certainly implicit in C means that only 3.4 outcomes in a million attempts are out of specification for a process. This low defect rate will lead to reliable, competitive products.

The concepts described in this section also apply to "attributes." Attribute measures are "yes, it passes" or "no, it doesn't pass" situations. The so-called "perfect order" in the distribution industry would be judged on attributes because it must possess predefined attributes (on time, complete, proper invoice, and so on). Certainly, a less-than-perfect order has the potential to generate unwanted transactions that add cost and waste time. A benefit of 3C is that it sets up replenishment order rules among partners, reducing the chances of error in orders.

An example illustrates these concepts. A part is specified to be 1-inch long with a tolerance range of ± 0.1 inch. Thus, any part between 0.9 and 1.1 inch is acceptable under this specification, as shown in Figure 17.5. The performance measures for the process used to cut the part to that length are capable of repeatedly making parts within that range. After measuring a sample of actual parts, distributions similar to those shown in Figure 17.5 could result.

For example, we calculate a sigma value of 0.02 inches for a sample distribution of measured parts. The process sigma is then:

Process sigma = ± [Process tolerance/(2 × process sigma)] = ± [0.2/(2 × 0.02)] = ± 5

Another measure is called the process capability, or C_p, calculated by dividing the same process tolerance range by six times the standard deviation as follows:

$$Cp = 0.2/(6 × 0.02) = 1.67$$

This value, which is greater than one, most closely matches C in Figure 17.5. It is well within the Six-Sigma capability and would produce fewer defects than 3.4 per million chances. A standard deviation of 0.033 would produce a curve like B in Figure 17.5 as long as the process was centered on the desired mean of 1.0 inch. This would also be a Six-Sigma process. Standard deviations greater than 0.033 produce C_p values less than 1.0. These curves look similar to A in Figure 17.5. The process is not capable of meeting the Six-Sigma standard.

Despite the poor performance, the "A" situation has long been accepted practice in manufacturing, distribution, and retail. For manufacturing, this situation gave rise to "receiving inspection" where manufacturers head off suppliers' defective goods from reaching its product lines. Quality procedures now call for 100 percent inspection of parts if the processes that produced those parts fall below standards, creating a very visible cost of operations. To combat the situation, Jack Welch, the former CEO of General Electric, built a strategy around achieving Six-Sigma processes. Some caution that Six Sigma, essentially a process control tool, is touted improperly as a strategy.

Figure 17.5 shows distributions centered on the specified mean—1 inch. What if they aren't centered? Figure 17.6 shows tight distributions, equivalent to acceptable values of C_p, but off the desired mean. The measure C_{pk} corrects for shifts in the mean even though the spread is acceptable. "A" in this case is centered above the mean. "B" is below, whereas "C" is acceptable because it is centered. Both "A" and "B" would have C_p ratings in the acceptable range, but C_{pk} would be unacceptable for both. "C" has an acceptable C_{pk} because it is centered.

Sometimes, only a small sample is available. This happens in the case of a new component or a new process. In these cases the process is untested under high volume conditions. So, managers will calculate P_k and P_{pk} using pilot production samples. A higher threshold is required. For example a C_{pk} threshold can be 1.33, while the P_{pk} threshold is 1.67.

The measures we just discussed are likely found for individual operations. Other commonly used performance measures gauge the overall process. *First-time*

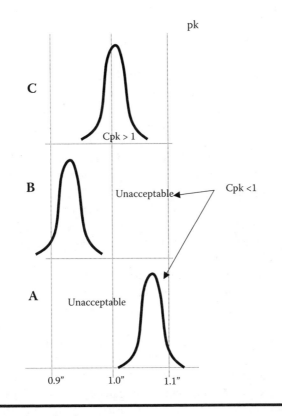

Figure 17.6   Meaning of Cpk.

capability (FTC) counts the number of acceptable products at each step in the process and at the end of the process. The constraint is that no rework can be done on the item at any point in the process. The picture provided is twofold. It shows how capable the collective process is, and it also points to possible bottlenecks that diminish capacity.

The equation for measuring FTC at the operation or process level is as follows:

FTC = (Quantity attempted – quantity rejected)/quantity attempted

FTC is often combined with a line speed evaluation. In manufacturing, this evaluation will confirm that the capacity required by the buyer is available. Line capacity is an issue with high-volume, closely linked supply chains. Often, the supplier is dedicating capacity, including machines and tooling, to fulfill the buyer's requirements. Line speed verification means producing product using the facilities and equipment when full-scale production begins. FTC can be calculated simultaneously. Product can also be measured to calculate process capabilities.

With low tolerance for error becoming more prevalent, collaboration along the supply chain becomes more crucial. Here are some examples in which quality issues play a part in joint trading partner decision making.

- **Designer versus doer.** The product designer, usually an engineer, must specify tolerances. Engineering is sometimes accused of "throwing the design over the wall" to manufacturing. SCM increasingly recognizes the need for the customer, designers, and operations people to work together to agree to and achieve process capabilities. Establishing collaborative relationships among trading partners to achieve the economies of the demand-driven supply chain will require the upstream partner to have capable processes.
- **Price versus quality.** The supplier selection decision may be driven by purchase price. However, the lowest purchase price may bring lower quality and bring on an abundance of hidden costs. Buying organizations must guard against this possibility. SCM practice will find new ways to reconcile conflicts between these two perspectives.
- **Old loyalties versus new blood.** There will be a time when the cord between the organization and a long-time supplier will have to be cut to assure the flow of quality components. When this should happen is often a gray area. Changing suppliers imposes a real cost on the buying organization. New sources have to be found; patterns of behavior have to be relearned.

The quality measures mentioned in this section emerged from manufacturing industry experience. They continue to find applications in the operations of non-manufacturing supply chain partners such as transportation, warehousing, and consolidation and distribution centers.

17.3.1.4 Design for Commonality

The demand-driven supply chain strategies at the top of Figure 17.3, postponement, and 3C work best when there is commonality in product designs. Some organizations do not design their products with this in mind because there are design constraints, or they are ignorant of the advantages. Commonality benefits exist from modular structures for complex products down to using common fasteners and other small components. These reduce raw material cost and simplify aftermarket service. Interestingly, chain restaurants have for years recognized the efficiency in combining a limited number of inputs into a variety of menu combinations. For example, Mexican restaurants, employing postponement, use refried beans, rice, guacamole, salsa fresca, various cheeses, and five or six preprepared meats in numerous menu offerings.

Postponement is especially good at reducing the inventory needed to maintain a certain level of customer service. The savings in inventory can be calculated. If a company sells two items that can be configured after orders come in, then it can reduce the cycling inventory—which excludes safety and dead stock—by 39 percent. This benefit is because postponement has eliminated the end-item forecasts and substituted last-minute configuration. Likewise, a postponement of five items into one common item reduces the inventory required to maintain customer service by 55 percent. So, the economics are compelling as shown in the table.

Consolidation from Postponement (Ratio)	Cycling Inventory Reduction (Percent)
2:1	39
3:1	44
4:1	50
5:1	55

Achieving commonality requires collaboration between sales, marketing, operations, and design functions. Designing its products with this in mind can make a manufacturer a more attractive partner to downstream retailers and distributors.

Postponement provides benefits such as those in the preceding table even if physical configuration changes are not needed. This comes by delaying (postponing) distribution to endpoints in the supply chain, such as individual retail stores. This is also the 3C approach, and it is the role a distributor plays in serving multiple retail stores from a centralized facility. Assuming each store sells different amounts of an item, holding stock at the distributor, whether it's internal or external, reduces the chances of dead stock at slower-selling stores and stockouts at faster-selling ones. This was the basis for Sam Walton's original Wal-Mart distribution strategy, in which one DC served ten or so stores within 250 miles, less than a day's drive away with the ability to return to the DC on the same day.

17.3.2 Management Improvements

Although operating improvements are most frequently assigned to technical staff, achieving management improvements requires managerial skills. Chapters 15 and 16 recommend frameworks for involving multiple functions and trading partners in initiatives to achieve the demand-driven supply chain. This involvement is important; some managers do not see operations as part of their job descriptions, yet their participation is necessary. The following subsections address issues using the demand-driven supply chain described in Tables 17.1 and 17.2. The decisions required are not technical in nature, but they do involve change, and must be understood and managed accordingly.

17.3.2.1 Synchronization and Fixed-Interval Planning

This category of management change could require widespread adjustments in many retailer and trading partner departments. For example, shifting to weekly, from monthly and quarterly, merchandise planning might require added staff and changes in systems, as well as changes in supplier behavior. It is also likely that synchronization would occur on a product-by-product or a customer-by-customer basis. This is because some product volumes are too low for such consideration, and some retail customers or suppliers may not want to participate. The result is tailored supply chains for individual "businesses within the business," such as those described in Chapter 12. In Chapter 15, West Marine tailored its replenishment schedules to correspond with the schedules of suppliers of different types of product.

Direct distribution from OEMs to selected retailer outlets will also strain some companies. This could require information links with the retailers and the ability to ship in smaller quantities—in this case, quantities similar to those distributed by former intermediaries. The reorder time for material is also shortened. This could require new procedures and relationships with suppliers. A company accustomed to a batch mentality must adjust to the fixed-interval discipline. This feature establishes a more continuous flow in the chain. It may also force a company to abandon department-level optimization. Costs such as transportation may increase with tighter control of inventory and the increased possibility of dispatching partially loaded delivery trucks or containers to customers. West Marine combated interruptions at its stores by picking up product at the suppliers and coordinating delivery.

17.3.2.2 Simplification

Many times, operating functions such as manufacturing and distribution must attempt to manufacture difficult products, manage complex distribution networks, or deal with poorly performing suppliers. West Marine is a good example. Our case from Table 17.2 shows that the demand-driven supply chain would bypass a distributor to create a direct path to the end-user, increasing the speed of information flow about retail consumption. Depending on the situation, this could require support from marketing, sales, financial, and operations managers.

The case did not deal with the key suppliers for any of several reasons stated earlier. However, the potential for improvement looks attractive. Improvement could be seen if the materials supplier were to synchronize with the new, shorter periods required by the manufacturer, who will be moving to a weekly cycle to meet the needs of its customer, the retailer. This is especially true because the current cycle is quarterly. If this does not happen, there will be a penalty in terms of excessive or insufficient raw material inventory for continuing to use this supplier.

17.4 Sponsoring the Demand-Driven Supply Chain

Leadership toward the goal of being demand driven can come from any one of the links in the chain. This "leader" must enlist other echelons in the effort. Leadership will depend on motivation, the ability to collaborate, the product category, opportunities for profit improvement, and the amount of business at stake. Depending on these variables, there are three likely leaders representing different supply chain echelons:

1. Retailers seeking to lower merchandise costs while assuring availability. They may take a category-by-category approach or a focus centered on store brands.
2. Independent distributors seeking a competitive edge by virtue of the service while lowering their cost at the same time.
3. OEMs who seek to improve their position while lowering market mediation costs for themselves if they bear the brunt for returns or for the retailer.

An OEM will find implementing the demand-driven supply chain attractive if it can do more business with lower inventories, while maintaining or achieving high levels of service. Some may employ the technique selectively with larger companies. According to data derived by Revere Data and the Securities and Exchange Commission, a number of large manufacturers sell a lot of merchandise to Wal-Mart.[6] Playtex Products, Clorox, Hasbro, and Revlon do over 20 percent of their business with the world's largest retailer. Can this be a "business within the business" with a demand-driven supply chain?

Retailers, probably the largest, might take the leadership role with selected OEMs. Alternatively, the retailer might set up pull systems through their captive distribution centers, ordering merchandise from most or all its suppliers based on demand. This would require negotiations with a large number of suppliers.

Independent distributors may have the most to gain as intermediaries by injecting demand-driven techniques into decision-making process. Indeed, those providing VMI services already do. The distributor may also have the most to gain because their profitability is closely tied to their ability to manage inventory.

17.5 Demand-Driven Supply Chain—Summary

Achieving the demand-driven supply chain gives trading partners a reason for collaborating and provides mutual advantages. Depending on the priority and the complexity of the chain, the journey could be a lengthy one, and so, the continuous improvement mentality is necessary. Also required are skills in working on multicompany improvement projects. It is likely that leadership for the demand-driven supply chain will lie with larger OEMs and distributors and include large retailers such as Wal-Mart. Members of these echelons understand the problem better and can influence product design. All can utilize demand-driven delivery as a competitive weapon in the dynamic retail supply chain.

Endnotes

1. Gomes, Lee, "Deciphering a Hot Tech Acronym: Can It Improve Software Building?" *The Wall Street Journal*, July 18, 2006, p. B4.
2. "Leveraging Lean Principles in a Service Parts Supply Chain: the Toyota Story," *CSCMP Explores ...*, Summer 2006.
3. Smith, Larry, "A CPFR Success Story," *Supply Chain Management Review*, March 2006, p. 35.
4. For further reading, see *3C: A Proven Alternative to MRPII for Optimizing Supply Chain Performance* Fernández-Rañada, Gurrola-Gal, & López-Tello and the *Handbook of Supply Chain Management, 2nd Edition* by James B. Ayers.
5. Monden, Yasuhiro, *Toyota Production System*, Norcross, Georgia: Institute of Industrial Engineers, 1983.
6. Hudson, Kris, "Wal-Mart Ripple Effect Strikes Again: Cutbacks Weigh on Supplier Earnings," *The Wall Street Journal*, April 27, 2006, p. C1.

Chapter 18

Product Tracking Along Retail Supply Chains

This chapter describes retail supply chain tracking tools categorized as "automatic identification and data capture" (AIDC) technologies.[1] Technical innovations, accompanied by an increasing number of solution providers, make this an area of increased attention and investment. The same technologies also create confusion among supply chain decision makers. The confusion arises in deciding which of the many proposed options is the "correct" one for a particular supply chain. Also, the economics of AIDC change continuously, with costs of implementation declining as technologies become more widespread.

Despite the confusion, channel masters such as Wal-Mart and the Department of Defense mandate increased use of radio frequency identification, or RFID, by their suppliers. RFID is a prominent AIDC technology; therefore, managers along the retail supply chain, including manufacturers and distributors, must be informed about its applications.

The retail industry already relies heavily on technology, a significant change over the last 40 years that occurred with the advent of the general-purpose business computer and scanner technologies. Each year a large retailer could easily have thousands of suppliers providing tens of thousands of stockkeeping units (SKUs) and hundreds of thousands of deliveries to hundreds of locations. The size of today's retailers such as Costco, Target, Best Buy, Walgreen's, and others has been made possible by electronic digital information processes. For any single company, these transactions generate millions—if not billions—of information exchanges in the form of forecasts, orders, shipping notices, receipt documentation, payments, and returns.

The need to track merchandise extends from the manufacturing process to the store shelf. In fact, according to Kerry Pauling, vice president of information systems at Wal-Mart, getting stock through the "last 90 feet" from the stockroom to the shelf is "where we often have breakdowns." An interesting example of potentially costly losses occurs in grocery stores. Customers often decide at the check stand against purchasing items they have previously selected. These may be perishables that, if not returned to refrigerators or freezers promptly, will spoil and become unsalable, yet the inventory tracking system has totally lost track of the whereabouts of these products. Keeping tabs on such complex, high-volume processes is daunting. Furthermore, in a global economy, trading partners in many countries are bolstering the need for standards that ensure efficient and timely information exchanges.

This chapter provides an overview of selected AIDC technologies, addressing technologies, and related standards. The contents include the following:

1. Standards for identification and tracking
2. RFID
3. The vision for integrated distribution and retail solutions

18.1 Low-Tech Retailing

Fred Abernathy is with the Center for Textile and Apparel Research at Harvard University. He has traced the growth of bar-code technology, an early AIDC technology. Bar codes, more technically known as Universal Product Codes (UPC), are the foundation standard for retail supply chain tracking. Abernathy describes the labor-intensive state of the retail supply chain before bar codes made their appearance.[2]

■ Merchandise was spread around—on the store floor, in the backroom, or in the warehouse.
■ Knowing what was actually selling was problematic.
■ Orders were placed six to nine months ahead of the selling season, well before trends in demand could be discerned.
■ Assistant buyers tracked inventory manually, a labor-intensive process.
■ Paper records reflected sales of categories, not individual SKUs, reducing the precision required for effective reordering.
■ The retailer, detached by long lead time and information gaps from manufacturers, carried the risks that go with stockouts or surpluses.

Before bar codes, "Kimball tickets," a small form of the old punch card technology, was the only real mechanization that existed for inventory tracking. These tickets were processed by a form of unit record equipment and, because of the many

Figure 18.1 Bar-code formats.

opportunities for human error, were far less than accurate. The advent of bar codes began the shift to automated tracking. In 1973, IBM was awarded the contract by the Uniform Grocery Product Code (UGPCC) Ad Hoc Committee and the consulting firm McKinsey & Company to develop a bar-code technology usable across the industry. In June 1974, at a store in Ohio, a 10-pack of Wrigley's chewing gum was the first item to cross a bar-code scanner. Subsequently, the retailer Kmart introduced bar codes for apparel in 1983. Others like Wal-Mart followed, bringing the spread of what Abernathy describes as "lean retailing." Improvements in computing technology abetted the spread by translating captured bar-code data to support merchandising decisions.

The initial UPC specification had 12 digits, 11 required by UGPCC plus one check digit. The check digit protects against errors in reading the codes. This version is the first shown in Figure 18.1. Most current U.S. bar codes use this format, or *symbology*. After submittal, the IBM team was asked to add a 13th digit that could be read without modifying equipment already in the field. This is the second version in Figure 18.1. This addition provided country identification, in effect enabling the worldwide spread of the UPC. The additional digit also led to the European Article Numbering, or EAN, system administered by EAN International (now GS1). Their standards are called the EAN*UCC standard. They cover bar codes, electronic data interchange (EDI) transaction sets, XML schemas, and other supply chain requirements.

As noted later, they promote the standard under the auspices of another organization, EPCglobal. EPC stands for *electronic product code*. In the automated identification space, participating organizations, standards, and products have proliferated, a potential confusion factor to those who have not followed the evolution.

In Figure 18.1, there are ten identifying digits plus "overhead" digits. These are for the check digit and identification functions. The EAN version has the two-digit number system code plus a check digit, whereas the UCC version has one identifier and one check digit. A manufacturer (or distributor or retailer) can have 99,999 SKUs by virtue of the five-digit product code. Adding to the complexity of the standards, each of these symbologies has variations for special circumstances. Many of these variations, some of which are described later, use techniques to shrink the space required for the bar code, enabling bar coding of small items.

Once a manufacturer, distributor, or retailer is assigned an EPC manager code, the organization is free to assign codes to products. This can be for internal or external use. In fact, some retail merchandise such as an apparel item may have multiple bar code identities as it passes along the supply chain. An example would be the product code for the original manufacturer and another for the retailer.

18.2 Beyond Basic Bar Codes

As older UCC and EAN formats have neared their capacities, standards for the 14-digit GTIN number (Global Trade Identification Number) have emerged. *GTIN* has become the umbrella term for all the bar code data structures such as those in Figure 18.1 and others needed for other data carriers such as RFID. This number identifies the manufacturer, product, version, and serial number. Where a number uses fewer than 14 digits, it is padded with zeros, encouraging migration to a uniform length in bar codes.

The voluntary nonprofit organization EPCglobal, Inc., is an independent body with a board of governors from leading supply chain "subscribers." The organization had its origin in the Auto-ID Center at MIT. GS1 and GS1 US, which set standards, are members. EPCglobal's mission is to support the deployment of radio frequency technology. EPCglobal refers to this as the EPCglobal Network™. The head of EPCglobal US, Mike Meranda, has described the role of the organization.[3] Meranda states, "standards development is not the destination." He notes that technology is "a tool to achieve a business objective." His organization uses five elements to promote its mission to the technical community:

1. Electronic Product Code™ (EPC)—the globally unique serial number that identifies items of all types along the supply chain.
2. ID System—the RFID tag that stores the EPC and the hardware needed to read the EPC. At the time of writing, Gen 2 ("Generation 2") was the standard, displacing Gen 1 technologies with better tag and reader technology.
3. EPC Middleware—software interfaces that manage supply chain read events and the handling of the information. Interfaces with EPC information services (#4 below) and enterprise systems.
4. EPC Information Services—enables information exchanges with trading partners through the EPCglobal network.
5. Discovery Services—tools that enable users to find data related to specific EPCs.

The core element, the EPC, includes items in the GTIN and adds extra digits for unique item identification, supporting what is called "item-level tracking" or ILT.

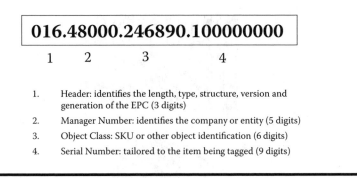

1.   Header: identifies the length, type, structure, version and generation of the EPC (3 digits)
2.   Manager Number: identifies the company or entity (5 digits)
3.   Object Class: SKU or other object identification (6 digits)
4.   Serial Number: tailored to the item being tagged (9 digits)

Figure 18.2   Electronic product code (EPC).

ILT aids in combating counterfeits, providing product quality documentation, and better managing inventory. A report in the publication *DC Velocity* describes emerging applications for ILT and the drivers behind them.[4]

■ Tagging innovative products such as new CDs and DVDs so they are easy to locate during their short introduction windows.
■ Documenting pharmaceutical movement through the supply chain. Example: Purdue Pharma shipping tagged bottles of OxyContin to Wal-Mart and a wholesaler.
■ Cost-effectively locating hard-to-find sizes and colors of upscale apparel items before a customer leaves the store because an item can't be found.
■ Theft reduction for high-value goods such as jewelry, rental skis, and electronics.
■ Expiration date tracking for food items such as cream cheese.
■ Monitoring temperatures along the supply chain.
■ Automatically playing a promotional video about the product when a customer picks up a merchandise item in the store.

Figure 18.2 shows components of the EPC. EPCglobal refers to this number as a "license plate." It can be assigned to "objects" in the supply chain such as individual items, cases, pallets, and locations. It is also compatible with existing numbering systems such as the GTIN. The "manager" number is assigned to companies wanting to use the bar-code system.

Although the basic 12- and 13-digit bar codes are familiar to most retail customers, other bar code formats exist that enable greater returns from the technology. These include the following:

■ Reduced space symbology (RSS), for placing bar codes on small items or adding needed information not available in regular bar codes while keeping a small footprint.

Figure 18.3   2D Bar code examples.

■ Two-dimensional (2-D) bar codes that, used with or without one-dimensional (1-D) codes such as UCC*EAN bar codes, provide around 2000 characters depending on the format. Figure 18.3 shows examples of the many available formats.

RSS formats include RSS-14, RSS Limited, and RSS Expanded, and finds application on smaller items such as individual pieces of fruit, cosmetics, jewelry, and so forth. Their appearance is similar to regular bar codes. Some formats have "double deck" or two lines of code to conserve space. Sometimes, the retailer needs to add information to basic bar codes in the same space provided by UCC*EAN bar codes. SKUs with limited shelf life such as dairy products and pharmaceuticals are examples and need to include expiration dates. Other applications include SKUs sold by weight such as meat and produce, items that require tracing, and promotion products eligible for coupons.

As shown in Figure 18.3, 2-D bar codes resemble postage stamps with a variety of patterns imprinted on them. Some applications combine conventional 1-D with 2-D data. Such uses described by the 2-D bar code company Dataintro Software include income tax returns, mixed SKU packing lists, and patient medical records. In these situations, the 1-D bar code provides the license plate identifier. The 2-D bar code provides the details. Other versions are designed for data capacity or for reading on high-speed conveyor lines.

Designing systems to read bar codes can be an engineering challenge. Intermec, a firm offering supply chain automation solutions, recommends different technologies depending on the nature of the item read, the potential for dirt on the bar code, whether the location is inside or outside, whether the bar code is 1-D or 2-D, and the distance over which the read must occur. Such complexities, plus the frequent need for labor to use the technology, are motivators for supply chain managers to turn to RFID technology although bar coding is considerably less expensive and, in some instances, can be used in conjunction with newer technologies.

18.3 Radio Frequency Identification

RFID applications already appear around us in the form of automatic car locks, road and bridge toll collection, subway fare collection, library materials checkout and return, animal identification microchips, and human implants of various sorts. Successful RFID implementation depends on collaboration among supply chain trading partners. For the distribution center or the retail store to use RFID, the manufacturer must place tags on its pallets, cartons, or individual items. What level—pallet, carton, or item—will vary, depending on item value, the cost of implementation, the need for control, and other factors.

18.3.1 The Retail Application

The most common RFID application in retail supply chains calls for placement of low-cost "passive" tags. These are part of open-loop systems. That is, the merchandise passes from company to company along the supply chain. The tag is passive if it has no energy source. "Active" tags, discussed later, have batteries or other power sources. These are often installed in closed-loop systems confined to a single company or small group of trading partners. The more expensive active tags are usually recycled for multiple trips through the process.

The energy required to transmit the passive tag's content is provided by the radio frequency energy transmitted by the reader. The reader transmits enough energy to cause the tag to respond with identifying data stored on the tag. The tag antenna length is half the wavelength of the operating frequency, so lower frequencies have larger antennas, the most visible part of the tag. The chip, in fact, is about the size of the head of a pin that can be seen as small dots near the center of the tags. Figure 18.4 shows examples of RFID tags.

The antennas on the passive tags have different sensitivity to the direction of the reader's signal. The tag signal is also affected by metal or liquids within and near the tagged product and the location of the tag on the product. Tags should be chosen with these factors in mind, as well as an understanding of how each tag will be scanned and where that will occur. For example, the four-dipole model (upper right in Figure 18.4) is less sensitive to orientation. With regard to capacity, a passive tag can hold up to hundreds of bits of data.

Passive Tags

1x4 Single Dipole Read/Write
(Symbol Technologies)

4x4 Dual Dipole Read/Write
(Symbol Technologies)

Active Tags

TC4S Active Tag
(Identec Limited)

Active Tag for Securing
Shipping Containers
(Savi Technology)

Figure 18.4   Passive and active RFID tags.

With RFID tags on each case on a pallet, a reader can identify all the cases without a person having to scan each case. Lower-frequency readers have a short range of a few inches. Higher-frequency readers have ranges up to about 30 feet. Like the bar-code system, designing an RFID application requires a number of considerations that depend on supply chain requirement and system costs, some of which are listed later in this chapter.

In a typical warehouse application, the reader will be placed at each dock door, or portal. The RFID data capture would take place as pallets are offloaded from the truck or railcar. Costs per portal can exceed $10,000, so implementing RFID has to be justified by savings in labor and improved tracking accuracy, particularly in a large warehouse with 100 doors. To minimize this cost, warehouses frequently have separate RFID portals near a group of loading docks. Items are unloaded from trucks into a receiving area and then pushed through, or placed on a conveyor to pass through, one of the RFID portals. Other applications call for handheld readers or readers on lift trucks. These provide added flexibility in exchange for a decreased investment.

The same economic hurdle exists at the store level—the need to lower the cost of tagging and reading enough so that improvements in labor cost and data utility can pay for the technology. Complicating matters is the fact that a company such as Wal-Mart dictates RFID to its manufacturers. However, the manufacturer may enjoy few direct benefits. The use of RFID tags may result in large orders from large retail chains; most benefits accrue further down the supply chain. In fact, manufacturer attachment of RFID tags without using the technology for its own purposes has been called "slap and ship." Section 18.4 describes an example of tracking stock as it moves from manufacturer to retail store shelf.

18.3.2 Active RFID

Active RFID tags include their own power supply. Two categories of these tags have internal power supplies in the form of batteries, an electric grid connection, or solar power. These are called active or semiactive (also called battery-assisted) tags. Active tags transmit to the reader, unlike passive tags, which use energy from the reader to respond. The semiactive tag is triggered by the reader but uses onboard power to respond. This increases the range over which it can be read. The read is also faster because the delay involved in responding is less. A speedy response is important if the tag is moving at high speed. Active tags can be read at distances of about 300 feet.

Often, the best applications for active RFID are closed-loop supply chain processes. The closed-loop application takes place in a single facility or company or in linked processes shared by trading partners. An example is an auto parts supplier and its assembly plant customer. The active tag tracks material shipped to its supplier and is removed after the part is assembled onto an automobile. Another example would be a laptop computer repair facility serving a retailer such as Best Buy where active RFID tracks laptop location through the repair process. In closed-loop applications, the tag is attached when the item enters the process, and removed when it leaves.

Both passive and active tags support capabilities for rewriting data over the life of the tag. A read-only (RO) tag is programmed at the factory where it's manufactured; no rewriting is possible. So, this type of tag finds limited use. A write-once, read-many (WORM) is written by the user and read throughout the supply chain. This is the most common type of tag. A read-write (RW) tag can be rewritten practically indefinitely.

An alternative passive tag technology called the Surface Acoustic Wave (SAW) has advantages over the microchips deployed in today's RFID tags. SAW chips utilize the piezoelectric effect, which relies on the fact that ceramic substances and some crystals generate voltage when mechanical stresses are applied to them. The transducer located on piezoelectric material generates a surface wave when excited by the reader's radio pulse. That surface wave is converted into acoustic wave pulses coded to the tag's data. The transducer then converts the waves back into a radio wave to send to the reader. The SAW technology has longer ranges, is more rugged, can be used around difficult materials such as metals and liquids, uses less power, and is more accurate.

18.3.3 RFID Applications

Engineering an RFID application must address a number of variables, including the following:

- The mission of the system—identification only, environmental sensing, or security
- The use for system data and interfacing systems that support data conversion

- The distance over which that must be read
- Antenna design to assure that tags can be read, and the orientation of containers to reader antennae
- The frequency to use for RF communication—generally, a choice between HF (3–30 MHz) and UHF (300 MHz–3GHz)
- Materials in the environment and atmospheric conditions that might interfere with reception
- Economic factors such as the cost of tags and readers and the return on investment (ROI)
- The need for rugged readers and tags in demanding locations such as warehouses
- The level of merchandise tagging (usually pallet, case, or individual item)
- Methods of attachment of tags to the pallets, cartons, or items to be read
- The frequency of data exchange, a determinant of battery life for active tags

Despite the complexity, RFID applications abound with usage application concepts seemingly limited only by the designer's imagination. The following are a few examples along the supply chain from manufacturers to end-users. Note that the examples are not necessarily spread all along the chain; finding a payoff from RFID often starts "bottom up."

- International Paper uses passive RFID tags at its 300,000-sq. ft. paper mill warehouse in Texarkana, Arkansas. The system follows the location of its large paper rolls and manages the loading of the rolls onto railcars and truck trailers. The system locates paper rolls to a confidence of plus or minus six inches. A continuously updated picture of loading status for 50 truck and rail dock doors enhances visibility.
- Volkswagen in Germany uses active RFID to track new vehicles through the final stages of preparation for customer delivery. Tags are attached after a vehicle is assembled and tracked in a closed-loop application through washing, vacuuming, cleaning, and quality control until the customer picks up the car.
- A chemical company uses semiactive tags to track the bulk containers required to deliver its product to customers, another closed-loop application. Because the containers must be returned, the visibility provided by the system has lowered the company's investment considerably by tracking the vessels and helped it recover the expensive containers that might not have returned.
- MTR Construction Ltd in Hong Kong is in the business of building and operating the Hong Kong rail system. It developed its RFID-based *octopus* card for riders on its trains. Now an octopus card can buy merchandise at

convenience stores, fast-food chains, supermarkets, and vending machines. Building on its experience, MTR added RFID tracking to construction material and construction equipment used in its many rail-related and commercial development projects. Tagged items are principally concrete shapes where the tags capture the results of quality testing to ensure the structural integrity of its buildings.

■ Startup Intelligent Global Pooling Systems (iGPS) has ordered five million Gen 2 passive RFID tags. The company will tag pallets. At 23 cents per tag, four will be placed at corners on each $55 pallet in the company's pool. The tags incorporate EPCglobal's Reusable Asset Identifier (GRAI) that uniquely identifies each pallet. The goal is real-time tracking of each pallet. The company has targeted monthly production at 400,000 pallets to be added to the pool.

These examples serve to illustrate the creativity leading to spread of RFID technology. They demonstrate that good returns are available if creativity is used to design the application. This particularly seems to be the case in closed-end approaches. The following sections focus on retail supply chain applications that are likely to find expanded deployment.

Two reports in early 2007 assess the viability of RFID in open-loop retail applications. Philip Lazo, vice president of Motorola's Global Products Group, delivered his assessment to a conference of supply chain professionals.[5] Lazo is an executive at Motorola's recently acquired Symbol Technologies business, a company serving the AIDC market. A *Wall Street Journal* article provided another assessment with consistent conclusions.[6] Table 18.1 summarizes those conclusions regarding the business case for RFID from these sources. The table shows benefits along the chain at retailer, distribution or transportation, and manufacturer echelons. The "most attractive" category refers to benefits that are most likely to justify RFID system costs at the time of the appraisal. The "emerging" category refers to benefits that seem, at the time of the appraisal, to be likely to justify RFID in a short time frame.

Perhaps the most compelling case is prevention of out-of-stock incidents at retailers. This is the last 90 feet along the long supply chain and the reason Wal-Mart established its Remix supply chain described in Chapter 12, Section 12.3. Promotions execution, the subject of a case later in this chapter (subsection 18.5.1), ensures that merchandise and displays are in place. These efforts usually accompany expensive advertising and promotion campaigns. RFID helps protect that investment. Asset utilization refers to assets used in transportation; a couple of the examples mentioned earlier focused on this benefit. Faster pack and pick was a benefit sought by International Paper for its paper rolls. Many of the other benefits arise from automation of processes displacing bar-code reading.

Table 18.1   RFID Justification—Early 2007

Justification	Retailer	Distribution/ Transportation	Manufacturer
Most attractive	Prevents out of stocks/lost sales Automated processing/ storage accuracy Promotions execution	Asset utilization	Promotional items
Emerging	Reduce shrinkage Inventory accuracy Product rotation Return tracking	Shipping/ receiving accuracy Faster pick and pack Electronic proof of delivery	Asset management Work-in-process tracking Recalls Shipping accuracy Cold-chain applications Chargebacks Maintenance/repair

18.4 Tracking in Transit

Total supply chain visibility requires knowledge of where the product is all along the chain, not just in controlled facilities. This means visibility requires in-transit tracking, a capability provided by what are called real-time location systems (RTLS). This tracking is not always just for identification purposes. Security measures may seek to ensure that a container from a distant supplier poses no security threat. Monitoring the integrity of the container seal and monitoring for signs of hazardous materials provides assurance regarding the supply chain shipment. To this end, the U.S. government has elicited the cooperation of supply chain participants in C-TPAT, or Customs-Trade Partnership Against Terrorism. Those collaborating in this effort agree to take preventive measures to protect against container tampering.

Some products require a "cold chain." Chapter 21, Section 21.1, describes these demanding chains. That is, the user must be assured that temperature limits are met throughout the chain. One way to ensure this is to monitor temperature in transit, at warehouses, and stores. This requires sensors attached to active RFID tags that keep track of temperature exposure as the product travels through its various intermediaries from manufacturer to retailer. Other types of sensors may monitor radioactivity, chemical environment, humidity, shocks, and vibration, as required.

Figure 18.5   Mitsui supply chain visibility tracking.

Yoshibumi Kotsuka of Mitsui & Company in the United States describes a test implementation for RTLS.[7] Kotsuka's position at his company is Director, Transportation and Logistics. His company provides services and financing related to export, import, and offshore trading. Since 2003, the company has pioneered applications with RFID in manufacturing, logistics, and retailing. Mitsui offers a service called *SCM Live* for tracking material movements in global supply chains.

Kotsuka identifies the following keys to success in implementing a supply chain visibility application:

- RFID tag data must be generated at the origin—where the goods are manufactured.
- Success requires cooperation among trading partners to avoid disruption and ensure ease of use.
- The solution must adhere to global standards and involve a blend of AIDC technologies. For example, his solutions include EDI, bar codes, active and passive RFID, and global positioning systems (GPS), among others.
- An infrastructure—such as Mitsui's *SCM Live*—must gather data generated by the system.
- Users must mine the data and put it to work to make decisions along the supply chain.

Mitsui piloted the deployment of tracking technology. The test was from points of origin at manufacturing centers at Guandong and Shenzhen in southern China across the ocean to U.S. ports at Long Beach and Los Angeles, and then on to inland distribution centers. This is a heavily traveled path for imports from China into the United States. Figure 18.5 depicts the path across several transportation links.

At the carton level, the manufacturer attached both bar codes and passive RFID. Each carton contained 16 individual items. Each pallet, which was also tracked with passive RFID, held 16 cartons, or 256 items. The pallets went into a container sealed with an active RFID tag and an "e-seal" security device from Savi

Technology. The device included intrusion detection, environmental monitoring, and weapons of mass destruction (WMD) sensors monitoring radiological, chemical, and biological threats.

The container was read at the portals of the Chinese port of Yantian—this was the port's entry gate for the inbound container and the gantry crane for outbound containers. It was likewise read upon arrival in southern California. The GPS tracked the containers across the Pacific Ocean en route to the United States. RFID at the distribution center's (DC's) portals recorded the containers' arrival at the warehouse. During ship and truck transit, GPS also tracked the vehicle, making the system aware of which pallets were in which truck.

The trial report concluded that 100 percent of both passive and active reads were successful. Intrusion detection and real-time tracking was also sustained throughout the transit. When exceptions, or "events," occurred, the system dispatched predetermined notifications to supply chain decision makers.

18.5 The Future of Product Tracking

This chapter began with a description of life before bar codes and the technologies deployed today. Bar codes economically contain individual, product-specific information, whereas RFID, at considerably more expense, allows for the tracking of inventories by supply chain participants on its way to the retailer. The chapter ends with a look into the not-so-distant future for retail locating systems.

18.5.1 Case Study for RFID Application

Procter & Gamble (P&G), through its Gillette subsidiary, has painted its picture of the future through experiments with RFID and the accompanying EPC.[8] The P&G EPC team has worked with retail partners to test RFID technology and to uncover the benefits that go with its implementation.

One test was the product launch of the Gillette Fusion razor. The test included two retail partners with over 400 stores. Tags were placed on Fusion cases, pallets, and displays. The displays were particularly critical to a successful product launch because they would be in prominent positions in the stores. The tagging also helped ensure that stores were adequately stocked to meet demand for the new product. Stores with RFID capability had considerably higher "display compliance rates" by day 3 of the launch. Compliance in this case was meeting the stores' commitments to deploy the displays and the adequacy of displays in terms of their numbers. The monitoring capability by RFID/EPC assured that the product was in place to support the demand generated by Fusion advertising and promotion.

Based on its experience, the P&G EPC team recommends RFID/EPC for certain "advantaged" merchandise. The best candidates are higher-value products with display modules to support time-sensitive product launches or promotions. Such display modules contain many individual units, and their proper placement in the store ensures higher levels of sales. The business case justification in this example lay not in internal savings at P&G or the retailer but in the collaborative space between them—making sure that P&G provides the product and the retailer deployed it on the store floor. This is not how many RFID applications are justified, with most relying on internal operating savings.

18.5.2 A Future RTLS System

Like many solutions in this space, teams of technology companies have collaborated to prepare their visions of the end-to-end retail solution. One such team includes ClickCommerce, VueTechnology, and Printronix. ClickCommerce is a supply chain management software company; VueTechnology provides enabling middleware; and Printronix markets RFID printers. They refer to their vision as the "agile supply chain." Features of the agile supply chain include the following:

- Passive RFID tags applied at both the item and case levels
- "Intelligent shelf" technology, where RFID readers monitor the contents of storage locations in warehouses and stores
- Automatic detection and reporting of out-of-stock items and shrinkage by monitoring the shelves
- A warehouse management system (WMS) to oversee movement at warehouse and retail store levels
- Several applications to translate RFID data into updates for the WMS
- Cost-effective printing of RFID tags at the manufacturer
- Direct feedback to warehouse material handlers when errors in stock putaway and picking are made
- Automated warehouse cycle counting for inventory
- A network inventory visibility system to monitor inventory within and between supply chain locations, creating notifications when exceptions occur

Figure 18.6 is an overview of the team's agile supply chain; Table 18.2 summarizes each step of the process. Once the commitment is made to item level tagging at the manufacturer, most of the downstream activities related to managing the inventory are automated. The agile supply chain also has the ability to sense shortages at the store or warehouse. This provides the benefit of maximizing revenue in the case of shortages at the retail level. It also signals to the supply chain when a product is not selling well, calling for cutbacks in production. However, the costs for RFID tagging are still high, so the use of this technology for lower-priced, lower-volume products still lies in the future.

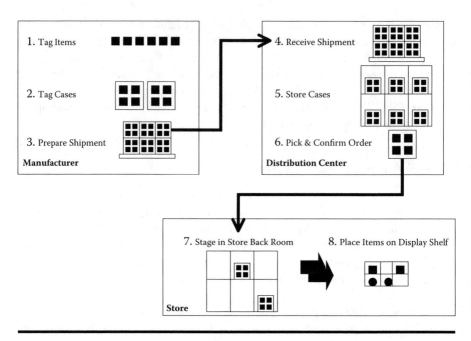

Figure 18.6   Vision for the agile supply chain.

On the operations side, incorrect picks or putaways are also signaled. The system can also match actual inventory with what should be there, resulting in the automation of inventory taking, potentially a cost savings justification for using this technology. Differences between book inventories and actual quantities can be indicative of shrinkage, poor execution, or quality problems.

18.6 Summary

The economic case for product tracking depends on the cost of tracking, paths to the customer, the value of the merchandise involved, and expected benefits. The visibility provided by using these technologies eases the work of matching supply and demand, particularly in reducing stockouts. This type of benefit is often subtle and unseen by potential users. Companies along the supply chain will continue to experiment with innovations in merchandise tracking. The purpose of this chapter is to heighten awareness of the alternatives that are now opening up and the challenges and opportunities that go with adapting tracking technology to one's supply chain.

Table 18.2   Process Steps for the Agile Supply Chain

Step #	Step Name	Step Description
At the Manufacturer		
1.	Tag items	An operator scans the bar code to generate passive item tags on a printer
2.	Tag cases	An operator associates individual items with a case
3.	Prepare shipment	An incoming order for several cases is filled. Order documentation identifies the items included
At the Warehouse		
4.	Receive shipment	The warehouse receives the shipment
5.	Store cases	The shipment is moved to intelligent shelves. Any errors in the shipment are detected. The WMS captures receipt of proper shipments
6.	Pick and confirm order	An order for one case is received. The WMS authorizes picking. A picking error is detected, and material handlers are redirected to pick the correct item. The shipment is transported to the store
At the Store		
7.	Stage in store back room	The item is staged for display shelves in the back room of the store on intelligent shelves
8.	Place items on display shelf	As sales occur, intelligent display shelves on the store floor are replenished from the staging shelves in the back room

Endnotes

1. The authors thank Mike Gerry for his review of this chapter.
2. Abernathy, Fred, "Marketing, Merchandising, and Retailing: The Role of Intermediaries in Global Value Chains," presentation at the University of Washington, June 6, 2004.
3. Quinn, Francis J. "Setting the Standards: An Interview with Mike Meranda," *Supply Chain Management Review,* October 2005, pp. 34–38.
4. Johnson, John R., "The Future is Now," *DC Velocity,* May 2006, pp. 57–60.

5. Lazo, Phillip, Keynote address at a Distribution Management Association (DMA) conference "How Technology is Impacting Today's Global Supply Chain," February 22, 2007, in Ontario, California.

6. Chopra, Sunil and Sodhi, ManMohan S., "In search of RFID's Sweet Spot," *The Wall Street Journal*, March 3–4, 2007, p. R10.

7. Kotsuka, Yoshibumi, "Case Study: Securing Cargo with E-Seals," presentation to RFID Journal Live 2006 conference, May 1–3 2006.

8. Cantwell, Dick, "Procter & Gamble's EPC Advantage Strategy," presentation to RFID Journal Live 2006 conference, May 1–3, 2006.

ACHIEVING FINANCIAL SUCCESS IN THE RETAIL SUPPLY CHAIN

Part 5 takes on the complexities of managing costs in multicompany supply chains. This is an ongoing quest that encompasses every link in the chain.

#	Name
19.	Understanding Supply Chain Costs
20.	Addressing Root Causes for Cost
21.	Multicompany Collaboration to Reduce Costs—Who, What, and How
22.	Retail Return Loops

The first problem is understanding where the costs are. This is the subject of Chapter 19. The chapter provides a methodology for profiling costs for targeted cost reduction efforts or identifying product profitability. Once costs are known, however, reductions won't succeed unless the root causes for the costs are understood. This is the topic of Chapter 20.

Because costs in one part of the supply chain may be due to actions at a trading partner, the need for collaboration is especially important if the common good is to be achieved. Chapter 21 defines how to identify the best trading partners for this effort and to structure mutually beneficial exchanges.

Chapter 22 addresses returns—a potential area of opportunity for cost reduction and enhanced customer satisfaction.

Chapter 19

Understanding Supply Chain Costs

The subject of this chapter, costs, affects decisions all along the supply chain.[1] Profitability is the ultimate measure of business success for all echelons, and managing supply chain cost is half the battle in fulfilling that mission. The other half is finding, marketing, and pricing profitable merchandise, merchandise that is in demand by end-users. Better cost numbers that support decision making related to merchandising and operations help execute both tasks.

However, many forces hinder gaining control over costs. One is the rise of "virtual manufacturers" that rely on partners—often in faraway places—to produce the products they design. Another force is the rise of strategies that offer extended product services. An example is the distributor, Arrow Electronics, and its efforts to earn more from services such as financing, on-site inventory management, parts tracking, and chip programming.[2] Such services move beyond the traditional low margin role of distributors, matching electronic component manufacturers with industrial customers.

Another task is evaluating "make-or-buy" decisions. An example is the specialty retailer weighing a proposal from a logistics service provider such as Argix Direct. Argix will execute four steps for specialty retailers—merchandise pickup at the source; sorting at the Argix distribution center; transport to one of 40 store delivery terminals; and, finally, store delivery. If a company is already doing these tasks in-house, it must understand the advantages and risks of outsourcing its work. For a smaller retailer, companies such as Argix offer an existing network, automated facilities, economies of scale in transportation, and up-to-date tracking systems. Unfortunately, companies offering such services or those considering buying them may get little help from their accounting departments. Their reporting formats are designed for financial reporting rather than managerial decision making.

This chapter describes how to apply the technique called activity-based costing (ABC) to make any number of decisions that require an understanding of supply chain costs. The reader can engage this chapter at two levels. The high-level alternative seeks knowledge of the role of activity-based costing in understanding costs, product profits, and partner contributions along supply chains. The alternative detail-level approach obliges the reader to examine the numbers presented in this chapter to better understand the mechanics of implementation. We've done our best here to make this as easy as possible.

19.1 Barriers to Cost Visibility

One would think that, being so important, the cost numbers that executives use to make supply chain decisions would be both timely and accurate. However, timely and accurate data is more the exception than the rule. The next sections explain a few of the reasons.

19.1.1 Understanding Costs Is Complicated

The first reason is that most companies are locked into single-company accounting systems. As mentioned earlier, these use decades-old cost accounting methods designed for financial reporting. The focus is on precision, not on accuracy or relevance. A primary reason for this situation is that accounting practices, in the U.S. in particular, are required to follow what are called Generally Accepted Accounting Principles, or GAAP. GAAP is designed to capture historical performance of the firm as a whole; it seldom accurately represents the current or future financial side of a specific process. Firms, guided by their chief financial officers, are adverse to duplication, so they steer away from creating additional numbers beyond the mandatory ones.

A second reason is that interactions between trading partners remain at arm's length. Partnerships, such as those described in Chapter 16, are unnatural, particularly in discussions about money. These discussions assume a "zero-sum" outcome where one party's financial gain is the other's loss. However, to make sizable gains in customer service and cost effectiveness, decision makers need to understand not only their own costs but also the costs of their trading partners. Depending on the relationship, partners may provide these voluntarily, certainly the best of situations. If not, estimates based on industry knowledge of prices along the chain or by supplemental research can approach reality, even if not exactly precise.

19.1.2 Partners Must Share Information

Sizable gains in service or cost reduction require cooperation to implement change among supply chain partners. The nature of the cooperation also varies from case to case. Depending on the situation, cooperation could include design changes for the product or its packaging, removal of process bottlenecks, capital investments, exchange of forecasts and sales data, modifying transportation and delivery methods, redesign of operating processes to achieve efficiencies, and other mutually advantageous measures.

However, there are real barriers to this collaboration beyond the willingness or ability to work together. Once sharing is agreed to, it can be difficult to decide what information is needed and how it should be applied to make decisions. This is compounded across company boundaries because of differences in accounting systems, industry practices, language, and geographical separation. This chapter describes a methodology for applying multicompany ABC for supply chain decision making. The following list summarizes possible applications for shared information:

- Assessing the profitability of a product or product category
- Adjusting retail markups* for different types of merchandise
- Finding and prioritizing opportunities for cost reduction through process improvement
- Comparing the profitability of private-label versus major-label brands
- Comparing the cost of goods purchased offshore to that of domestic producers
- Working with partners to assess new technologies such as RFID
- Negotiating prices and cost sharing

The preceding list should signal the reader that ABC applications are numerous, so the modest effort required to calculate activity-based costs is usually well worth the effort.

19.1.3 ABC Needs a "Makeover"

Note the use of the term "modest" in the previous section to describe the effort required to use ABC. Many organizations have pursued ABC efforts that required large investments in setting up and maintaining numbers that were ultimately little used to make decisions. Today's practitioners, including Robert S. Kaplan

---

* A *markup* is a factor added to the merchandise cost of an item to cover expenses and profit. Most retailers define markup as the percentage of the selling price consisting of margin. For example, if a retailer marked up an item that cost $2 by 50 percent, the selling price would be $4. Selling price − cost = markup. Markup $/Selling price $ = markup percentage.

who introduced ABC in 1987, advise streamlined procedures.[3] Douglas Hicks, who reviewed this chapter, has long argued for what he calls the simplified *abc* approach.[4] This alternative approach, also called Time-Based ABC, moves away from the paper-intensive time reporting required by earlier approaches. In essence, the new method creates *unit times* for each activity through direct measurement or other industrial engineering techniques. This facilitates measurement of capacity utilization. As an example, people in a work unit can produce a unit of output in one labor hour per unit, the unit time. The capacity of the work unit is 60 hours a day—equivalent to about nine employees, considering downtime. If actual output is 45 units, there is extra capacity for growth, work additions, or staff cutbacks. This approach may call to mind older work measurement approaches that used stopwatches to browbeat employees into being more productive. That approach is not necessary; knowledge of work unit output and capacity is fundamental to managing workflow. Employee participation and agreement to unit times should be sought as well as their buy-in to the process.

This simpler approach is a "snapshot," not a movie. That is, cost data is assembled with a purpose—as part of an improvement project, for example. So, assembling ABC costs becomes part of the project; it is not an ongoing "movie" that has to be maintained alongside a conventional accounting system.

The methodology described here also recommends the use of both *top-down* and *bottom-up* cost numbers. Top down means all costs are included and are assigned to broad company processes. Bottom up turns to the *unit time* approach to understand the cost of individual processes.

In describing ABC, clarification of terminology is in order. Practitioners in strategic planning and project management use the word *activity* in different ways. Loosely, it can mean an operation of some kind or a process or a set of processes. This view was described in Chapter 13 in relation to *activity systems*, a tool for developing strategies. There, activities were groups of operating processes that are the basis of the company's strategy for competing. In project management, an "activity" is an element of work performed during a project.

The activity in activity-based costing is also an operating process that can cross department and company boundaries. Activities are expressed as verb phrases, such as *put away pallet*, in a warehouse, or *sell merchandise*, in a store. These activities produce a "deliverable" that defines the activity or process "driver." In the case of a process called *pallet put away*, this deliverable and driver might be a pallet transfer from the loading dock to a storage space. For the *sell merchandise*, the driver might be *dollars sold* or *items sold*.

Other supply chain drivers include customer sales in a retail store, pallets, purchase orders, shipments, customer inquiries, and so forth. So, if a warehouse requires a unit time of *10 minutes per pallet* to perform the putaway activity, this time, in turn, can be translated into a unit cost. That cost could include labor, equipment in the form of the forklift, and facilities in the form of the warehouse itself.

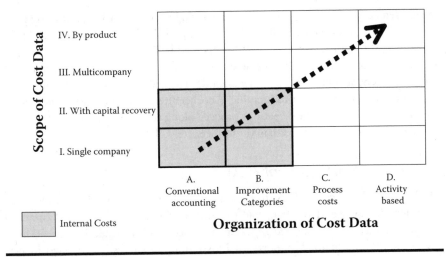

Figure 19.1   Migration to activity-based cost by product.

19.2 Goal: Activity-Based Costing by Product

Doing all the things that are possible with ABC requires development and manipulation of financial data. Figure 19.1 illustrates with an arrow the path from the current state using conventional accounting to the goal of activity-based cost by product. While there are other paths, the explanations in this chapter assume a team follows the diagonal shown in the figure. The vertical axis, *span of cost data*, has four levels defining *what* cost data is collected. The horizontal axis has levels for *organizing and presenting* cost data. The improvement team, if its charter were focused on cost reduction, may decide that III-C (Multicompany process cost) is sufficient to achieve its goals. Another team, with a charter to purge unprofitable products, will need activity-based costs by product or product category (IV-D).

Numbers gathered in the shaded area in the lower left of the Figure 19.1 grid are top-down costs incurred inside the organization. "Top down," mentioned earlier, means all costs are collected, not just costs for selected processes or products targeted for improvement. These top-down costs point to opportunities for improvement because higher-cost activities signal areas of improvement potential. They are also suitable for assessing product profitability at the company level or to support make-or-buy decisions. The unshaded area is bottom up and moves outside the company on a process-by-process basis to explore well-defined process improvement (III-C) or product profitability (IV-D) opportunities.

An example of III-C ABC application is justifying a CPFR (Collaborative Planning, Forecasting, and Replenishment) initiative described in Chapter 15, Section 15.2.3. In another example from Chapter 15, West Marine took over its inbound transportation function to better coordinate shipment arrival at stores. This reduced the hidden costs of interruptions in store working routines. At III-C, trading partners say, "This process cost $5,000,000; we can reduce that by 15 percent." At the IV-D level, the trading partners say, "Process A adds $123 to the cost of our widget. We aren't competitive in widgets. Here are ideas for reducing widget demands for Process A." Or, the team can jointly conclude that widgets will never be profitable and should be cut from the product line. Another alternative is boosting the price if the market permits. The next sections proceed along the arrow in Figure 19.1 using a case to describe how activity-based numbers are collected.

19.2.1 The Starting Point (I-A)

The lower left-hand corner (I-A) in Figure 19.1 is the single-company, conventional approach. Its span and presentation are sufficient to produce standard financial reports such as those described in Chapter 2, Section 2.1. Table 19.1 is a typical income statement financial report; for illustration, cost data is expressed in percentage, not absolute, terms. Confined to one company, the conventional approach reports costs by broad categories such as "direct labor," "costs of goods sold," "general and administrative," and "overhead." Overhead often includes depreciation charges to cover the cost of capital employed in the business. A common approach, using what is called straight-line depreciation, is to divide the initial cost of the asset by the life of the asset in years.

Table 19.1 Conventional Accounting (I-A)

1.	Gross revenue	100	
2.	Returns and discounts		5
3.	Net revenue (#1 less #2)	95	
4.	Direct labor expense		5
5.	Indirect labor expense		10
6.	Overhead expense		15
7.	Material/merchandise expense		50
8.	Cost of goods sold (#4 + #5 + #6 + #7)	80	
9.	Gross margin (#3 less #8)	15	
10.	General and administration expense		10
11.	Profit before tax (#8 less #9)	5	

Note: Figures are percentages.

The income statement follows accounting principles used by retail and industrial companies. In this model, many costs are allocated. A common example is the allocation of "overhead" to a "direct labor" base. This occurs despite the fact that direct labor in retailing, manufacturing, and other industries has shrunk. Also, direct labor costs may not cause, or "drive," the overhead costs. The failing in this method is that no costs are assigned to the "activities" that "consume" the resources reported. This I-A approach has a number of shortcomings with respect to SCM:

- It is limited to *one company*, and supply chain processes, by definition, cross company boundaries.
- Cost accounts are built on reporting from individual budget centers—usually the organization's functional units (e.g., purchasing, receiving, planning, store), not the processes that generate the cost (e.g., put away pallet, pick line item, or sell merchandise).
- The costs are not useful for analyzing the activities/processes that produce the cost.
- Current practices under-report capital costs associated with the activity/process by omitting the cost of capital. These costs include facilities, equipment, and working capital.

The following sections move along the path of the arrow in Figure 19.1. Each level—II-B, III-C, and IV-D—adds further insights for decision making.

19.2.2 Department Costs with Capital Recovery (II-B)

To move from conventional accounting, the initiating company should assemble all its own costs—the top-down approach. It should then sort them in a way to call attention to opportunities for cost reduction. Box II-B in Figure 19.1 represents this position. This step can best be accomplished by assigning internal costs, usually in the form of budget "cost centers," to improvement categories amenable to common cost-cutting approaches (B on the horizontal axis). This level also adds the cost of capital to fixed assets and working capital accounts (II on the vertical axis).

Table 19.2 lists cost categories that apply across the retail supply chain regardless of echelon—retailer, distributor, OEM, or second-tier supplier. The recommended list includes four workforce costs, recurring costs that include the cost of capital, and three categories of purchased item costs. For retailers, most of the purchased item costs are for the merchandise they sell. In fact, these may dwarf the costs of internal operations. However, effectively managing internal operating processes makes the difference in customer service and profitability—particularly if one's competitors pay similar prices for the same merchandise. The variation that exists among retailers was illustrated in Table 3.3 in Chapter 3.

Table 19.2   Improvement Categories

Category	Description	Environment
Workforce Costs		
Direct labor	Labor that "touches" the product. Examples: retail salespeople, purchasing, assembly workers, and material handling	Customer-facing or product-producing. Easily measured. May be suitable for automation. Low level of decision making. Repetitive work
Indirect labor	Direct support activity such as janitorial, transportation, and material handling. Often allocated	Less easily measured support staff. May be outsourced
Administrative/ clerical	Detached from direct activity. Managers, assistants, accounting staff, receptionists, and sales administration. Often allocated	Overhead required to support customer-serving processes. Hard to control or evaluate
Technical/ professional	Engineers, merchandising staff, information technology support, logistics planners, and other white-collar functions	Requires decision making. Involved in process- and product-related decisions. Hard to control or evaluate
Recurring Costs	Annualized costs of capacity— generally plant and equipment or working capital. Other fixed expenses such as corporate accounting or executive positions	Normally not assigned to processes. Often in the General and Administrative category or allocated through overhead
Purchased Item Costs		
Services	Manufacturing, accounting, consulting, transportation, and engineering support	Supplements or displaces staff by providing skills and services
Specialized material/ merchandise	Material or merchandise made to company specification. Private label brands, unique components for products	Few suppliers. Marked by a need for collaboration over design and replenishment
Commodity material/ merchandise	Products or material bought by many companies. Low-technology, off-the-shelf design	Provided by multiple sources, including distributors, where comparison is easy. Easily verified market price

Why separate costs into categories? We noted earlier that cost reduction techniques for each category are different. Table 19.2 describes the environmental characteristics of each cost category. In manufacturing, as an example, *direct labor* is often a target for cost reduction. Many manufacturers focus on this category using industrial engineering and operations research tools even though this category may be a small proportion of overall product cost. For manufacturers and retailers, hard-to-measure administrative and technical groups offer more potential for increased efficiency and effectiveness, but making improvements in these groups requires a wider skill set. This includes understanding not only the work content but also the effectiveness of the function, the role of incentives, the quality of decisions, the importance of work skills, and the potential for automation.

Box II-B also upgrades capital recovery reporting to account for the cost of money to acquire the asset. These costs fit into the Recurring Costs category in Table 19.2. Capital items include assets such as plant and equipment as well as working capital such as inventory and accounts receivable. Calculating the cost of capital utilizes a rate of interest, or "discount rate." Many companies refer to this as the *hurdle rate* that any investment must meet to be approved. Companies often calculate the hurdle rate by averaging the rates of interest paid to those financing the enterprise—banks, leaseholders, shareholders, mortgage holders, franchisees, and bond investors.

Applying the discount rate, the resulting calculation is the *equivalent uniform annual cost* (EUAC) for the asset. This approach has variations including EVA[5] (Economic Value Added) and residual income. EUAC effectively converts the investment cost into an expense. Practitioners use tables or calculators because the equations that calculate EUAC are complex.

Table 19.3 provides examples of EUAC calculations for different assets. Example #1 is a $1,000,000 capital equipment item such as a production machine or warehouse conveyor. In this example, tax accounting rules allow writing the equipment off over 10 years. Current accounting doesn't allow the cost of capital to be added to the cost of operating equipment. But experience shows that, due to rapid obsolescence, this equipment has a likely "economic" life of only three years. Taking this and a 15 percent cost of capital into account, Example #1 shows an increase from $100,000 to $350,000 in the annual cost of the asset. Note that, for leased equipment, the lease payments may sufficiently reflect the EUAC because the leaser builds those costs into its lease rate.

The discount rate and asset life for dissimilar assets will vary in the same company. Example #2 in Table 19.3 shows comparable numbers for a building, which could be a store, a warehouse, corporate headquarters, or a factory. For example, a building asset may be less risky for the manufacturer or retailer because the building, but not the equipment, has a market value if the company sold the asset. For this reason, a lower cost of capital, in this case 10 percent, and a longer economic life, ten years instead of three in Example 1, are appropriate. Again, rent paid for a leased facility may capture these costs.

Table 19.3   Calculation of Capital Cost (II-B)

#	Example	Conventional Annual Expense	Equivalent Uniform Annual Expense (EUAC)
Fixed Assets			
1	Equipment item cost: $1,000,000	$100,000 based on a 10-year accounting life with straight-line depreciation	$350,000 based on a 3-year economic life and a 15 percent cost of capital
2	Building cost: $20,000,000	$400,000 based on a 50-year accounting life	$3,200,000 based on a 10-year economic life and a 10 percent cost of capital
Working Capital Assets			
3	Inventory $50,000,000	$0 in the income statement, displayed on the balance sheet	$12,500,000 recognizing interest, shrinkage, obsolescence, handling, and storage
4	Accounts receivable $25,000,000	$0 in the income statement, displayed on the balance sheet	$5,000,000 based on interest, collection costs, potential returns, and bad debt history

Examples #3 and #4 are working capital assets that should also be converted to expenses. Example #3 is inventory that, with conventional accounting, is only recognized on the balance sheet. So, some managers may consider inventory to be "free." On the contrary, the cost of carrying inventory can be huge in retail supply chains. Despite its size, the cost of inventory is often not accurately calculated or assigned to the process steps that create it. Herman Miller, described in Chapter 10, Section 10.1, recognized this need in reengineering its supply chain.

Sometimes, supply chain negotiations between trading partners center on transferring the cost of inventory to upstream companies. Dell, for example, pays suppliers after the customer pays them for its direct sales. Dell shares forecasts and sales data with those suppliers to help them lower inventory. Retailer Costco, listed in Table 3.3 (Chapter 3), follows a similar practice—producing, like Dell, a negative cash-to-cash cycle. In Example #3, the company has assigned a 25 percent per year cost to the inventory—a typical value that captures storage, financing, obsolescence, insurance, and other costs.

Example #4 in Table 19.3 is for the asset, Accounts Receivable. It is the money owed the company due to the delay between customer billing and customer payment, often a major item for retailers such as Macy's and Target that maintain house interest-paying charge accounts. This account also should be converted to an EUAC. Although it's an asset, high receivables may highlight unprofitable customers or lines of business. Some companies will use the cost of capital with an allowance for nonpaying customers added on. In Example #4, a 20 percent cost is assigned to the Accounts Receivable balance.

There is considerable latitude for presenting cost information at the II-B level. Table 19.4 presents a top-down example for a vertically integrated retail company. The table maps organization costs to improvement categories. Vertically integrated, in this case, means the company has merchandising, retail, distribution, and manufacturing operations. Because of its size, it has assembled numbers for each of its principal operations (columns 2–5). The data in the columns in Table 19.4 are summarized as follows:

1. Cost categories from Table 19.2 subdivided into workforce costs, recurring costs, and purchased items categories.
2. Costs for the merchandising department that selects and purchases merchandise. Note that merchandising is assigned the cost of merchandise and inventories as shown in the working capital line (#7). There is a division of merchandise cost into specialized and commodity material categories. The former represents fashion, or innovative merchandise and the latter staples, or functional, merchandise.
3. Costs for internal manufacturing operation that makes an exclusive product line of merchandise, called the widget line.
4. Costs for internal distribution centers (DC) supplying the chain's stores.
5. Costs for the company's retail stores.

Table 19.4 shows the costs that are either incurred or controlled by each of the four functions. Note that the merchandising group (column 2) is responsible for merchandise expenditures because it selects the merchandise, negotiates with suppliers, and plans replenishment. The merchandise department is also assigned the cost of inventory ($350 million) because its source selection and replenishment decisions determine the amount of inventory in the company's DCs and stores.

The captive manufacturing operation (column 3) produces the widget line for sale only in company stores. The costs of production are included in the merchandise costs in column 2. This in effect treats the manufacturing operation as an independent supplier. The company DCs (column 4) are assigned only operating costs and are not charged for the merchandise that flows through the facility. Because the DC contracts for transportation, it is responsible for these costs under "services." The DCs also incur a modest working capital expense for packaging and displays. The retail outlets (column 5) handle stock at their locations and sell merchandise to customers. However, the merchandise department decides what the store will carry and generates the orders that dispatch merchandise from the DCs to those stores.

Table 19.4 also assigns "drivers" to the organization functions (lines #12 and #13). A driver is selected as a workload indicator because costs increase more or less directly as the driver volume increases. Precision in deciding what driver to

Table 19.4 Vertically Integrated Retailer Costs ($millions)

	1	2	3	4	5	6
		Retailer Merchandising Department	*Manufacturing Operation*	*Distribution Centers*	*Retail Outlets*	*Total Cost by Improvement Category*
Work Force Costs						
1.	Direct labor	$1	$8	$12	$35	$56
2.	Indirect labor	$1	$15	$2	$5	$23
3.	Administration/ clerical	$2	$2	$2	$8	$14
4.	Technical/ professional	$30	$4	$1	$2	$37
Recurring Costs						
5.	Equipment	$1	$10	$15	$2	$28
6.	Facilities	$1	$6	$30	$80	$117
7.	Working capital	$350	$4	$10	$0	$364
Purchased Items						
8.	Services	$5	$3	$20	$3	$31
9.	Specialized material, merchandise	$300	$80	$5	$3	$388
10.	Commodity material, merchandise	$500	$20	$3	$5	$528
11.	**Total:**	**$1,191**	**$152**	**$100**	**$143**	**$1,586**
12.	Driver	Categories Managed	Units Produced	Pallets Handled	# Items Sold	
13.	Quantity	250	500,000	400,000	15,000,000	
14.	Cost per unit ($)	$4,764,000	$304	$250	$10	
15.	Excluding merchandise ($)	$1,564,000				

use is secondary to finding a "mostly correct" parameter. As an example, the merchandising driver is *categories managed.* Each category increases the quantity of work, inventory, replenishment activity, and merchandise cost. Dividing the total assigned cost by the volume—in this case the number of categories managed is 250—produces the baseline activity cost of about $4.8 million per category. Internal costs that don't include merchandise purchases (lines #9 and #10) for operating the department are just under $1.6 million per category (line #15). Other driver candidates for the merchandise function could include *# SKUs, $ merchandise cost,* or *# of suppliers.*

If an analysis team were examining the workings of the merchandising department, they might use different drivers for different processes. For example, sourcing processes might use *# categories,* whereas inventory planning processes might use *# SKUs.*

For the manufacturing operation (column 3), the driver is the number of product units manufactured annually, in this case 500,000. The activity cost per unit is $304. The DCs' cost is $250 per pallet handled. This includes both inbound and outbound pallets. Later, we develop separate figures for inbound and outbound pallets.

The retail operations of the company employ *# items sold* as a driver. This produces a cost of $10 per transaction, regardless of the value of the transaction or the product. The sales staff is considered "direct labor." Some retailers who employ a more consultative sale might assign the sales staff to the "technical/professional" category. Later, we'll show how to treat differences in selling time for different types of product—in this case, innovative, functional, and the widget line.

The presentation in Table 19.4 enables quick analysis to set baselines to measure improvement efforts or to make comparisons with alternatives. For example, a company such as Argix Direct could supplant the internal DCs. So, this data would be helpful in evaluating a decision to outsource. Table 19.5 provides examples of such ratios. What emerges from the analysis is a higher end specialty retailer with merchandise cost per item sold of $53 with a salesperson selling about 66 items a day.

Table 19.5   Key Ratios—Vertically Integrated Retailer

# of sales people at $40K each	875
# of employees at $50K each	2,600
# Items sold/person/day	65.9
Merchandise cost per item	$53
Merchandise cost per product category	$3,200,000
Inbound/outbound pallets per category	1600
Purchases as percentage of cost	60

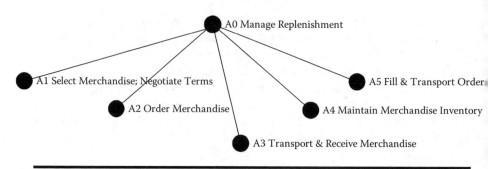

Figure 19.2   IDEF$_0$ node tree process definition.

A process flowchart is useful at the II-B level. Figures 19.2 and 19.3 provide a process view of the retailer's merchandising, distribution, and retail operations. The flowchart format is called IDEF$_0$—a modeling language supported in business process documentation tools. The node tree in Figure 19.2 summarizes the process. The detailed chart in Figure 19.3 shows inputs, outputs, mechanisms, and controls for each process step. The IDEF format is "top down" and useful for "drilling down" into subprocesses that merit further investigation.

19.2.3 Multicompany Process Cost (III-C)

At the next level (III-C in Figure 19.1), the path moves to multicompany accounting focused on individual processes. IDEF is also useful for scoping and documenting these processes. The perspective transitions from an organization to a process view of improvement categories using the process steps in Figures 19.2 and 19.3. A process for analyzing and comparing costs includes the following steps:

1. Set process boundaries.
2. Prepare a process flowchart and description.
3. Decide what cost categories to include.
4. Assign unit costs to activity/process steps. Use engineering studies, interview data, and estimates as needed.
5. Analyze the findings; prepare conclusions and recommendations.

Data from Table 19.6 illustrates how to execute these steps. This is a multicompany example in that the case involves a cost comparison with a potential third-party logistics service provider. The logistics service provider has proposed to assume responsibility for the distribution centers at our retailer. The provider claims to have better material management systems to cut inventories, economies of scale for transportation services, and automated facilities that cut labor costs. Using the case, the following sections execute the five steps just listed.

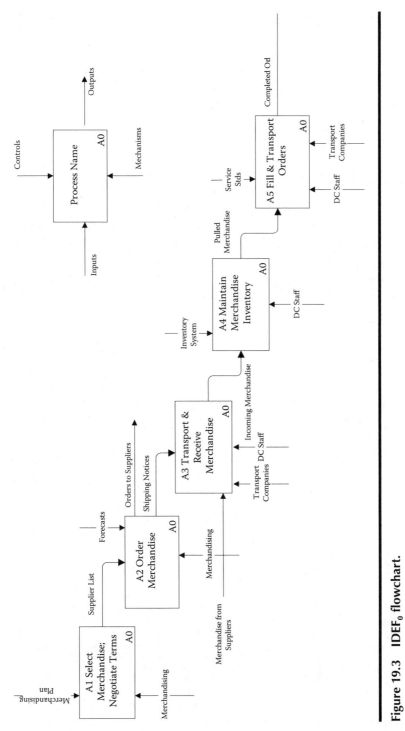

Figure 19.3   IDEF₀ flowchart.

Table 19.6 Process Costs ($millions except per pallet figures)

		A1 Select Merchandise; Negotiate Terms	A2 Order Merchandise	A3 Receive and Store Incoming Merchandise	A4 Fill Store Orders and Transport Merchandise	A5 Stock and Sell Merchandise in Stores	Total	Cost per Pallet ($)*
1.	External trading partner proposal	Not included in process	$3, Technical and professional	$10, Labor and transportation	$250, Labor, recurring inventory turns	Not included in process	$263	$657
2.	Internal: all departments	Not included in process	$10	$38	$394		$442	$1105
3.	Merchandising department	—	$10, Technical and professional		$350, Working capital		$360	
4.	Distribution centers	—	—	$6, Direct labor; $10, transportation services; $22, Factory/ equipment	$6, Direct labor; $10, transportation services; other labor, $5; $23, Factory/ equipment		$82	
	Comments:		Replenishment planner reductions	Covers inbound side of DC operations	Covers outbound side of DC operations			

*For 400,000 pallets per year

19.2.3.1 Set Process Boundaries

Any improvement project should have a meaningful, but not overreaching, scope definition. Otherwise, the project team may fail. It may also "under-reach," taking on a mission that is too limited when weighed against the potential for improvement. As part of its proposal, the third-party provider has estimated its costs for the process steps described in Figures 19.2 and 19.3. Because our own vertically integrated retail company has not had a process view of its costs, it must uncover how costs in departments/improvement categories are distributed to process steps (Level C on the horizontal axis of Figure 19.1). Table 19.6 shows the resulting analysis that identifies affected processes in the Merchandising and Distribution departments.

19.2.3.2 Document Process Flow

Industrial engineers and other practitioners have a number of tools for representing processes. A popular alternative is the "swim lane," or cross-functional flowchart, where flow is charted across organization groups. Another is the $IDEF_0$ format introduced earlier and used here to illustrate process documentation. The node tree in Figure 19.2 is "top down," meaning, each level of activities can be decomposed into its components depending on the needs of the project. In Figure 19.2, there is one level of decomposition of the top-level process, *A0 Manage Product Categories*. The decomposition is into five subprocesses or activities that show how merchandise replenishment operates.

The second $IDEF_0$ representation is the flowchart in Figure 19.3. Each step in the process from the node tree is linked with other steps. The user-friendly documentation of process steps includes inputs, outputs, controls, and mechanisms. A team that understands how the company's processes really work can develop such a flowchart fairly quickly. This process should also evaluate which processes work and which do not. As the team prepares flowcharts, members should also explore why there are differences between the company's as-is cost and the third-party provider's proposed costs.

19.2.3.3 Decide What Cost Categories to Include

This step relies on the scope of the analysis. Because the team is chartered to look at operating processes, they decide to include the following categories:

- All the labor categories that employ people in the process—rows 1–4 from Table 19.4. This includes people from merchandising who order merchandise, and the DCs who handle merchandise.
- Recurring costs that apply to the process—rows 5–7 in Table 19.4. This would include equipment and facilities employed at the warehouses as well as inventory-carrying costs. In fact, the service provider is "promising" considerable inventory decreases in the order of $100 million annually.

■ Services related to the process, particularly for transportation—row 8 in Table 19.4. The service provider expects that its existing transportation network enjoys economies of scale.

19.2.3.4 Assign Costs to Process Steps

Table 19.6 assigns internal costs to the process steps for comparison with the service provider's proposal. Using process steps provides a common ground for discussion across company boundaries. Row 1 shows process costs of $263 million for the service provider. Teams won't always have a neat comparison to make with an external entity. However, in similar situations, using a standard process like this one will enable responders to document their expected costs. An improvement team can also use row 1 to enter their cost estimates if best practices were utilized.

Row 2 lists costs of the process steps from the merchandising department and the internal DCs. Beneath these totals are the components from each department (rows 3 and 4). As indicated earlier, absolute accuracy is not essential, and probably not feasible. What is needed is certainty that the numbers are sufficiently accurate for decision making regarding sourcing or process improvements. The cost comparison on a per-pallet basis is $657 for the third-party provider and $1105 for the retail company, including planning, transportation, inventory-carrying costs, and material handling capital and labor.

19.2.3.5 Analyze Findings

The gap is certainly a great one. Much of the gap is due, not to labor costs, but to working capital and facilities/equipment utilization. Do the division of responsibility or department measures promote overinvestment in our company? Are the tools for planning and forecasting doing the job that is needed? The gap for planning staff as part of activity A2 is also great—$3 million for the service provider, $10 million for our company.

The questions posed to those evaluating the proposal include the following:

1. Does the service provider have better processes than we do?
2. Should we transfer our work to the service provider or should the company adapt the service provider's methods to our own business?

From the activity-based numbers, the answer to #1 is "most certainly." The answer to #2 is more complex. If the reasons for better performance can be adapted to the organization, it makes sense to implement the practices that produce the better result. Other alternatives include reassignment of process responsibilities and measures of performance. However, if the service provider is capable in terms of capacity, provides quality service, and is willing, the function is an excellent candidate for outsourcing some or all of the company's requirements.

19.3 Activity-Based Costs by Product (IV-D)

As noted earlier, the requirements for cost analysis are often fulfilled at the level (III-C) just described. This is particularly true if process improvement is the primary goal. Note there has been little mention of prices or profits from the sale of merchandise. Adding these factors is the mission of level IV-D in Figure 19.1. At the IV-D level, merchandise costs are captured by activity and measured against market prices to assess profitability. Without such data, the actual profitability of specific products lines is likely to be cloudy.

Such data becomes useful in price negotiations with merchandise suppliers. The data also supports efforts to rationalize the product line by purging unprofitable merchandise. Another application is price setting. As suggested at the beginning of this chapter, retailers may base their prices on across-the-board markups of their purchase costs. This method, although simple to apply, puts the retailer at risk of undercutting by competitors with a better knowledge of their costs. At best, the retailer's most profitable products subsidize the unseen laggards.

Accomplishing this requires some calculations because different processes, such as those shown in Figures 19.2 and 19.3, will have different cost drivers. Also, our product lines will differ in the amount of resources needed to support them. For example, selling specialized fashion, or innovative merchandise usually takes more sales time than selling functional products. Our retail case in this section sold three product types: specialized merchandise, commodity merchandise, and the widget line that it manufactured itself. These will form the basis of our example in the next section, which describes a method for calculating activity costs by product.

19.3.1 Gather Product Line Information

With prices and profitability in the picture, data on the product lines selected for analysis provides a foundation. The example of needed data in Table 19.7 shows three product lines—innovative, functional, and the widget line. Lines #1 through #3 capture revenue and profitability figures. Lines #4 through #6 show the cost driver quantities for each product line. Those identified were *number of categories, # pallets handled,* and *# items sold.* Lines #7 through #10 show the profitability of the overall business; the ABC analysis will show the contribution of each product line, taking into account the merchandising, distribution, and the selling costs for each line.

19.3.2 Adjust Unit Costs and Volumes Through Engineering Studies

Table 19.8 is another picture of the company cost structure. Rather than organizational units (Table 19.4), this presentation shows costs for process activities.

Table 19.7 Gathering Product Line Metrics

		Product Type			
		Innovative	Functional	Widget Line	Total/Average
1.	Retail sales (annual)	$750,000,000	$714,285,714	$608,000,000	$2,072,285,714
2.	$ Annual merchandise cost	$300,000,000	$500,000,000	$152,000,000	$952,000,000
3.	Profit margin (percent)	60	30	75	46
4.	Number of categories	20	180	50	$250
5.	# Pallets handled	60,000	240,000	100,000	400,000
6.	# Items sold	3,000,000	7,000,000	5,000,000	15,000,000
7.	Average unit cost	$100	$71	$30	$63
8.	Average selling price	$250	$102	$122	$138
9.	Total operating expense		$1,586,000,000		
10.	Pretax operating profit		$486,285,714		

Populating this table requires estimates or engineering studies that allocate organization unit costs to the processes. It is also a time to examine assumptions about unit volumes and the distribution of work. Table 19.8 shows two such adjustments—one for the workload in pallets handled that are now divided between incoming and outgoing pallets. The second is for the distribution of work among store staff.

In Table 19.8, the number of outgoing pallets (Process A4) is found to be three times the number of incoming pallets (Process A3). The numbers (100,000 and 300,000) are on Line #13. This imbalance is due to smaller loads on each outgoing pallet and the requirements for sophisticated sorting systems to assemble those loads. Also, a salesforce analysis engineering study (Lines 16–18) in the stores shows that salespeople spend about half their time selling innovative products. The rest of the time is divided between the widget line and functional products. The time required for each unit sold is $24, $9, and $4, respectively. These average to $10 on a volume-weighted basis.

For Process A1, which encompasses product selection and sourcing, there are two costs per unit (lines 14 and 15). The first includes the cost of the merchandise; the second excludes it, reflecting the operational cost of the process without the merchandise cost included.

19.3.3 Calculate Product Line Profitability

The cost of the drivers can be used to calculate each product line cost. Table 19.9 performs this task using the driver unit costs (column #2) and the driver quantities associated with each product line from Table 19.7. This produces the total cost of each activity by product, shown in Columns 6–8 of Table 19.9. The cost per unit is calculated by dividing by the volume of product sold in each category, line 6 in Table 19.7. The results are shown in Columns 9–11 of Table 19.9.

Table 19.10 summarizes the unit costs for each activity by product line. The box outlines these costs. A profitability analysis by product line highlights costs and profitability. What the analysis shows is that two product lines (innovative and the widget line) are profitable. Functional products, as a whole, are not. Options based on the analysis include the following:

- Accept that some products are unprofitable but need to be carried to fill out the product line.
- Search the functional category further and drop the lowest-profit items.
- Cut internal costs for merchandising and ordering material. These are the highest-price activities.
- Transfer logistics for functional products to the third-party service provider. Retain control over innovative products and the widget line.

Table 19.8   Calculation of Cost Drivers

	A1 Select Merchandise; Negotiate Terms	A2 Order Merchandise	A3 Receive and Store Incoming Merchandise	A4 Fill Store Orders and Transport Merchandise	A5 Stock and Sell Merchandise in Stores	Total
Workforce Costs						
1. Direct labor	$0	$1	$6	$6	$35	$48
2. Indirect labor	$1	$0	$1	$1	$5	$8
3. Administration/clerical	$1	$1	$1	$1	$8	$12
4. Technical/professional	$20	$10	$1	$0	$2	$33
Recurring Costs						
5. Equipment	$0	$1	$5	$10	$2	$18
6. Facilities	$1	$0	$10	$20	$80	$111
7. Working capital	$150	$200	$0	$10	$0	$360

Purchased Items

8. Services	$4	$1	$8	$12	$3	$28
9. Specialized material, merchandise	$300	$0	$0	$5	$3	$308
10. Commodity material, merchandise	$500	$0	$0	$3	$5	$508
11. **Total:**	**$977**	**$214**	**$32**	**$68**	**$143**	**$1,434**
12. Cost driver	Categories Managed		Pallets Handled		# Items Sold	
13. Quantity	250		100,000	300,000	15,000,000	
14. Cost per unit ($)	$3,908,000	$856,000	$320	$227	$10	
15. Excluding merchandise ($)	$708,000					

Sales Force Analysis

16. Innovative	$24
17. Functional	$4
18. Widget Line	$9

Note: Costs are in $millions.

Table 19.9 Calculation of Unit Costs by Activity

		1	2	3	4	5	6	7	8	9	10	11
	Activity/Process	Driver	Cost per Driver Unit ($) (Table 19.8, Row 14)	# Drivers—Innovative (Table 19.7, Rows 4–6)	# Drivers—Functional (Table 19.7, Rows 4–6)	# Drivers—Widget Line (Table 19.7, Rows 4–6)	Activity Cost—Innovative ($millions) (#3×#1)	Activity Cost—Functional ($millions) (#4×#1)	Activity Costs—Widget Line ($millions) (#5×#1)	Activity Cost per Unit—Innovative ($)	Activity Cost per Unit—Functional ($)	Activity Cost per Unit—Widget Line ($)
A1	Select merchandise; negotiate terms (with merchandise cost)	# Categories	$3,908,000	20	180	50	$78	$703	$195	$26	$100	$39
A1	Select merchandise; negotiate terms (without merchandise cost)	# Categories	$708,000	20	180	50	$14	$127	$35	$5	$18	$7
A2	Order merchandise	# Categories	$856,000	20	180	50	$17	$154	$43	$6	$22	$9
A3	Receive and store incoming merchandise	# Pallets handled	$320	20,000	80,000	25,000	$6	$26	$8	$2	$4	$2
A4	Fill store orders and transport merchandise	# Pallets handled	$227	40,000	160,000	75,000	$9	$36	$17	$3	$5	$3
A5	Stock and sell merchandise in stores	# Items sold	$10	3,000,000	7,000,000	5,000,000	$29	$67	$48	$24	$4	$9

Table 19.10 Product Line Profitability

Product	1 Average Unit Selling Price	2 Purchase Cost	3 Merchandising Cost A1	4 Order Cost A2	5 Inbound Logistics Cost A3	6 Outbound Logistics Cost A4	7 Selling Cost A5	Total Activity Cost per Unit Sold	8 Profit per Unit ($)	9 Units Sold	10 Total Profit ($millions)	11 Cost Markup (percent)
Innovative	$250	$100	$5	$6	$2	$3	$24	$39	$111	3,000,000	$332	139
Functional	$102	$71	$18	$22	$4	$5	$4	$53	($23)	7,000,000	($158)	174
Widget line	$122	$30	$7	$9	$2	$3	$9	$29	$62	5,000,000	$310	196

The last option recognizes that a focused provider might best handle the high volume of these products. The company might retain responsibility for the "crown jewels," at least until the service provider has proven its effectiveness.

19.4 Understanding Costs—Summary

This chapter describes a methodology for applying the ABC tool to a vertically integrated retail enterprise. Each organization will have to weigh the value of pursuing the ABC effort for its own business. However, it is increasingly intractable to confine one's perspective to one's own organization. This is especially so as companies continue to outsource traditional operations. In a supply chain world, a broader view of cost is needed. Also, the use of across-the-board markups will inevitably overprice some and underprice other merchandise. This leaves a retailer susceptible to the competitor with better knowledge of costs, even if that retailer has no cost advantage. A sharper pencil is the solution; ABC is the tool.

Endnotes

1. The authors thank Douglas T. Hicks for his review and comments on this chapter.
2. Nelson, Brett, "Stuck in the Middle," *Forbes,* August 15, 2005, pp. 88 and 89.
3. Kaplan, Robert S. and Anderson, Steven R., "Time-Driven Activity-Based Costing," *Harvard Business Review,* November 2004, pp. 131–138.
4. Hicks, Douglas T., *Activity-Based Costing: Making it Work for Small and Mid-Sized Companies,* 2nd edition, New York: John Wiley, 1999.
5. EVA is a registered trademark of Stern Stewart & Co., a global consulting firm.

Chapter 20

Barriers to Addressing Root Causes for Cost

This book's Part 4, Supply Chain Process Improvement, describes ways to enlist one's organization, trading partners, and process designers in the effort to become more competitive. This includes better service to customers, lower cost, and increased profits. Chapter 19 in this section, Part 5, attacked the issue of identifying, through activity-based costing (ABC), costs that are often hidden. Once costs are documented with ABC, tools in this chapter will guide teams to the next steps. Topics of the chapter include root causes for costs and the barriers that exist in addressing them.[1]

20.1 Root Causes for Supply Chain Cost

The list of root causes for cost addressed in this book is the following:

1. *Lack of clarity.* As described in Chapter 19, this root cause includes ways cost accounts are organized and presented; these often obscure cost drivers. ABC is a solution for this root cause.
2. *Variability.* The variability root cause includes anything in the supply chain that creates uncertainty in operations such as missed deliveries, demand fluctuations, unforeseen demand, and poor quality material arriving at the doorstep. Such uncertainty generates costs that show up in contingency inventory; overtime pay; expedited freight; lost sales; returned products; and, at the retail level, lost customers.

3. *Product design.* A product's cost is "baked in" during design through decisions related to material choices, component obsolescence, suppliers, and ease of fabrication and assembly. Leaving such considerations out of the design will increase costs.

4. *Lack of Information sharing.* Information exchanges range from operating costs as part of cost reduction collaboration to sharing operating data needed to make day-to-day decisions.

5. *Weak links.* Managing links encompasses make-or-buy decisions, the choice of partners, options to make or buy, and the connections between one partner and another.

6. *Unintended consequences.* The best of intentions can produce bad results. An effort to reduce costs in one area of the supply chain might raise costs elsewhere. For example, choosing the lowest-price supplier might not result in the lowest total cost because that partner might practice some of the cost-raising practices just described.

Most incidents of waste in supply chains can be tracked to one or more of these six causes. Chapter 21 addresses #5 and #6 in greater depth, focusing on when and how to enlist trading partners in the effort to reduce cost.

Identifying and addressing root causes of costs should be an essential part of any supply chain improvement project. The model for implementing supply chain change, introduced in Figure 15.1 (Chapter 15), points to the need to uncover the gap between where we are and where we want to be. Definition of a "gap" includes cost in addition to service, delivery, and flexibility. The model also notes the barriers that exist in making that transition. This book defines *barriers* as factors that can be overcome if properly managed. A *constraint,* as previously defined, is a "given," and beyond our power to change.

Table 20.1 lists chapters and sections that prescribe methods to address costs attributable to these root causes. This chapter seeks to explain why root causes do not get addressed in many supply chains. Table 20.2 serves as a guide. It lists five barriers and the principal root causes that apply to each barrier. The remainder of this chapter will prescribe approaches to overcome these barriers.

20.2 No Focus

Supply chain projects are, by definition, ambitious. The need for formal project management rises when attempting great things beyond the boundaries of one's own company. This was seen in the West Marine case introduced in Chapter 15. At West Marine and many other companies, focus was achieved in a crisis brought on by too-fast growth. Sometimes, a crisis does not exist to jumpstart the process and sustain it, so a focused effort that includes disciplined project management should

Table 20.1 Root Causes for Cost

	Root Cause for Cost	What It Is	Chapter or Section Addressed
1.	Lack of clarity	An inability to attach costs to processes. Cost accounting obscurity and inaccuracies. Lack of sharing of costs	11.1 The product life cycle 11.2 Innovative and functional products 11.3 Market mediation costs 12.2 Market segments 17.2 The path from forecast-driven to demand-driven 19 Understanding supply chain costs
2.	Variability	Any variable factor that affects supply chain flow	17.3.1.1 Lean supply chain approaches 17.3.1.2 Constraint management
3.	Product design	Designs that are hard to manufacture, maintain, or service	17. 3.1.3 Quality improvements 17.3.1.4 Design for commonality
4.	Insufficient information sharing	Failures to provide or to manage for information accuracy	17.3.2.1 Synchronization and fixed-interval planning 18 Product tracking along retail supply chains
5.	Weak links	Poorly performing trading partners or trading partner interfaces	14 Retail SCM — skills required 16 Collaboration with supply chain partners 21 Multicompany collaboration to reduce costs — who, what, and how
6.	Unintended consequences	Well-intentioned actions that hurt more than help	12.3 Spheres — modules for supply chain design 13 Activity systems and process definition 15. Organizing to improve supply chain performance 17.3.2.2 Simplification 21 Multicompany Collaboration to reduce costs — who, what, and how

Table 20.2 Root Causes and Related Barriers

			Barriers to Cost Reduction				
			No Focus	Confusion	Motivators	Boundaries	Rigidity
Root Causes for Cost	1	Clarity	•		•		•
	2	Variability		•	•		
	3	Product or service design	•	•			•
	4	Information sharing		•		•	
	5	Weak links		•		•	
	6	Unintended Consequences		•	•	•	•

be present. Disciplined project management for large projects requires a top-down commitment because a bottom-up continuous improvement mentality will not be sufficient if strategy-level changes are needed.

Unfortunately, many retail supply chain companies give half-hearted support, if any, to project management. There are no commonly understood project management practices adopted by the company. Improvement efforts are "bootstrapped," that is, assigned to employees already working in other roles to complete in whatever time is left over after their regular duties are completed. This often means no time at all.

When "teams" from various departments meet on occasion to work on the project, the result may be muddled. Total Quality Management (TQM) and more recent Six Sigma efforts are like this. Managers tout success in terms of "number of people trained" or "number of projects launched." Also, in manufacturing companies, the engineering department is a frequent omission. They are needed to address #3 on our list of root causes for cost in Table 20.2. In summary, we have not deployed the right "army" to uproot the root causes.

An unintended result is a superficial effort with local savings far below the potential of a focused project with broad participation. A common response is "We don't have the budget for a dedicated team." Fair enough, but do not expect meaningful results. With a focused approach to a limited number of projects, more improvement will be achieved. The following sections describe two solutions for this barrier: Project Management Basics and Team Building.

20.2.1 *Project Management Basics*

Projects are displacing ongoing, repetitive operations as a share of all work. Consequently, most of us need to better understand how to manage projects. *Projects are* "temporary efforts that produce a product, service, or result." In fact, there is a "body of knowledge" for managing projects maintained by the Project Management Institute.[2] In a bow to the impact of globalization, the guide is available in French, German, Chinese, Italian, Spanish, Portuguese, Japanese, and English.

A start for a retail supply chain project is establishing a project infrastructure within the company using this body of knowledge.[3] Making this commitment recognizes that the challenge requires a dedicated effort and raises the visibility of the effort. Definition of the reason for a "project" is important to achieving focus. How we define the deliverable makes a difference in how we do the project. For example, a *product* definition for a supply chain project might be, "establish a truck route between point A and point B." A *service* definition might be, "establish transportation links between point A and point B." A *result* definition might be, "lower logistics costs between point A and point B." The first, the product definition, is very specific and easily verified. However, it is limited in the choice of method employed. The second, the service definition, opens options to the project manager. For example, roads, railways, or air options are candidates. The third, the result definition, expands the options to not only transportation links but also logistics services such as warehouses, common carriers, and so forth.

In framing the expected project, the company has a huge opportunity to declare its intent if it wants to reduce costs. This is by emphasizing the "result" sought, not the means to achieve it. DaimlerChrysler did this when it was formed by merger, with visible displays of the cost reduction achieved exhibited widely. A technology company did the same thing for a bill of material (BOM) cost reduction effort. The result was a series of measures ranging from value engineering to renegotiated prices that slashed material cost by 20 percent annually on a base of $250 million. As described in Chapters 15 and 16, retailer West Marine followed a two-stage approach, starting in its own operation and then involving its trading partners in pursuing what they called "breakthroughs."

20.2.2 *Team Building*

Startup is the time to select key project-team members. As recommended in Chapter 16, Section 16.4, insiders should include a project manager and staff (if necessary), a steering committee, and a design team. Supply chain partner-participants should include the "keepers," those you want for long-term relationships. This is an excellent time to rationalize a supplier base or review distribution channels for poor-performing partners and unprofitable products. Keep in mind that an important criterion for being a "keeper" is the willingness of the partner to collaborate on cost reduction efforts.

The project manager, if a significant impact is sought, should be dedicated. Company executives should populate the steering committees with the CEO or COO included for the most important efforts. The design team is a mid-level management team who will do the early work on the project. Participating functions, depending on the echelon organization and project needs, could include merchandise planning, engineering, finance, planning, procurement, distribution, and manufacturing.

It is not too early to start a "Stage 3" multicompany steering committee as described in Chapter 6, Section 6.7.2. Supply chain cost reduction is a multicompany effort; costs include any incurred all along the chain, not just in one's own company. Some suppliers may greet this with suspicion. That is why creating a dialog early on is important. It should be emphasized with suppliers that this is not a quarterly business review where price reductions are sought, but a focused effort seeking direct solutions.

20.3 Confusion

A second barrier is confusion within management, the project team, and among partners about what the mission is. The opportunities for confusion are many. In particular, there may be different ideas about just what is included and what is not—what is called "scope" in the project management discipline. In fact, some of these are related to varying definitions of the supply chain, certainly a source of confusion. If there are ongoing efforts already underway, there can also be confusion about whether a proposed new project is already underway in another form.

Another source of confusion is technology—often for the purpose of sharing information. There is no shortage of "solutions providers" ready to solve problems. Many managers do not have the time and training to match all these solutions to the needs of their supply chains. In particular, proposed claims for software are confusing and may be inappropriate for the business. Retailers are particularly prone to problems in this area because most of industry's business information technology was originally developed not for merchandise-based businesses but for manufacturing companies. When there is pressure to accomplish something, however, the current management fashion or slickly marketed software package may be the easy choice, absent an understanding of the real needs.

Often, product design is overlooked as a possible root cause for costs. Managers are confused because the "horse is already out of the barn" in cases of products already in the marketplace. Closing the door does not solve the problem. Cost reduction is a reactive strategy to high cost. The most effective cost reduction effort would have been cost avoidance captured during product design. Here we describe two actions to avoid confusion: promoting SCM and the graduated approach.

20.3.1 Promoting SCM

Often, people in supply chain functions are second-class citizens, considered unimportant strategically. This may be particularly true in retail organizations where merchandising, not operations, is the priority. In a recent visit to a technology company further up the supply chain, it was apparent that the "supply chain" department managers had a huge inferiority complex. The company's fortune was based on high-tech products, and engineering and finance ruled the roost. Many supply chain functions were afterthoughts and taken for granted. Because of this attitude toward SCM functions, there was little interest inside the group for going outside their comfort zone—purchasing, warehousing, and distribution.

20.3.2 Graduated Approach

A source of confusion mentioned earlier is matching the right solution with the real problem. This is complicated if the supply chain is extended, with three to eight partners and the accompanying interfaces. Each partner has two internal interfaces, represented by departments or important processes. We are now up to six interfaces for a simpler chain and sixteen for a lengthier one. At each interface, decisions to replenish and stock are made. The discussion of the demand-driven supply chain in Chapter 17 provided an example.

The as-is review of the supply chain will uncover sources of delay that extend the lead time for a product. As described in Chapter 17, they should also uncover the degree to which planning decisions are based on forecasts or on actual demand. Long lead times, naturally, make forecast-based planning a necessity. Shorter lead times make demand-driven decisions possible. Figure 17.3 and the accompanying discussion described a programmatic way of shifting to demand-driven decision making. The approach also yields requirements for technology, including information systems, where they are needed along the chain. The multicompany steering committee can review and approve proposals for these solutions.

20.4 Motivators

Implicit or explicit performance measures drive reward and punishment in an organization. Although many organizations are turning to broader approaches such as the balanced scorecard, most organizations still stress company financial success as their essential measure. This is natural because the company that does not make money has failed in one of its most important missions—to earn a return for its investors.

However, currently used tools for financial measurement are outmoded. Accountants concoct their budgets following accounting practices developed decades ago, with performance in internal supply chain functions tied to budget adherence. A typical result is an oft-encountered measure like "supply chain costs as a percentage of sales." Broader measures, such as those including multiple companies, are hard to come by. Chapter 19 describes how to use Activity-Based Costing (ABC) to address this issue.

Excellence in SCM requires something different. Defining better measures and what is needed in terms of flexibility, described in the following sections, will motivate desirable results from the project team.

20.4.1 Measures

Selected performance metrics for a retail supply chain organization can drive dysfunctional behavior, resulting in unintended consequences. If the measure is "percentage of sales," just mentioned, the person being measured will surely ratchet down on supply chain costs without regard to the fallout or increased costs in other parts of the business, often on the critical sales floor. The broader supply chain mission of matching supply and demand is lost. For example, if the company is selling hot products with short life cycles, the cost-conscious supply chain manager, trying to reduce transportation cost, will leave money on the table and destroy customer goodwill. Ample inventories, expedited airfreight, and extra manufacturing capacity can be a good thing if it means supply is chasing fast-growing demand or trying to maximize the return from a rapid fashion cycle.

The commodity or staple product manager or buyer whose measure is lowest price paid for merchandise also may make bad source-selection decisions. In addition to quarterly price decreases, one company shifted raw material inventory to its suppliers to relieve its own balance sheet. Total supply chain costs remained the same, and ultimately showed up in the price paid by the consumer at the retail level.

Another OEM, in the last two weeks of each quarter, turned production control over to corporate finance—not because they were great schedulers but to book as much business as possible by the end of the accounting period. The result was a crash program that pulled finished products out of inventory and reconfigured them to get them out the door. A lot of work was duplicated, and the company was exposed to shortages in the next quarter.

Another public company nearing the end of its fiscal year put its high-ticket products on sale at a large discount to boost year-end earnings. The manufacturing vice president was alarmed but went along as a "team player." This cost him his job. The plant choked on the fire-sale orders, and the new year brought the pink slip. The stock also collapsed as the factory dropped further and further behind its sales commitments.

20.4.2 Flexibility Defined

Perhaps it is unrealistic to purge all of these bad habits; however, it is possible to manage them better. To address situations like the ones described, marketing strategies for each product line should define the need for supply chain "flexibility." Section 6.5 in Chapter 6 recommends how to do this.

If final demand is uncertain or fluctuates up and down—and it's hard to conjure up a product that does not fit this situation—then flexibility is the most important supply chain design objective. Achieving other objectives in the categories of cost and customer service depend on supply chain flexibility.

If one asked 100 people what supply chain "flexibility" means, that person might get 150 different answers. American Production and Inventory Control Society (APICS), for supply chains, defines *flexibility* as the ability to neutralize the risks of variability in demand, supply, cycle time, and other factors during up or down volume changes. So, consequences, such as added cost or reduced responsiveness, from any of these sources of variability will be minimal in a flexible supply chain.

The SCOR model uses time and volume change to gauge flexibility. An example is "so much volume change" in "such and such" time. As with the APICS definition, changes must also occur without cost or inventory penalties. So, upside production flexibility is defined as "the number of days to achieve an unplanned sustainable 20 percent increase in production." Interestingly, downside production flexibility is defined as the "percentage order reduction sustainable at 30 days prior to shipping with no inventory or cost penalties." It's strange that upside flexibility is expressed as number of days, whereas downside flexibility is defined as percentage of production.

Although the process may be complex, a multicompany steering committee, in a process such as that described in Chapter 16, Section 16.4, will make a strong contribution by defining supply chain flexibility requirements. This "strategic" definition should be in terms the supply chain partners most affected by changes in demand can understand and embrace, providing clear direction for investments and performance measures.

20.5 Boundaries

At the risk of being too obvious, boundaries make supply chain improvement difficult. Therefore, they are "barriers" in both the literal and figurative sense. At the basic level, the individual, whether a front-line worker or the CEO, exercises a high level of control over his or her immediate environment. As additional players are introduced into a business process, an individual's control and visibility diminishes. By extension, the same is true for the company level where several work groups take part, and certainly for the supply chain level where multiple companies are involved. West Marine, in taking back control of its inbound material flow, eliminated a troublesome boundary—coordinating supplier deliveries—that had disrupted its stores' operations.

Effective SCM means we must manage improvement not only across our own department boundaries but also across company boundaries. To be successful, we must somehow enlist those in other departments in our own company and those in our partners' organizations to assist in developing the new strategy. This requires skills that many lack, such as an inclination to be proactive in leading change, powers of persuasion, and creativity in devising "win-win" solutions in collaboration with partners.

An example of the impact of boundaries is the bullwhip effect. Small changes in final, end-user demand are amplified into wide swings in demand as one goes up the chain. West Marine was motivated to work with its suppliers to eliminate supply chain bullwhips. Prior to the effort, supply chain synchronization was not incorporated in the design of participant linkages, an example of weak links. That said, the latest and greatest technology is even less likely to fit the differing levels of capability along the chain. So, unless our company is a channel master that dictates to partners, such as West Marine or Wal-Mart, we are stuck with supply chain performance levels determined by the weakest link. The next sections describe the divide-and-conquer approach and mechanisms for multicompany participation.

20.5.1 Divide and Conquer

This approach encourages organizations to bite off one piece of their supply chain at a time. It builds a firewall around what might be a risky endeavor if too much is undertaken at once. It also allows the company to focus limited resources on priority supply chain activities. Retailer West Marine almost did not recover from its too rapid effort to integrate the operations of a merger partner with its own.

As an example of this approach, companies may serve more than one customer segment. These segments have different requirements for customer service, products, and so forth. Also, companies differ in terms of the importance of various supply chain functions. A retailer specializing in high fashion or a high tech, engineering-intensive company depends heavily on its suppliers, but a manufacturer relying on commodity products or a discount retailer depends less on individual supplier relationships because there are multiple suppliers for their products.

A company can divide and conquer by carving its supply chain into "spheres" as described in Chapter 12. The term refers to three-dimensional customer–product–operations combinations. These define multiple supply chains in a single company set aside for focused improvement. The divide-and-conquer strategy creates workable projects and reduces the risk of designing a "one-size-fits-all" supply chain. It is also a tool for setting priorities if resources are limited. The highest-priority first project can address the needs of the most important "businesses within the business."

20.5.2 Multicompany Participation

Once a piece of the supply chain has been chosen for a makeover, the willingness of a partner to cooperate will be put to the test. If a multicompany steering committee does not exist, then it should be formed. Partners whose operations are important must contribute to gain full benefit from the effort. Contributions will take various forms; examples include the following:

- Providing information on and guarding the integrity of the retail format
- Supplying data for process flowcharts for cost and time across the chain
- Providing points of contact across boundaries in a variety of functions, the "diamond" model of Figure 16.1 (Chapter 16)
- Costs and cost-driver information
- Technology improvements that would enhance the supply chain
- Ideas for cost reduction that address root causes
- Contracting that encourages ideas for cost reduction

Balky partners are an occupational hazard. A company's steering committee should anticipate lack of cooperation and have a contingency plan in place. Such a plan should include the work-around option, partner replacement, or suspension of the effort until cooperation is forthcoming. The major mistake is not confronting the situation and allowing the effort to muddle along when success is doubtful.

20.6 Rigidity

The press reminds us frequently that the pace of change, or "clockspeed,"[4] has quickened. Fashion-oriented and technology industries have always had to move at fast clockspeeds, whereas the older, so-called staple or smokestack industries have poked along. In the latter, slowness afflicts decision-making speed. Changes in the environment, if they are even detected, are not translated into timely action plans. Of course, initiation of new supply chain projects or modifying ongoing ones is also slow.

Clockspeeds have increased, whereas processes for decision making have not. A barrier exists if company processes continue to move more slowly than the pace of change needed to stay competitive. Slowness may be a symptom of a conservative, isolated management. It can also be the symptom of fast-paced environments where no one has time to reflect about the longer term. Such organizations are unlikely to unlock their doors for supply chain partners.

One wholesale distributor of electronic products, Merisel, contracted for an ambitious enterprise resource planning (ERP) system. A constraint was that all the built-in forms and reports had to be identical to the legacy system format. This and other project pitfalls led to the unintended consequences of overruns and a resulting unique high-maintenance system. The financial bleeding triggered a rapid pullback in the company's fortunes, putting the company out of business.

Rigidity is both subtle and unsubtle. Subtle rigidity besets the mindsets of people in the organization and is hard to identify. The solution is changed mindsets, often not an easy task. Unsubtle rigidity produces slowness in coping with needed change during the execution of supply chain change projects.

20.6.1 Mindset Changes

Supply chain change projects surface in many instances where a steering committee or management team will face a subtle change decision. How they decide reflects their collective mindset and values. The electronic product distributor discussed earlier had one such decision. Essentially, that decision was to change the software or the way people worked. The choice to change the software, not retrain the people, mucked up the software implementation and irreparably damaged the company.

The solution to this barrier lies in bringing in new mindsets through replacement or addition of people. Often, facilitating consultants fill a "devil's advocate" role to help a client team make the shift. There are no objective yardsticks for measuring mindsets. In fact, a positive mindset for implementing effective supply chain change might be measured by the absence of the barriers described in this chapter. Obstacles to change exist at two levels: the mindset level and the technical level. Life is easier if the mindset for change is in place, so that the team can tackle the technical level. If the mindset is not in place, a team must work on shifting ways of thinking before attempting technical solutions.

20.6.2 Changing the Project

Another rigidity source comes from sticking too long with a previously developed project plan. To many project managers, persistence through thick or thin is a virtue. These managers take pride in staying the course despite the fact that forces for change are hard at work.

Postmortem research into ERP implementation projects supports this proposition.[5] Professors Robert Austin of the Harvard Business School and Richard Nolan of the University of Washington Business School maintain that executives drop the ball when they treat large-scale ERP implementations as "rigid" IT projects. A better model, they suggest, is the new business venture. Such a venture needs to change frequently in response to new circumstance. The Project Management Body of Knowledge (PMBOK), cited earlier, refers to this as "progressive elaboration" requiring processes to realign the project with each new reality.

To be successful, supply chain projects must have well-oiled change management processes. In addition to changing project tasks and schedules, management must also be willing to change people or add people with absent skills. The steering committee should also avoid giving a project team too long a leash. Coming back for regular approvals is a good way of making sure the effort has not run amok.

20.7 Barriers to Cost Reduction—Summary

Awareness of barriers to improvement is the first step toward neutralizing them. This chapter has described five barriers to supply chain cost reduction and described ways to counter or circumvent them. The barriers act to keep us from dealing with the six root causes of cost listed in Table 20.2. The threat here is wasted time and effort on ineffectual supply chain improvement efforts. Also lost is competitive advantage that can never be recovered, a life-threatening consequence.

Endnotes

1. Many of the ideas for this chapter were previously published in the following article: Ayers, James B., "Costs: Getting to the Root Causes," *Supply Chain Management Review*, November–December, 2003, pp. 24–30.
2. *PMBOK Guide*, 2000 Ed., Project Management Institute: 2000. PMBOK stands for Project Management Body of Knowledge.
3. For a description of how to do this, see *Supply Chain Project Management* by James B. Ayers, published by St. Lucie Press, Boca Raton, in 2003.
4. A term originated by Charles Fine of MIT.
5. Cliffe, Sarah, "ERP Implementation: How to Avoid $100 Million Write-Offs," *Harvard Business Review*, January–February 1999, pp. 16 and 17.

Chapter 21

Multicompany Collaboration to Reduce Costs—Who, What, AND How

This chapter guides the reader toward decisions about *who, what,* and *how* for retail supply chain collaboration among trading partners in efforts to reduce costs.[1] The "who" discussion presents a screening process for confirming which partners are worth the teaming effort. The "what" discussion focuses on the type of collaboration using model information exchange and decision making described in Chapter 16, Section 16.1.2. The "how" lists types of collaboration appropriate for initiation by different supply chain partners—retailers, service providers, distributors, or manufacturers.

Chapter 20 listed root causes for costs and reasons why they are not addressed. In particular, three of the root causes—confusion, weak links, and unintended consequences—likely involve trading partners. Being multicompany in nature, these root causes can be the most challenging to fix. Despite the difficulty, multicompany partnerships to reduce cost are bound to increase as the globalization of retail markets increases. And, as if there are not enough options now, more will come into being as trading partners become creative in implementing new solutions.

21.1 Case Study—Frozen and Refrigerated Foods "Cold Chain"

Models of demanding supply chains already exist. One of the most demanding is that for frozen and refrigerated foods, the so-called "cold chain."[2] According to the Grocery Manufacturers Association (GMA), the U.S. consumer packaged goods industry annually generates $2.1 trillion in revenue. Of this, GMA members generate about $680 billion, and frozen food sales by manufacturers are about $28 billion. The refrigerated segment is thought to be larger in revenues than the frozen segment, and both have higher growth rates of dollar sales volume than all food categories. Important retail supply chain issues that are related to frozen and refrigerated food are:

- Temperature variance control (a quality issue)
- Higher costs of warehousing and transportation versus dry products sold at ambient temperatures (financial)
- Dating and stock rotation (quality)
- The necessity for high inventory turnover and effective application of just-in-time concepts (financial and quality)
- Frequent requirements for store door delivery from manufacturers/processors (financial and quality)
- Alternatives for self distribution versus use of wholesalers (financial)
- Feasibility of using Automatic Identification and Data Capture (AIDC) technologies (bar coding/radio frequency identification [RFID]) with moisture and frost on the packaging (quality and cost effectiveness)
- The potential for tracking temperatures with sensors as merchandise moves through the chain—an application with near-term feasibility as described in Chapter 18, Sections 18.3 and 18.4.

These are just some of the issues for frozen and chilled food products. The following are examples of projects aimed at dealing with these issues. They illustrate the breadth of projects required of a demanding supply chain.

1. *Retail grocery store door-delivery ice cream manufacturer*: Larger or outside warehouses versus tighter production scheduling and safety stocks; separate storage from odorous products such as fresh fish, due to the pickup of the odor in the ice cream
2. *Retail chain of ice cream parlors*: Use of contract co-packers or self manufacturing; product dating due to "freezer" burn; implementation of time-of-day delivery precision
3. *Refrigerated fruit juice processor*: Multistop scheduling of less-than-truckload (LTL) deliveries and automatic product identification
4. *Dairy food products processors*: Scheduling and routing of delivery vehicles for fluid milk, ice cream, yogurt, and sour cream

5. *Frozen microwave dinner entrees*: National location of plants and warehouses to minimize overall supply chain costs
6. *Refrigerated third-party logistics (3PL) "public warehouses"*: Outsourced inventory customer service to chain distribution centers
7. *Frozen and refrigerated food warehouses*: Order processing and warehouse productivity

The retail part of the supply chain requires higher turnover and higher levels of service than the manufacturing/processing echelon of the supply chain. Comparing the supply chain performance metrics for retail supermarket, mass merchandisers, convenience stores, and food-service (restaurant) chains illustrates the differences.

	Metrics	Processing/ Manufacturing	Retail Stores/ Outlets
1.	Annual inventory turns	5–10	20–50
2.	Fill rates	85–95 percent	98–99 percent
3.	On-time delivery	90 percent	95–99 percent

In summary, frozen and refrigerated products require more resources to plan, schedule, store, deliver, and manage than other food products as well as other categories of mass merchandise. In addition to service, the amount of care and quality provided need to be at higher levels due to the perishable nature of the product and the demand that there be little variance in temperature all throughout the temperature-controlled chain.

21.2 Recognize Root Causes

The need for collaboration is obvious in the frozen and refrigerated food cold chain, but it is not always so in others. However, once the desire for collaboration has been established, the sponsoring company needs to pursue correction of root causes for cost. An article in the *Harvard Business Review* by V.G. Narayanan and Ananth Raman reports cases and research as examples of several of these causes.[3]

■ *Confusion.* Technology company Cisco relied on subcontract manufacturers. These manufacturers had incentives to build inventories of parts, not what Cisco was selling. A sales slump left too much material in the supply chain and ambiguous accountability for the unneeded inventory. In fact, it was not clear what was actually ordered and what was actually made. Cisco had to take the write-offs.
■ *Confusion.* There are "hidden actions" that are not shared by trading partners. The authors point to manufacturer Whirlpool not knowing whether retailer

Sears is pushing its own Kenmore brand instead of Whirlpool, making it hard to plan for efficient production.

- *Confusion and weak links.* One party often possesses information or knowledge that its trading partner does not possess. This particularly applies to cost information. Suppliers fear that retailers will use that information to negotiate lower prices.
- *Unintended consequences.* The authors conducted research of over 50 supply chains. It found that incentives were not aligned, so companies acted in their own interest, not the joint interests of themselves and their trading partners.
- *Unintended consequences.* Badly designed incentives play a role in adding costs. The authors describe a Canadian bakery that paid deliverymen for sales based on their allotted space in stores. The deliverymen's incentives promoted overstocking, necessitating disposal of large quantities of stale pastries.

Narayanan and Raman recommend correcting the relationships by targeting these hidden actions, information gaps, and incentives. Their solutions include rewriting contracts, documenting costs with activity-based costing to develop appropriate charges, and collaborating on information sharing and tracking. This chapter offers specific suggestions for pursuing these ends.

Just how one's trading partners should be involved with a company will depend on their relative power in the relationship, the business arrangements among partners, and how broadly and deeply they interact. The chapter refers to a number of concepts ("whats") and methodologies ("hows") already described elsewhere. For ready reference, Table 21.1 lists candidate collaboration topics described elsewhere in this book.

21.3 Types of Collaboration

Figure 16.3 in Chapter 16 depicted different types of collaboration. These types vary in terms of the need for mutual adjustment during the collaboration and the associated risks. As needs for adjustment increase, more intense collaboration is required. The four levels of collaboration described in Section 16.1.2, ranked from lower to higher levels, were the following:

- *Data exchange collaboration* where partners exchange information as required to complete day-to-day transactions. Data exchange can have two forms: one-way (type A) or two-way (type B). These types of collaboration are often automated and seek to improve supply chain speed and efficiency.
- *Cooperative collaboration* (type C) where partners share systems and tools so each partner has simultaneous access to information needed for decision making. One or both will make an independent decision after the sharing. Examples include sharing sales and forecasting data provided by a system

Table 21.1 Candidate Topics for Collaboration

	Partnership Topics	Topics Defined	Chapter or Section Addressed
1.	Product-related collaboration	Considerations related to the base (physical) product and extended (related services) product	11.1 The Product life cycle 11.2 Innovative and functional products
2.	Market-related collaboration	Understanding the needs of different customers and end-users	12.2 Market segments 13.1 Activity system example
3.	Demand-driven supply chain	Process designs that utilize actual demand rather than forecasts, in decision-making, leading to the "lean" supply chain	13.2 Defining processes 17 The demand-driven supply chain
4.	Partnership types and structures	Nature of the multicompany relationship and governance	12.3 Spheres—Modules for supply chain design 14 Retail SCM—skills required 15.2 Continuous improvement cycles 15.3 S&OP process and functional roles 16 Collaboration with supply chain partners
5.	Financial incentives	Recognizing opportunities and rewarding	11.3 Market mediation costs 19 Accounting for supply chain costs 20 Addressing root causes for cost
6.	New technology	Innovations in merchandise tracking, transportation, and handling	18 Product tracking along retail supply chains

to personal interactions for capacity planning and product development. A non-supply chain example is consulting a stockbroker about the purchase of a security. The broker must understand the investor's goals and recommend the "right" investment, but the investor must ultimately decide what to purchase.

◾ *Cognitive collaboration* (type D) involves joint, concurrent intellectual, and cognitive activity between partners to reach joint decisions. This level includes "knowledge" exchanges included in this book's definition of supply chain flows in Chapter 1. Such collaboration could change the "space" in the supply chain, lead to new products, or produce investments in facilities and information systems. In this case the broker and investor invest together.

Using inputs from this book, sourcing-team brainstorming, and other sources, Table 21.2 lists examples of trading partner collaboration candidates of each type. The mission of the list is to trigger ideas for innovation in trading-partner relationships. The next section describes a methodology for confirming the trading partners with whom the company wants to collaborate. Following that discussion, this chapter will explain the options presented in Table 21.2 in greater depth.

21.4 Who—Rationalizing the Customer/Supplier Base

Pursuing multicompany partnerships should start with a review of existing and candidate trading partners. This look should confirm that you desire a relationship in any form—collaborative or not—with any particular trading partner. A helpful tool from the inventory management discipline is called inventory ABC analysis or distribution. Note that this version of ABC shouldn't be confused with the other "ABC" described in Chapter 19 that stands for *activity-based costing*.

Many companies use ABC inventory analysis to sort products or SKUs (stock-keeping units) into category *A*, *B*, or *C*, based on parameters such as total sales performance for a retailer or distributor, or percentage of the cost of goods sold for a manufacturer. This type of analysis is particularly useful for nonfashion or staple merchandise. Note that manufacturers might use the term *SKU* to refer to their raw materials, and the term "products" as the finished goods they ship to distributors and retailers. A distributor might use either term; but SKU is common for both incoming and outgoing merchandise when an SKU is not converted but passes through en route from manufacturers to retailers. However, distributors moving into new space in the supply chain may convert an incoming SKU into multiple SKUs for individual retailers. A retailer might use "SKUs," "products," or even product "categories" in applying an ABC inventory analysis.

Another available tool for spend analysis is the United Nations Standard Products and Services Code (UNSPSC). The UNSPSC allows its users to generate eight-digit codes for over 20,000 products and services. Having common codes puts

Table 21.2 Candidates for Collaboration by Type—What's and How's

Type	Name	Candidate Multicompany Collaborative Tools	2nd Tier Supplier	OEM	Distributor	Retailer	Service Providers
A	One-Way Data Exchange	**Prearranged exception notices:**					
		■ Inventory shortages/excesses			•	•	
		■ Missing product/SKUs			•	•	
		■ Excessive backlogs	•	•			•
		■ Capacity problems	•	•		•	•
		■ POS exception data		•	•		•
		■ Transportation bottlenecks			•	•	•
		■ Other exceptions	•	•			
B	Two-Way Data Exchange	**Information sharing:**					
		■ Production schedule sharing	•	•			
		■ Forecasts as committed orders		•			
		Product & service related quality:					
		■ Specification flexibility	•	•			
		■ Tolerance relaxation	•	•			
		■ Reporting against standards	•	•			
		■ Backup inventory availability	•	•	•	•	
		Transportation & warehousing:					
		■ Freight consolidations		•	•		•
		■ Transportation coordination		•			•
		■ Warehousing services	•		•	•	•
		■ Production staging			•	•	•
		■ Customs /freight forwarding			•		
		Life cycle product data:					
		■ Configuration status		•		•	
		■ Repair history		•		•	
		■ Asset management		•		•	

Table 21.2 (continued)   Candidates for Collaboration by Type—What's and How's

Type	Name	Candidate Multicompany Collaborative Tools	2nd Tier Supplier	OEM	Distributor	Retailer	Service Providers
C	Cooperative Collaboration	**Process improvements:**					
		■ Yield improvement	•	•		•	•
		■ Synchronized replenishment		•		•	
		■ Technologies like RFID				•	
		■ Direct-to-store shipments					
		■ Supplier process qualification		•			
		Financial incentives:					
		■ Incentives to reduce costs	•	•		•	
		■ Consignment inventory		•		•	
		■ Contract terms					
		Collaborative analysis:					
		■ Inputs for QFD analysis		•		•	•
		■ Activity-based costing support		•		•	•
		■ Multicompany teams		•		•	
		■ Flexibility definition		•			
		Compliance services:					
		■ Quality audits		•			•
		■ Social compliance audits		•		•	•
		■ Consulting services					•

	Collaboration items	1	2	3	4	5
D — Cognitive Collaboration	**Collaboration strategy:**					
	■ Activity system construction		•		•	
	■ Providing a core competency		•		•	
	■ Service agreements/guarantees		•		•	
	■ Long-term contracts		•			
	New product development:					
	■ Avoidance of capital costs		•			
	■ Financing new product		•			
	■ Product design support		•			•
	■ Sourcing /component selection		•			•
	■ Packaging configurations		•		•	
	■ Component commonality					
	Demand-driven supply chain:					
	■ Data sharing/synchronization		•		•	
	■ Addition/deletion of echelons		•		•	•
	■ Supplier consolidation		•		•	•
	■ Postponement – configuration		•			
	■ Postponement – location				•	
	■ Inspection reductions		•			
	■ Tooling design		•			
	Life cycle product support:					
	■ Vendor-managed inventory		•		•	
	■ Configuration management		•		•	
	■ Repair/return support		•		•	
	■ Repair parts stocking		•			
	■ Component refurbishment		•		•	
	■ Technical support		•			

Note: • Indicates likely originators of collaborations.

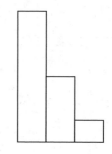

Item Value   65% 25% 10%
No. of Items 10% 25% 65%

Figure 21.1   ABC inventory strategies.

buyers and sellers on common ground when identifying just exactly what is bought and sold. Coding purchases this way eliminates a source of confusion—that of identifying what is purchased. The eight-digit codes can be extended with other company-specific information.

Regardless of the application, a typical product/SKU split will have about 65 percent of total value (in cost, contribution margin, "importance," or revenue) in the *A* category. *B* items may account for another 25 percent, and *C* items for 10 percent. The percentage of items in each category is reversed, with about 10% of the product/SKUs being the high-value *A* items, *B* items about 25 percent of all the items, and low-value *C* items the remaining 65 percent of products/SKUs.

Dividing products and SKUs into categories enables tailored strategies for sourcing, replenishment, handling, and storage (Figure 21.1). *A* products/SKUs receive focused attention for source selection and replenishment. Depending on classification criteria, they likely generate most of the merchandise cost and inventory investment. From a customer loyalty point of view, *A*-item stockouts may also carry the highest penalty. This isn't always the case; Wal-Mart set up a Remix supply chain to avoid stockouts for critical everyday items. Chapter 12, Section 12.3, describes the Wal-Mart effort. Shortages of critical or hard-to-find *C* items sometimes cause manufacturing operations to halt because no one has paid attention to their availability. Because *C*s are low cost, their transaction costs represent a higher proportion of the total cost of managing them. So, management of *C* items focuses on developing efficient processes. In retail supply chains, the retailer is more likely to purchase *A* items directly from the manufacturer and *C* items from a distributor. *B* items may follow either path, depending on the volumes involved and supply chain economics.

Figure 21.2 illustrates the landscape for product–supplier strategies using the ABC approach. The table can be interpreted to match the perspective of any player in a retail supply chain: retailers, distributors, OEM manufacturers, service providers and second-tier component suppliers. Figure 21.2 employs the ABC approach to sort *both* SKUs and suppliers, a technique conceived by David Malmberg of CGR

Suppliers

		a	b	c
Products/SKU's	**A**	Major OEM manufacturers supplying high price products/SKUs to distributors or stores. Collaboration of all types. **Aa**	Manufacturers or distributors supplying innovative niche product. Alternate sources unlikely. Product life cycle collaboration. **Ab**	A company has produced a new product with high market potential. Sole source. Future growth attractive. Help supplier with design/production. **Ac**
	B	Manufacturer or distributor of mid-priced merchandise. Apply activity-based costing. A & B collaboration. **Ba**	For high performing suppliers, add business to convert from "b" to "a". Type A & B collaboration. **Bb**	Search out alternative sources. Justify continuing relationship with activity-based costing. **Bc**
	C	Manufacturer or distributor of consumer packaged goods or small items. Type A & B collaboration. **Ca**	Explore moving business to an "a" supplier or, for good performers, expand role. Apply activity-based costing. **Cb**	A supplier/product combination that's a candidate for elimination. Use activity-based costing to make case. **Cc**

Figure 21.2   Product supplier landscape.

Management Consultants. In the figure, capital letters in italics stand for products/SKUs, and small letters in regular type stand for suppliers. As mentioned earlier, *A* products/SKUs are usually high-price or profit products. But they can also be *A*'s by virtue of their importance in the company's strategy for the future—like a new product just launched into the market. *A*'s are likely in the growth or maturity stages of the product life cycle shown in Figure 11.1 in Chapter 11. *B*'s have moderate volumes or importance; *C*'s are usually low-value and high-volume commodities. Sometimes, more than one supplier provides a particular SKU. So, there may be two providers of an *A* product/SKU; one might be an "a" supplier, the other a "b". Likewise an "a" supplier, like a large distributor, may provide nothing other than "*C*" products/SKUs.

An "a" supplier will often supply *A* SKUs. *A* items residing with many small "c" suppliers may be a signal to reduce suppliers. This would be even more the case if the SKUs are *C* items, and the suppliers are "c" suppliers. Freeing the company of many small suppliers will reduce hidden transaction costs. The other ABC, activity-based costing is a good way to document these costs. Note that parameters for supplier classification need not be the same as those for products/SKUs. For example, a "b" supplier might supply a high-margin critical *A* product to a retailer or an important proprietary technology for a manufacturer. This relationship may be a critical one for innovative products promising high growth, thereby promoting the "b" supplier to the "a" list.

Figure 21.2 lists examples and suggests forms of collaboration that might fit each combination of product/SKU and supplier. Higher forms of collaboration (Types C and D) are particularly suitable for all *A* products/SKUs. Indeed, one might define

Figure 21.3 Product supplier strategies.

A products/SKUs as ones requiring such collaboration. *C* products, on the other hand, are amenable to data sharing to streamline replenishment (Type A and B collaboration) or shifting from direct purchase to purchase from a distributor.

The lower right-hand corner of Figure 21.2 (cell *C*c) represents commodity products from low-volume suppliers. An ABC analysis might prove them uneconomical. Moving their business to another larger supplier (an "a" or a "b") could make sense. For the retailer or distributor, low-profit "c" products might also be dropped.

Figure 21.3 suggests what directions collaboration might take. Space does not permit an all-inclusive list. There are two types of strategy in Figure 21.3—one that applies to products/SKUs, and the other that applies to suppliers. Strategies for products/SKUs are in italics; those for suppliers are in regular type. For example, the *A*a cell suggests pursuing a demand-driven supply chain, as described in Chapter 17, for high-volume product/SKUs. For a supplier strategy, financial incentives are suggested for cost reductions that apply to all the products from that supplier. A vendor-managed inventory (VMI) arrangement might also be negotiated with a supplier of multiple products/SKUs. The same strategies could apply to the *B*a cell. For a high-performing "b" supplier of *A* products, more business with that supplier might be justified if the supplier offers products/SKUs that aren't currently purchased.

The *C*a cell could include a distributor providing a lot of small-value parts. The total volume of multiple *C* items makes the distributor an "a" supplier. Perhaps there are too many distributors or manufacturers if a large amount of *C* products/SKUs is purchased from "b" and "c" suppliers.

21.5 What and How—Pursuing Partnership Opportunities

This section describes in further detail the collaboration scenarios listed in Table 21.2. Five participating supply chain links are shown on Table 21.2: 2nd-tier suppliers, OEM manufacturers, distributors, retailers, and logistics service providers. Examples of the latter category include transportation companies, customs brokers, quality inspection services, freight forwarders, and sourcing companies. An example of the last category is Li and Fung Limited in Hong Kong. This company describes itself as a trading company that manages the supply chain for high-volume, time-sensitive consumer goods. Its services, much of it for apparel merchandise, include product design, sourcing, production planning, quality assurance, and export documentation from any of 40 countries where it operates.

Dots on Table 21.2 show where in the supply chain collaboration initiatives might originate. For example, if all four participants are marked, that collaborative action could be initiated at any link in the chain. If just the retailer is marked, then the collaboration could include any of the other echelons. For example, for a *C*-item shortage, just the distributor might be involved. But for an *A* item, the OEM and the 2nd-tier supplier of the item might be involved.

21.5.1 Type A: One-Way Data Exchange Collaboration

Although there is little exotic about one-way exchanges, they can be quite valuable in alerting trading partners to exception situations. Rapid notification of exceptions can head off bigger problems if the condition causing the exception is not corrected. The list in Table 21.2 is an example of exception conditions. Such reports are often prearranged by partners along the chain and generated according to agreed-to business rules. Terms for these arrangements include "proactive" systems and workflow. The rules are a by-product of process designs that have built-in collaboration mechanisms. The communications should be directed at decision makers responsible for reacting to the reported condition, such as an out-of-stock condition.

Inventory mismatches in the form of shortages or excesses are reported by distributors or retailers—those closest to end-user demand. These notices signal upstream manufacturing partners to slow down or speed up. Missing products/SKUs refers to mismatches between what was ordered and what arrived. These can be generated at the OEM, distributor, or retailer levels. Backlogs or capacity problems normally occur in manufacturing, but they can also occur when a supply chain manager such as Li and Fung detects a problem.

Point of Sales (POS) data must originate at the retailer. It does not necessarily have to be streaming data but can be automatically screened to detect conditions when customer demand is running ahead or behind forecasts. Distributors, supply chain managers, and transportation companies might trigger transportation bottleneck reports. Because the world of exceptions is quite broad, any participant might consider generation of exception reports as a feature in its extended product service offerings.

21.5.2 Type B: Two-Way Data Exchange Collaboration

This category covers communications that, although routine, require responses to the originating supply chain partner. A common area of collaboration in manufacturing is production scheduling and forecasting, often under the CPFR banner. As described in Chapters 15 and 16, West Marine issued its forecasts in the form of committed orders. This is shown as a reasonable method for both the OEM manufacturer to its supplier or the retailer, like West Marine, to the OEM or the distributor. By accepting the forecast, the receiving partner is agreeing to meet its commitment.

The area of product and service quality is an area of potential two-way collaboration. Specification flexibility is important in product design to assure that suppliers have the processing capability to meet the specification. It also applies to assuring that components specified in a product are not at the end of their production lives, especially important in fast-changing electronics. Relaxation of tolerances might occur in production when specifications not critical to product function can be relaxed.

Reporting exceptions to service standards for completeness of orders is a useful technique to spur corrective actions. This can occur at the second tier, OEM, and distributor levels. Many manufacturers and distributors are now contracted to carry inventory to service retailers; reporting the status for critical items is an option for two-way communication.

The transportation and warehousing category deals with merchandise moving through the supply chain. So, transportation and warehousing exchanges can occur at several points, but which points will depend on the supply chain partner with the biggest stake in having the visibility. This can be an OEM, distributor, retailer, or a service provider providing visibility as an extended product service. Second-tier manufacturers, distributors, or logistics service providers can support production staging. This staging serves manufacturers' production lines or retailers' stores. Often, the staging involves added services such as store labels, material kitting for production, or light assembly. Customs and freight-forwarding reports from logistics service providers are another forum for two-way communications.

Long-lived retail merchandise such as personal computers, televisions, cameras, autos, and other expensive items require support over their product life cycles in the form of warranties, recall notices, rebates, repairs, and software upgrades. End-user registrations, returns, service contracts, and OEM warranties trigger the requirement for collaboration. The retailer and OEM need to establish responsibilities for these, and they may vary by product categories. In actual operations, the end-user will trigger these events that require retailers or OEM manufacturers to respond. Chapter 22 discusses the category of aftermarket processes in more detail.

21.5.3 Cooperative Collaboration

This category is more intense two-way collaboration. This collaboration is more likely to go on personally, by phone or face to face, rather than through message exchanges. An example is an effort in manufacturing to increase process yields. Small increases in first-pass yield bring outsized benefits in capacity and profit. Often, this requires collaboration between a supplier and its OEM customer. The collaboration should address root causes for yield losses, including too tight specifications from the OEM. These can be caused by variations in processes such as those that are targets of Six Sigma initiatives described in Chapter 17.

Synchronized replenishment seeks to eliminate bullwhips or to employ pull-type replenishment rules such as those in 3C. The retailer, OEM, or supply chain manager could orchestrate the synchronization for all or part of the supply chain. Technology deployments are more likely to be less democratic. Technology such as RFID will likely proliferate if demanded by strong retailers who have the best chance of capturing savings from the technology. The same applies to direct-to-store delivery service provided by OEM manufacturers and distributors, thereby avoiding distribution-center processing. Supplier-process qualifications are likely driven by OEMs to assure reliable components from their suppliers.

The research by Narayanan and Raman highlights the importance of aligning financial incentives.[4] A second-tier supplier or a third-part supply chain manager might propose such incentives to the OEM manufacturer. Consignment inventory rules might avoid a situation like that faced by Cisco where order tracking disappeared and excess inventory caused write-offs. The OEM and the retailer may want to set the rules for inventory for their upstream suppliers. The same applies to other contract terms designed to avoid mismatched incentives.

Collaborative analysis encompasses supply chain efforts directed at improvement. A manufacturer may ask retailers or its customers for inputs into product design. These efforts could employ Quality Function Deployment (QFD) as a way of displaying the "voice of the customer" inputs. Chapter 7, Section 7.5, describes the approach. Activity-based costing inputs could help assure alignment of incentives and provide a clear picture of where supply chain costs reside. These, in turn, could lead to contract terms that reduce conflicts of interest.

The retailer, OEM, or supply chain manager could initiate an effort to define flexibility. The collaboration would set operating ranges for products, SKUs, or categories for capacity setting and response to changes in sales levels. Beyond basic capabilities, flexibility is the most important property of a supply chain. This is because end-user demand fluctuates for all but the simplest products, and other measures such as cost, quality, and delivery depend on being flexible enough to respond accordingly.

A final category for cooperative collaboration is compliance with quality assurance, standards for worker protection, and supply chain troubleshooting. OEM manufacturers will need to collaborate with their suppliers or their supply chain managers to assure compliance. Retailers also are aware of the downfalls of not considering worker conditions in the factories that supply them. This is particularly true in those overseas labor surplus regions, even if these suppliers are two or three organizations removed from the retailer. Nike, after being highly criticized for poor labor practices overseas, totally overhauled its product specifications and its supply chain to meet customer expectations in this area. The supply chain manager and other specialized providers can fill a consulting role to assist OEMs and retailers in designing products and establishing the logistics required to put merchandise on shelves in appropriate quantities.

21.5.4 Cognitive Collaboration

This category encompasses high-level decisions made at key points in a relationship. Such points include initiation of the partnership, planning a new product, making decisions on what to make and what to buy, and setting up the supply chain. In fact, the lower levels of collaboration (A, B, and C) will have been considered, and presumably designed, during cognitive collaborations.

Collaboration strategy addresses the basic, up-front need for supply chain partners to work together. These are likely to be initiated by OEM manufacturers or retailers for their supply chain zones—second-tier suppliers and service providers to the OEM, and distributors and OEMs for the retailer. An example is Wal-Mart's reliance on drug distributor McKesson for vendor-managed inventory services. In some cases, OEMs and retailers may collaborate in the design of an activity system for a new product, service, or territory. These arrangements may lead to service agreements in exchange for business guarantees. An OEM may seek second-tier suppliers for their core competencies leading to long-term contracts.

New products bring a host of options for collaboration for the OEM manufacturer. This includes choices of suppliers, outsourcing supply chain activities to service providers, and working with the retailer on packaging and tracking technologies such as bar codes and RFID. The collaboration includes the base product, associated extended products, and design and financing of the means of production.

The demand-driven supply chain, by definition, requires collaboration among trading partners. The effort ideally will be driven from the retailer or retailers closest to customers. The OEM may also initiate such efforts, especially if there is high degree of component commonality or an extensive supply network.

The OEM would likely lead postponement decisions related to configuration—seeking to commit to final configuration as close to final assembly as possible. However, postponement related to location is the logical domain of the retailer. This type of postponement delays shipments from the distributor (or retailer distribution center) until customer demand signals the retailer to send merchandise to individual stores. This is also consistent with vendor-managed inventory arrangements between retailer and distributor. Inspection and tooling are opportunities to lower cost through automation and elimination of non-value-adding steps in the process.

Product life-cycle support also requires collaborative decisions. OEMs will initiate requirements for repair parts stocking and component refurbishment. This need is common for large-ticket items where rebuilt parts can be recycled after their initial replacement. For many big-ticket items, this is a lucrative business. Options abound for handling initial warranty repairs and long-term repairs. For example, for laptop computers, Best Buy might do long-term warranty repairs in-house or farm the work out to contractors, or in some cases, return the computers to the manufacturers for service.

21.6 Multicompany Collaboration to Reduce Cost—Summary

The process for initiating or bolstering efforts to collaborate with trading partners is a three-step process. First there is a need to screen both upstream and downstream trading partners. This may lead to pruning unprofitable products, categories or SKUs or trading partners that drive up costs. Second, the types of collaboration needed (A, B, C, D) should be derived from company strategies for operations. This might include analysis of costs with activity-based costing, customer requirements with QFD, or an activity system design. Finally, the collaborative tools must be chosen. Table 21.2, along with sections and chapters listed in Table 21.1, provide a candidate list of area for collaboration.

Endnotes

1. The authors thank David Malmberg for his review of this chapter and his contributions to the analytical framework described in Chapter 21.
2. The authors wish to thank Peter A. Crosby for contributing the cold chain example.
3. Narayanan, V.G. and Raman, Ananth, "Aligning Incentives in Supply Chains," *Harvard Business Review*, November 2004, pp. 94–102.
4. Ibid.

Chapter 22

Retail Return Loops

This chapter explores issues that are, for many supply chains, becoming more important. These deal with the "return loop." When the *forward* supply chain has delivered a product to an end-user, merchandise, for varying reasons, journeys back through the *reverse* or *return* supply chain. Returns or reverse flows also address issues of sustainability wherein some products must be disposed of in environmentally friendly ways. This is particularly true of products that degrade chemically. Currently, tires and technology products are examples of the types that use the return loop at the end of their usable life.

The return loop is also a service element that is important to many customers and end-users. Convenient returns reduce purchase risk when buying from a retailer. Customers may also place considerable value on aftermarket service for equipment repair and maintenance. For durable products, manufacturers and retailers find that aftermarket services are more profitable than initial sales. Retailers or OEMs price many products lower in the beginning because the real source of profit will come from the aftermarket. For example, cell phones, cameras, and computer printers require ongoing investment in consumables after purchase in the form of minutes, film or photo paper, and ink cartridges, respectively.

22.1 GENCO Case Study—the Rise of the Return Loop

GENCO is a U.S. supply chain services provider specializing in reverse logistics. The company, based in Pittsburgh, is privately held and maintains 26 million sq. ft. of warehouse space in 90 facilities and employs 5500 "team members." The company, whose revenues are about $400 million, offers several services related to reverse supply chain logistics. These include an online auction of returned merchandise, software to manage return flows, disposition of damaged merchandise, warehouse and transportation services, and consulting in reverse logistics.

GENCO pursued returns after providing forward flow logistics services since 1898. In an interview, GENCO's CEO, Herb Shear, recounted how his company was drawn into reverse logistics.[1] As with many new business opportunities, GENCO's move into reverse logistics started with a customer request. In 1988, the customer, a discount drug retailer, sought a place to store merchandise returning to its warehouses. Service to that customer evolved into developing software to scan incoming items, identify the merchandise and the store where they originated, and charge back the items to the manufacturer where possible. The first large retailer to buy the software was Target; other large retailers followed, transforming GENCO from a regional into a national company.

22.2 Types of Returns

The GENCO case demonstrates that reverse-logistics consciousness is a relatively recent phenomenon, and examination of the types of returns demonstrates the potential for complexity. The Supply Chain Council's Supply Chain Operations Reference (SCOR) model lists three types of returns. The types are listed in the following text along with other observations produced by a publication of the Council of Supply Chain Management Professionals (CSCMP) authored by Dale Rogers and Ronald Tibben-Lembke of the University of Nevada Reno.[2] These authors add a fourth type of return, the recapture of assets required for shipment, such as special containers, pallets, and totes. This is a routine feature in forward supply chain design, so it's not included here.

1. *Return defective products.* Interpreted broadly beyond outright defects, this return category also includes cases of customer or end-user "remorse" and mind changes. Included are items that are hard to install or did not fit properly, product recalls, and environmentally hazardous material.
2. *Return an MRO (maintenance, repair, or overhaul) product.* In retail, this type includes high-value items needing repair or periodic maintenance. Rogers and Tibben-Lembke include product refurbishment and remanufacturing in this category. For appliances, this service can be done on site; for automobiles, at a dealer location or at a contract repair center. Often, such returns must be authorized through a *return merchandise authorization* (RMA).
3. *Return excess products.* Examples include unsold merchandise sold on consignment, and obsolete product.

Figure 22.1 is an adaptation of Figure 1.1 in Chapter 1 that depicts the forward supply chain. Figure 22.1 traces both forward and reverse flows for base, or physical, products. Depending on the product, returns can occur between the end-user and the retailer, or from the end-user back to the OEM manufacturer. Product

Figure 22.1 Physical flows in return loops.

component flows occur further upstream from the OEM back to first-tier suppliers. A third-party reverse-logistics provider, such as GENCO, may play a role anywhere in this flow. Indeed, transactions associated with reverse flows for many products outnumber those for forward flows.

Figure 22.2 models return processes using a three-step process. Large numbers mark each step.

1. *End-user originates return action appropriate to the product.* This is one of the three types described earlier, with the product landing at the retailer, the OEM, a return center operated by the OEM, first-tier supplier, distributor, retailer, or a returns service provider.
2. *Receiver processes the return.* It could process the item back into the forward supply chain without modification ("no fault found"), repair or refurbish the product, or remove the item from the chain for disposal.
3. *Product moves to a forward return path or to disposal.* Paths shown include regular forward paths, a discount or auction option, or direct shipment to end-users. This requires a decision based on the action taken, available channels for return, and the nature of the product.

In Figure 22.2, a "regular channel" shown at the upper right can be through the retailer or by the Internet or catalog. A discount channel can include all of the previously discussed types, including "factory stores" or sales to brokers. The "direct-to-end-user" channel is shipment back to the party originating the return—especially appropriate for returning or replacing expensive merchandise.

Table 22.1 provides examples of reverse flows for different types of retail merchandise. These examples illustrate the multitude of paths in return-loop supply

Figure 22.2   Disposition of returned merchandise.

chains. For each example, there's a reason for the origin of the return and identification of common configurations of related processes.

22.3 Opportunities in Returns

The return loop, for many products, is an afterthought, but the cost and service implications of returns make the design of their processes important. This section describes some of the opportunities available from better design of the return processes. Table 22.2 outlines these opportunities.

22.3.1 Reduced Returns

An organization that has returns should adopt a "lean" philosophy by treating returns as a form of "waste," but this can only be done if root causes for returns are addressed. For example, Section 21.2 described a bakery with unaligned compensation for its delivery staff. The incentive arrangement based on total sales without considering "scrap" led to overstocking and returns of unsold product. An apparel manufacturer using multiple Chinese manufacturers sold products with varying

Table 22.1   Examples of Return Loops

#	Example/Reason	1 Originator	2 Processor	3 Return Path/Disposal
1.	Clothing return (doesn't fit, changed mind, etc.)	Customer, end-user	Retail outlet where sold	Same-store resale
2.	Laptop repair (manufacturer's warranty)	End-user	OEM	Direct shipment
3.	Laptop repair (extended retailer warranty)	End-user	Retailer or service provider	Direct shipment
4.	Books on consignment (unsold, surplus)	Retailer	OEM (publisher)	Regular-channel resale or disposal
5.	Bakery goods (unsold, no longer fresh)	Retailer	OEM (bakery)	Disposal or discount channel
6.	Defective part from 1st-tier supplier	OEM manufacturer	1st-tier supplier	Repair, replace, or dispose of (scrap)
7.	Car battery end of life	End-user	Retailer (dealer garage)	Dispose through approved processor or recycling center

sizing standards. The inconsistencies raised returns because buyers found that garments did not fit properly. Attacking returns with a programmatic Six Sigma approach, such as that described in Chapter 17, should reduce processing costs and overproduction.

Another avoidance technique is targeting "no-fault-found" situations. These take the form of both returned products at the retail level and between first- and second-tier suppliers. The latter can sometimes be addressed by assuring that quality measurements are consistent between suppliers and OEMs. The former might be reduced by better instructions and troubleshooting direction. Information systems, designed around the return process, can also reduce returns. First, they assure that end-user returns are eligible under warranty and sales terms. Second, such systems alert partners to problems and track what is coming in and where it is. They can also help to diagnose problems in the system or the product so that they can be resolved.

Table 22.2   Opportunities in Returns

#	Opportunity	Suggested Strategies
1.	Reduced returns	Understand and mitigate root causes for returns
2.	Improved customer service	Emphasize extended product features that reduce end-user risk
3.	Collaboration with partners	Cooperate in returns to achieve forward process improvement
4.	Customer feedback	Gather early indications with base product or its use
5.	Material source	Use recycled components as parts
6.	Environmental mitigation	Control environmental impact of your product; reduce liability
7.	Additional business	Expand service beyond your own product line
8.	Cash-to-cash cycle reduction	Tighten investment in product circulating in return loops
9.	Process standardization	Assure consistency. Provide economies of scale

22.3.2 Improved Customer Service

The return level is an inverse measure of customer satisfaction—more returns equates to less satisfaction. Smooth returns processing is also an index of the ease of doing business with one's company, whether retailer, distributor, or manufacturer. For example, some customers find comfort in a "clicks-and-bricks" model used by retailers such as Eddie Bauer. They know they can return their Internet purchases to the retailer's stores, which makes them more willing to take the "risk" of shopping online and buying products sight unseen. This should be a powerful incentive to improve returns processing.

22.3.3 Collaboration with Partners

A supply chain approach to returns requires multicompany collaboration. Such collaboration in the returns domain can build on or lead to collaboration on forward supply chain processes. One aspect of the collaboration can include the determination of which services the OEM and the retailer will provide. Data generated using activity-based costing (ABC), described in Chapter 19, will aid the discussion. This may be particularly necessary because financial reporting of cost in many return processes is weak or nonexistent.

Financial flows are another aspect of collaboration; this topic includes pricing and credits for returned items. For many products such as tires and batteries, there is a fee paid by the customer to cover the cost of recycling or disposal. The conditions for issuing an RMA may also be negotiated between the retailer and the OEM to control what is returned and where it is returned.

22.3.4 *Customer Feedback*

An understanding of customer feedback provides rich "voice-of-the-customer" information to improve product design, adjust merchandise assortments, and respond to customer priorities. For example, Rogers and Tibben-Lembke cite IKEA. Customer feedback led to development of easy-to-understand instructions for its knockdown furniture that the customer has to assemble.[3] Better instructions reduced returns by frustrated assemblers of the product.

22.3.5 *Material Source*

For durable goods and parts, the return loop is a source of refurbished and remanufactured product. For example, Amazon offers both new and recycled books for sale at various prices. For a prior book by one of the authors, the site offers new books for about $77 and used ones for $40. However, many retailers and OEMs take a casual approach to this source of revenue. This does not mean there are no players taking advantage of this role. Smaller remanufacturers or generic part makers often refurbish previously owned goods for resale, a practice reinforced by growing interest in sustainability as discussed in Chapter 5. Auto manufacturers in the U.S. compete actively in the aftermarket by touting the reliability of their "authentic," and usually pricier, products. Pulling in more of this business may be an option to consider.

22.3.6 *Environmental Mitigation*

If a product presents an environmental hazard, then close control of the return process can limit liability. It may also, through process reengineering, produce product designs and material substitutions that lower the cost of product ownership and produce recycled material for new production. As described in Chapter 5, retailers are making environmental sustainability an important mission. Wal-Mart recently announced its intention of becoming a totally "green" company.

22.3.7 Additional Business

Some vertically integrated retailers may choose to handle their own reverse supply chain activities. However, as there are service providers in the form of contract manufacturers serving the forward supply chain, there are service providers doing the same for reverse supply chains. GENCO, described at the beginning of this chapter, is an example. A company that decides to operate its own reverse supply chain might also do so for others as a service provider, creating another line of business.

22.3.8 Cash-to-Cash Cycle Reduction

Improvements in this metric, introduced in Chapter 3, Section 3.3, result from reductions in cycle-time in return processes. Too often, returned merchandise is put aside for processing "when time is available." If it is not available, then both customer service and cash flow may suffer. A related problem, according to Rogers and Tibben-Lembke, is accounting for returns.[4] For example, the retail store is measured on sales, but returns cut into sales. So, returns are bad news to stores, and, if salespeople are paid on commission, for their paychecks. This may cause underreporting of returns, although most store operations capture this information. More common is inaccurate recording of reasons for returns.

22.3.9 Process Standardization

Returns processes will vary as merchandise is sold in different chains, different countries, and in a variety of store types. Added control at the retailer, distributor, or OEM level assures consistent processes. Rogers and Tibben-Lembke point to the potential for centralized returns centers, or CRCs, as ways to shorten cycle times and enforce consistent process guidelines. Benefits cited by the authors include the following:

- Retail-store space savings by moving returns out of the store quickly or bypassing it altogether
- Screening out items that have to be discarded, saving the expense of their transport back up the supply chain
- An extended product service by the manufacturer or distributor trying to win business from a retailer
- Shorter cycle times because the dedicated facility has returns as its primary mission
- An ability to spot trends in returns and better understanding of root causes for returns. For the manufacturer or distributor, this could lead to quicker correction of root-cause process problems that cause returns

22.4 Return Loops—Summary

Return-loop opportunities abound for the many retailers and the trading partners that serve them. If these opportunities are being overlooked, addressing returns can pay off in customer satisfaction, market share, end-user feedback, lower cost of sales, and lower working capital. With the movement to a sustainable business model, return loops can also be the source of new profits, reduced liability risk, and improved image with customers and end-users.

Endnotes

1. MacDonald, Mitch, "A Fortune in Reversal," *DC Velocity,* October 2006, pp. 25–30.
2. Rogers, Dale S. and Tibben-Lembke, Ronald S., "Returns Management and Reverse Logistics for Competitive Advantage," *CSCMP Explores ...,* Winter, 2006.
3. Ibid., p. 7.
4. Ibid., p. 13.

GLOSSARY

Glossary

3C alternative to MRP: A method that uses capacity, commonality, and consumption as a basis for control of material in the supply chain. The technique decreases the dependence of the supply chain on forecast accuracy by shifting inventory decision to considerations of actual demand and capacity.

3D bar code: A microscopic bar code used to protect high-value items.

4PL/LLP: 4PL is a trademarked term from the consulting firm, Accenture. It describes an integrator of supply chain service providers to deliver a comprehensive solution. The Lead Logistics Provider (LLP) is a company's primary supply chain services provider. Clifford Lynch quoted in *DC Velocity*, July 2005, page 57.

5S: A foundation for visual controls in a production operation. Characteristic of lean manufacturing. The approach includes the following:

1. Sort (organization): what is needed and not needed
2. Stabilize (orderliness): a place for everything and everything in its place
3. Shine (cleanliness): keeping the workplace clean
4. Standardize (adherence): maintains and monitors the above
5. Sustain (self-discipline): sticking to the rules, scrupulously

Source: Best Manufacturing Practices Center of Excellence

ABC inventory classification: Division of inventory into groups based on decreasing order of annual dollar volume (annual units × projected volume). "A" items are 10 to 20 percent of items but 50 to 70 percent of dollar volume. "B" items are about 20 percent of items and 20 percent of dollar volume. "C" items are 60 to 70 percent of items but only 10 to 30 percent of value.

The classification points to places where attention can be focused for improvement. The same principle can be applied to products, product categories, suppliers, customers, and sales. In classification efforts, one must decide at what level the classification should be completed. This will depend on the product's configuration.

Adapted from *APICS Dictionary*, 10th Ed.

ABCD analysis: Technique for analyzing technical and administrative functions. "A" activities add value to the customer and require decision-making discretion. "B" activities require decision making but don't add value. "C" activities don't require decision making but do add value. "D" items don't require decision making and don't add value. The classification is useful for process analysis and deciding how to remove or automate activities.

Accordion Theory: Fluctuations in breadth (wide or narrow) and depth (broad or narrow) of retail product mix according to the strategy of the retailer.
Adapted from *Retailing Management,* 5th Ed.

Action plan: A plan that defines a project or projects. They are part of programs or initiatives.

Activity (project management context): An element of work performed during a project. It has an expected duration, cost, and resource requirement. An activity can be subdivided into to tasks. Activity definitions describe what has to be done to produce deliverables. Formerly called a "work item."
Adapted from the *PMBOK Guide,* 2000 Ed.

Activity-Based Costing, Management (ABC, ABM): A method to plan, measure, and control expenses associated with managing and monitoring the supply chain; specific techniques for assigning cost in business processes to activities. ABC is seen to overcome many of the shortcomings of conventional accounting methodologies. *Time-Driven Activity-Based Costing,* from Robert S. Kaplan and Steven R. Anderson, simplifies the administration of ABC.

Activity system: A term originated by Michael Porter in defining networks of activities that provide a sustainable competitive advantage. These networks can constitute a supply chain. An activity in this context is a feature of the company's strategy that makes it distinctive. Activities, in turn, are supported by supply chain and other company processes. In this book, groups of supporting processes make up activities.

Agent: A party that negotiates supply chain transactions that does not take title to the goods.

Agile enterprise: Companies that employ rapid customer/supplier partnering to achieve a short-product development life cycle.
Agility merges competencies in cost, quality, dependability, and flexibility.
APICS Dictionary, 10th Ed.

AIDC (Automatic Identification and Data Capture): A set of technologies to track material movement in the supply chain. Technologies include bar codes, RFID, GPS, and others. Also ADC, automatic data capture. Includes bar codes, RFID, biometrics, magnetic strips, and voice recognition.
Adapted from *Wikipedia.*

Allocation: The process of deciding which customers should receive products or services that are in short supply.

APICS: International not-for-profit offering programs and materials for individual and organizational education, standards of excellence, and integrated resource management topics. Formerly called American Production and Inventory Control Society, now The Educational Society for Resource Management.

Apparel Matrix: Inventory category.

Application area: With respect to project management, an application area is a discipline where project management theory and practice applies. This book adapts SCM to project management. Other example application areas include construction, defense acquisition, and software development.

Approved Material List (AML): A list of approved suppliers and materials. Some companies seek to expand the AML to increase options for product design and to avoid single-source or end-of-life components.

APS: Advanced Planning System. Systems that plan actual logistics and production over short, immediate, and long term periods. Can be separate from or built into MRP/ERP systems. The APS can generate different scenarios for decision support. Components include demand planning, production planning, production scheduling, distribution planning, and transportation planning.
   Adapted from *APICS Dictionary,* 10th Ed.

AS2: Messages notifying of inbound items and contents. Transmitted by Internet. Used by smaller companies due to lower cost.

As-is: The current state, such as how processes in the supply chain process, are currently performed.

ASN (Advance Ship Notification): Messages notifying of inbound items and contents. Transmitted by EDI. Used by larger companies.

ASQC: The American Society for Quantity Control

Assemble-to-order: An environment where products or services are assembled after receipt of an order. This is useful where there are a large number of options consisting of common components. A basket of groceries is an example. Made-to-order computers are another. In a VAT analysis, this approach might be tried for "T" type product structures.
   Adapted from *APICS Dictionary,* 10th Ed.

Assortment: The items carried within a category. Can include sizes, styles, and colors of items. Collaboration is often required when setting up and making changes to the assortment.

ATP: Available to promise. The uncommitted portion of inventory and planned production maintained in the master schedule.
   Adapted from *APICS Dictionary,* 10th Ed.

Auctions online: Online negotiations among qualified suppliers. Usually facilitated by software applications.

Balanced Scorecard: An approach to measurement that cascades measures from the top down through the organization. The method uses four perspectives to achieve balance. These are financial, customer, internal business, and innovation and learning.

Bar coding: An automatic identification technology that uses parallel dark bars and spaces to represent characters. Bar coding is an important element in automating the tracking of material in the supply chain. Also called the Universal Product Code.

Barrier: An obstacle that hinders the organization's ability to reach its objectives. Many barriers are hidden. Barriers, unlike constraints, can be managed through project planning and execution.

Batch-and-queue system: Refers to a production management system that relies on large batches of material. This leads to large queues while waiting to complete a production step. Such systems are characterized by high work in process inventory and low velocity production.

Benchmarking: A search for those best practices that will lead to superior performance. Benchmarking is usually executed with those who perform a targeted activity the best, regardless of the industry they are in. Internal benchmarking makes comparisons within an organization, such as developing best practices from several stores who perform similar functions.

Best of Breed: This term refers to a specialized supply chain application such as demand management or a warehouse management application. These are standalone, and compete with similar functions that are part of integrated enterprise-level applications such as those from JD Edwards, SAP, or Oracle.

Bill of Material items: Inventory category. Assemblies and subassemblies.

"Blue Ocean Strategy": In strategic planning, a strategy that makes competitors irrelevant by creating a "monopoly" in the marketplace. The title of a book describing the strategy by W. Chan Kim and Renée Mauborgne.

Bluetooth: A technology that uses radio frequency standards for wireless communication between computers and their peripherals. A line-of-site connection is not necessary.

BOM: Bill of material in manufacturing industry.
  Beginning of month in retail.

BPM: Business Process Management. Broadly, BPM focuses on improving business processes rather than functions or costs. Narrowly, BPMI (Business Process Management Initiative) is a nonprofit group promoting open standards for information technology used in business processes.

BPO: Business Process Outsourcing. Contracting out for support services beyond information technology. Examples include human resources, finance and accounting, and logistics services.

Bracket pricing: The use of brackets for order volumes. Each bracket has a different price per unit, with larger orders having lower prices per unit. Such prices usually recognize economies in logistics and other supply chain processes.

Brand, Branding: Vision, position, "space" in the market. Establishing a brand name is a primary way to compete in many industries. SCM can support the strategy for establishing a brand image. Also includes brand equity, or value of the brand.

Breadman: A term applied to "automatic" replacement of inventory by third-party logistics providers, normally distributors. The analogy is the breadman who replenishes stock in the grocery store on a regularly scheduled basis. A related term is "milk run." The term can also apply to types of vendor-managed inventory.

Break-even analysis: A calculation that produces the volume required to make a profit on a product. This is called the break-even point. It is also used to calculate the volume required to pay for a cost reduction.

Adapted from *Retailing Management,* 5th Ed.

Buffer stock: See Safety stock.

Bullwhip effect: A term coined by Dr. Hau Lee of Stanford. It describes the phenomenon in which small changes in final demand for a product produce wide swings in production upstream in the supply chain.

Business model: A model answers questions such as the following: "Who is the customer?" "What does the customer value?" "How do we make money in this business?" "What is the underlying economic logic that explains how we deliver value to customers?" A *strategy* defines how the organization competes. Competing effectively requires being different from your competitors.

Why Business Models Matter, *Harvard Business Review,* May 2002.

Business Process Reengineering (BPR): Taking a holistic customer-focused systems view to changing processes in the organization. BPR encompasses vision for the organization's future, workflow along the supply chain, information technology, organization theory, The internet, computer-supported collaboration, and other approaches.

Buyback: The purchase of a competitor's stock at a retailer in order to substitute the buying company's product.

The purchase of a retailer's slow-moving stock by the manufacturer.

Adapted from *Retailing Management,* 5th Ed.

Capacity strategy: A strategic choice for adjusting strategy to business levels. A "leading" strategy adds capacity in anticipation of demand. A "lag" strategy waits until the demand has materialized. A "tracking" strategy means attempts to match capacity and demand.

Adapted from *APICS Dictionary,* 10th Ed.

Such a strategy should consider product life-cycle position and profitability.

Capital recovery costs: The equivalent expense to recover the cost of an investment, such as that for fixed assets and working capital. The calculation normally uses asset life, salvage value, and the cost of capital to make the conversion. Also called "equivalent uniform annual cash flow."

Cash-to-cash cycle time: The time between payments for product components to suppliers and the time customers make payments. This parameter has become an important measure of supply chain performance, reflecting both financial and inventory management process performance. Most have negative measures ranging from 30 to 80 days. Some, notably Dell, have a positive cycle time, meaning they collect payments from customers before they have to pay suppliers.

Category: Items that are substitutes for each other. There are many ways to determine categories.

Adapted from *Retailing Management,* 5th Ed.

Category captain: Supplier who works with a retailer to improve customer satisfaction and profits across a category.

Adapted from *Retailing Management,* 5th Ed.

Category management: A structure that focuses on management of products or product families. With respect to SCM, this could also include incoming material, production planning, and distribution shifting away from a structure based on commodities or manufacturing plants.

Cause-and-effect diagram (fishbone diagram): A tool that uses a graphical description of contributing elements to identify root causes of process variation.

Cellular manufacturing: A manufacturing process that produces families of parts within a single line or cell of machines with operators who work only within the line or cell. The cellular concept is applicable to administrative and technical process. In this context, it means clustering unlike operations to increase processing velocity.

Center of Excellence (COE): A formal or informal committee that focuses on benchmarking and continuous improvement. Has expertise in identifying project management tools.

Adapted from Strategic Planning for Project Management

Centralized Return Center (CRC): Process facility to handle returned merchandise. The CRC collects the items and makes decisions on its processing based on retailer and manufacturer guidelines.

Adapted from Rogers, Dale S. and Tibben-Lembke, Ronald S., Returns management and reverse logistics for competitive advantage, *CSCMP Explores* ..., Winter, 2006.

Certified partner: A trading partner that has met its customer's supplier requirements.

Certified supplier: A supplier that has been approved for providing defined components for manufacturing or distribution. Certification levels may have varying conditions related to quality management, such as needs for quality control. Suppliers are often qualified before financial terms are negotiated.

Channel: A group of businesses that take ownership title to products or facilitate exchange during the marketing process from the original manufacturer to the final buyer. Effective SCM requires an understanding of the needs of each customer and segment and the correct channel to reach them.

Channel master: The single, most powerful company in a supply chain. The channel master dictates terms of trade for the channel. The presence of a master depends on the nature of the industry and competition. Channel mastery is often the goal of SCM programs.

Charter: A document that authorizes a project. It enables the project manager to apply resources to project activities.

Adapted from *PMBOK Guide,* 2000 Ed.

CLM: Council of Logistics Management. A worldwide professional organization of logistics personnel. CLM has contributed heavily to the discussion of supply chain issues. Beginning January 1, 2005, the organization was renamed the Council of Supply Chain Management Professionals (CSCMP).

Closed-loop supply chain: A supply chain that with finite boundaries. Such a situation provides a domain for implementation of advanced RFID and other technologies. Examples are single companies in which parts containers are tracked or high volume flows between two trading partners, where benefits can be readily identified.

Closeout: An offer of discontinued or slow-moving merchandise at a discount. Often made in bulk quantities.

Collaboration: CGR defines it as joint planning and execution of supply chain activities. These activities can range from new product development to day-to-day operations. Collaboration includes all aspects of the relationship related to physical movement, information sharing, financial flows, and exchange of intellectual property. Collaboration is also defined as internal between people and functions, and external between supply chain companies.

The Supply Chain Council defines collaboration as:

> *A relationship built on trust that is benchmarked by the commitment to the team objective and where consensus may not always be achievable but where nothing takes place without the commitment of all involved.*

Collaborative execution systems: Category of application software that enables the effective coordination and flow of information across the entire value chain. Automating tasks required to manage each transaction and providing real-time visibility to information, collaborative execution systems are designed to improve productivity and reliability.

Collaboratory: A term coined by participants in the Supply Chain Council's SCOR update technical committee. It refers to the entity that includes the business, cultural, and system environment needed to build and operate a linkage between partners.

Comparative Advantage: This concept, sometimes called a "theory" or a "law," holds that trading partners gain when countries specialize in what they can do most efficiently (use the fewest labor and capital resources) and trade for the products they don't produce as efficiently. This is not to be confused with absolute advantage, where a trading partner can make all products more efficiently than others. Absolute advantage would hold that the best producer should not specialize, making everything and not trading for any goods.

Concurrent engineering: The process of coordinating product and process, including supply chain, development. Also called simultaneous engineering.

Configuration: The arrangement of components specified to produce an assembly.

APICS Dictionary, 10th Ed.

Configuration has a major impact on supply chain design. For example, different configurations affect postponement strategies. In application of the 3C approach, configuration figures in commonality among end items.

Configurator: A system used by design-to-order, make-to-order, or assemble-to-order companies. They enable direct customer or sales engineer configuration of the product. Configurators can generate solid models, drawings, costs, and bills of material.

Adapted from *APICS Dictionary,* 10th Ed.

Consignment:

1. A shipment by a common carrier.
2. Terms of a contract in which a supplier is not paid until the goods are used or sold.

APICS Dictionary, 10th Ed.

Consignment inventory: Inventory provided for sale but not paid for until it is sold to an end-user/customer.

Constant-cycle (fixed-cycle) reorder model: An inventory reorder pattern with fixed time intervals and variable quantities. Advantages include:

- Better for close operations with minimal transportation requirements.
- Can take advantage of EOQ economies for operations involving high setup costs.
- Fast, doesn't require counting or tracking of inventory.
- Simplicity. Compatible with visible signaling. Examples are the two-bin system and Kan-Ban approaches.
- Easier to predict time requirements once orders are placed.

Disadvantages include that the model can cause excess inventory in the system. It is better for low-cost, "C" items. Some companies expense items in this category.

Handbook of Supply Chain Management

Constant-quantity (fixed-quantity) reorder model: An inventory reorder pattern with fixed-quantity delivered variable time intervals.

Advantages include:

- Establishes a regular rhythm in the supply chain.
- Decreases variability from uncertainty about schedules.
- Can take advantage of setup economies when setup times depend on sequence, for example paint lines where different color sequences require different setup efforts.

Disadvantages arise when variation in quantities can cause production to run behind. One must also track production through the chain, with a requirement to know usage at various points to signal correct quantity. The approach fits higher-value "A" items.

Constraint: Any element that prevents a system from achieving a higher level of performance. Constraints can be of many kinds, including physical steps in production and the limits on customer desire for the product. Constraints are "givens" or limitations that can't be changed in the course of designing or redesigning a supply chain. A barrier is an obstacle that may be mitigated by management action.

Continuous Replenishment Planning (CRP): The practice of partnering between distribution channel members that changes the traditional replenishment process from traditional purchase orders based on economic order quantities, to the replenishment of products based on actual and forecasted product demand.

Control points: In the theory of constraints, these are strategic locations that are tightly planned and scheduled. Other work centers are not, simplifying scheduling and control.

Adapted from *APICS Dictionary,* 10th Ed.

Cooperative advertising (co-op): Joint advertising agreements between supply chain partners (OEMs and retailers).

Core assortment: A large proportion of stock carried by every store in a chain. Seen to be essential to the image of the store.

Adapted from *Retailing Management,* 5th Ed.

Core competence: An organizational capability that can be applied to a variety of core and end products. The capability is usually technology based, but can also be competence in facets of supply chain management.

Core processes (project management context): Processes with clear dependencies that are likely to be performed in the same order on most projects. These processes may be iterated several times. Examples are scope planning, performance reporting, and project phase initiation.

Adapted from *PMBOK Guide,* 2000 Ed.

Cost baseline: A time-phased estimate of cost. It is used to monitor performance on cost throughout the project.

Adapted from *PMBOK Guide,* 2000 Ed.

Cost driver: In activity-based costing, volume variable used to calculate the total cost of an activity or process. The activity cost may be expressed in a unit cost—(cost)/(unit of volume). The unit of volume used is the cost driver.

Cost of Quality (COQ): COQ may be viewed as a subset of activity-based costing and can provide the information necessary to drive service improvements and reduce costs. Components of COQ usually include prevention, detection, and correction. Some will divide correction into internal (before-the-sale) and external (after-the-sale) components.

Country Portfolio Analysis (CPA): An analysis of country market attractiveness using statistics such as income, population, and product consumption. It is recommended that this analysis be adjusted for cultural, administrative, geographic, and economic distance. Distance Still Matters, *Harvard Business Review,* Sept. 2001, pp. 129–147.

Cp, Cpk: Process capability and the index of capability, respectively. Typically, a process is considered "capable" when capability and/or the capability index are 1.33 or greater.

Cp = (upper - lower specification limit)/6s where s = standard deviation of process output.

Cpk = (mean - nearer specification)/3s

CPFR®: Collaborative Planning Forecasting and Replenishment. A set of business processes used for supply chain collaboration. The term is a trademark of the sponsoring organization, the Voluntary Interindustry Commerce Standards (VICS) Association

CPIO: Chief Process Improvement Officer. A senior management role to lead the reengineering of processes. Facilitates process improvement across internal and external boundaries.

AMR Research

Critical path: The series of activities that determines the duration of a project. It is the longest path through the project. The Critical Path Method (CPM) is a technique to predict the project's duration by analyzing the path of activities with the least amount of scheduling flexibility.

Adapted from *PMBOK Guide,* 2000 Ed.

Critical to Quality (CTQ): A feature in a product that's important to customers. Such a feature can be translated to processes for delivering the feature. The term is used in connection with Six-Sigma efforts to improve processes.

CRM: Customer Relationship Management. "CRM aligns business processes with customer strategies to build customer loyalty and increase profits over time."

(Quoted from: Rigby, Darrell K., Reichheld, Frederick F., and Schefter, Phil, Avoid the Four Perils of CRM, *Harvard Business Review,* Feb. 2002, pp. 101–109.)

Computer applications that deal with the "front office" interface between the company and its customers.

Cross docking: At a warehouse or distribution center, providing quick turn-around of incoming stock by backing supplies truck up to loading dock where merchandise is immediately transferred to retailer's distribution truck. This avoids storing inventory for any time in the warehouse.

CSCMP: Council of Supply Chain Management Professionals. Formerly the Council of Logistics Management.

CTP: Capable to promise. The ability to commit to orders with available capacity and inventory.

Adapted from *APICS Dictionary,* 10th Ed.

Customer: A person or organization that decides to purchase a product or service or that receives a product or service if no purchase is involved, such as an internal customer for information. An end-user is the person or organization that uses or consumes the product or service. The end-user is not necessarily the customer or buyer.

Customer service ratio: In a make-to-stock company, the percentage of items or dollars shipped on schedule. In a make-to-order company, the percentage of

items or dollars shipped on time. Synonymous terms include fill rate and customer service level.

Customer-centric organization: An organizational structure built around customer segments. Desirable when segments have different requirements, style-driven products with short product lives requiring fast responses, and higher-margin products.

Handbook of Supply Chain Management

Customer-centric supply chain: Supply chains or organizations whose construct centers on the requirements of targeted customer segments. Alternatives are functional and product-centric supply chains.

Customs-Trade Partnership Against Terrorism (C-TPAT): A voluntary government-business initiative to build cooperative relationships that strengthen international and U.S. border security. The effort involves owners of the international supply chain such as importers, carriers, consolidators, licensed customs brokers, and manufacturers.

Adapted from http://www.cbp.gov/xp/cgov/import/commercial_enforcement/ctpat/.

Cycle time: A property of processes along the supply chain. The minimum theoretical cycle time for a product's supply chain is the sum of individual process cycle times.

Cycle-time reduction is achieved through process reengineering, including new technology along the chain. Examples include automated sharing of information about final demand, introducing postponement through product design, and automation in production processes.

Lead time is a market-oriented property that is driven by competitive forces. A competitor that works to reduce cycle time can also end up with the shortest lead time. Throughput time is a synonym.

Data warehouse: A repository for data organized in a format that is suitable for ad hoc query processing. Data warehouses are built from operational databases used for day-to-day business processes. The operational data is "cleaned" and transformed in such a way that it is amenable to fast retrieval and efficient analysis. A single-purpose data warehouse is sometimes referred to as a data mart.

Dealer: A representative of a manufacturer or distributor who directly services end-users/customers.

Decomposition (forecasting): A method of forecasting where data is divided into trend, seasonal, and cyclical components. Another component may be random—where no pattern exists. Forecasts are made using each component.

Adapted from *APICS Dictionary,* 10th Ed.

Decomposition (WBS, IDEF): Breaking a category down into lower levels for sharper definition of requirements. The term can apply to project scope, activities, tasks, and projects. IDEF decomposes functions in a supply chain in a similar way.

Adapted from *PMBOK Guide,* 2000 Ed.

Deficiency, discrepancy: Failure of a quality system to comply with requirements.

DELIVER processes: SCOR processes to provide finished goods and services to customers.

Deliverable: Any measurable, tangible, verifiable outcome, result, or item produced to complete a project or part of a project. Often refers to a work product delivered to and approved by a sponsor or customer.

  Adapted from *PMBOK Guide,* 2000 Ed.

Demand: End-user requirements for a product or service. This is what would be consumed if sufficient product were available at prices that yield a profit. End-users aren't necessarily purchasers who pay for a product. A "customer" may buy a product or service on behalf of the end-user.

Demand chain: A term sometimes applied to the "outgoing" side of the business. Supply chain, in this context, only applies to the "incoming" side. To the end-user, all activities to produce the product or service are part of the supply chain.

Demand flow®: A technique to speed product final assembly. Demand flow uses the concept of a "pile of parts" that can be assembled in response to actual customer orders. The term is trademarked by the John Costanza Institute of Technology.

Demand-driven supply chain: A term developed by CGR that applies to supply chains using tools that enable decisions to be made on the basis of actual customer demand rather than forecasts. The extent to which a supply chain is "demand driven" is measurable. Most supply chains will require some level of forecasting for advanced planning. However, it is desirable to reduce dependence on these forecasts.

Dependent demand: See Independent demand.

Derived demand: See Independent demand.

Design team: A team, usually of operations managers involved in included supply chain processes, which designs new supply chains. Design teams may be called upon to develop spheres, activity systems, requirements for IT systems, and process improvements.

Discount: A price reduction to promote or clear inventory of an item.

Discounted cash flow: A method of financial analysis that recognizes the time value of money as measured by the cost of capital. DCF is used to convert capital costs into "equivalent uniform cash flows." This makes it possible to combine expense and capital items when weighing capital investments.

Disintermediation: The elimination of echelons or stages in the supply chain. This can reduce cycle time and operating expense. The term is often used with respect to distribution and the number of warehouses a product passes through between the manufacturer and the end-user/customer.

Distribution Requirements Planning (DRP): Replenishment procedures at distribution control points. Can use MRP logic or other rules.

DMIAC: Define, measure, analyze, improve, and control. A process for implementing supply chain changes associated with the Six-Sigma improvement process.

A Foundation for Operational Excellence, *Supply Chain Management Review,* March/April 2003

Downstream: The end of the supply chain nearest to end-users. Upstream refers to the beginnings of the supply chain, probably suppliers of components or raw materials. Some reverse this convention.

Driving force: A strategic planning concept developed by Michel Robert. The concept holds that there is one and only one driving force around which a company competes. Company management may acknowledge this; however, often it is not.

Drumbeat: The pace at which an organization produces product. Used to pace all the operations in a factory or in a supply chain. Similar to takt time.

Drum–buffer–rope: In the theory of constraints, a generalized process to manage resources to maximize throughput. The "drum" sets the pace of production to match the system's constraint. "Buffers" protect the system from disruption and uncertainty. They are often placed to assure that the constraint always has work. The "rope" communicates between the constraint and the gating operation that controls release of work into the system.

The model can be applied at the factory and supply chain levels.

Adapted from *APICS Dictionary,* 10th Ed.

DSD (Direct Shipment to Stores): A form of disintermediation in which a manufacturer or distributor ships directly to a customer's stores often bypassing that customer's distribution centers.

EAN*UCC: European Article Numbering/Uniform Code Council. Standard codes for supply chain commerce administered by EAN International, now GS1, and the Uniform Code Council, Inc., now GS1 U.S. The latter is U.S. based and, since 2002, is a member of GS1. Joining facilitated the generation of global standards.

Early manufacturing and supplier involvement (EMI/ESI): Inclusion of the manufacturing department and suppliers in product design. The result is a more producible and durable design.

EAS tags: Electronic article surveillance tags. A tag that is part of a price tag that protects merchandise against shoplifting. The tag is deactivated when the purchase is made. The manufacturer often installs it.

Adapted from *Retailing Management,* 5th Ed.

Echelon: A term that refers to layers of distribution or to stages in the process. Each echelon can include the storage, transportation, and handling of the product between the source (presumably a factory) and its point of use. A trend is toward reducing echelons to speed the supply chain and reduce its cost. Also, competitors at any echelon may seek to add services, reducing the roles of other echelons.

E-Commerce: Electronic commerce has come to mean many different things to many different people. Originally, the term meant selling things online. The term has evolved to mean conducting business online, which can include customer service functions, sales, marketing, public relations, advertising, and more.

Economic Order Quantity (EOQ): A fixed order quantity model that determines the amount of an item to be purchased or manufactured at one time. The model minimizes the combined costs of acquiring and carrying inventory. When production rates are closer to consumption rates as in a synchronized supply chain, the production quantity approaches infinity or continuous operation. INCLUDEPICTURE \d "Images/Assets/dotclear.gif"

Economic Value Added (EVA®): The dollar amount of value added by an enterprise over a specified period of time. EVA takes into account the capital employed in the business. EVA is a trademarked term by Stern Stewart.

ECR: Efficient Consumer Response. Refers to technologies to match supply and demand in the retail sector.

EDLP: Every day low prices. A pricing strategy that calls for continuing lower prices with few sales. A high–low pricing strategy uses premium prices and sales.

Electronic Data Interchange (EDI): The computer-to-computer transmission of business information between trading partners. The information should be organized in standard file formats or transaction sets following guidelines administered by the Uniform Code Council (UCC). Standards have been developed for all regular business-to-business communication, including purchase orders, invoices, shipping notices, and funds transfer. By eliminating the clerical, mailing, and other costs associated with paper-based information, EDI reduces costs, time delays, and errors.

Source: *ECR Best Practices Report*

Electronic Draft Capture (EDC): Integration with leading credit card services to reduce fraud and error. Microsoft.

Enable process: A SCOR process that prepares, maintains, or manages information, relationships, or other factors to support planning and execution processes. EP processes enable PLAN processes, ES enable SOURCE processes, and so on. EP.1 establishes and manages PLAN rules, ES.1 plans SOURCE rules, and so on.

Enable sphere: Spheres that involve activities used by product-producing spheres. These are often supporting activities. Customer requirements are set by the needs of the product-producing spheres. Examples can include support systems, organization, logistics services, and sourcing.

End-user: The person or organization that uses or consumes a product or service. The end-user is at the end of the supply chain. The user is not necessarily the customer or buyer of the product or service.

Engineer-to-order: Products that need unique engineering design, customization, or new materials. Each order results in a unique bill of material, some unique part numbers, and custom routings.

Adapted from *APICS Dictionary,* 10th Ed.

Enterprise Resource Planning (ERP): ERP systems are comprised of software programs that tie together all of an enterprises various functions—such as finance, manufacturing, sales, distribution, procurement, and human resources. This software also provides for the analysis of the data from these areas to plan production, forecast sales, and analyze quality.

EPC: Electronic Product Code(. Industrywide standards for RFID communication of product information through standards organization, EPCglobal, Inc. (EPCglobal is a joint venture between GS1 and GS1 US. It is a unique number that identifies a specific item in the supply chain. The EPC is stored on RFID tag, which combines a silicon chip and an antenna. EPC data can include changing data such as origin and production date, much like a GTIN (Global Trade Identification Number). The EPC identifies the manufacturer, product, version, and serial number. A large amount of related data can be stored in a linked database. The items referred to can be individual items, cases, or pallets.

Adapted from the GCI Glossary

EPCglobal Network: Organization that grew out of the Auto-ID Center, an academic research project headquartered at the Massachusetts Institute of Technology (MIT). The focus is on RFID identification using Electronic Product Codes (EPC). UCC and EAN (Standard setters GS1 US & GS1) are participants.

Adapted from epcglobalinc.org

Event: An occurrence in the supply chain that triggers the need for action. Supply chain event management (SCEM) refers to software solutions that monitor operating data to determine if such an event has occurred.

Execution process: A SCOR process that changes the state of material goods. It includes scheduling/sequencing, transforming products through manufacturing processes, and moving products.

Executive information system: Software providing operating information for direct access by executive users.

Extended product: Those features of a product that aren't part of the base, or physical, product. Many supply chain attributes are extended product features such as availability of product, method of delivery, customer service, ability to return the product, and so forth.

Adapted from *Handbook of Supply Chain Management*

Facilitating processes (project management context): Processes that may or may not be needed, depending on the needs of the project. These are likely to be performed intermittently or as needed. Examples include staff acquisition, risk response planning, team development, and solicitation of suppliers.

Fashion product: A product has high margins and uncertain demand. The supply chain for such products should be designed for responsiveness to demand, rather than efficiency. The term, innovative product, includes fashions, new technology, and other fast-growing products.

Five focusing steps: A theory of constraints process to continuously evaluate the production system and market mix to make the most of the system constraints. There are five steps:

1. Identify constraints in the system.
2. Decide how to exploit the constraint.
3. Subordinate nonconstraints to the constraints.
4. Elevate the constraints in the system.
5. Return to step 1 if the constraint is broken.

Adapted from *APICS Dictionary,* 10th Ed.

Flexibility: The ability to change or react with little penalty in time, effort, cost, or performance. Categories of flexibility include product mix variation, volume variations, labor flexibility, design-change flexibility, and routing flexibility.

David Upton, *California Management Review*

Focused factory: A concept originated by Wickham Skinner arguing that factories or parts of factories perform best if they are designed to fulfill customer requirements as efficiently as possible. The focused factory uses manufacturing capability to support strategies for competing.

Forecast error: The difference between actual and forecast demand, stated as an absolute value or a percentage. Forecast errors are used to adjust production and inventory plans in supply chains with high dependence on forecasts for decision making.

Source: *APICS Dictionary,* 10th Ed.

Forecastable demand: Applies to certain patterns of demand that contain enough history to provide a forecast of future demand. The opposite is lumpy demand, for which forecasting isn't possible.

Form Factor: A term used to describe product features that has different meanings depending on the product. Commonly includes linear dimensions and configuration of a product.

Adapted from *Wikipedia*

Format: The design of a store or other retail outlet. Includes layout, décor, location, advertising and promotion, product selection, and services provided.

Fourth-party logistics service provider: A fully integrated supply chain partner who plays a substantial role in its customers' supply chain operations. Some, such as UPS Logistics, evolve from their parent company. Some are joint ventures such as Vector, a joint venture between General Motors and CNF. Others focus on specific industries, such as Li & Fung for apparel.

Collaborative Global Logistics by William W. Goldsborough.

Freight forwarder: This is a manager or handler for the shipment of goods. The responsibilities of a freight forwarder include arranging shipment details and completing documentation. Because of their brokering role, freight forwarders have a good understanding of market trends and insurance and transport alternatives.

Frontline team: A group of people working in a process who test new designs and provide recommendations for process design and changes.

Functional organization: An organizational structure built around functional tasks such as marketing, accounting, manufacturing, and customer service. Works best where product lines are narrow or mature businesses. Not a good alternative where speed is required or products and customers have diverse requirements.

Handbook of Supply Chain Management

Functional product: A category of product with lower margins and low uncertainty regarding demand. The supply chains for these products should be designed for the lowest possible cost. This type of product is also called a staple or a frequently purchased consumer good (FPCG). (See innovative product.)

Fuzzy front end: Refers to the beginning of the development cycle when new product and service concepts are not clear. Many organizations are defining processes and systems to manage the "fuzziness" of the front end of new product development cycle.

GCI: Global Commerce Initiative. An effort by retailers and manufacturers to implement best practices and standards in supply chains. Effort includes a global data dictionary.

Adapted from GCI Web site

Gemba: Japanese term meaning "the place where truth can be found." Refers to going to the manufacturing flow or the customer's place of business to observe what takes place and what needs improving.

Adapted from *Wikipedia*

Glass pipeline: A term describing a supply chain in which the visibility over the status of the product is high. One is able to track physical movement through the pipeline easily.

Global Positioning System (GPS): A satellite technology for tacking position. Supply chain tracking systems use GPS for locating materials along the supply chain.

Globalization: Doing business across country boundaries. In the supply chain context, this can include upstream sourcing and downstream channels to customers or both.

GMROI: Gross Margin Return on Investment. A financial performance measure that incorporates sales, profit margin, and assets employed. It is calculated by multiplying the traditional gross margin by the ratio of Net Sales to Average Inventory. (Gross Margin/Net Sales) × (Net Sales/Average Inventory). The latter is also called the sales-to-stock ratio.

Adapted from *Retailing Management,* 5th Ed.

Greenfield vision: An ideal state based on specifications for future operations. The greenfield should ignore constraints inherent in the current situation. It should serve as a "stretch" target for implementing improvements in the supply chain. The use of the greenfield approach is based on the premise that, without ambitious targets, only incremental change will occur.

Group technology: A technique used to develop manufacturing cells that are similar but not identical. The practice gains economies that are spread over a large volume of similar parts, each of which has relative low volume. The routing in the work cells need not be the same for each part. The technique can be broadly applied in designing supply chain logistics processes.

Lean Direction, Society of Manufacturing Engineers, February 9, 2004

GSMP: The Global Standards Management Process. Development and maintenance of the EAN•UCC System.

Adapted from GCI Glossary

GTAG: Global TAG. An RFID standard developed by EAN*UCC. The standard addresses data content specifications and performance guidelines.

GTIN: Global Trade Identification Number. UCC/GS1 global data structures that employ 14 digits. Currently, GTIN is used exclusively within bar codes, but could be used in other data carriers such RFID. For North America, the UPC is the existing form of GTIN. Current standards covered include: EAN/UCC-8, UCC-12, EAN/UCC-13, and EAN/UCC-14. Products at every level of product configuration (consumer selling unit, case level, inner pack level, pallet, shipper, etc.) require a unique GTIN.

Adapted from "http://www.gtin.info/"

Hedge stock: A form of safety stock implemented for a specific period. Reasons can include interruptions due to strikes, price increases, or a currency reevaluation.

Adapted from *APICS Dictionary,* 10th Ed.

Heijunka: Heijunka, or production smoothing, is a technique used to adapt production to fluctuating customer demand. The Japanese word Heijunka (pronounced hey June kah), means literally "make flat and level." Customer demand must be met with the customers preferred delivery times, but customer demand is "bumpy" whereas factories prefer "level" or stable production. So, a manufacturer needs to try and smooth out these bumps in production.

The main tool for smoothing is frequent changing of the model mix on a given line. TPS advocates small batches of many models over short periods of time, requiring fast changeovers.

Adapted from Frederick Stimson Harriman at FredHarriman.com

High–low: A pricing strategy that relies on both premium prices and sales over a product's life cycle. The opposite is EDLP, or every day low prices.

Adapted from *Retailing Management,* 5th Ed.

Hosted Software Vendors (HSV): A model of offering software packages over the Internet. The term has supplanted "ASP." Applications can be in categories such as accounting and CRM or vertical solutions for specific industries.
Adapted from *Infoworld,* Jan. 20, 2003, p. 35.

HPC: High Productivity Computing.

IDEF: Integrated Computer-Aided Manufacturing (ICAM) DEFinition methods are used to perform modeling activities in support of enterprise integration. The original IDEF methods were developed for the purpose of enhancing communication among people who needed to decide how their existing systems were to be integrated. The technique of decomposing a process into activities is useful for supply chain process analysis. The product is a "node tree" of supply chain process functions. IDEF0 modeling is supported by Visio software.

Implosion: The process of determining where a component is used. Implosions can be single level; showing only the parents of the next higher level; or multilevel, showing the ultimate top-level parents
Adapted from *APICS Dictionary,* 10th Ed.

Independent, dependent demand, derived demand: Independent demand is driven by end-user or customer needs. It comes from outside the sphere or enterprise. Dependent demand is derived from independent demand by a direct link between the end product through the bill of materials and triggers replenishment within the sphere or enterprise. Derived demand also depends on final demand but is not directly linked through the bill of materials, such as steel being derived from the sale of automobiles.
APICS Dictionary, Mentzer & Moon, SCMR May/June 2004

Inert stock: A term used by CGR to define slow-moving categories of inventory. Components can include defective items, obsolete items, "stranded" odd-quantity components with no demand, and lumpy demand items. The inert category can be a large portion of total inventory. Reducing it may require a concerted effort on several fronts.

Initiative: A broad program to improve supply chain operations. Initiatives can last several years and evolve with changing requirements. An initiative can have multiple projects. A synonym is program.

Innovative product: An innovative product has high margins and uncertain demand. The supply chain for such products should be designed for responsiveness to demand, rather than efficiency. Also called a fashion product in retail. (See functional product.)

Integrated supply: An alliance or long-term commitment between two or more organizations for the purpose of achieving specific business objectives by maximizing the effectiveness of each participant's resources. The relationship is based upon trust, dedication to common goals, and an understanding of each other's individual expectations and values.

Integration: The extent to which components of the production process are inextricably linked. A software design concept that allows users to move easily between applications.

Supply Chain Integration. Coordinated data sharing between companies to improve customer service and reduce cost.

Adapted from *Supply Chain Management in the Retail Industry.*

Interleaving: Task interleaving is a warehouse productivity improvement technique in which software directs workers to perform unrelated tasks such as putaway and picking where feasible. This reduces travel time in the warehouse. *Supply Chain Digest,* Logistics Ed.

International Standards Organization (ISO): An international organization charged with setting broad-ranging standards that can lead to certification including those of process discipline, RFID, and communications.

Internationalization: The process of designing a software or Internet application to handle different linguistic and cultural conventions without additional engineering. Central to internationalization is the separation of language and cultural data from the source code.

globalization.com

Inventory turnover: Ratio of sales (at cost) to average stock. Can be calculated by multiplying sales-to-stock ratio by (1-gross margin). Usually intended for performance measurement over an annual period. Adjustments are required for shorter selling periods. If the average inventory required to support a six-month sales effort that produces $200,000 in monthly sales ($1,200,000 total sales) is $100,000 at cost, the sales-to-stock ratio is 2. The inventory turns calculated conventionally are $1,200,000/($100,000/2) = 24 turns.

Adapted from *Retailing Management,* 5th Ed.

Inventory turns: The number of times each year that the inventory turns over. It can be in units, but is more often in dollars. It is computed by dividing the average inventory level into the annual cost of goods sold.

Issue, Issues List: Issues are questions that define the scope of the supply chain strategy. A running list keeps track of these issues and the response implicit in the strategy. Issues are often tracked in categories such as financial, organization and measures, product development, processes, and so forth.

Item Level Tagging (ILT): RFID passive tag attachment to individual items. Used to combat counterfeiting, track expiration dates, support inventory control, provide rapid checkout, and track product quality, among others.

Jikoda: A principle of the Toyota Production System that allows workers to stop the production line in the event of defects.

Joint replenishment: Coordination of lot sizing and order release for related items. The purpose is to take advantage for setup, shipping, and quantity discounts. It applies to material ordering, group technology production, and distribution. The commonality component of the 3C approach is a form of joint replenishment.

Adapted from *APICS Dictionary,* 10th Ed.

Just in Time (JIT): A philosophy of manufacturing based on planning elimination of all waste and continuous improvement of productivity. It encompasses the successful execution of all manufacturing activities required to produce a final product, from design engineering to delivery and including all stages of conversion from raw material onward. The primary elements of just in time are to have only the required inventory when needed; to improve quality to zero defects; to reduce lead times by reducing setup times, queue lengths, and lot sizes; to incrementally revise the operations themselves; and to accomplish these things at minimum cost. In the broad sense, it applies to all forms of manufacturing, job shop, and process, as well as repetitive.

Adapted from *APICS Dictionary,* 10th Ed.

Kaikaku: Innovation. As applied in lean approaches to operations, the implementation of novel, original, and likely more radical change. Contrasts with kaizen or continuous improvement.

Kaizen: A Japanese word that means loosely translated, constant improvement.

Kaizen Blitz: Conceived of as five days and one night applying Toyota Production System principles that include process observation, cycle time calculation, calculation of takt time, calculation of value-added fraction, elimination of work, and preparation of standard worksheets.

Lean Directions, Society of Manufacturing Engineers

Kanban: A method of just-in-time production that uses standard containers or lots sizes with a single card attached to each. It is a pull system in which work centers signal with a card that they wish to withdraw parts from feeding operations or suppliers. The Japanese word Kanban, loosely translated, means card, billboard, or sign. The term is often used synonymously for the specific scheduling system developed and used by the Toyota Corporation in Japan.

Adapted from *APICS Dictionary,* 10th Ed.

Kano Model: The model describes three different types of quality. The first is basic quality, items that one assumes are part of a product. The second is performance quality. The customer will be able to articulate this type of quality and can be captured by surveys. The third is excitement quality that is unexpected and cannot be articulated by the customer. The supply chain has the potential for assuring all three types of quality.

Source: The *QFD Handbook*

Key characteristic: A feature whose variation has the greatest impact on the fit, performance, or service life of the finished product from the perspective of the customer. Key characteristics are a tool to help decide where to focus limited resources. They are used for process improvement purposes. Key characteristics may or may not be "critical characteristics" that affect product safety.

Key process parameter: A process input that is controllable and that has a high statistical correlation with the variation in a part key characteristic. Key process parameters are most effectively determined by the use of designed experiments.

Knowledge management: Refers to efforts to capture the "knowledge" resident in an organization. Such efforts are often centered on information technology. Some have dismissed knowledge management as a fad, but the concept has value in supply chain management across multiple enterprises.

KPI: Key performance indicator. Measures of supply chain performance.

Lead time: Lead time is associated with a product or service delivered by the supply chain. It is "imposed" on the supply chain by the competitive environment. It is driven by customer expectations, supply chain innovations, and competitive pressure.

All these factors are in constant motion, moving toward "faster, cheaper, better." Competitors that can't deliver products and services within the established lead time will likely perish. Competitors that have the shortest lead time have an advantage.

Lean enterprise: A term coined by James Womack and Daniel Jones to extend the idea of "lean manufacturing" along the supply chain, including production partners. The lean enterprise is operationally synchronized with end-user demand. (Womack and Jones were the originators of the "lean" terminology.)

Adapted from *APICS Dictionary,* 10th Ed.

Lean manufacturing: Production approach based on using multiskilled workers, highly flexible machines, and very adaptable organizations and procedures to manufacture an increasing variety of products while continually decreasing costs. "Lean" means more productive use of labor, material, and inventory along the supply chain.

Legacy systems: A network or hierarchical database system, usually running on a mainframe. Replacement of legacy systems is often a motivator for installing new supply chain information systems. Implementing supply chain improvements may be limited by the capabilities of legacy systems.

Level (of a product): Components of product structure. Each level is coded with the end item as the 0 level. Level 1 has level 0 components; level 2 has level 1 components, and so forth. Also see Decomposition.

Adapted from *APICS Dictionary,* 10th Ed.

Level 1 processes: SCOR has five core management processes: PLAN, SOURCE, MAKE, DELIVER, and RETURN. There are separate definitions in this table for each. When used in SCOR, these core processes are spelled with capital letters.

Level of Effort (LOE): A support-type activity that is hard to measure. It is usually characterized as a uniform rate of activity.

Adapted from *PMBOK Guide,* 2000 Ed.

Level plant loading: Efforts to reduce variability in production at the business unit and supply chain levels. Level plant loading is considered a best practice for achieving effective supply chains. Drumbeat and takt time are related terms.

Levels (SCOR): SCOR processes decompose to three levels. Level 1 is composed of the five core management processes. Level 2 is the configuration level and depends on supply chain design. Level 2 process examples are a letter and a number, such as PP for plan supply chain and M1 for make-to-stock. Configuration types include ake-to-stock, ake-to-order, and engineer-to-order. Level 3 activities are process elements supporting level 2. Level 4 processes are company specific and fall outside SCOR.

Localization: The process of adapting a product to the requirements of a target locale. This involves the translation of the user interface (UI)—including text messages, icons, buttons, etc., of the online help, and of any documentation and packaging, and the addition of cultural data and language-dependent components, such as spell checkers, input methods, and so forth.
globalization.com

Logistics management: That part of supply chain management that plans, implements, and controls the efficient, effective forward and reverses flow and storage of goods, services, and related information between the point of origin and the point of consumption to meet customers' requirements. Council of Logistics Management

Lot Matrix: Inventory category.

Lot operation cycle time: Length of time from the start of setup to the end of cleanup for a production lot at a given operation.
APICS Dictionary, 10th Ed.

Lumpy demand: An infrequently occurring demand that can't be forecast. The usual result is a need to carry an insurance level of stock. Also called "discontinuous demand."

Maintained markup: The markup a retailer actually makes over the life of the product. It is expected to cover direct costs of selling the product, shrinkage, and discounts offered as the product ages and to provide a profit. This may differ from the initial markup which is set when the product is originally put on the floor.

Maintenance, Repair, and Overhaul (MRO): A class of activity occurring after the sale of the product. MRO often demands special supply chain design and can be an important factor in the success of a product that has a long life cycle.

MAKE processes: SCOR processes that transform material into finished products.

Make-to-order: A production environment where the product is made after receipt of the order. The product is often a combination of standard and custom items. Make-to-order is similar to assemble-to-order.
Adapted from *APICS Dictionary,* 10th Ed.

Make-to-stock: An environment where products are finished before receipt of a customer order. The customer orders are filled from stock. Production orders replenish the stock.
Adapted from *APICS Dictionary,* 10th Ed.

Manufacturing Execution System (MES): An MES is a manufacturing software application, not a "MIS" system. MES focuses on execution and management of production processes. It provides synchronization of the following as they are used to make the product: labor, machinery and equipment, tooling, and other resources, e.g., power, raw material, and work-in-process inventory. MES usually operates in time increments from subshift to real time.

MES applications may serve as interfaces between MRP scheduling applications and machine controllers. They also collect quality and production data.

Manufacturing strategy: The concept that manufacturing can support other strategies for competing, such as product, marketing, and financial strategies. A related term is a "supply chain strategy" where supply chain design contributes to competitiveness.

Market mediation cost: The often hidden cost to a business due to mismatches in supply and demand. Too much supply causes discounts; too little causes lost profits from unmade sales.

Mass customization: Creation of individual variations of a high-volume product with many options for configuration.

Matrix bill of material (BOM): A method for identifying common components. Components are arranged on one dimension; end products on the other. This is a useful tool for establishing commonality in applying the 3C methodology.

Maturity model: A framework for measuring progress toward some goal. The model consists of descriptive "levels" to help users assess their progress toward higher levels of maturity. Harold Kerzner's project management maturity model (PMMM) has five levels: common language, common processes, singular methodology, benchmarking, and continuous improvement.

Mean absolute deviation (MAD): The average of absolute values of the deviations between observed and expected values. MAD can be calculated to evaluate forecasting processes as the difference between actual sales and forecasts.

Merchandise management: The process of providing the right product in the right quantity in the right place at the right time. (This definition is similar to Supply Chain Management.)

Adapted from *Retailing Management,* 5th Ed.

Merge-in-transit: A technique for combining order components from various sources while those components are in transit from sources to customers.

Milestone: A significant event in the project usually associated with completion of a deliverable.

Adapted from *PMBOK Guide,* 2000 Ed.

Milk run: A transportation link in the supply chain characterized by regularly scheduled shipments to one or more points. By combining shipments, more frequent shipments are economically feasible. The milk run lowers the incremental cost of filling an order, enabling continuous flow in the supply chain.

Minimum Shelf Quantity: Also MSQ. The quantity of stock to maintain at a shelf location.

Min-max: A type of order point replenishment where the reorder point is the "min," and the "max" sets the order quantity.

Mixed-model production: A production scheme where the production line product mix matches what is sold each day.

Monopsony: A market dominated by a few large customers who have power over pricing. The effect is to put pressure on suppliers to these customers for price reductions. Examples cited in this context include tobacco companies, blueberry processors, and Wal-Mart. Antitrust focus is on monopoly situations where control of end-user markets is deemed excessive. Monopsony suits are less frequent.
The Wall Street Journal, January 27, 2004, p. A1.

MRP, MRP II: Materials Requirement Planning—a concept developed in the 1970s to make use of high-speed computers to model the requirements of material for a manufacturing operation. It is viewed as a method for planning all resources of a manufacturing company. It addresses operational planning in units, financial planning in dollars, and has simulation capability. Output from MRP is integrated with financial reports, purchase commitments, shipping budgets, and inventory projections. "Closed-loop" MRP implies feedback to keep plans valid with regard to constraints such as capacity.
Adapted from *APICS Dictionary,* 10th Ed.

Network diagram: A logical display of project activities. It shows sequence and dependencies among activities.
Adapted from *PMBOK Guide,* 2000 Ed.

Noninventory items: Inventory category. Services and warranties.

NTEP: National Type Evaluation Program. Standards for weights and measures to protect commerce. Administered in the United States by the National Council on Weights and Measures (NCWM). Program provides a one-stop evaluation process that satisfies the initial requirements for introduction of weighing and measuring devices.

Offshoring: The movement of operations from one country to another within the same company. Outsourcing transfers responsibility for a process to another entity that may be in the same country or not. Often, outsourcing involves a transfer of employees as well.

Operation: A step in a process. Can include a changing of physical configuration, a quality control action, temporary or long-term storage, an administrative task, or transportation.

Operational excellence (OE): A term used by Michael Porter in discussions of strategy. His contention is the OE is a necessary but not sufficient condition for sustained competitiveness. It reflects the belief that "you can't save your way to prosperity." Porter advocates the development of activity systems to distinguish the company from its competitors.

Optimization: The application of operations research tools to a supply chain function. Examples include distribution planning (warehouse location and transportation planning) and planning a scheduling production. Optimization technology applies in complex supply chains and when the potential for improvement justifies its use.

Order penetration point: The point in a product's flow where an item is earmarked for a particular customer. Downstream processes are driven by customer orders; upstream processes are driven by forecasts and plans. However, the plans themselves can reflect actual customer orders in a demand-driven supply chain.
Adapted from *APICS Dictionary,* 10th Ed.

Outsourcing: The transfer of responsibility for a process to another entity that may be in the same country or not. Often, outsourcing involves a transfer of employees as well. Offshoring moves a process to another country, but retains the process within the company.

P:D ratio: According to the APICS Dictionary, 10th Ed., "P" is the manufacturing lead-time. "D" is the customer required delivery time. If the ratio exceeds 1.0, the customer order will be delayed or production will start as a result of a forecast (make-to-stock). The demand-driven supply chain approach argues that different segments of the supply chain can be driven by either forecasts or actual demand. In general, actual demand is more desirable than forecasts. In this book, we use cycle time to refer to processes for manufacture and distribution, and lead time as a market-driven requirement for delivery.

Panelization: A construction practice of fabricating building components in a factory and assembling them at a building site. A case is the 2000 panels (140 truckloads) for the Salt Lake City library fabricated in Mexico.
The Wall Street Journal, March 3, 2004, p. B1.

Partner: An entity with which one does business, either upstream or downstream in the supply chain, whose performance is important to your success. The relationship between you and the partner may or may not include partnering.

Partnering: A management approach used by two or more organizations, often, but not always, a buyer and a seller, to achieve mutual business objectives by maximizing the effectiveness of each partners resources. Partnerships can take a number of forms from arms-length sharing of information to acquisition. Examples include collaboration in design, measures to reduce cost, and simplified replenishment procedures.

Partnership classification: A classification of partnerships has three dimensions: purpose, direction, and choice. The purpose defines whether the partnership creates new space or not. Direction refers to the supply chain. Horizontal means partners are at the same echelon. Vertical is a partnership along the supply chain—probably between customer and supplier. Choice refers to the relative strength of each partner. A "many to one" means your company has many competitors and you are seeking a partnership with a dominant partner.
Handbook of Supply Chain Management

PDCA: Plan–Do–Check–Act. Also called the Shewhart Cycle for implementing process improvement.

Perfect Order: A flexibly defined metric that measures error rates in filling customer orders. Components include the completeness and correctness of the items picked, the delivery of the order on time, delivery without damage, and proper invoicing and collection.

Adapted from www.supplychainmetric.com.

Performance-based pricing: Basing prices on value to the customer, not necessarily what the product costs. The supply chain can influence value to the customer. Applies specifically to "innovative" products as opposed to "functional" ones where prices are cost driven in competitive markets.

Periodic replenishment: Aggregating requirements to place deliveries of varying quantities at evenly spaced time intervals, rather than variably spaced deliveries of equal quantities. The term fixed cycle also refers to this method. The milk run is also a tool for implementing this approach.

Adapted from *APICS Dictionary,* 10th Ed.

Phase: A project phase is a collection of logically related project activities, usually culminating in a deliverable.

Adapted from *PMBOK Guide,* 2000 Ed.

PLAN processes: SCOR processes that balance supply and demand. PP processes cover long-range planning at the supply chain level. PS, PM, PD, and PR cover shorter-term planning for source, make, deliver, and return.

Planning process: A SCOR process that aligns expected resources with expected demand.

Planogram: Diagram that shows the location of specific SKUs in a retail store. Uses drawings, computer-generated graphics, or photographs.

Adapted from *Retailing Management,* 5th Ed.

PMMM: Project Management Maturity Model. A five-level model developed by Dr. Harold Kernzner. The levels are common language, common processes, singular methodology, benchmarking, and continuous improvement.

Point of Sale (POS):

1. Place where the purchase is made at the checkout stand or scanning terminals in a retail store. The acronym POS frequently is used to describe the sales data generated at the checkout scanners. Source: ECR Best Practices Report
2. The relief of inventory and computation of sales data at a time and place of sale, generally through the use of bar-coding or magnetic media equipment. *APICS Dictionary,* 10th Ed.

Point-to-point integration: Building a customized computer connection. The software for such integration is usually expensive to build and maintain. When systems change on either side of the connection, expensive changes are needed.

Portfolio, PPM: A set of initiatives or projects being pursued to improve supply chains. Portfolio management is deciding the priority of the projects and making resources available for their completion. PPM stands for Project Portfolio Management.

Postponement: A product or supply chain design strategy that shifts product differentiation closer to the end-user. The approach encompasses identity changes such as assembly or packaging.

Adapted from *APICS Dictionary,* 10th Ed.

Price-taker: A buying organization that typically takes the low price every time. Generally requires a functional supply chain in the face of competitive alternatives. Prices often become the basis for selection in online auctions.

Private-label brand: An exclusive brand made for and sold by a retail enterprise.

Privatization: Transfer of product or service delivery from the public to the private sector.

Privatization is the transfer of assets or service delivery from the government to the private sector. Privatization runs a broad range, sometimes leaving little government involvement, and other times creating partnerships between government and private service providers where government is still the dominant player.

Privatization.org

Proactive systems: An approach to designing information systems to focus on the needs of decision makers. The approach may rely on computer-based tools to disseminate the needed information. Non-computer-based approaches may also be used.

Process owner: The central figure in organizations organized around processes. Owners are charged with end-to-end responsibility and authority for a cross-functional process.

Process, process group (project management context): A series of actions bringing about a result. A process either manages the project itself (a project-management process) or creates the output of the project (a product-oriented process). In the former group are initiating, planning, controlling, and closing process groups. Project-management processes call for project-management knowledge and practice expertise. In the latter are executing processes. Executing processes call for application-area knowledge and practice expertise.

From *The American Heritage Dictionary of the English Language,* 3rd Ed., Boston: Houghton Mifflin Company, 1992, and *PMBOK Guide,* 2000 Ed.

Process type: At Level 2, SCOR uses three processes types: planning, execution, and enable. Planning processes are preceded by a P, Enable by an E, and Execution by S (Source), M (Make), and D (Deliver).

Product description: In a project, the product description documents the characteristics of the physical product, service, or result sought in pursuing the project. It is established prior to project initiation and should be embellished as the project progresses. The product description should have sufficient detail to support project planning throughout the project.

Adapted from *PMBOK Guide,* 2000 Ed.

Product group, product line, product family: A grouping of products or SKU's for planning and forecasting requirements.

Product life cycle: A well-known marketing concept that holds that products pass through phases in their market lives. The phases are inception, growth, maturity, and decline. The presence of the product life cycle has implications for supply chain design.

Product pipeline, product funnel: Visual models of the way new products are developed. The concept infers a repetitive pattern for producing products. SCM should be a part of the product-development process.

Product-centric organization: An organization structure built around different product lines. Preferred in cases of multiple products with different technologies, homogeneous customer bases, and capital-intensive and cost-driven businesses.

Handbook of Supply Chain Management

Product-centric supply chain: Supply chains or organizations whose construct centers on the production of products. Alternatives are functional and customer-centric supply chains.

Product-producing sphere: A sphere that produces products for external customers. The other type is an enable sphere that provides a support service. The product-producing sphere is a "business inside the business." It merits its own supply chain design.

Product tree: A graphical representation of the product and its SKUs. The tree can also show manufacturing locations and multiple geographic markets for the same or similar SKU.

Program: A group of related projects managed in a coordinated way. A synonym is initiative. A program can include project and ongoing operations work. For example, a new product program includes product design (a temporary project) and ongoing manufacturing and sales (an operation).

Adapted from *PMBOK Guide*, 2000 Ed.

Handbook of Supply Chain Management

Progressive elaboration: A property of projects that arises from the "temporary" and "unique" nature of projects. At the beginning of a project, the resulting product, service, or result is defined broadly. As the project proceeds, the final result is "progressively elaborated." For example, a building project progressively proceeds from concept to design on paper to construction.

Adapted from *PMBOK Guide*, 2000 Ed.

Project: An organized change effort usually associated with an initiative or program, with a manager, budget, objectives, and schedule. A project is temporary and produces a unique product, service, or result. Several projects may support an initiative or program. Action plans define the goals for the project.

Adapted from *PMBOK Guide*, 2000 Ed., and the *Handbook of Supply Chain Management*

Project life cycle: A collection of generally sequential project phases needed for control of the project. Life-cycle phases generally include the initial phase, intermediate phase, and final phase. Different industries define these differently. For example, the construction industry might call the initial phase "feasibility," and the final phase "turnover and startup." A software project might start with "business requirements" and finish with "test and deploy."

Adapted from *PMBOK Guide*, 2000 Ed.

Project manager: A person responsible for managing a project. The project-management function may rest with an individual for smaller projects, and with a larger project office for larger ones. The project manager function coordinates the logistics involved in the project, including the activities of steering committees, design teams, and employee teams testing new ways of working.

Project manufacturing: Manufacturing processes designed for large, often unique, products requiring custom design. These processes require flexible processes and multiple engineering changes.

Adapted from *APICS Dictionary*, 10th Ed.

Project office: A permanent line function for project manager with expertise in project-management processes and tools, a repository of lessons learned, and a champion for project-management methodology. A project office can administer a larger supply chain project.

Adapted from *Strategic Planning for Project Management*

Promotion: A term used by CGR to describe risk pooling to lower inventories. In promotion, products, product families, or SKUs are moved higher in the tree (promoted) to concentrate demand.

Promotion: Activities to inform customers about a product or service. Also used in connection with short-term efforts to increase sales of a product or service.

Provider Service Models (PSMs): A tool for defining the staffing requirements to meet defined service objectives. Often used in managing the staff required to support operations focused on delivering services.

Public warehouse: A warehouse that is rented or leased. Services are provided under contract or on a fee-for-service basis.

Adapted from *APICS Dictionary*, 10th Ed.

Pull system: In production, replenishment only when items are taken for use as a result of a pull signal. For material control, an issue of material is made only in response to a pull signal from a using entity. Similarly, in distribution, a pull signal comes from the downstream warehouses close to the end-user.

Adapted from *APICS Dictionary*, 10th Ed.

Push-and-pull systems: Production control systems are often describes as "push" where decisions are based on forecasts, or "pull" where decisions are based on actual demand. A demand-driven supply chain is an example of a pull system. Most organizations try to move from "push" to "pull" decision making.

Push system: In production, replenishment from a schedule driven by forecast requirements. In material control, it is the issue of material based on forecast requirements. In distribution, replenishment is based on forecasts likely to be generated centrally.

Adapted from *APICS Dictionary*, 10th Ed.

QR Code: A two-dimension data exchange medium such as a bar code with more information.

> "Enterprise Integration in Japan," *CASA/SME Blue Book,* 2004.

Qualitative risk analysis: Use of tools to identify the probability and potential outcomes to identify high- , moderate- , and low-risk conditions to set priorities for response planning.

> Adapted from *PMBOK Guide,* 2000 Ed.

Quality Function Deployment (QFD): A system engineering process that transforms the desires of the customer/user into the language, required, at all project levels, to implement a product. It also provides the glue necessary, at all project levels, to tie it all together and to manage it. Finally, it is an excellent method for assuring that the customer obtains high value from your product, actually the intended purpose of QFD.

Quality standard: A set of rules for those seeking to qualify under the standard. Standards are either general or industry-specific. Standards bring consistent practice to large numbers of participants in the supply chain.

Quality threshold: The expected features of a product and its supply chain. Any participant must at least operate at the threshold to maintain market share. Those falling below the threshold lose market share and may have to exit the business.

Quantitative risk analysis: Measurement of probability distributions and potential results to calculate a distribution of possible outcomes.

> Adapted from *PMBOK Guide,* 2000 Ed.

Quick response program (QRP): A program to shorten cycle times in supply chains. Elements include strong relationships among trading partners, elimination of waste, and the use of technology for information exchange.

> *APICS Illustrated Dictionary*

Radio frequency (RF)/ automatic data collection: Technology frequently deployed in distribution centers for rapid processing of operating information.

RAG: A system for better shop-floor control through use of Red, Amber, and Green lights. Red calls for "urgent action." Amber for "going out of control," which is on the borderline, and Green is for "no problem." RAG is used with kanban systems, inventory management, customer service, and statistical process control.

> *Lean Directions,* Society of Manufacturing Engineers

Rapid replenishment: Denotes frequent or fast response to signals for inventory restocking. Rapid replenishment enables demand-driven supply chain approaches.

Real-Time Location Systems (RTLS): Technologies capable of locating and tracking assets along the supply chain. Such systems must have fixed reference points for ranging or must use triangulation. Applications that track people carrying small electronic tags.

Reduced Space Symbology (RSS): Bar-code technology allows greater use of bar codes on smaller products with limited space for bar-code labels.

Reengineering: Analysis, redesign, and implementation of process changes. Can involve new technology, new methods of performing process steps, and organizational change to support the process. The idea of reengineering should not be confused with downsizing or staffing cutbacks, although they may occur in conjunction with process change. Also, **Business process reengineering.**

Replenishment cycle time: The total time from the moment a need is identified until the product is available for use. The *APICS Dictionary*, 10th Ed., uses "lead time" to define this. Here we refer to cycle time as a physical property and lead time as a market-determined property, or expectation by customers for performance.
    Adapted from *APICS Dictionary*, 10th Ed.

Representative product: A typical product flowing through a process that is used as the basis for process design. The term is applied in developing manufacturing cells or maps of supply chains with many product variations.
    Source: Bourton Group

Reseller: A party that sells to end-users/customers. Many add value to manufactured products and software.

Return Merchandise (Material) Authorization (RMA): Documentation required before a customer can return purchased items to the retailer or OEM manufacturer. This is to allow for on-the-phone troubleshooting and assuring that the cause wasn't customer-induced damage.
    Adapted from *Wikipedia*

RETURN processes: SCOR processes addressing return and receipt of products for repair, overhaul or refurbishment, or for resale. Includes postdelivery customer support.

Reverse logistics: The processing of returned merchandise from end-users. This process includes matching returned-goods authorizations, and sorting salvageable, repairable, and nonsalvageable inventories. The flows involved reverse typical flows of physical goods, information, and funds in the supply chain. The purpose is to either recapture value or dispose of the merchandise.

RFID: Radio Frequency Identification. Emerging technology that uses passive (short-range) or active (battery-powered long-range) tags to identify inventory items. RFID allows for distance reading of product information.

Risk: An uncertain event or condition that could have a positive or negative effect on a project's objectives. Risk identification determines what risks might affect the project; a risk management plan will help manage project risks.
    Adapted from *PMBOK Guide*, 2000 Ed.

Risk pooling: The process of reducing risk among customers by pooling stock, reducing the total inventory required to provide a customer service level. CGR uses the term promotion to describe movement up the product tree resulting in pooling of lower levels of inventory.
    Adapted from *APICS Dictionary*, 10th Ed.

Routing Guide: An instruction from a retailer regarding shipping to its locations. Increasingly, the guides have become complex as retailers seek to reduce their costs and improve their services. VICS is seeking to standardize terminology and content.

Adapted from VICS standard

S&OP or S&IOP: Sales, (inventory), and operations planning. Processes for matching supply and demand. Usually an intermediate (1–3) planning horizon. Also refers to a category of software to perform these tasks.

Safety factor, safety stock: Factor used to calculate the amount of inventory required providing for uncertainty in forecasts. This is a numerical value based on a service standard, such as 95 percent certainty that orders will be filled. The factor usually ranges between 1 and 3 and is applied to the mean absolute deviation (MAD) or standard deviation (σ) to compute the safety stock required.

The need for safety stock is reduced from risk pooling, more frequent replenishment, or taking advantage of commonality among SKUs using the 3C methodology.

Safety stock: A quantity of stock planned to be in inventory to protect against demand fluctuations. The level of safety stock is a function of the uncertainty of the demand forecast during the replenishment period and uncertainties in the length of time required for replenishment. High uncertainty (such as for an innovative product) and longer lead times increase the need for safety stock. Also referred to as "buffer stock."

Sales-to-stock ratio: Ratio used in merchandise budgeting to calculate GMROI, which is the product of Gross Margin times the Sales-to-Stock ratio. Sales in the ratio are at retail, whereas stock is at cost. The sales-to-stock ratio may be calculated from required GMROI, and anticipated contribution margins from merchandise sales.

Adapted from *Retailing Management,* 5th Ed.

Scan-based trading: Supplier retention of ownership until the merchandise is sold (scanned). The effect is to shift inventory cost and control to the manufacturer or distributor. Some see benefits and risks for manufacturers. Manufacturers may enjoy more business and will have increased visibility into final demand. Other might see a threat to the manufacturer.

Adapted from *Wikipedia*

Scan-based trading: The practice of shifting risk from retailers to manufacturers. The manufacturer is paid when merchandise is sold (scanned). Similar to consignment sales.

Schedule baseline: The approved schedule developed in project planning. It is the standard by which subsequent progress is measured. Throughout the project, the baseline is updated based on actual progress.

Adapted from *PMBOK Guide,* 2000 Ed.

Schema: From the Greek for "form" or "figure." The organization or structure of a database. It is the product of data modeling. In retail supply chains, the term refers to the information objects used in commerce, such as a freight invoice, a receiving advice, or a replenishment request. Plural is schemata.

SCO: Supply chain orientation. A term coined by the University of Tennessee Supply Chain Research Group. It is a management philosophy that recognizes the implications of proactively managing both the upstream and downstream flows of products, services, finances, and information. See Chapter 2.

Scope: The sum of the products and services to be provided by a project. Product scope includes the features and functions in the products and services produced by the project. Project scope is what has to be done in the project to produce those features and functions.

    Adapted from *PMBOK Guide,* 2000 Ed.

SCOR: Supply Chain Operations Reference model. An activity model developed by the Supply Chain Council to standardize descriptions of supply chain processes.

SCPM: Supply Chain Event Management. Used to describe software that tracks supply chain operations. Includes Supply Chain Event Management (SCEM) and Supply Chain Performance Management (SCPM).

    ARC Advisory Group

Segmentation, segment: Breaking the market down into definable subcategories. For instance, Coca-Cola may segment its audience based on frequency (one can a month or five cans a day), location (Bangkok or Bangladesh), and many other criteria. Supply chains should be designed with the differing needs of multiple segments in mind.

Sell–Source–Ship (3S): A supply chain characterization in which the seller doesn't hold inventory. Once an order is placed, the seller channels orders to single or multiple sources. This is the opposite of the Buy–Hold–Sell model in which the seller does hold inventory.

Seven wastes: Shigeo Shingo developed these waste categories as part of the just-in-time philosophy: overproduction, waiting, transportation, stocks, motion, defects, and processing.

Single Minute Exchange of Dies (SMED): A theory and the techniques for performing setup operations in fewer than ten minutes, the number of minutes expressed in a single digit. The SMED philosophy is important in moving from "batch-" to "flow-" oriented supply chains.

Single sourcing: Selection of one supplier when there are alternatives.

    Adapted from *Supply Chain Management in the Retail Industry*

Six Sigma: Sigma is a letter in the Greek alphabet. The term sigma is used to designate the distribution or spread about the mean (average) of any process or procedure.

    For a business or manufacturing process, the sigma value is a metric that indicates how well that process is performing. The higher the sigma value, the better. Sigma measures the capability of the process to perform defect-free work. A defect is anything that results in customer dissatisfaction. The sigma scale of measure is perfectly correlated to such characteristics as defects-per-unit, parts-per million defective, and the probability of a failure/error.

A Six-Sigma capability means no more than 3.4 parts per-million defects. Recently, Six Sigma programs have become more general in their approach, reflecting overall efforts to make improvement as well as error-free production.

SKU (Stockkeeping unit): An inventory item whose status is maintained in an inventory-tracking systems. In the distribution system, different SKUs may represent the same item at different locations. Pronounced "skew." For clothing, SKU definition includes size, color, and style (configuration).

Adapted from *APICS Dictionary,* 10th Ed.

Slotting allowance (fee): Fee paid by a manufacturer to a retailer for shelf space.

SOA: Service-Oriented Architecture. An approach to developing software that capitalizes on the ability to reuses software modules. In the supply chain context, this practice is an example of commonality and postponement.

SOAP: Simple Object Access Protocol. An XML-based communications protocol between Web services. The protocol allows programs to communicate via standard Internet HTTP.

WWW Consortium.

Sole sourcing: Purchasing from one supplier when there are no alternatives.

Adapted from *Supply Chain Management in the Retail Industry*

SOURCE processes: SCOR processes related to incoming material and services.

Specification: A description of performance required from the supply chain for a process based on an evaluation of the as-is. The specification only states what is required, not how that goal will be reached.

Sphere: A description of entities derived by dividing complex supply chain operations for the purposes of improvement. A sphere consists of market–product–operations combinations, or "businesses within the business." There are two types of spheres: product-producing and enable. The former has external customers. The latter provides support to multiple product-producing spheres and has internal customers.

A related, but not synonymous, term from the Supply Chain Council is "threads."

Handbook of Supply Chain Management

Sponsor: An executive champion for a supply chain improvement effort. The level of the individual will depend on the level of the project—functional (department level), business unit level, or supply chain level.

Stage 3 supply chain organization: Stage 3 refers to the multicompany organization needed to implement supply chain-level changes. A common goal, multicompany staffing, a third-party "honest broker," creative win-win contracting, and a senior management steering committee mark stage 3.

Stage gate approach to product development: Formal processes used for the development of new products and services in companies of all sizes. It includes: (1) clearly defined stages in which specific tasks are undertaken, (2) the development of compelling, comprehensive business cases, rigorous, and demanding, (3) go/no-go decision points at the end of each stage using clearly defined measurable criteria, and (4) the objective review of actual versus planned performance for every new product, after its introduction to the marketplace.

Adapted from *Winning at New Products*

Staple product: A category of product with lower margins and low uncertainty regarding demand. The supply chains for these products should be designed for the lowest possible cost. This type of product is also called a functional product or a frequently purchased consumer good (FPCG). (See innovative product.)

Statement of Work (SOW): A narrative description of products or services to be supplied, often part of contract terms.

Adapted from *PMBOK Guide,* 2000 Ed.

Statistical Process Control (SPC): A set of techniques and tools that help characterize patterns of variation. By understanding these patterns, a business can determine sources of variation and minimize them, resulting in a more consistent product or service. Many customers are demanding consistency as a measure of high quality. The proper use of SPC provides a powerful way to assure that the customer gets the desired consistency time after time.

Steering committee: An executive level group responsible for SCM projects. The steering committee makes decisions and sets policies. Membership depends on the levels represented: level 1 is functional, or departmental; level 2 is the business unit level; level 3 is the multicompany or supply chain level. The steering committee is responsible for project results. It will also make important organization-related decisions. A project may have two steering committees. The first is inside the company that initiates the project. Later a multicompany steering committee may oversee intercompany relationships including processes and terms of agreements.

Stock-to-sales ratio: Ratio of expected sales for a period to the inventory (at retail price) needed to support the sales. Corresponds to the weeks of supply or months of supply. Used in merchandise budget planning to set beginning-of-period inventory that drives replenishment requirement for the prior period. See also sales-to-stock ratio.

Adapted from *Retailing Management,* 5th Ed.

Strategic sourcing: The use of the overall acquisition function as a tool for strategic improvement rather than one focused on transactions only. Involves both cost reduction from better purchasing and effective partnerships across the supply chain.

Strategy: The ways in which the company will be different from competitors. Strategy is different from a business model that defines the customers, their needs, and the underlying economic logic for the organization.

Why Business Models Matter, *Harvard Business Review,* May 2002.

Subproject: A smaller portion of a larger project. A subproject is likely to be managed just like a standalone project

Adapted from the *PMBOK Guide,* 2000 Ed.

Supplier clustering: Deliberate sole sourcing of remote suppliers within a small geographic area to gain economies in shipping.

Adapted from *APICS Dictionary,* 10th Ed.

Supply chain:

1. Life-cycle processes comprising physical, information, financial, and knowledge flows whose purpose is to satisfy end-user requirements with products and services from multiple, linked suppliers.
2. The global network used to deliver products and services from raw materials to end customers through an engineered flow of information, physical distribution, and cash.

APICS Dictionary, 10th Ed.

Supply Chain Council (SCC): A nonprofit association of companies interested in supply chain management (SCM). The Council was incorporated in June 1997 as a not-for-profit trade association. The Council offers members an opportunity to improve the effectiveness of supply chain relationships from the customer's customer to the supplier's supplier. Its primary mission is to develop and maintain its Supply Chain Operations Reference Model, or SCOR.

Supply Chain design: According to the *APICS Dictionary* 10th Ed., facets of design include selection of partners, location and capacity of warehouse and production facilities, the products, the modes of transportation, and supporting information systems.

Supply Chain Event Management (SCEM): Software feature that monitors supply chain transaction data for predefined "exceptions" or events that require intervention. An example could be a late order. In such a case, the SCEM software would alert designated parties to inform them and suggest interventions.

Supply Chain Management (SCM):

1. Design, maintenance, and operation of supply chain processes, including those that make up extended product features, for satisfaction of end-user needs.
2. The design, planning, execution, control, and monitoring of supply chain activities with the objective of creating net value, building a competitive infrastructure, leveraging worldwide logistics, synchronizing supply with demand, and measuring performance globally.

APICS Dictionary, 10th Ed.

3. Encompasses the planning and management of all activities involved in sourcing and procurement, conversion, and all logistics management activities. Importantly, it also includes coordination and collaboration with channel partners, which can be suppliers, intermediaries, third-party service providers, and customers. In essence, supply chain management integrates supply and demand management within and across companies. CSCMP.

Supply chain orientation: The idea of viewing the coordination of a supply chain from an overall system perspective with each of the tactical activities of distribution flows viewed within a broader strategic context. Actual implementation of supply chain orientation is supply chain management.
Council of Logistics Management

Supply chain strategy: The idea that supply chain design should support overall strategies for competing—that supply chain operations themselves can be used to differentiate a company's products and services and can protect it from competitors.

Surface Acoustical Wave (SAW) RFID: An emerging RFID technology that offers advantages over microchip-based technology.

SWOT Analysis: Strengths, Weaknesses, Opportunities, Threats. A technique to use in planning to identify issues related to competition.

Synchronized supply chain: A general vision of having all links in the supply chain producing at the same rate as customer demand. Obstacles include coordination, batch size limitations in production, and inability to share information. However, synchronization is a useful goal because it is likely to provide high levels of customer service at low cost relative to unsynchronized supply chains. The term is somewhat synonymous with a lean supply chain.

Tag: Notifications or commands written into Web documents.
WWW Consortium.
A small object attached to or incorporated into a product, animal, or person. The tags contain silicon chips and antennas to receive and respond to radio-frequency queries. Passive tags require no internal power source; active tags require a power source.
Adapted from *Wikipedia.*

Tag-along Items: Inventory category.

Takt time: The interval that sets the pace of production to match the rate of customer demand. It is the "heartbeat" of the lean production system. The term is derived from the German expression for a metronome beat.
Adapted from *APICS Dictionary,* 10th Ed.

Target costing: A strategic profit-planning and cost management system that incorporates a strict focus on customer wants, needs, and values, and translates them into delivered products and services. A variation is using cost as a design criterion in product development.

Task: The lowest level of effort on a project. Not included in a work breakdown structure but could be part of the decomposition of work by individuals responsible for the work.
Adapted from *PMBOK Guide,* 2000 Ed.

TCP/IP: Transmission control protocol/Internet protocol. The communications protocol used by the Internet.

Template: An activity list containing skills, resources, deliverables, dependencies, and risks that is appropriate for reuse from one project to another.
Adapted from *PMBOK Guide,* 2000 Ed.

TEU: Twenty-foot equivalent unit. The standard for measuring ocean-shipping containers. The dimensions are 20' × 8' × 8'6" (6.1 m × 2.44 m × 2.59 m). Two TEUs are one FEU (forty-foot equivalent unit).

Theory of Constraints (TOC): A portfolio of management philosophies, management disciplines, and industry-specific "best practices" developed over the past 20 years by physicist Dr. Eliyahu M. Goldratt and his associates.

Third-party logistics (3PL) provider: A company specializing in performing logistics-related services for its customers. Examples include warehouse, transportation, and product assembly.

Thread: A multientity supply chain that uses different Level 2 SCOR execution processes. For example, a make-to-stock company supplies a make-to-order company. Sphere is a related work with a broader meaning in Section I.

Throughput: In the theory of constraints, the rate at which the system generates money through sales. This does not necessarily mean output in terms of physical production, so it excludes inventory building.

Adapted from *APICS Dictionary*, 10th Ed.

To-be: The future state, or how a supply chain process will be performed in the future. Determined after examining trade-offs between an ideal goal (greenfield) and constraints standing in the way of implementing that ideal.

Total Cost of Ownership (TCO): All the costs associated with buying, supporting, and operating a product or a component.

Total Productive Maintenance (TPM): A systematic approach to minimizing machine "downtime" resulting from unexpected breakdowns. TPM emphasizes the role of the machine operator, who becomes more involved with routine checks and fine-tuning. TPM enables machinery to operate more efficiently and reliably, decreasing the risk of a "broken link" in the supply chain.

Total Quality Management (TQM): An approach that involves all employees in continually improving products and work processes to achieve customer satisfaction and world-class performance. TQM is generally associated with "bottom-up" incremental improvement.

Toyota Production System: A manufacturing process model developed by Toyota that contributed to reputation for quality in the auto industry. The Toyota Production System was built on three key factors that differentiated it from practices being employed by their competitors in the auto industry: (1) reduced lot sizes, leading to production flexibility, (2) controlling parts required in production to enable them to be provided when and where they are needed for specific tasks, (3) arranging production equipment in the order that people work, and value is added instead of grouping by equipment function. All these elements involved suppliers and customers to some extent.

Traceability: An attribute that allows for ongoing location of items in the supply chain.

Tracking signal: A signal that forecasting techniques should be reevaluated.

Handbook of MRP II and JIT

Transfer pricing: The pricing of goods and services between entities in the supply chain. These entities can be internal or with outside organizations. Supply chain partnerships require agreements on pricing.

Triad: This concept from a research paper by Alan Rugman and Alain Verbeke shows that few so-called multinationals in the North America–European Union–Japan "triad" focus on home or regional markets. The conclusion is that these multinationals are not really global and leave much autonomy to national or regional decision makers.

Trigger, trigger events: An indication a risk has occurred or is about to occur. A trigger may activate a risk response or a replanning of supply chain operations.

TRIZ: Russian acronym for Theory of Incentive Problem Solving. TRIZ is a methodology for eliminating conflicts that arise in product design.
Source: *QFD Handbook*

Truckload/less than truckload carriers (LTL): Carriers that cater to the needs of different classes of shippers. "Truckload only" carriers generally serve larger shippers. LTL carriers generally serve smaller shippers.

Two-bin system: An inventory rule that calls for a new order when one bin (either real or conceptual) runs out. The second bin then becomes the source of new requirements. The reorder quantity is equal to the bin size and depends on lead times and usage quantities. The method is one of the simplest to implement and lends itself to visual approaches.

Unit time: In activity-based costing, the labor required expressed in time or money to process one unit of a driver through an activity or process.

UNSPSC: United Nations Standard Products and Services Code. An open, standard, voluntary method for codifying products and services. Uses two-digit codes to define segments, families, classes, and commodities. For example, a "photocopier" is in Segment 44, Office Equipment and Accessories and Supplies, Family 10, Office Machines, Class 15 Duplicating Machines, and Commodity 01, Photocopiers. So, the UNSPSC would be 44101501. Codes are utilized to analyze spend categories.
Adapted from "Introduction and Overview UNSPSC" a presentation available from the UNSPSC.

UPC: Universal Product Code found on products in the form of a bar code. Used for identification throughout the supply chain.

Upstream: A reference to the "front-end" component and raw material suppliers in the supply chain. Downstream is the end of the supply chain nearest to end-users. Some reverse this convention.

Utility computing: Acquiring systems capability on a pay-as-you-go basis. This reduces the investment required by the user. "Grid computing" relies increases computing resource utilization by linking together computing resources into a grid capable of executing large computing tasks.
SupplyDemandChain Executive, January 18, 2004.

Value chain: The source of strategic advantage within the firm. It stems from the many discrete activities a firm performs, including those associated with the supply chain. Value is created through cost efficiencies or differentiation from competitors. Value will be reflected in the profitability of value-chain (or supply chain) members. Those making the highest profits are, by definition, adding the most value.

    Adapted from Competitive Advantage: Creating and Sustaining Superior Performance by Michael Porter

Value-Added Network (VAN): A network for automated information sharing between trading partners. Can be administered by a third party. Uses standards for common transactions.

Variable costing: An accounting approach to support management decision making. Variable costs normally consist of direct labor and material plus variable overhead. Fixed overhead, which is allocated, is not included, although it is included in the cost of goods sold, the basis for inventory costing.

    Variable costing is more valid in making decisions related to make or buy, economic order quantities, and other decisions. Supply chain design may transform variable into fixed costs. For example, a milk run will be made regardless of a decision to replenish for any single SKU. Therefore, the reorder cost (including transportation) assumption related to the decision should be reduced accordingly.

    The approach is consistent with the theory of constraints, which maintains that operating expense is relatively fixed over a range of production.

VAT analysis: Analysis of product structure from the theory of constraints. A "V" structure has a few raw materials and many products. An "A" structure has many raw materials and a few end products. A "T" structure has numerous similar finished products assembled from common components.

    Describing the product structure is a foundation for supply chain design.

    Adapted from *APICS Dictionary,* 10th Ed.

Velocity: A term that describes how much time a unit of production spends in actual process steps as a percent of total time in the process. It is also the ratio between cycle time and lead time. Low velocities mean much of the time required for processing is spent in waiting on value-adding steps in the process. A goal of supply chain design is often to increase velocity. The term is increasingly applied to administrative as well as physical processing.

Vendor-Managed Inventory (VMI); Vendor-Managed Replenishment (VMR): The practice of partnering between distribution channel members that changes the traditional replenishment process from distributor-generated purchase orders, based on economic order quantities, to the replenishment of products based on actual and forecasted product demand. Source: CRP Best

    A process by which a supplier automatically replenishes customer stock based on actual sales or shipments. Also called continuous replenishment. *APICS Dictionary,* 10th Ed.

Some practitioners view VMR as an enhancement of VMI, requiring more collaboration.

VICS: Voluntary Interindustry Commerce Standards Association. Maintains CPFR and other processes for commerce. Promotes a "vision for the future" in which products move through the global supply chain. Promotes voluntary rather than compulsory standards.

Adapted from http://www.vics.org/home.

Virtual enterprise: A team of individual companies organized to meet a market opportunity as if they were all part of the same company with a common goal.

Virtual private network (VPN): A private network that uses Internet technology. It is only accessible by authorized users. It is seen as a cost-effective alternative to dedicated lines.

Virtual value chain: The virtual, information-based equivalent of the value-chain model where value is created by gathering, selecting, synthesizing, and distributing information.

From *Harvard Business Review,* "Exploiting the Virtual Value Chain," J.F. Rayport and J.J. Sviokla, November–December, 1995.

Voice of the customer: A component of quality function deployment (QFD) that provides customers' requirements as the basis for design of a product or process.

Voice-directed picking: In warehouses, delivering orders to stock pickers via a wireless network. Such orders are usually produced by warehouse management systems. Usually, data is transmitted from the WMS; the picker's terminal translates the data into voice messages.

Voucher item: Inventory category. Gift card/gift certificate.

W3C: World Wide Web Consortium. An organization of public and private sector organizations that maintains standards for the World Wide Web (WWW). WWW Consortium.

Wall-to-wall inventory: A technique in which material enters a plant and is processed into finished goods without entering a formal stock area. Also four-wall inventory.

APICS Dictionary, 10th Ed.

Warehouse Management System (WMS): A system that tracks and controls the movement of inventory through the warehouse, from receiving to shipping. Many WMS systems also plan transportation requirements into and out of the warehouse. The WMS allows visibility to the quantity and location of inventory, as well as the age of the inventory, to give a current and accurate picture of the Available to Promise (ATP).

Web services: Supply chain application-to-application communications delivered over the Internet. These reduce the cost and complexity of forming links between supply chain partners and customers for products in the chain. They use shared standards to speed the job of developing links.

Adapted from "The Strategic Value of Web Services" in *The McKinsey Quarterly,* and "Business Processes and Web Services" by Alan Kotok.

Weight Item: Inventory category.

WERC: The Warehousing Educational and Research Council. An international professional association dedicated to the advancement and education of people involved in the management of warehouses and distribution facilities.

Wireless Fidelity (Wi-Fi): A technology that follows the IEEE 802.11x standard for wireless communication over the Internet. The technology uses "hot spots" where personal computers, particularly laptops, and other devices can access the Internet.

Work Breakdown Structure (WBS): A deliverable-oriented grouping of project elements that organizes and defines the total work scope of the project. Descending levels add detailed definition to the project work.

Adapted from *PMBOK Guide,* 2000 Ed.

Work flow: A class of software application that includes automation of the flow of information according to process rules. Similar to, but not as encompassing as, a proactive systems approach in which the requirements of decision makers are part of the redesign of the supply chain.

Work in progress (WIP): Units of production that have started, but not finished, the production process. Material entering the factory usually starts as raw material, then becomes WIP, and then proceeds to finished goods. High WIP levels are characteristic of long cycle times or low velocity in production.

Work package: A deliverable at the lowest level of the Work Breakdown Structure, when that deliverable may be assigned to another project manager. A work package can be divided into activities.

Adapted from the *PMBOK Guide,* 2000 Ed.

World class: Being the best in your industry on enough competitive factors to achieve profit goals and be considered one of the best in satisfying customers.

World Trade Organization (WTO): A global international organization (over 140 countries) dealing with the rules of trade between nations. WTO agreements, negotiated and signed by the bulk of the trading nations, are ratified in their legislative bodies. The goal is to help producers of goods and services, exporters, and importers conduct their business.

XML: Extensible markup language. This is a flexible cousin of the HTML, the format for Web pages. HTML just describes how the document will look. XML describes what's in the document and is not concerned about the display but the organization of the information. XML enables transfer of data among databases and Web sites without losing descriptive information. It also speeds searches because the search engines can look at tags rather than lengthy text. A standard syntax is required in order for companies to share information.

"Explaining XML", *Harvard Business Review,* July–August 2000.

Yield management: Using price and other promotions to maximize the return on investment. Usually infers a fixed capacity, such as airline seats, that is filled with customers from segments paying different prices.

BIBLIOGRAPHY

Bibliography

A Guide to the Project Management Body of Knowledge (PMBOK Guide), Newtown Square: Project Management Institute, 2000.

Abernathy, Fred, "Marketing, Merchandising, and Retailing: The Role of Intermediaries in Global Value Chains," presentation at the University of Washington, June 6, 2004.

Agrawal, Mani, Kumaresh, T.V., and Mercer, Glenn A., "The False Promise of Mass Customization," *The McKinsey Quarterly*, 2001, Number 3.

Andraski, Joe, Joe Andraski discusses collaborative planning, forecasting and replenishment with Larry Smith of West Marine, Interview Transcript at www.vics.org/committess/cpfr.

Ansberry, Clare and Aeppel, Timothy, "Surviving the Onslaught," *The Wall Street Journal*, October 6, 2003, p. B1.

Arntzen, Bruce C. and Shumway, Herbert M., Driven by Demand: A Case Study, available at www.manufacturing.net, January 1, 2002.

Arruñada, Benito and Vázquez, Xosé H. "When Your Contract Manufacturer Becomes Your Competitor," *Harvard Business Review*, September 2006, pp. 135–145.

"As U.S. Quotas Fall, Latin Pants Makers Seek Leg Up on Asia," *The Wall Street Journal*, June 16, 2004, p. A1.

Ayers, James B. and Malmberg, David R., "Supply chain systems: are your ready?" *Information Strategy: The Executive's Journal*, Fall 2002, pp. 18–27.

Ayers, James B., Backbone of the lean enterprise, SME Technical Paper TP04PUB138, Detroit: Society of Manufacturing Engineers, 2004.

Ayers, James B., "Costs: Getting to the Root Causes," *Supply Chain Management Review*, November–December, 2003, pp. 24–30.

Ayers, James B., Gustin, Craig and Stephens, "Scott, Reengineering the supply chain," *Information Strategy: The Executive's Journal*, Fall, 1997 (14/1), pp. 13–18.

Ayers, James B., *Handbook of Supply Chain Management* (2nd edition), Boca Raton, FL: Auerbach Publications, 2006.

Ayers, James B., *Making Supply Chain Management Work: Design, Implementation, Partnerships, Technology, and Profits*, Boca Raton, FL: Auerbach Publications, 2002.

Ayers, James B., *Supply Chain Management (SCM), the Wheel and the Manufacturing Engineer*, Detroit: Society of Manufacturing Engineers, 2002.

Ayers, James B., *Supply Chain Project Management: a Structured Collaborative and Measurable Approach*, Boca Raton, FL: St. Lucie Press, 2004.

Ayers, James B., "Supply Chain Strategies," *Information Strategy: The Executive's Journal,* (15/2) Winter, 1999, pp. 2–10.

Ayers, James, Rooting out supply chain costs, *Optimize,* October 2003, available at www.optimizemagazine.com.

Banker, Steve and Snitkin, Sid, "A Foundation for Operational Excellence," *Supply Chain Management Review,* March–April 2003, pp. 42–48.

Beavers, Alex N., *Roadmap to the e-Factory,* Boca Raton, FL: Auerbach Publications, 2000.

Beer, Michael and Eisenstat, Russell A., "How to Have an Honest Conversation about Business Strategy," *Harvard Business Review,* February 2004, pp. 82–89.

Bensaou, M. and Earl, Michael, "The Right Mind-Set for Managing Information Technology," *Harvard Business Review,* September–October 1998, pp. 119–128.

Bermudez, John, "Supply Chain Management: More Than Just Technology," *Supply Chain Management Review,* March–April 2002, pp. 15–16.

Bhagwati, Jagdish, *In Defense of Globalization,* Oxford: Oxford University Press, 2004.

Bhote, Keki R., *Strategic Supply Management: A Blueprint for Revitalizing the Manufacturer–Supplier Partnership,* New York, AMACOM, 1989.

Blackman, Andrew, "Is consensus wisdom on Oracle—"buy"—wrong?" *The Wall Street Journal,* May 12, 2004, p. C3.

Blackwell, Roger D., *From Mind to Market: Reinventing the Supply Chain,* New York: Harper Collins Publishers, 1997.

Blumberg, Donald F., *Managing High-Tech Services Using a CRM Strategy,* Boca Raton, FL: St. Lucie Press, 2003.

Bowersox, D.J. and Closs, David J., *Logistical Management: the Integrated Supply Chain Process,* McGraw Hill, 1996.

"Breakthrough Ideas for 2004," *Harvard Business Review,* February 2004, pp. 13–37.

Brussee, Warren, *Statistics for Six Sigma Made Easy!* New York: McGraw-Hill, 2004.

Burt, David N., "Managing Suppliers Up To Speed," *Harvard Business Review,* July–August 1989.

Buss, Dale, "Little giants," *Chief Executive,* May 2004, available at www.chiefexecutive.com.

Cahill, Joseph B., "Whirlpool Experiences Shipping Delays over Computer Glitches in SAP software," *Wall Street Journal,* November 3, 1999, p. A3.

Camp, Robert C. *Benchmarking,* Milwaukee: ASQC Quality Press, 1989.

Campoy, Ann and Rhoads, Christopher, "As EU Expands, It Re-Examines Old Ways: Sleepy Economy of Europe May Get Jolt by Low Prices and Vigor of New Members, *The Wall Street Journal,* April 29, 2004, p. A14.

Cantwell, Dick, "Procter & Gamble's EPC Advantage Strategy," presentation to RFID Journal Live 2006 conference, May 1–3 2006.

Cavinato, Joseph L., "What's Your Supply Chain Type?" *Supply Chain Management Review,* May–June 2002, pp. 60–66.

Chakravorti, Bhaskar, "The New Rules for Bringing Innovations to Market," *Harvard Business Review,* March 2004, pp. 59–67.

Chapman, Timothy L., Dempsey, Jack J., Ramsdell, Glenn, and Bell, Trudy E., "Purchasing's Big Moment—After a Merger," *The McKinsey Quarterly,* 1998, Number 1, pp. 56–65.

Christensen, Clayton M., The law of conservation of attractive profits, *Harvard Business Review,* February 2004, pp. 17–18.

Cliffe, Sarah, "ERP Implementation: How to Avoid $100 million Write-Offs," *Harvard Business Review,* January–February 1999, pp. 16–17.

Conner, Martin P., "The Supply Chain's Role in Leveraging PLM," *Supply Chain Management Review,* March 2004, pp. 36–43.

Cooper, Robert G., *Winning at New Products,* 3rd edition, New York: Perseus Publishing Company, 2001.

Cooper, Robin and Chew, W. Bruce, "Control Tomorrow's Costs through Today's Designs," *Harvard Business Review,* January–February 1996.

Corcoran, Elizabeth, "Making over Motorola," *Forbes,* December 13, 2004, pp. 102–108.

Council of Supply Chain Management Professionals, *Supply Chain Management Process Standards,* Council of Supply Chain Management Professionals, 2004. The standards are in six volumes: *Plan Processes, Source Processes, Make Processes, Deliver Processes, Return Processes, Enable Processes.*

Cox III, James F. and Blackstone, Jr., John H., *APICS Dictionary,* 10th ed., Alexandria: APICS—The Educational Society for Resource Management, 2002.

DC Velocity Staff, "The Rainmakers," *DC Velocity,* July 2006, pp. 33–49.

Denend, Lyn, West Marine: driving growth through shipshape supply chain management, Stanford Graduate School of Business Case Study GS-34, 2005.

Duffy, Mike, "How Gillette Cleaned Up Its Supply Chain," *Supply Chain Management Review,* April 2004, pp. 20–27.

Dyer, Jeffrey H., "How Chrysler Created an American Keiretsu," *Harvard Business Review,* July–August 1996, pp. 42–56.

Dyer, Jeffrey H., Kale, Prashant and Singh, Harbir, "When to Ally & When to Acquire," *Harvard Business Review,* July–August 2004, pp. 109–115.

Eisenhardt, Kathleen M. and Brown, Shona L., "Patching: Restitching Business Portfolios in Dynamic Markets," *Harvard Business Review,* May–June 1999, pp. 72–82.

Fahey, Jonathon, "Just in Time Meets Just Right," *Forbes,* July 5, 2004, pp. 66–68.

Farrell, Diana, "The Real New Economy," *Harvard Business Review,* October 2003, pp. 104–112.

Fawcett, Stanely E., Magnan, Gregory M., and Williams, Alvin J., "Supply Chain Trust Is Within Your Grasp," *Supply Chain Management Review,* March 2004, pp. 20–26.

Feitzinger, Edward and Lee, Hau, "Mass Customization at Hewlett-Packard: The Power of Postponement," *Harvard Business Review,* January–February 1997, pp. 116–121.

Feld, Charlie S. and Stoddard, Donna B., "Getting IT Right," *Harvard Business Review,* February 2004, pp. 72–79.

Ferdows, Kasra, Lewis, Michael A., and Machuca, Jose A.D., "Rapid-Fire Fulfillment," *Harvard Business Review,* November 2004.

Fernández-Rañada, Miguel, Gurrola-Gal, F. Xavier, and López-Tello, Enrique, *3C: A Proven Alternative to MRPII for Optimizing Supply Chain Performance,* Boca Raton, FL: St. Lucie Press, 2000.

Fish, Lynn A. and Forrest, Wayne C., "The Seven Success Factors of RFID," *Supply Chain Management Review,* September 2006, pp. 26–32.

Fisher, Marshall L., Hammond, Janice H., Obermeyer, Walter R., and Raman, Ananth, "Making Supply Meet Demand in an Uncertain World," *Harvard Business Review,* May–June 1994.

Fisher, Marshall L., "What is the Right Supply Chain for Your Product?" *Harvard Business Review*, (75/2), March–April 1997, pp. 105–116.

Fites, Donald V., "Make Your Dealers Your Partners," *Harvard Business Review*, March–April 1996.

Ford, Henry, Henry Ford on continuous improvement, *Lean Directions*, available at www.sme.org, July 9, 2003.

Foster, Thomas A., "The trends changing the face of logistics outsourcing worldwide," *Global Logistics & Supply Chain Strategies*, June 2004, pp. 32–43.

Friedman, Thomas L., *The World is Flat: A Brief History of the Twenty-first Century*, New York, Farrar, Straus and Giroux, 2005.

Geary, Steve, Childerhouse, Paul and Towill, Denis, "Uncertainty and the Seamless Supply Chain," *Supply Chain Management Review*. July–August 2002, pp. 52–61.

Ghemawat, Pankaj and Ghadar, Fariborz, "The Dubious Logic of Global Megamergers," *Harvard Business Review*, July–August 2000, pp. 64–72.

Ghemawat, Pankaj, "Distance Still Matters: The Hard Reality of Global Expansion," *Harvard Business Review*, September 2001, pp. 137–147.

Gibson, Brian J., Rutner, Stephen, M. and Manrodt, Karl B., "How Trigger Events Can Get the CEO's Attention," *Supply Chain Management Review*, November 2005, pp. 40–45.

Gilliland, Michael, "Is Forecasting a Waste of Time?" *Supply Chain Management Review*, July–August 2002, pp. 16–23.

Global Reporting Initiative, *Sustainability Reporting Guidelines*, Version 3.0, 2006.

Goldratt, Eliyahu M. and Cox, Jeff, *The Goal*, Croton-on-Hudson: North River Press, 1984.

Goldratt, Eliyahu M. and Fox, Robert E., *The Race*, Croton-on-Hudson: North River Press, 1986.

Goldsborough, William W., *Collaborative Global Logistics*, Report R860, SRI Consulting Business Intelligence, 2002.

Gouillart, Francis J. and Sturdivant, Frederick D., "Spend a Day in the Life of Your Customers," *Harvard Business Review*, January–February 1994.

Gould, Stephen A., "How to Source Logistics Services Strategically," *Supply Chain Management Review*, September–October 2003, pp. 48–54.

Gupta, Rajat and Wendler, Jim, "Leading Change: An Interview with the CEO of P&G," *The McKinsey Quarterly*, Web exclusive July 2005.

Hagel III, John and Brown, John Seely, "Your Next IT Strategy," *Harvard Business Review* (79/9), October 2001, pp. 105–113.

Hamel, Gary and Prahalad, C.K., "Strategic Intent," *Harvard Business Review*, (67/3) May–June, 1989, pp. 63–76.

Hamel, Gary and Prahalad, C.K., "The Core Competency of the Corporation," *Harvard Business Review*, (68/3) May–June 1990, pp. 79–90.

Hammer, Michael, "Deep Change: How Operational Innovation Can Transform Your Company," *Harvard Business Review*, April 2004, pp. 84–93.

Harbison, John R. and Pekar, Peter, *Smart Alliances: a Practical Guide to Repeatable Success*, San Francisco, CA: Jossey-Bass, 1998.

Hauser, John R. and Clausing, Don, "The House of Quality," *Harvard Business Review*, (66/3), May–June 1988, pp. 63–73.

Hayes, Robert H. and Pisano, Gary P., "Beyond World-Class: The New Manufacturing Strategy," *Harvard Business Review*, January–February 1994.

Hayes, Robert H. and Wheelwright, Steven C. *Restoring Our Competitive Edge: Competing Through Manufacturing*, New York, John Wiley & Sons, 1984.

Hayes, Robert H., Wheelwright Steven C., and Clark, Kim B. *Dynamic Manufacturing: Creating the Learning Organization*, New York: Free Press, 1988.

Hicks, Douglas T., *Activity-Based Costing: Making it Work for Small and Mid-Sized Companies*, 2nd ed., New York: John Wiley & Sons, 1999.

Hofman, Debra, "Getting to World-Class Supply Chain Measurement," *Supply Chain Management Review*, October 2006, pp. 18–24.

Hope, Jeremy and Fraser, Robin, "Who Needs Budgets?" *Harvard Business Review*, February 2003, pp. 108–115.

House, Charles H. and Price, Raymond L., "The Return Map: Tracking Product Teams," *Harvard Business Review*, January–February 1991, pp. 92–100.

Hugos, Michael and Thomas, Chris, *Supply Chain Management in the Retail Industry*, Hoboken: John Wiley & Sons, 2006.

Hyland, Tricia, Logistics is not supply chain management, *CLO/Chief Logistics Officer*, October 2002, pp. 32–34.

Iansiti, Marco and Levien, Roy, "Strategy as Ecology," *Harvard Business School*, March 2004, pp. 69–78.

Iansiti, Marco and West, Jonathan, "Technology Integration: Turning Great Research into Great Products," *Harvard Business Review*, (75/3), May–June 1997, 69–79.

Imai, Masaaki, *Kaizen*, New York: Random House, 1986.

"In bow to retailers' new clout, Levi Strauss makes alterations," *The Wall Street Journal*, June 17, 2004, p. A1.

Ittner, Christopher D. and Larcker, David F., "Coming up Short on Nonfinancial Performance Measurement," *Harvard Business Review*, November 2003, pp. 88–95.

Iverson, Steven, "When Clear Communication Matters," *World Trade*, July 2004, pp. 58–59.

Jackson, Bill and Winkler, Conrad, "Building the advantaged supply network, *strategy + business*," September 15, 2004, www.strategy-business.com/resilience/rr00011.

Jennings, Dana and Kling, Greg, "Integration of Disparate Enterprise IT Systems," presented to Supply Chain World Conference sponsored by the Supply Chain Council, April 1999.

Johansson, Juliet E., Krishnamurthy, Chandru, and Schlissberg, Henry E., "Solving the Solutions Problem," *The McKinsey Quarterly*, 2003, Number 3.

Johnston, Peter, Onsite manufacturing is a lean strategic advantage, *Lean Directions*, September 9, 2003, available at www.sme.org.

Juran, J. M., *Juran on Quality by Design*, New York: The Free Press, 1992.

Jutras, Cindy M. *ERP Optimization: Using Your Existing System to Support Profitable E-Business Initiatives*, Boca Raton, FL: St. Lucie Press, 2003.

Kahn, Gabriel, "Invisible Supplier Has Penny's Shirts All Buttoned Up," *The Wall Street Journal*, September 11, 2003, p. A1.

Kahn, Gabriel, "Tiger's New Threads," *The Wall Street Journal*, March 26, 2004, p. B1.

Kaplan, Robert S. and Norton, David P., "Measuring the Strategic Readiness of Intangible Assets," *Harvard Business Review*, February 2004, pp. 52–63.

Kaplan, Robert S. and Norton, David P., "The Balanced Scorecard—Measures That Drive Performance," *Harvard Business Review*, January–February 1992, pp. 71–79.

Kaplan, Robert S. and Anderson, Steven R., "Time-Driven Activity-Based Costing," *Harvard Business Review*, November 2004, pp. 131–138.

Kerzner, Harold, *Project Management: A Systems Approach to Planning, Scheduling, and Controlling*, 7th edition, New York: John Wiley & Sons, 2001.

Kerzner, Harold, *Strategic Planning for Project Management: Using a Project Management Maturity Model*, New York: John Wiley & Sons, 2001.

Kim, W. Chan and Mauborgne, Renee, "Creating New Market Space," *Harvard Business Review*, (77/1), January–February 1999, pp. 83–93.

Kim, W. Chan and Mauborgne, Renee, "Value Innovation: The Strategic Logic of High Growth," *Harvard Business Review*, July–August 2004, pp. 172–180. (First published in 1997.)

Knemeyer, A. Michael, Corsi, Thomas M., and Murphey, Paul R., "Logistics Outsourcing Relationships: Customer Perspectives," *Journal of Business Logistics*, Vol. 24, No. 1, 2003, pp. 77–109.

Knemeyer, A. Michael, Corsi, Thomas M., and Murphy, Paul R., "Logistics Outsourcing Relationships: Customer Perspectives," *Journal of Business Logistics*, 2003, pp. 77–109.

Kotsuka, Yoshibumi, "Case Study: Securing Cargo with E-Seals," presentation to RFID Journal Live 2006 conference, May 1–3, 2006.

Kumar, Nirmalya, "The Power of Trust in Manufacturer-Retailer Relationships," *Harvard Business Review*, November–December 1996.

Lahiri, Sandip, *RFID Sourcebook*, Upper Saddle River, NJ: IBM Press, 2006.

Lambert, Douglas A. and Knemeyer, A. Michael, "We're in this Together," *Harvard Business Review*, December 2004, pp. 114–122.

Laseter, Tim and Oliver, Keith, "When Will Supply Chain Management Grow Up?" *strategy + business*, Issue 32, Fall 2003, http://www.strategy-business.com/reprints/03304.

Lee, Hau I., "The Triple-A Supply Chain," *Harvard Business Review*, October 2004, pp. 102–114.

Lee, Hau L. "What Constitutes Supply Chain Integration?," *IEEM Network News*, Stanford University School of Engineering, Summer 1998.

Leimanis, Eriks, *APICS Illustrated Dictionary–11th Edition*, APICS—The Educational Society for Resource Management, 2004.

Levitt, Theodore, "Marketing Myopia," *Harvard Business Review*, July–August 2004, pp. 138–149. (First published in 1960.)

Levy, Michael and Weitz, Barton A., *Retailing Management* (5th edition), New Delhi: Tata McGraw-Hill, 2004.

Lewin, Marsha, Kennedy, Keith, and Ayers, Jim; "Transformation through Proactive Systems: A Case Study, *Information Strategy: the Executive's Journal*, (12/3), Spring 1996, pp. 29–35.

Lewis, William W., *The Power of Productivity*, Chicago, IL: University of Chicago Press, 2004.

Liker, Jeffrey V. and Choi, Thomas Y., "Building Deep Supplier Relationships," *Harvard Business Review*, December 2004, pp. 104–113.

Luhnow, David, "As Jobs Move East, Plants in Mexico Retool to Compete," *Wall Street Journal*, March 5, 2004, p. A1.

Lutz, Robert A., *Guts*, New York: John Wiley & Sons, 1998.

Magretta, Joan, "Why Business Models Matter," *Harvard Business Review,* May 2002, pp. 87–92.

Marglin, Stephen A., "Outsourcing Common Sense," *Los Angeles Times,* April 25, 2004, p. M3.

McAfee, R. Bruce, Glassman, Myron, and Honeycutt, Jr., Earl D., The Effects of Culture and Human Resource Management Policies on Supply Chain Management Strategy," *Journal of Business Logistics,* 2002, pp. 1–18.

McCormack, Kevin P., Johnson, William C., Walker, William T., *Supply Chain Networks and Business Process Orientation: Advanced Strategies and Best Practices,* Boca Raton, FL: APICS/St. Lucie Press, 2003.

McGee, Ken, "Give Me That Real-Time Information," *Harvard Business Review,* April 2004, pp. 26.

McGrath, Rita Gunther and MacMillan, Ian C., "Discovery-Driven Planning," *Harvard Business Review,* July–August 1995. pp. 44–54.

McWilliams, Gary, "Lean Machine: How Dell Fine-Tunes its PC Pricing to Gain Edge in a Slow Market," *The Wall Street Journal,* June 8, 2001, p. A1.

Mentzer, John J. and Moon, Mark A., "Understanding Demand," *Supply Chain Management Review,* May-June 2004, pp. 38–43.

Mercer, Glenn A., "Don't Just Optimize—Unbundled," *The McKinsey Quarterly,* 1994, Number 3, pp. 103–116.

Moffett, Sebastion, "Canon Manufacturing Strategy Pays Off with Strong Earnings," *The Wall Street Journal,* January 30, 2004, p. B3.

Monden, Yasuhiro, *Toyota Production System,* Norcross, Georgia: Institute of Industrial Engineers, 1983.

Montcrief, Bob and Stonich, Mark, Supply chain practice maturity model and performance assessment, a presentation by the Performance Management Group (PMG) and Pittiglio Rabin Todd & McGrath (PRTM), November 6, 2001.

Moody, Kavin W., New meaning to IT alignment, *Information Systems Management,* Fall 2003, pp. 30–35.

Moore, Geoffrey A., "Innovating within Established Enterprises," *Harvard Business Review,* July–August 2004, pp. 86–92.

Morais, Richard C., "I Want It Yesterday," *Forbes,* November 24, 2003, pp. 134–136.

Morris, Steven A. and McManus, Denise Johnson, "Information Infrastructure Centrality in the Agile Organization," *Information Systems Management,* Fall 2002, pp. 8–12.

Muller, JoAnn, "Global Motors," *Forbes,* January 12, 2004, pp. 62–68.

Myerson, Judith M., *Enterprise Systems Integration Second Edition,* Boca Raton, FL: Auerbach Publishers, 2002.

Naik, Sapna, *Fight for Consumer Mind Space: Dynamics in Food Retailer-Supplier Relationships,* Rabobank International Food &Agribusiness Research and Advisory, May 2004.

Narayanan, V.G. and Raman, Ananth, "Aligning Incentives in Supply Chains," *Harvard Business Review,* November 2004, pp. 94–102.

Narus, James. A. and Anderson, James C., "Rethinking Distribution: Adaptive Channels," *Harvard Business Review,* July–August 1996.

"New Study Reveals Changes in Supply Chain Management Best Practices," *Supplier Selection & Management Report,* Institute of Management & Administration (IOMA), November 2004, p. 1.

Norek, Christopher D., "Throwing it into Reverse," *DC Velocity*, January 2003, pp. 54–58.

Nunes, Paul F. and Cespedes, Frank V., "The Customer Has Escaped," *Harvard Business Review*, November 2003, pp. 96–105.

O'Brien, Kevin P., Value Chain Report—Cats & Dogs: Objective Approaches to SKU Rationalization, available at www.iwvaluechain.com, October, 7, 2002.

O'Brien, Kevin, Vendor-managed inventory in low-volume environments, *Industry Week's the Value Chain*, available at www.valuechain.com, July 7, 2003.

Outsourcing 101 (editorial), *The Wall Street Journal*, May 27, 2004, p. A20.

Parker, Bob, "Building a 'House of Productivity,'" *Supply Chain Management Review*, March 2004, pp. 12–13.

Parker, Ginny, "Going Global Can Hit Snags, Vodafone Finds," *The Wall Street Journal*, June 16, 2004, p. B1.

Petroff, John N., *Handbook of MRPII and JIT: Strategies for Total Manufacturing Control*, Englewood Cliffs, NJ: Prentice-Hall, 1993.

Poirier, Charles C., "The Path to Supply Chain Leadership," *Supply Chain Management Review*, (2/3), Fall 1998. pp. 16–26.

Poirier, Charles, "Achieving Supply Chain Connectivity," *Supply Chain Management Review*, November–December 2002, pp. 16–22.

Porter, Michael E., *Competitive Advantage: Creating and Sustaining Superior Performance*, New York: The Free Press, 1985.

Porter, Michael E., *Competitive Strategy: Techniques for Analyzing Industries and Competitors*, New York: The Free Press, 1980.

Porter, Michael E., "Strategy and the Internet," *Harvard Business Review*, (79/3) March 2001, pp. 62–78.

Porter, Michael E., "What Is Strategy?" *Harvard Business Review*, (74/6) November–December 1996, pp. 61–78.

Porter, Michael E. and Kramer, Mark R., "Strategy and Society," *Harvard Business Review*, December 2005, pp 78–92.

Prohalad, C.K, and Ramaswamy, Venkatram, The collaboration continuum: understand the full goals and complexity of collaboration before moving forward, November 2001, available at www.optimizemagazine.com.

Project Management Institute, *A Guide to the Project Management Body of Knowledge (PMBOK Guide—2000 Edition)*, Newtown Square, PA: Project Management Institute, 2000.

Ptak, Carol A., Schragenheim, Eli, *ERP: Tools, Techniques, and Applications for Integrating the Supply Chain*, Boca Raton, FL: St. Lucie Press, 2000.

Quinn, Francis, "Alliance Builder: An Interview with Lorraine Segal," *Supply Chain Management Review*, April 2004, pp. 43–47.

Quinn, Francis J., "Ready for the Digital Future? An interview with M. Eric Johnson," *Supply Chain Management Review*, July–August 2006, pp. 26–32.

Rangan, V. Kasturi, "The Promise and Rewards of Channel Stewardship," *Supply Chain Management Review*, July–August 2006, pp. 42–49.

Rayport, Jeffrey F. and Sviokla, John J., "Exploiting the Virtual Value Chain," *Harvard Business Review*, November–December 1995.

Reichheld, Frederick F., "The One Number You Need to Grow," *Harvard Business Review*, December 2003, pp. 46–64.

ReVelle, Jack B., *Manufacturing Handbook of Best Practices: an Innovation, Productivity, and Quality Focus*, Boca Raton, FL: APICS/St. Lucie Press, 2002.

ReVelle, Jack B., Moran, John W., and Cox, Charles A., *The QFD Handbook*. New York: John Wiley & Sons, 1998.

Rice, Jr., James B. and Hoppe, Richard M., "Supply Chain vs. Supply Chain—The Hype and the Reality," *Supply Chain Management Review*, September–October 2001, pp. 46–54.

Rigby, Darrell K., Reichheld, Frederick F., and Schefter, Phil, "Avoid the Four Perils of CRM," *Harvard Business Review*, February 2002, pp. 101–109.

Riggs, David A. and Robbins, Sharon L., *The Executive's Guide to Supply Chain Management: Building Supply Chain Thinking into All Business Processes*, New York, AMA-COM, 1998.

Robb, Drew, "The Virtual Enterprise: How Companies use Technology to Stay in Control of a Virtual Supply Chain," *Information Strategy: the Executive's Journal*, Summer 2003, pp. 6–11.

Robert, Michel, *Strategy Pure & Simple II*, New York: McGraw-Hill, 1998.

Roche, Eileen, "Explaining XML," *Harvard Business Review*, (78/4), July–August 2000, p. 18.

Rogers, Dale S. and Tibben-Lembke, Ronald S., "Returns management and reverse logistics for competitive advantage," *CSCMP Explores ... ,* Winter, 2006.

Ross, David F., *Competing through Supply Chain Management: Creating Market-Winning Strategies through Supply Chain Partnerships*, Chapman & Hall Material Management Series, 1997.

Ross, Jeanne W. and Weill, Peter, "Six IT Decisions your IT People Shouldn't Make," *Harvard Business Review*, November 2002, pp. 85–91.

Roztocki, N. and Needy, K.L., An integrated activity-based costing and economic value added system as an engineering management tool for manufacturers, 1998 ASEM National Conference Proceedings, Virginia Beach, October 1–3, 1998, pp. 77–84.

Rugman, Alan M. and Verbeke, Alain, *Regional Multinationals and Triad Strategy*, August 5, 2202.

Rutner, Stephen, Waller, Matthew A., and Mentzer, John T., "A Practical Look at RFID," *Supply Chain Management Review*, January–February 2004.

Schragenheim, Eli and Dettmer, H. William, *Manufacturing at Warp Speed: Optimizing Supply Chain Financial Performance*, Boca Raton, FL: APICS/St. Lucie Press, 2001.

Schroeder, Michael, "Outsourcing May Create U.S. jobs," *The Wall Street Journal*, March 30, 2004, p. A2.

Shapiro, Benson P., Rangan, V. Kasturi, and Sviokla, John J., "Staple Yourself to an Order," *Harvard Business Review*, July–August 2004, pp. 162–171. (First published in 1992)

Shirouzu, Norihiko, "Chain Reaction: Big Three's Outsourcing Plan: Make Parts Suppliers Do It," *The Wall Street Journal*, June 10, 2004, p. A1.

Skinner, Wickham. "The Focused Factory," *Harvard Business Review*, May–June, 1974.

Slater, Derek, "The Ties That Bolt," *CIO Magazine*, April 15, 1999.

Slone, Reuben E., "Leading a Supply Chain Turnaround," *Harvard Business Review*, October 2004, pp.114–121.

Smeltzer, Larry R. and Manship, Jennifer A., "How Good Are Your Cost Reduction Measures?" *Supply Chain Management Review*, May–June 2003, pp. 28–33.

Smith, Rob, *Global Supply Chain Performance And Risk Optimization: The Value Of Real Options Flexibility Demonstrated In The Global Automotive Industry,* Weisbaden: Deutscher Universitäts-Verlag GmbH, 2002.

Smith, Larry, "A CPFR Success Story," *Supply Chain Management Review,* March 2006, pp. 29–36.

Smith, Hedrick and Young, Rick, "Is Wal-Mart good for America?" Frontline program available at http://www.pbs.org/wgbh/pages/frontline/shows/walmart/, Hedrick Smith Productions, 2004.

Snyder, Bill, "When Should You Sell the Factory?" *Stanford Business,* November 2003, p. 31.

Soloman, Ira and Peecher, Mark E., "Does Your Auditor Understand Your Business?" *The Wall Street Journal,* May 25, 2004, p. B2.

Spear, Seven and Bowen, H. Kent, "Decoding the DNA of the Toyota Production System," *Harvard Business Review,* September–October, 1999, pp. 97–106.

Spear, Steven J., "Learning to Lead at Toyota," *Harvard Business Review,* May 2004, pp. 78–86.

Stalk, Jr., George and Lachenauer, Rob, "Hardball: Five Killer Strategies for Trouncing the Competition," *Harvard Business Review,* April 2004.

Starinsky, Robert W., *Maximizing Business Performance through Software Packages: Best Practices for Justification, Selection, and Implementation,* Boca Raton, FL: Auerbach Publishers, 2003.

Swank, Cynthia Karen, "The Lean Service Machine," *Harvard Business Review,* October 2003, pp. 123–129.

Thurm, Scott, "Lesson in India: Not Every Job Translates Overseas," *The Wall Street Journal,* March 3, 2004, p. A1.

Timme, Stephen G., "The Real Cost of Holding Inventory," *Supply Chain Management Review,* July–August 2003, pp. 30–37.

Tinnirello, Paul C., *Project Management,* Boca Raton, FL: Auerbach Publications, 2000.

Trebilcock, Bob, "The Seven Deadly Sins of Reverse Logistics," *Logistics Management,* June 1, 2002, available at www.manufacturing.net.

Turbide, Dave, "What is APS?," *Midrange ERP,* January–February 1998.

Turrettini, John, "Remade in America," *Forbes,* January 12, 2004, p. 190.

Upton, David M. and McAfee, Andrew, "The Real Virtual Factory," *Harvard Business Review,* July–August 1996.

Upton, David M., "The Management of Flexibility," *California Management Review,* (36/2), Winter 1994, pp. 72–89.

Upton, David M., "What Really Makes Factories Flexible," *Harvard Business Review,* July–August 1995.

Vitasek, Kate L., Manrodt, Karl B., and Kelly, Mark, "Solving the Supply Demand Mismatch," *Supply Chain Management Review,* September–October 2003, pp. 58–64.

Vitasek, Kate, Manrodt, Karl B., and Abbott, Jeff, "What Makes a Lean Supply Chain?" *Supply Chain Management Review,* October 2005, pp. 39–45.

W. Chan Kim and Renée Mauborgne, *Blue Ocean Strategy,* Boston, MA: Harvard Business School Press, 2005.

Walker, Marcus, "Reunification Policies Flopped, Germany Admits, as East Faces Competition," *The Wall Street Journal,* April 29, 2004, p. A14.

Walker, William T., *Supply Chain Architecture: a Blueprint for Networking the Flow of Material, Information, and Cash*, Boca Raton, FL: CRC Press, 2005.

Walton, Mary, *The Deming Management Method*, New York: The Putnam Publishing Group, 1986.

Wheelwright, Steven C. and Clark, Kim B., *Revolutionizing Product Development*, New York: Free Press, 1992.

Whelan, David, "The Slipper Solution," *Forbes*, May 24, 2004, p. 64

White, Erin, "For Retailer Mango, Frenzied "Fast Fashion" Proves Sweet," *The Wall Street Journal*, May 28, 2004, p. B1.

Witte, Carl L., Grünhagen, Marko, and Clarke, Richard L., "The Integration of EDI and the Internet," *Information Systems Management*, Fall 2003, pp. 58–65.

Wohleber, Curt, "The Shopping Cart," *Invention & Technology*, Summer 2004, pp.10–11.

Wolf, Martin, *Why Globalization Works*, New Haven, CT: Yale University Press, 2004.

Womack, James P. and Jones, Daniel T., "Beyond Toyota: How to Root Out Waste and Pursue Perfection," *Harvard Business Review*, September–October 1996, pp. 140–158.

Womack, James P. and Jones, Daniel T., "From Lean Production to the Lean Enterprise," *Harvard Business Review*, March–April 1994, pp. 93–103.

Womack, Jim, Taking a value stream walk at Firm "A", *Lean Directions*, available at www.sme.org, May 8, 2003.

Woods, John A. and Marien, Edward J., *The Supply Chain Yearbook*, 2001 edition, New York: McGraw-Hill, 2001.

Zook, Chris and Allen, James, "Growth Outside the Core," *Harvard Business Review*, December 2003, pp. 66–73.

INDEX

Index